LARGE SCALE
RORSCHACH TECHNIQUES

PUBLICATION NUMBER 82

AMERICAN LECTURE SERIES

A Monograph in

AMERICAN LECTURES IN PSYCHOLOGY

Edited by

M. R. HARROWER, Ph.D.

Research and Consulting Psychologist
New York, New York

LARGE SCALE

RORSCHACH TECHNIQUES

(Second Edition)

*A Manual for the Group Rorschach
and Multiple Choice Tests*

By

M. R. HARROWER, Ph.D.

*Research and Consulting Psychologist
New York City*

and

M. E. STEINER, M.A.

*Research Psychologist, General Electric Company
Bridgeport, Connecticut*

With Contributions by

FLOYD O. DUE, M.D.

*Assistant Clinical Professor of Psychiatry
University of California Medical School*

BEATRICE A. WRIGHT, Ph.D.

*Assistant Professor of Psychology
San Francisco State College*

M. ERIK WRIGHT, Ph.D., M.D.

*Professor of Clinical Psychology
Department of Psychiatry, University of Kansas Medical School
Department of Psychology, University of Kansas*

CHARLES C THOMAS · PUBLISHER

Springfield · Illinois · U. S. A.

CHARLES C THOMAS · PUBLISHER

BANNERSTONE HOUSE
301-327 EAST LAWRENCE AVENUE, SPRINGFIELD, ILLINOIS, U. S. A.

Published simultaneously in The British Commonwealth of Nations by
BLACKWELL SCIENTIFIC PUBLICATIONS, LTD., OXFORD, ENGLAND

Published simultaneously in Canada by
THE RYERSON PRESS, TORONTO

Printed in the United States of America

Acknowledgments

THE AUTHORS are indebted to the editors of the *Journal of Consulting Psychology,* the *Journal of Genetic Psychology,* the *Journal of Clinical Psychology,* and *Psychosomatic Medicine* for permission to include in this book portions of articles which have appeared in these journals and to Alfred A Knopf, Inc., for permission to include a section of PART IV which is appearing in *Projective Psychology* edited by L. E. Abt and L. Bellak.

In connection with obtaining the group records analyzed in PART II, we wish to thank the staff of the School of Nursing at the Royal Victoria Hospital, Montreal; Dr. John McIntosh, Secretary of the Faculty of Medicine, McGill University; Dr. Ralph Banay, for making possible our work at Sing Sing Prison; Dr. Bernard Glueck, and Dr. Herbert Jasper for arranging the rather unusual opportunities to obtain group records from psychotic patients.

We are most grateful to the members of the departments of Neuropsychiatry and Student Health at the University of Wisconsin for cooperating so fully with us during the experimental work in connection with the Multiple Choice Test. Dr. Hans Reese and Dr. Annette Washburne, in particular, were more than cooperative and most helpful to us in securing relevant clinical material.

To Dr. Wilder Penfield we owe a very special debt for the opportunities which he afforded for work both clinical and experimental with the Rorschach method. Not so long ago the Rorschach was an unknown quantity in Canadian medicine. It got a unique chance to prove its merits in the Montreal Neurological Institute. The open-mindedness and interest which characterized the reception of our efforts, both clinical and experimental, greatly facilitated the development of these new techniques.

The gratitude which we feel toward the Josiah Macy Jr. Foundation for the continued grants which made this work possible is hard to express. Particularly we wish to thank the Medical Director, Dr. Frank Fremont-Smith, for his insight into and belief in the practical usefulness of ideas which, in their initial stages, might well have seemed impossible of attainment, for the continual help and encouragement which he gave throughout the progress of the study, and for specific suggestions which were incorporated in the final form of the Multiple Choice Test.

M. R. H.
M. E. S.

Contents

Part III. A Multiple Choice Test for Screening Purposes

Part IV. Recent Developments in Group Techniques For the Rorschach Test

Part V. An Analysis of Content

Part VI. A Statistical Study of "Card-Pull"

List of Tables

ix

LARGE SCALE
RORSCHACH TECHNIQUES

Introduction

A N INEVITABLE difficulty confronts the writer who must deal with investigations involving a specialized technique. Shall he speak to a relatively small group whom he can assume is familiar with the procedure in question and knows the grammar of the scientific language which is spoken, or shall he aim at a far wider audience by attempting to educate them in the first half of the book to a point where they can be specialists in the second?

The consideration of problems involving the use of the Rorschach method of personality diagnosis presents just such a dilemma. It is a specialized technique which must be mastered before its results are properly understood and before modification of its original methodology can be appreciated.

In writing a manual for the *group Rorschach* we have, therefore, had to make our choice, and since there now exist several alternative sources in English (1) (2) (3) from which the would-be Rorschach worker can instruct himself on the technique proper, we have decided to assume a knowledge of such aspects of the test as are common to both the original (individual) method and its present modification (group method). In other words *we will make no attempt here to give specific instruction in the scoring of Rorschach records per se or to deal with the interpretive principles which are the essence of the method regardless of its manner of administration.*[1]

We do not feel that this must constitute a warning to the effect that only the Rorschach expert need concern himself with this book. Rather it will be our aim in the final chapters to show that the group method of administration, combined with the Multiple Choice Test which has been developed, may bring at least some aspects of the Rorschach technique into fields where to date its use has not even been contemplated. For in this Multiple Choice Test we have a simple and objective procedure which will allow the psychologist, psychiatrist, educator, social worker, or probation officer, *without any Rorschach training,* to profit by the experience of Rorschach and subsequent workers. The development of such a short objective test

[1] The best and most systematic presentations of the Rorschach method will be found in *The Rorschach Technique* by Bruno Klopfer and Douglas Kelley and in *Rorschach's Test* by Samuel J. Beck. (8)

was, of course, possible only after the analysis of group records presented in Part II of this book, and after the accumulation of a large number of individual records derived from various sources, clinical and otherwise. Thus, in presenting this new test together with the norms for the group Rorschach, we hope to show that it is not only a simple and practical method in itself, but that it grew out of a detailed study and is based on statistical findings.

We have a fourfold purpose then in this book. In PART I we are concerned with a brief history of the development of the group procedure and with a consideration of the uses to which it is being put at the present time (Section I). We have also discussed in detail the technical aspects of the administration of the test, the problem of the inquiry and the scoring of the records (Sections II and III). While parts of this material may be found elsewhere (4) (5), it seemed advisable to include it here so that all necessary information for the use of the test could be found in one place.

In PART II we have presented an experimental investigation from which norms for the new method may be derived. We have analyzed the responses in terms of *location,* and *determinants.* (In Part V, in order not to disrupt the continuity of our general presentation, will be found the *List of Content* which may be compared with the lists for the individual method, compiled by Beck (6) and Hertz (7).) One of our main concerns in these sections has been to study each card separately so that we now possess information about the kind of perceptual experience which each card most readily evokes. A card by card comparison of individual and group records is also included. Lists of the *popular answers* derived from this statistical study, the frequency with which failures occur in each of the cards, a consideration of the distribution of *anatomical answers* within the ten cards, and the like have been discussed.

The records of three hundred and forty subjects provided the material for this analysis. The total number of the responses which we dealt with was 8,526. While our main interest and concern was with providing norms for the *college age group* (224 subjects), we contrasted this experimental group with three others. We examined one other "normal," unselected group of 34 male subjects (age range 26-58 years) referred to in the tables as the *adults,* and two selected groups of persons whose behavior in some form or another showed marked deviations from the normal, namely 41 patients from a sanatarium, *psychotics and psychopathic personalities* (male and female).

and 41 *inmates from a large penal institution* (male). The comparison which can be made between these groups enhances the interest of
the material; for in considering the graphs of the determinants and
the locations, it is possible to see what features of the cards emerge
as common to all four groups on the one hand, and what features may
be said to show the imprint of the characteristics of one particular
group on the other.

Since the number of *college age subjects* was considerably larger
than that of the other groups, we broke down this total into five
sub-groups, each with different training, namely medical students,
student nurses, aviation cadets in training, and male and female
students in a college of arts.

We have presented the results in some cases in both graphic and
tabular form, feeling that these two methods fulfill very different
functions. The graphs allow for comparisons to be made at a glance
between cards and between groups of subjects. They show immediately the interrelationship of the various factors and the dominance
of any particular perceptual component. On the other hand the tables
make for a more accurate presentation and are correct to one decimal
place.

PART III is concerned with the Multiple Choice Test which was
derived from the material presented in PARTS I and II. This test,
even in its preliminary form, was found to be of use not only to
educators and counselors as suggested above, but also to persons
concerned with problems of military selection, classification and
rehabilitation, as well as to workers in the industrial field. We have,
therefore, added a brief report on some of the findings in these
various fields which have been published or made available to us,
and have included three papers devoted to various phases of the use
of the test in military psychiatry by Due, Wright and Wright.

PART IV presents an account of recent developments in group
techniques for the Rorschach test in industry, in the hospital or
clinical setting, in education and in the Armed Forces. Suggested
modification of group procedures are also included.

PART V, as mentioned above, is given over entirely to the *List of
Content,* which will obviously be used only for reference.

In PART VI a comparison of "card-pull," or the perceptual properties of the Rorschach inkblots which predispose the subject to the use
of particular scoring variables, is made between group administered
tests to our four main groups of subjects—college age group, adults,

prison inmates, psychotics and psychopathic personalities—and individually administered tests to adolescent groups of subjects.

REFERENCES

1. Rorschach, Hermann: *Psychodiagnostik*. Fourth edition. Bern, Switzerland, Hans Huber, 1942, 226 pp.
2. Klopfer, Bruno and Kelley, D. M.: *The Rorschach technique*. New York, Book Co., 1942, viii + 436 pp.
3. Bochner, R. and Halpern, F.: *The Clinical Application of the Rorschach Test*. New York, Grune and Stratton, 1942, x+216 pp.
4. Harrower, M. R. and Steiner, M. E.: Modification of the Rorschach method for use as a group test. *Rorschach Res. Exch.*, 5:130-144, 1941. Also in: *J. Genet. Psychol.*, 62:119-133, 1943.
5. Harrower, M. R.: Directions for administration of the Rorschach group test. *Rorschach Res. Exch.*, 5:145-153, 1941. Also in *J. Genet. Psychol.*, 62:105-117, 1943.
6. Beck, Samuel: Introduction to the Rorschach method: A manual of personality study. *Am. Orthopsychiat. Ass. Monog.*, 1937, 1:xv+278 pp.
7. Hertz, Marguerite: *Frequency tables to be used in scoring the Rorschach inkblot test*. Revised edition. Cleveland, Ohio, Department of Psychology, Western Reserve University, 1942, 275 pp.
8. Beck, Samuel: *Rorschach's Test*. New York. Grune and Stratton. 1944, xiii+223 pp.

PART I

THE GROUP RORSCHACH—
DEVELOPMENT, ADMINISTRATION,
SCORING

The Development of the Group Rorschach

W ITH THE outbreak of the war it became evident that Rorschach workers possessed a tool which, if properly used, could be of value in problems of classification, selection, and screening of military personnel on the one hand, and in clinical problems such as the differential diagnosis of hysteria and malingering from cerebral trauma on the other.[1]

It was, however, equally clear at that time that technical barriers prevented the wide-spread use of the test, not the least of these being the amount of time required for its administration to large numbers of persons. At this point necessity proved the mother of invention and to obviate this outstanding difficulty the *group method* was devised (2).

The essence of the *group method* is contained in the following ideas: the important features of a Rorschach record can be obtained if the subject *writes down what he sees* in the ten ink blots when these *are projected on a screen in front of him,* instead of reporting his perceptions to the examiner. In doing this he may be a member of a large group of several hundred persons who are also engaged in recording their responses in this way. Moreover, by *locating his own responses* on diagrams of the blots, and by writing additional information about his responses following their spontaneous recording, he will provide the examiner with the material on locations and determinants which is needed for accurate scoring and which is usually obtained in the inquiry period described and advocated by Klopfer (3).

We will discuss in Section II the detailed procedure for administra-

---

[1] An early publication (1) has shown the differentiating potentialities of the Rorschach method with regard to subdural hematoma and neurotic individuals. The authors state: ". . . this technic can be an excellent diagnostic aid in borderline and puzzling cases. A fairly characteristic picture is expected in the 'dull' syndrome similar to the findings in intracranial tumors by Harrower. In differential diagnosis the anxiety and conversion neuroses are likely to give a typically neurotic performance with color shock, lack of human movement and the predominance of animal movement over human movement."

tion of the group method, a procedure which was selected from many experimental sessions in which the variables were systematically altered. Summarized briefly, however, at this stage we may say that the procedure consists in showing *slides of the ten Rorschach cards* for *three minutes* each in the upright position. The *number of subjects* tested is limited only by the size of the auditorium provided each seat gives an uninterrupted and undistorted view of the screen, and that the front row is some 10 or 12 feet distant from it. *Sufficient light* comes in most cases (where the lantern is strong enough) from the slides themselves, but this can be supplemented by indirect lighting from the back of the hall if necessary. Specially *prepared booklets** with ten blank pages for recording and small diagrams of each card (at one stage hidden by a flap) for use in the inquiry period were used. *Instructions* were essentially the same as those described by Rorschach (4) and subsequent workers, except for technical details about the use of the booklets and the nature of the slides. Following the recording of responses for each of the ten slides, a second half hour period was devoted to the accurate delineation of the areas used in these responses on the small diagrams and to giving additional information concerning the answers. This procedure was found practical and effective not only with college students but with adults of below average intelligence (prison inmates with I.Q.'s from 70 to 90), high school students, and even institutionalized psychotics. The instructions naturally varied slightly with the nature of the group tested, and the more specific inquiry was reserved for groups where the level of intelligence made such a procedure productive.

Once the underlying principle of the group method is understood and once the truth of the assumption that it provides one with essentially the same information as the individual method has been demonstrated, it is clear that minor deviations in technique, in materials, in administration and scoring will matter as little here as they do when the test is given individually. Whether the blots are projected as slides as in the majority of investigations to date, or whether the cards themselves are projected by means of an epidiascope, for example, is immaterial. Whether the responses are recorded in the prepared booklet, such as we have used and recommended, or on plain paper (5), (6) with diagrams of various sizes attached is equally inconsequential. Whether the instructions are given by the examiner in

---

* The booklets now supplied *do not have the flap which hides the diagrams.* This proved unnecessary experimentally and complicated their production.

person or are written out on slides and projected along with the blots, or are given from victrola records[2] or are mimeographed and made available to each subject independently is again unimportant provided that the method that is chosen is suitable for the group being tested. Just as the individual procedure receives a variety of treatment in the hands of its users and yet "delivers the goods" so the group method seems capable of many minor modifications provided the basic ideas are retained.

The most recent development in group procedure will, perhaps prove the most practical of all. Using a new series of inkblots (devised by the authors as a parallel set) individual booklets will be prepared in which full-sized, colored and uncolored, blots will be available for each subject. Thus slides are unnecessary, for each person tested has his own set of blots and records his responses on the other half of the open double page. These blots utilized in a military investigation will shortly, we hope, be available for general use.

What Are the Group Records Like?

Four questions very naturally come to mind when such a drastic change in a previously sacrosanct procedure as the Rorschach method has occurred. First, what are records taken under these new conditions like? What sort of protocol will the normal and the various abnormal personalities give? How does the experience of looking at slides differ from that of looking at cards? And so on. The best answer to this question undoubtedly is to take the group test oneself, to experience group conditions and make a direct comparison from "within." Then one should read through the group and individual records of some person with whom one is acquainted and compare the information that can be derived from each. For the moment, however, a comparison of the four records in Table I will provide a good introduction. These records should be compared one with another and then mentally with the records of similar types of subjects from one's own clinical experience, i.e., should be mentally compared with the *individual* records of normal persons, the organic patient, the neurotic, and the psychopath.

Of the many hundred "normal" records which could equally well have been given at this point the one quoted is chosen merely for its brevity and for the obvious use of some of the main determinants which can be seen despite the absence of scoring.

---

[2] Bigelow, R. B. and Lindner, R. and Chapman, K. have adopted the above methods.

TABLE I

Comparison of Responses Obtained by Group Administration of the Rorschach From Four Individuals Varying Widely in Personal Adjustment

WELL ADJUSTED INDIVIDUAL Age 20	PROFOUNDLY MALADJUSTED INDIVIDUAL. RECENT SUICIDE ATTEMPT Age 20	INDIVIDUAL WITH ORGANIC CEREBRAL LESION Age 40	PSYCHOPATHIC PERSONALITY SCHIZOID TYPE Age 20
Card	*Card*	*Card*	*Card*
I Face of glossy black cat like a Hallowe'en decoration.	I Butterfly.	I This is a black bug, also very large.	I Possibly the brain pattern (physical) of some animal.
II Two people talking over a small table, possibly twins, with clothing, hats, and hair styles the same. Arms folded on the table. Salt and pepper between them.	II	II This is also a large bug with black and red colors on it. Laid out flat on paper.	II Two scotties, nose to nose, in copulation with the heat of passion flaming above them. Fire also indicates the area of orgasm.
III Two figures, women according to their shoes, maids possibly. They are lifting some heavy object. In the middle is a red butterfly upside down. (D)	III Head of two birds. (d)	III This looks to be a bug with parts taken away, also black and red.	III Two blacks working over the carcass of a shark, tossing out foeti and viscera which appear to be atavistic lungs.
IV Face of some insect highly magnified. (D)	IV X-ray of spine.	IV This looks to be a black bug of some sort or other laid out flat on paper with two arms.	IV A good representation of a vampire bat.
V Bat with wings outstretched.	V Bat.	V This is a bug or butterfly laid out flat with two long legs and two long horns.	V Pools of blood obstructing the view of disengaged human limbs.

6

TABLE 1 (Continued)

VI Old-fashioned warming pan for bed. The handle at the top has a fringe of fur attached. Also a fur rug and the handle of a mace.	VI Oil well.	VI This I would say is possibly a bug also of a different kind, black in color and large.	VI Radio antenna with ether distribution represented by lacerator radiating from the top of blot and magnetic fluid permeating the soil beneath.
VII Two women about the middle of the 19th Century. Both pointing in different directions.	VII Charms.	VII This as I see it is a very hard thing to describe as a dead bug that has been for a long time.	VII A graph representing the similarity of pattern and the paths a human life may follow. At base, the first major event is birth, in poverty, in wealth. Second major event is maturation and its ramifications. The last event being inevitable and complete inertness reached by all living things good or bad.
VIII Crest of some institution or family, two animals flanking a crown. The crown is standing on an orange and red base.	VIII	VIII This is also a bug of some sort that has been laid away for safe keeping and has faded in color.	VIII Mirror image of marmot leaping from life, the red area, of vibrance to death, the jagged area.
IX Red and green figures. Chinese dragons or devils, standing on lower red base, possibly smoke or flame.	IX X-ray.	IX This bug has five or six different colors. Also very large in size I am sure.	IX If side view is taken a man is sitting smoking his pipe pondering over a map of Corsica with bloody clouds looming up behind him.
X The cross section of a red tulip upside down. (D) There are blue flowers on each side. (D) There are also yellow and orange buds of some other plant.	X Fish. (D)	X This is also a large bug spread out very large in size with about six different colors.	X Mantis, male and female in the act of coitus. (D)

It is also of interest that the three abnormal records were correctly diagnosed by "blind analysis" from large groups when it was not known that such abnormal individuals were taking part. With one exception the subjects are all the same age.

Even at their face value without benefit of scoring it can be seen that these four records represent very different Rorschach personalities, and that each of the abnormal records presents its own striking differences from the normal. The marked perseveration will be noticed in the record of the organic; the failures on cards II and VIII characterize the record of the neurotic individual; while strange symbolism and bizarre answers pervade the record of the psychopath. Even the sentence structure and the choice of words is significantly different in the four records—a difference which comes to light by the group method.

Are the Records Different Under the Two Methods?

The second question which comes to mind concerns the differences, if any, which would result from the change of method in any individual's case. Granted that records are recognizably normal or abnormal (a vitally important fact in screening) are there nonetheless differences in a given record in the distribution of the responses (where locations and determinants are concerned) which can be proved to be the result of change of method and of that alone?

In order to answer this conclusively one and the same individual should be able to take the test both ways, each for the first time! Unfortunately this is not possible in the nature of things, so we are left to make the best of two alternative procedures. Either we can make the *same subjects* take the test both ways, arranging them in control and experimental groups so as to isolate the inevitable factor of repetition and contrast it with the factor of change of method, or one can take *two different groups,* matching them subject for subject as nearly as possible and give each of these groups the test under the different conditions. Both of these procedures have been undertaken, the first as part of our development of the method (2), the second by Hertzman (7).

In our original study (2) the 110 subjects who took part were divided into four groups, two *control* groups who repeated the individual and group test respectively and two *experimental* groups who took in the one case the group test followed by the individual, and in the other, the individual test followed by the group test. All repetitions occurred within five days of taking the first test in order to rule out any change in personality due to development or a change in life situation.

The most striking finding which emerged from our study was the fact that the only consistent changes which occurred were those which occurred as a result of *repeating the test* and not as the result of the change in method. That is, the *same* changes occurred in the second test among the control subjects *where no change of method had been introduced,* as occurred in both experimental groups, *i.e.,* regardless of which method was used in the repeat test! These changes were a decrease in the W percentage and a corresponding rise in the percentages of D, d, and Dd, and a slight but consistent decrease in CF responses with a corresponding rise in FC.

It is not true, of course, that the records of any individual were identical on the two occasions. Changes in F% and even a reversal of the M:C ratio were sometimes noted, but such changes could not be ascribed to the fact that the method had changed, for they occurred equally frequently when the method had remained the same, as in the control groups.

Hertzman (7) has shown in a careful and detailed analysis in which he followed the alternative procedure of working with matched subjects that certain differences emerged between his groups which, since no repetition was involved, could not be explained in this way. These differences, however, were in his opinion much less important than the significant similarity between the two tests. Two of the differences which he found in the group test, namely fewer responses given and fewer shading responses, interestingly enough, appeared as changes in the reverse direction in the groups studied by Munroe (8) and Buckle (9), namely *more* responses in the group test and an increase in texture responses! It is probable that the character of the groups studied affects some changes more than is realized.

Where Can Such a Test Be Used?

The third question which one naturally asks is where can this test be used and what types of subjects are capable of taking it?

Devised primarily for military use the test has, during the years of its availability, been tried out in connection with a variety of problems involving military personnel. Psychologists in station hospitals, rehabilitation centers, and the like are trying it and in many cases have incorporated it into their regular program. The published reports of these projects will probably not be available for some time. We may mention, however, one or two of those which have appeared in print. The group method has been used in the Australian Air Force as a report of Buckle and Cook indicates (10).

Under the direction of Klopfer and Sender group Rorschach examinations were given every two weeks as part of the program in one unit of the Signal Corps. The use to which the test was put in this case was for the "purposes of adding information concerning personality adjustment and emotional stability to other information derived from psychological tests, experience background and progress in training. The objective was to provide as much evidence concerning the nature of the assignment best suited to the individual as possible" (12). A comment on this study received by Dr. Klopfer from the commanding officer may be quoted in this connection: "The use of the group Rorschach psychodiagnostic technique in evaluation of the qualifications of student officers for assignment is proving extremely valuable. When used in conjunction with our other psychological tests, it provides an opportunity to observe the interplay between intelligence and personality and to estimate the emotional stability of the officers under stress and responsibility. This knowledge allows us to recommend assignment according to the best interest of the service" (15).

Hertzman and Seitz have had considerable success with the group method in high altitude studies in which changes in personality occur. Hertzman (11) has reported "In a current experiment the group Rorschach has been shown to be a sensitive indicator of changes in adjustment occurring under high altitude conditions. The experiment, which is one of a series, has indicated that the group test is at least as adequate an indicator of changes as the individual test had previously been found to be for similar conditions."

Ross, Dancey and Brown (13) report the use of the group Rorschach with parachute troopers in training in Canada. In this investigation it was shown that ". . . the group of 35 men after failure to complete training have been shown to give Rorschach scores significantly more unstable and more neurotic than the group of 65 studied at the outset of training." The authors conclude, however, that ". . . the group Rorschach, by itself, cannot provide a criterion for prediction of the remaining paratroopers unlikely to complete their course when these have already been selected by personal interview."

The method has also been found of value in child guidance clinics and guidance centers. Krugman (16), for example, reports: "At the senior high school level the group method serves a useful purpose.

The writer recently participated in a rather intensive study of 650 boys, in the third and fourth years of the academic high schools of New York City, who were enrolled in advanced pre-flight aviation courses. Among the battery of psychological tests employed was the group Rorschach." . . . "Although far from complete, preliminary results indicate that, although the group test will probably not yield as many data as the individual Rorschach would have, the data yielded possess far greater usefulness for personality evaluation than any other pencil-paper 'personality' test now know to the writer and his colleagues."

In hospitals there are several studies in progress as, for example, that referred to by Hirning (17) on allergy patients and by the same author in connection with rehabilitation of tubercular patients.

Surprisingly enough the method can be used successfully in institutions for psychotic patients. Even quite seriously disturbed patients may be brought to take the test under group conditions when, because of suspicion or an extremely negativistic attitude, the individual method has failed.

In this connection it has been pointed out that some of the psychoneurotic casualties who were unable to take the individual Rorschach have become "caught up" in the group administration of the test so that they are able to participate. The darkened room and the feeling of companionship with the other patients involved in the same activity apparently broke down the barriers of resistance. For example, Hutt (23) states: "When the rate of intake (of patients) did not permit the use of the individual Rorschach, the writer adopted a modified group Rorschach test. This was essential in order to set up quickly some group therapy and group activity programs for the reconditioning of the neurotic casualty. It was soon found that the modified group method yielded leads for therapy and were not readily obtainable in all individual Rorschachs. Moreover, the group situation seemed to facilitate responses in the cases of some soldiers who were reluctant to respond in an individual setting. The method used may be described briefly as follows: "Approximately 15 soldiers were examined at one sitting in a fairly large room. A brief orientation was given about the 'ink-blot' test and they were then asked to write their spontaneous responses to each of the blots as they were projected upon the screen, using one-half of the page. After all ten blots had been shown in this manner, they were projected upon the screen over again as part of the inquiry. (The soldiers used the other half of the page for this purpose.) Finally, the Harrower Multiple Choice Test was administered as a kind of 'testing the limits.' The clinical interpretations obtained in this manner upon 114 cases agreed essentially in 82% of these cases with the total clinical finding as approved by the psychiatrist in charge."

Prisons and reformatories have also put the method to use. Some aspects of the studies made at Sing Sing by the authors (18) (24) may be quoted here. Two groups of prisoners were examined. One group was composed of sex offenders, the other group contained persons serving terms for murder, burglary, grand larceny and forgery. "No information concerning any of the prisoners serving sentences was given to the Rorschach examiner until their performance in the test had been reported. The range of intelligence quotients in the two groups was between 77 and 140 with approximately 50% scoring 100 or below. (These ratings had been previously obtained and were taken from case histories.)

"It is interesting to note that the cooperation of these prisoners in both groups was excellent. No antagonism was shown toward the examiner, or skepticism concerning the purpose of the test. In fact so eager were all the participants to make themselves useful and to receive special attention that there were not nearly sufficient small 'jobs' in connection with the test to go around. In consequence of this good cooperation the instructions were carried out carefully and with considerably greater accuracy than had been found in other more privileged groups.

"A survey of the results obtained revealed many points of interest, both in regard to the feasibility of using such a method of personality evaluation in penal institutions and in regard to theoretical questions pertaining to the group method of the Rorschach test. It showed, for instance, that the group procedure is a perfectly suitable test for persons of below average intelligence. Twenty-five per cent of those tested had IQ's within the 70-90 range, and all records obtained from these persons were of such a nature that they could be scored and evaluated without difficulty.

"It was also demonstrated, as will of course be anticipated, that no typical or uniform 'criminal personality' existed among the prisoners. Neither can it be said that a 'typical personality' was found as to murder, burglary, and the like. The record of each of the 40 subjects was as diverse and 'individual' as any record obtained from an unselected group of a similar number might be. Some persons demonstrated very profound psychological disturbances; a few showed well-adjusted personalities; the majority showed considerable deviation from the normal but this deviation took a variety of forms. By and large the more disturbed personalities were found in the group of sex offenders" (24).

However, as will be shown in PART II where the records of these prisoners are analyzed, certain consistent deviations from comparable groups of normals stand out clearly, chief of these being the marked predominance of the explosive and more primitive type of emotional responses over the more adjusted and well-integrated ones. (CF higher than FC)

Lindner and Chapman (19) (20) have also reported the routine use of the group method at the Lewisburg Penitentiary, finding it of considerable value.

Interesting research projects include a study of different professional and vocational groups. Harrower and Cox (21) reported an investigation in which organists, metallurgists, commercial artists, engineers, clergymen, social workers, and insurance salesmen took part. They report: "Inasmuch as the groups were small, any differentiation between groups would have to be made with a statistical method set up for such a purpose. A modified form of Fisher's analysis of variance, developed by Dr. Robert W. B. Jackson, was used, in conjunction with Snedecor's Tables, which give the 5% and 1% points for the distribution of F. Inasmuch as this study is largely exploratory, the 5% point was used, as indicative of differences worthy of further investigation."

Some of their results may be seen in the following quotation:

"An examination of the approach the various professions took to their problems is interesting. The social workers, the clergymen, and the metallurgists took the most systematic and analytical approach to the problem, using first a whole response and then breaking it down into the detail responses; the artists and insurance salesmen took the least systematic approach, picking out whatever first struck their fancy.

"Among other tentative interpretations on the basis of group averages, one might postulate the artist as one who seeks in his work whole effects, details being incidental; his mind is rather undisciplined. The organist not only seeks whole effects, but is also concerned about details: his approach is much more systematic than that of the artist, suggesting that music is something more than an art, that it is to a degree a science. The metallurgist differs from the engineer in that he is a detailist, his major concern being his own particular aspect of the work, while the engineer sees his work as a whole. The clergyman and the social worker are very systematic in their approach to a problem, for they differ in that the clergyman seeks generalities rather than specific applications: the former is more introspective than the latter. The insurance salesman gives evidence of considerable drive: he does not express as creatively as he might. The engineer takes a more general approach to problems than does the metallurgist."

The study of Piotrowski and Candee on the selection of outstanding mechanical workers is also of great interest. These authors were

TABLE II

Personality Rating	Number	Work Good or Work Satisfactory	Poor Work Several Failures Dropped
Excellent .... Above average .... Average .... Just below average.......	94	86% (81)	14% (13)
Poor and very poor.......	14	7% (1)	93% (13)

able to differentiate correctly 88% of the 78 cases in terms of their being outstanding or poor mechanical workers. In an early article Piotrowski (22) reports: "The Rorschach ratings of seventy-eight workers were compared with ratings made independently by the foremen. The investigation indicates that general personality traits have a bearing even on mechanical work." . . . "The results which have been gained with the specific vocational use of the Rorschach method justify the hope that this specific use will be a promising field of exploration for vocational psychologists."

The use of the group Rorschach in schools and colleges has grown considerably during the past years. Utilization of the method for guidance, screening, or research in personality is in progress in many educational institutions at the present time and validation studies on the group method at the Brush Foundation have already been published by Hertz (6). Examination of all entering freshmen at McGill University was undertaken by the authors some years ago and results are available which show the relationship between academic performance and the evaluation of personality as seen in the group Rorschach records (15). In addition to a detailed personality description an over-all personality rating was given to each student ranging from "excellent" to "very poor."

Of the 108 students examined 94 fell between "excellent" and "just below average," while 14 showed severe personality difficulties or inadequacies. Of those with "poor" or "very poor" personalities,

TABLE III

PREDICTION OF POSSIBLE DISTURBANCE DUE TO ANXIETY	RESULTS
"Basic potentialities better than 'poor' group, but at present disturbed and anxious. If this continues . . . likely to produce detrimental effect on studies. If they can work out of their difficulties they will probably make the grade."	U. Failed all subjects. "Worried and could not attend." Referred for psychiatric examination: anxiety state diagnosed.
	A. Age 40. Has wife and family and serious financial worries. "Carried outside employment. Extensive lung shadows found over which he worried a great deal."

PREDICTION OF POSSIBLE DISTURBANCE DUE TO EMOTIONAL INSTABILITY	IMMEDIATE REPORT
"For his age this man is not stable or adjusted. Although he has considerable driving power, he nonetheless shows an immature personality structure. He has not yet successfully integrated his drive into a constructive scheme of work. Emotionally he is still explosive. For general purposes he has adequate self-control, but this control is achieved at the cost of considerable strain. A poor risk."	"The report includes some surprises as, for example, Mr. Z. who is an older man with a successful career behind him and a personality of considerable energy."
	Report one year later:
	"Mr. Z. did not write any of his examinations as he felt he was not prepared. He was required to retire. He was a curious individual with a great deal of drive and I think your analysis of him hit him off extremely well."

93% had been in some kind of academic difficulty by the end of the first year and a half while only 14% of those without severe personality difficulties had been in similar trouble.

Table II epitomizes some of the findings from the above mentioned study. The manner in which these results were obtained may perhaps be mentioned. The names of all those who did outstanding work and those who did extremely poor work (failed in many subjects or were dropped) were sent to the Rorschach examiner by the secretary to the faculty of medicine. Those who fell into neither of these groups but whose work was satisfactory were not mentioned by name. Among the 86%, therefore, are included the names of those who did exceptionally good work and those whose names were not mentioned.

Sometimes specific predictions were verified in an interesting way as, for example, those that commented on an individual's anxiety or emotional immaturity, as may be seen in Table III on page 15.

The most thorough work in this field has been done by Munroe whose studies at Sarah Lawrence College are well known (14). Some of her early results are quoted here in considerable detail since they are not only an excellent example of what can be expected from the group method in the hands of the expert, but because they raise the very interesting question of the interrelation of intelligence and personality in academic success and failure. The "check list" devised by Munroe and discussed below is an extremely valuable asset for the handling of a large number of group records systematically and objectively.* Munroe summarized some of her findings as follows:

"Large-scale application of the Rorschach test, using the group method of administration developed by Harrower and some means of rapid assessment, is still a new venture. I think that I can contribute most to the discussion of this problem by reporting developments in our experimentation with such use of the test at Sarah Lawrence College. Perhaps the most immediate interest of our results is further confirmation of the validity of the Group Rorschach. I would like, however, to draw your attention to the special way in which we used the group test, because the results seem to have important implications for more general problems of selection and of test construction.

"The Rorschach is a versatile instrument. The raw responses to the ink blots reflect so much of the personality that many lines of differentiation in personality analysis can be developed. Until recently, the fully trained expert has used all the data in the test with as much clinical insight as he could muster. This is undoubtedly the ideal procedure, because the examiner has at his disposal fairly good norms for single items and key relationships of data. He also has a knowledge of how clinical syndromes are expressed in the test, which is unfortunately no more uniform from one subject to the next than the symptomatology of two schizophrenics is identical. Bringing all this material together into a sound diagnosis takes time and skill— the same order of skill that a psychiatrist must have in sorting the data of case history and interview into a significant picture of the personality.

---

* See footnote p. 21.

"Large-scale testing does not permit the necessary time for this type of evaluation, and large-scale testing must ultimately be done by psychologists less elaborately trained. Moreover, the Rorschach is being used in new fields for new purposes. Efforts are being made in several directions, therefore, to reach more objective criteria for special conditions or special aptitudes. The 'neurotic signs' developed by Harrower represent one example of this trend. She found that diagnosed psychoneurotics actually deviate from normals more frequently on nine items than on any others. Most neurotics and few normals have more than four of these 'signs.' Similar work has been done or is in progress on patients with organic brain conditions, on schizophrenics, on psychopaths, etc. Piotrowski and his colleagues have statistically isolated three 'signs' important for success in shop-work. Bigelow and also Molish have compared the protocols of successful and unsuccessful aviation cadets to determine objectively which items differentiate these groups most adequately. Such investigations can clarify, objectify, and, at times, for some purposes even supplant the general clinical evaluation described above. All of these efforts are directed, however, toward the diagnosis of *specific* conditions.

"Before coming to the discussion of our different procedure at Sarah Lawrence, I should also mention the kind of work Harrower has done in quickly predicting success in medical school. Indeed, I have done it myself in giving to students a rating that I called specific academic prediction. Harrower obtained excellent results. Our results were also very good. Out of 45 ratings, aimed at predicting academic performance, 39 were 'on the nose' according to the general average established for the student's work during the first year; only one was badly discrepant. Nevertheless, I feel that these ratings, however successful, did not adequately meet the necessary criteria for large-scale testing. They were highly composite affairs, based not only upon our knowledge of the students through their protocols, but also upon our awareness of the specific requirements of the academic situation. Our method was essentially 'clinical,' dependent upon our personal insight. I am sure Harrower would agree that future development of large-scale work should envisage both a more objective approach to the evaluation of the student and more precise knowledge of what the situation demands.

"We have already tried to be more precise in one direction at Sarah Lawrence, though in a manner which may sound paradoxical and is certainly very different from the investigations mentioned above aimed at specific diagnosis. What we did was to give each student a quantitative rating on 'general adjustment,' *excluding* so far as possible her adaptation to specific academic requirements; indeed, excluding the selection of any particular type of personality. (We will discuss at some length, later, the objective criteria in the test for this rating. It seems preferable to describe first what it is and how it works.) Unintelligent and unintellectual girls, introverts and extroverts, aggressive and timid individuals, complicated and simple souls were all rated 'adequate' provided the personality seemed to be functioning well. 'Functioning well' meant initially—to be frank—nothing more than having a 'good' Rorschach protocol. This criterion is, on reflection, pretty sound. The test was developed by clinicians who knew mental disturbance in variety and had no particular axe to grind in defining normality. Indeed, they did not define it at all, except 'operationally.' Reflection on the nature of the test suggests that what a good protocol means essentially is a reasonable balance or integration between the impulsive and controlling forces in the personality. Control must be adequate but not excessive or too repressive. Great latitude is allowed in type and intensity of impulse and type of control, but their relationship must be sound. In behavioral terms we defined adjustment very simply as the ability to 'get along' reasonably well with reasonable inner comfort. Occasionally, we rated a girl badly adjusted with an asterisk to indicate that she gets along well, but at too high a cost to her own comfort.

"I shall depend primarily on our experimental results to show that this apparently vague concept of 'general adjustment' does mean something that is empirically rather precise, useful, and measurable. I must first describe the experiment. For two successive years (1940 and 1941), we administered the Rorschach to the entire entering class at Sarah Lawrence College (225 girls in all), under carefully controlled conditions. Teachers were not informed of test results in order to guarantee complete independence of judgment. (Beginning this year the test is being used on a practical basis. A feature of the work not presented here is a descriptive sketch of each student. Ratings and sketches are now available to teachers.) Evaluations from the test were made 'blind,' i.e., with no information about the student except her response to the ink blots. The test ratings were compared in June with the ordinary college records of academic performance and explicit notation of emotional difficulty—chiefly the list of girls brought to the attention of the college psychiatrist. His advice is frequently sought by teachers in cases of minor maladjustment without referring the student directly.

"The adjustment ratings were very successful in predicting adjustment. Out of 100 girls rated 'adequate' (A or B on a scale running from A to E), only three appeared on any list of students in any sort of trouble, and two of these had minor upsets quickly solved. On the other hand, out of 33 students brought to the attention of the college psychiatrist, 30 had been rated as moderate or severe problems, 20 of them as severe problems. Many of these cases were not at all serious, of course, and with one striking exception, the Rorschach rating corresponded well with the psychiatrist's estimate of degree of difficulty. Ten of the 13 girls rated in the worst category by the Rorschach in 1941 either failed outright in their studies or had prolonged psychiatric attention, and the others were spontaneously described by teachers as rather neurotic.

"Of greater interest to the present discussion, however, is the fact that 18 out of 19 students who were either dismissed or conditioned in their freshman year had poor adjustment ratings. Half of these girls were above the median on the ACE (American Council on Education Psychological Examinations, an intelligence test) one quarter above the 90th percentile. Thus outright academic failure in the freshman year seems far more closely related to problems of adjustment than to lack of intelligence. (This statement must not be reduced to the absurd. All entering students have a certain minimum of intelligence.)

"The adjustment rating predicted degree of academic success *short of actual failure* as well as the intelligence test, but no better. Seventy-four per cent of the adjustment ratings and 71% of the ACE scores (for purposes of comparability, the total distribution of ACE scores was reduced to five groups ranging from bad to good, numerically equivalent to the Rorschach ratings E to A) tallied with the academic average, excluding the cases of failure and conditioning. The point that I find most significant, however, is the relationship between the two tests. Failures in the prediction of each measure can be at least partially explained by the other. The small group of unadjusted girls who did satisfactory work all stood above the median on the ACE. Conversely, with very few exceptions, the adjusted girls whose work was on the poor side stood in the bottom quartile on the ACE. *The two tests seem to measure demonstrably different things, both of which are important in academic performance.* An effort to *combine* them yields the following very suggestive results:

"1. When the two measures point in the same direction, good or bad, their combined predictive power is almost perfect. No 'adequately adjusted' student with a good ACE score failed. No 'poorly adjusted' student with a low ACE score did fully satisfactory work. There were very few discrepancies with external measures of performance even of a minor degree.

"2. Girls with 'adequate' adjustment ratings and low ACE scores form a group which includes neither superior scholars nor outright failures. Half of them proved to be weak students and several were rejected for return as juniors, although their work for the two lower years was considered passable. Many of them made valuable contributions to the college as *people* and seemed to profit by their education as much as girls who got better grades. In short, this group causes no serious trouble, but is likely to do mediocre work, at best, and, at worst, to trail along near the bottom academically.

"3. The most unpredictable group consists of girls with poor adjustment ratings and high ACE scores. This group contributes half of the dramatic failures and more than its quota of girls who just squeak by. It also accounts for several very superior students. Statistically speaking, girls in this category are poor risks. To eliminate them altogether is both impracticable, because there are too many, and undesirable, because one would eliminate the very good along with the very bad. These girls are probably the square pegs who need square holes, but an impressive number of them are well worth any special attention or tolerance required. Looking beyond the academic scene, it is probable that a good many distinguished, creative people—scholars, artists, aviators, etc., would do as badly on any general adjustment tests as the crackpots and dismal neurotics we would like to rule out.

"Sensible procedure might be to avoid 'speaking statistically' about this group and devote whatever time is available for selection to individual study of each case. Some types of maladjustment are likely to prove difficult in all situations. More specific identification of what is wrong will suffice to cut out these cases. Other types must be studied more carefully to determine whether their assets are especially important for the situation under consideration and their difficulties such as can be handled.

"In spite of the fact that our evidence is too limited in scope to warrant safe generalization to other fields, it does, to my mind, suggest a useful hypothesis. Fragmentary observations strongly support the idea that the same problems obtain elsewhere. I should like to urge further experimentation with the concept of 'general adjustment,' as an empirical entity, to be measured separately and then combined with appropriate indicators of the special qualities required for any job in some such manner as that outlined above. It is not enough simply to screen out the mentally ill, and to measure special aptitudes or character traits independently. The concept of adjustment applied to the entire range of cases can probably be made to show, in a quick, practicable manner, the actual relationship between general personality factors and assets for a particular job. Prediction of success or failure could be made from a statistical combination of test scores with great accuracy in the majority of cases. The small group where errors are most likely to occur is isolated for more intensive study and the problem to be considered is clearly posed.

"A further advantage of the concept is that the adjustment measure can be used in new contexts, as desired, with different sets of special data. A composite measure, oriented toward a particular situation but including personality factors (like our academic ratings and probably Piotrowski's signs), is less suitable for prediction in other fields. I should, perhaps, also emphasize the idea that 'special data' could include not only aptitude tests, but also tests of personality configuration like the Rorschach itself differently analyzed, physiological measures and items from the case history.

"That our results are not due exclusively to the magic of ink blots is shown by the fact that Mrs. Schmidl-Waehner obtained similar findings with an adjustment rating based upon her method of evaluating spontaneous drawings. Once the goal is clearly set, it should be possible to devise other techniques of measurement, possibly more practicable for large-scale use.

"This statement brings us back to the problem mentioned earlier of making the Rorschach evaluation more objective. Unlikely as it may seem, 'general adjustment' is a rather simple thing to measure by the test. After all, we defined the term originally as having a 'good' protocol and elaborated our psychological concepts after the fact, when we found that this definition worked out well in practice. To our own surprise, we found that the method we have developed for quick inspection of the protocol actually yielded a *numerical score* of impressive validity independent of our expert judgment.

"What we did was to prepare a mimeographed check list of 30 items generally considered significant in Rorschach diagnosis* (Note:

---

* Munroe's check list is now included, for the examiner's convenience, in the Group Rorschach test booklets designed for use with this manual.

these items remain in technical Rorschach terms—F%, color shock, CF:FC, etc. They are not translated into judgments of behavior. The reader unfamiliar with the test must be content to assume that this abracadabra makes sense if it actually works.) Its original purpose was merely to provide a guide for *systematic* review of the whole personality as represented in the test, and a way of recording our findings quickly for future reference. We tried to omit nothing of general importance and also to include only the major points in each sector of evaluation—color, form, movement, shading, content, etc. Our method of recording was to enter a check against any item on the list where the protocol under consideration showed a marked deviation from the usual. Two or even three checks were entered when the deviation was very marked. Thus normal reaction to the appearance of color received no check, mild color shock one check, severe color shock two or three checks.

"The rating discussed above is based upon a qualitative evaluation of all the data we were able to grasp in a short time, and it is more discriminating than the quantitative method now to be presented. Looking over our material, however, we found that simply *adding up the number of checks on the list for each student gave us a figure which corresponded well with the external criteria used to check the ratings.*

"Sixty-four students out of 121 had six checks or less. None of these girls was markedly disturbed and only one had even a mild, temporary upset. Conversely, the group of 31 girls who had more than 10 checks, included all but two of 19 students who showed fairly serious difficulties, academic or personal. In fact, only four of these girls did entirely satisfactory work and the descriptive comments of teachers suggested that none of them could be considered well adjusted.

"It does not seem possible, by *counting*, to evaluate degree of disturbance among the 31 girls having more than 10 checks. To date, this finer discrimination can be made only by the judgment of the examiner based on more complicated analysis. Reduction of a group of 121 to 30 for more careful study is of great practical importance, however, especially since filling out the check list seems to require far less experience and skill than orthodox use of the Rorschach. A rough knowledge of the scoring system is sufficient.

"In comparison with this method, we also tried out Harrower's criterion of 'neurotic signs,' equally objective and somewhat quicker. Students having not more than one 'neurotic sign' kept out of trouble to the same degree as those having not more than six checks. No other discrimination could be made by the 'signs,' however. Girls with two 'signs' had difficulties almost as often as those with three or four. This finding is not surprising if the neurotic signs are actually a measure of overt psychoneurosis. Very few college students have the open symptomatology characteristic of diagnosed patients. Neurosis *narrowly defined* is by no means the only reason for failure to handle life situations effectively.

"Reflection on the nature of the check list suggests that it works because, by design, it offers a *systematic* and *comprehensive* coverage of the resources of the personality. Adding up checks, therefore, becomes a meaningful procedure. Upward of 10 single checks scattered all over the lot actually mean a diffuse disturbance very likely to reduce the person's effectiveness—and very likely to be missed by the 'neurotic signs.' More serious difficulty in one or more sectors of adjustment, represented by double checks and a multiplication of checks in the same area, is reflected in a high score, *unless* all the other resources of the personality are functioning unusually well. A subject with marked difficulty in external relations will have a high number of checks in the color area. To keep the total number below 10 his handling of all other aspects of the test must be almost perfectly sound. An adequate score means that *other resources have been tested and found good.*

"As a rule, there is good correspondence between the neurotic signs and the check list—as would be expected from the fact that the check list includes all the signs. Discrepancies are likely to be clinically significant—a measure of the fact that secondary factors in the personality are either contributing unduly to its inadequacy, or on the contrary are functioning so well that the subject can handle his difficulties effectively. Our material suggests that, for unselected groups, it is worth while to spend the small amount of extra time required for recording the supplementary data.

"In passing, I would like to throw out the suggestion that such tests as the Bernreuter predict 'adjustment' badly, not so much because they are questionnaires as because the questions they ask are neither comprehensive nor systematic. Some types of failure in adaptive mechanisms are overemphasized, others neglected. Statistical item analysis does not handle this problem at all unless the experimental 'bad' group presents a single syndrome. These questionnaires have avowedly started with a list of symptoms and traits, not with an over-all concept of personality resources nor even clinical neurotic entities. Items have been retained when they occurred frequently in a heterogeneous 'bad' group. If we are correct in ascribing the observed success of the check list to its systematically inclusive character, it seems plausible to account for the observed inadequacy of the Bernreuter by the unsystematic character of its construction. (The Bernreuter was given to the group of 225 girls here discussed. Its prediction of emotional difficulty was somewhat better than chance, but not much. Failures in predictions did not show the relationship to the ACE described above for the Rorschach—nor was the large group of adjusted girls clearly delimited.) A psychiatrist would understand at once that a person may have few of the "frequent" neurotic symptoms and still be very neurotic, and that some quite adequate persons may be consistently on the introverted side—a trend which scores strong neurotic tendency on the Bernreuter.

"Again, our experimental material does not permit sound generalization. It seems likely, however, that our adjustment rating succeeded beyond other attempts of the sort, not so much because it was based on ink blots, as because of the way personality data are handled in the Rorschach and especially in our check list. The survey of the personality is complex, systematic and comprehensive. A questionnaire constructed on similar principles might very well serve the same purpose.

"In summary, then, our findings suggest that a measure of general adjustment can profitably be separated from capacity to deal with a particular situation such as academic work and recombined with measures of specific qualities for prediction of actual success in a given field. This method may well improve statistical prediction markedly in the majority of cases and isolate for intensive examination the small group where failures in prediction are frequent.

"A numerical figure of good validity was obtained by adding up deviant items on a check list, thus providing a relatively objective means of using the Rorschach. The success of this check list is probably due to its systematic, comprehensive survey of personality resources. Such balanced comprehensiveness is proposed as a basic— and heretofore neglected—principle in the construction of adjustment inventories" (25).*

What Are the Advantages of Such a Procedure?

The final question which we may ask is: what advantages accrue to the use of such a method? Before answering this let us admit that

* See also (26).

certain nuances in a record, obtainable by the individual method, will probably never be available under group conditions. The fact remains, however, that, even if a blunter weapon, we have in the group method an enormously powerful one. Quite apart from the practical advantages which pertain to the shortened time of administration, the amount of material which any one examiner can acquire in a relatively short space of time is startling when compared with the slow accumulation of individual records. To acquire several hundreds of records by the individual method in order that certain questions could be answered statistically was a major operation in itself. A similar number of records can now be acquired in a few hours. The availability of such large numbers of records opens up new avenues of research which in turn will greatly enlarge our understanding of the psychological processes involved in the original method of Hermann Rorschach.

REFERENCES

1. Abbott, W. D., Due, Floyd O. and Nosik, W. A.: Subdural hematoma and effusion as a result of blast injuries. *J. Am. Med. A., 121*:739-741, 1943.
2. Harrower, M. R. and Steiner, M. E.: Modification of the Rorschach method for use as a group test. *Rorschach Res. Exch., 5*:130-144, 1947. Also in: *J. Genet. Psychol., 62*:119-133, 1943.
3. Klopfer, Bruno and Kelley, D. M.: *The Rorschach Technique.* New York, World Book Co., 1943, viii+436 pp.
4. Rorschach, Hermann: *Psychodiagnostik.* Fourth edition, Bern, Switzerland, Hans Huber, 1942, 226 pp.
5. Sender, Sadie: The influence of variations in the Rorschach group method administration upon the scorability of the records. *Rorschach Res. Exch., 7*:54-69, 1943.
6. Hertz, Marguerite: A modification of the Rorschach inkblot test for large scale application. *J. Orthopsy., 13*:191-211, 1943.
7. Hertzman, Max: A comparison of the individual and group Rorschach tests. *Rorschach Res. Exch., 6*:89-108, 1942.
8. Munroe, Ruth: The group method with college students. Paper read at the meeting of the Rorschach Institute, New York, 1942.
9. Personal communication.
10. Buckle, D. F. and Cook, P. H.: Group Rorschach method: Technique. *Rorschach Res. Exch., 7*:159 ff, 1943.
11. Hertzman, Max and Seitz, Clifford: Rorschach reactions at high altitudes. *J. Psychol., 14*:245-257, 1942.
12. Personal communication.
13. Ross, W. D.; Dancey, T. E.; and, Brown, F. T.: Rorschach scores of parachute troopers in training. *Bull. Canad. Psychol. A., 3*: 2:26-27, 1943.
14. Munroe, Ruth: An experiment in large scale testing by a modification of the Rorschach method. *J. Psychol., 13*:229-263, 1942.
15. Harrower, M. R.: The Rorschach method in the study of personality. *Ann. New York Acad. Sc., 44*:569-583, 1943.

16. Krugman, Morris: The Rorschach in child guidance. *J. Consult. Psychol.,* 7: 2:80-88, 1943.
17. Hirning, L. C.: Report of the research committee. *Rorschach Res. Exch., 6:*177, 1942.
18. Banay, Ralph S.: Psychiatric technique and rehabilitation. *Yearbook Amer. Probat. A.,* 1942.
19. Lindner, R. M. and Chapman, K. W.: An eclectic group method. *Rorschach Res. Exch., 6:*139-146, 1942.
20. Lindner, R. M.: A further contribution to the group Rorschach. *Rorschach Res. Exch.,* 7:2-15, 1943.
21. Harrower, George, and Cox, Kenneth: The results obtained from a number of occupational groupings on the professional level with the Rorschach group method. *Bull. Canad. Psychol. A., 3:* 2:31-33, 1943.
22. Piotrowski, Zygmunt: Use of the Rorschach in vocational selection. *J. Consult. Psychol.,* 7: 2:97-102, 1943.
23. Hutt, Max: Some notes on the usefulness of the Rorschach method and the Rorschach as a group test. (Paper read at the symposium on the use of the Rorschach method in the armed forces, 1944.)
24. Harrower, M. R.: Personality testing in penal institutions. *Probation,* 22: *1:*1-6, 1943.
25. Munroe, Ruth: Discussion of the paper, "The Rorschach method in the study of personality," *Ann. New York Acad. Sc., 44:*583-588, 1943.
26. Munroe, Ruth: Prediction of the Adjustment and Academic Performance of College Students by a Modification of the Rorschach Method. *Appl. Psychol. Monog. No. 7,* Stanford Univ. Press, 1944.

Directions for the Administration of the Group Rorschach

A DMINISTRATION of the *Group Rorschach* is not a formidable or difficult task. Anyone who has given the test under the usual conditions will find that he is easily able to cope with a group of subjects once he has familiarized himself with the procedure.

So much depends, indeed, upon the particular examiner's rapport with his particular group that we are inclined to say that no absolutely hard and fast rules can be laid down. If an examiner finds himself forced, for instance, to alter, add, or omit some part of the following procedure or instructions, he is probably doing what is right for his own set-up and group of subjects and need not be disturbed. This is not tantamount to saying that the test cannot be standardized, but rather that here, as in the individual procedure, the spirit rather than the letter of the law must be followed. If one understands the kind of written response that is needed in order that the record may be properly scored and evaluated, it is not hard to deal with the situations which arise in order to be sure that each record is as complete as possible.

Since the general procedure has been briefly outlined in the previous chapter, we may now turn to a consideration of the details one by one.

Slides

Carefully reproduced slides of the 10 Rorschach cards[1] whether in the regular lantern size (3¼ inches by 4 inches) or on the 35 mm. Kodachrome roll film have been found to be satisfactory. For larger

---

[1] The reproductions of the Rorschach cards were originally made for our use by Mr. H. S. Hayden, F.R.P.S. Cards II, III, VIII, IX and X were made on Kodachrome cut film; Cards I, IV, V, VI and VII on Ilford lantern plates. All sets of slides were checked by the experimenters, as it was found that slight differences in shading, imperceptible to persons not familiar with the cards, were sufficient to give a wrong "flavor" to the blot. Slide 7 for example, if slightly too dark, may lose its "cloudiness." The set used in our initial experiments has been taken as the standard, and subsequent sets have been equated with it. Both slides and booklets are now obtainable from The Psychological Corporation, 522 Fifth Ave., New York 18, N. Y.

auditoriums the regular sized slides are recommended, but in small class rooms the 35 mm films are equally good. It is also possible to use the cards themselves in an epidiascope, provided the epidiascope is in good condition and reproduces a clear and complete picture.

Projector

A standard sized projector placed so as to produce an image of approximately five feet by six feet seems very satisfactory for large auditoriums. In general, however, it will be found that the usual position of the projector in the auditorium in question may be accepted as the correct one. Thus no hard and fast rule can be laid down as to the exact size of the image thrown on the screen. There is one important point in this connection, *i.e.*, that the examiner looks at the image from all the side seats (so as to be sure that there is no distortion from too great an angle) and from the front and back seats (to check on the possibility of too marked a discrepancy in size between these two positions). In a very large auditorium the seats in the front two rows and back rows may have to be discarded.

Visibility of the Image to All Subjects

McCulloch (1) has made an interesting suggestion in connection with the seating arrangements and their effect on the results; namely, that inasmuch as subjects differing in visual acuity are scattered with respect to their distance from the screen, it would be well to include a standardized lantern slide of a Snellen chart and have each subject record the lowest line of letters legible to him. He states:

"A correlation of the letters actually visible to the particular subjects under these circumstances, with their tendency to respond to forms as a whole or to pick out details, might indicate that a purely extraneous type of response was obtained. The lack of such a correlation would of course indicate its insignificance." In order to settle the question experimentally, Dr. McCulloch has prepared lantern slides in which the entire height of the standard Snellin chart occupies the same height as the Rorschach blot on the slide.

In the same way we might add here that it would be advantageous to include, as a standard preliminary, one of the Ishihara charts in order to detect those persons with color blindness or color weakness in the group.

The Screen

The screen that is already in use in the auditorium will be found in most cases to be satisfactory provided it is in good condition. Beaded screens give very brilliant images from the center of the hall, but give definitely less saturated images from the sides. If the screen is beaded, therefore, subjects must be seated in the center of the hall only.

Lighting

This phase of the work constituted somewhat of a problem. In order that the slides may be seen to the best advantage, the room or auditorium should be as dark as possible. On the other hand, of course, some light is necessary for the recording of responses. Our first idea was to use one dim light somewhere in the auditorium but we found rather to our surprise that the light from the slides themselves was sufficient to enable our subjects to write their responses. That this was possible may have been partly due to the fact that our auditorium was built up in tiers so that for no person was the light obscured by the individual in front of him. We therefore must emphasize that this was a condition which was possible in our auditorium but which perhaps would not be possible in others.

We tried out one variation but found it unsatisfactory. This was to switch the light off and on alternately for periods of 30 seconds, requesting observation during the dark period, and recording during the light period. Interestingly enough those subjects submitted to this variation unanimously requested to be allowed to write in the dark. Porbably the best suggestion is to have one dim light available at the back of the hall shielded so that it does not shine directly on the screen, but bright enough to afford some guidance in the matter of recording. We always stressed the fact that handwriting need not be neat, and to our knowledge no difficulty arose in this connection. All answers, incidentally, were perfectly legible. When the slides were changed, the light in the projector was extinguished momentarily, thus contributing to, rather than lessening, the dark adaptation. This is a minor point, however, and it is quite possible that a momentary period of brighter light would have been a better interlude than the momentary total darkness.

Time

After considerable experimentation a three-minute exposure of each card was decided on. Time intervals shorter than three minutes were not long enough for the average subject. Intervals longer than three minutes were unnecessary except in a very few individual cases. If, however, there is no time limit to the experiment as a whole, there is no reason why more time might not be allowed to each card.

One of the aims in this particular experiment was to see whether the whole test could be completed within approximately one hour, and having discovered that this was possible, we kept the total time constant for all our groups.

Turning the Slides

In the same way it might be said that if a longer total time is to be allowed, each slide might well be exposed for perhaps one minute in the reverse position in addition to the three minutes in the usual position. Our experience on this point, however, leads us to conclude that not enough was gained by this turning to justify the extension of the time limit we had set for the test. It is also interesting to note that certain answers were given as if the cards had been turned, the subjects turning their heads so as to get the impression more clearly.

Manner of Recording Responses

Special booklets were prepared for the subjects to write in, all answers pertaining to one slide being written on one page, and the pages turned as the slides changed. Originally the pages were folded so as to conceal the diagrams used in localizing the responses. This proved unnecessary and the booklets now used are not folded. Hertz (2) and Sender (3) have suggested other types of recording blanks.

Instructions

It may be valuable at this point to outline in chronological order the series of events as they took place. When our subjects arrived in the auditorium they found in each seat a pencil and the booklet in which the answers were to be recorded. A notice on the blackboard stated: "Do not open the booklets you will find on the seats." The examiner waiting in front of the auditorium chatted informally with the subjects as they came in, calling attention to the notice on the board and to the pencils they would find together with the booklets. When all subjects were seated, the examiner mounted the platform, called for their attention and the test proper began.

We have said previously that the instructions were similar to those given in the individual test. Perhaps it is well in this connection, however, to be more specific and to "dot all the i's." While we feel that there can be no set formula, we advocate some such statement as the following to open the procedure:

"The test which you are about to take is rather an interesting one and I think you will enjoy it. All you have to do is to look at some slides which will be projected on the screen and write down what you see. Now the point about these slides is that they are nothing more or less than reproductions of ink blots. Probably all of you at one time or another have shaken your pen on a piece of paper, caused a blot of ink, and on folding the paper produced a weird splotch which may or may not have resembled something that you recognized. Now these slides are nothing more than reproductions of ink blots formed in this way. Your task is simply to write down what these splotches remind you of, resemble, or might be. You will see each

DIAGRAM OF SLIDE USED TO EXPLAIN THE
LOCATION OF RESPONSES

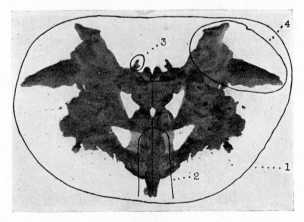

FIGURE 1

of these slides or blots for three minutes and you may write your answers at your own time. Is that understood? It may help you later in the test if you make a point of numbering your answers to each side as you write them down."

After instructions about the nature of the ink blots, the booklets were described and explained. It was emphasized that a page should be turned each time the slides changed; that is, all answers to a given slide should be recorded on a separate page.

The ten slides were then shown in the usual order for three minutes. Between each slide we paused to be sure that all the pages had been turned. When the tenth slide had been shown for three minutes the lights in the auditorium were all put on, the examiner again mounted the platform and after a few informal remarks explained the next phase of the task.

INSTRUCTIONS FOR THE LOCATING OF RESPONSES

"Well, this is the first part of the experiment. Now we shall go on to the second. I'm sure you will have seen a lot of amusing and different things in the various inkblots, but one of the important aspects of this test is the fact that I must know as accurately as possible just what it is you have seen and where it is you have seen it. In order that you can do this, you will find on each page a little diagram representing the slide." At this point Slide I with various areas marked off on it was thrown on the screen and the examiner continued:

"Now perhaps some of you saw on this particular slide a butterfly, and then perhaps you also saw the legs of some person in the center here, and perhaps a boxing glove in this little protuberance here or a dog's head here on the side. (While speaking of these objects the examiner points to the areas referred to which are encircled by a dark line on the slide.) Your next task, therefore, is to number your own answers, if you forgot to do so before, and then with your pencil to draw a line around the area where you saw that particular object and attach to that area the number of the answer you are describing. For example, let us suppose you have seen just those four things which I mentioned. You would put a number 1 by 'a butterfly' draw a line all the way around the miniature ink blot and put a number 1 beside this line. If 'somebody's legs' was your second answer, you would number that 2, draw a careful pencil line around the area on the diagram and attach a number 2 to it. In other words you will do for all your own answers what has been done for these hypothetical answers on the screen."

INSTRUCTIONS FOR OBTAINING ADDED INFORMATION

After the instructions concerning the *recording of the location* of responses have been given, Slide VIII may be thrown on the screen and *added information concerning the responses* may be asked for. Our instructions at this point were something of this sort:

"Before you begin to mark off your answers, there is something else you have to do for me. You have to help me reconstruct as accurately as possible the kind of experiences you have been having or some of the characteristics of the things you saw. You might, for instance, have seen two bears or two animals here on the side. You might have seen two flags here in the center, or you might have called these same parts two cushions. This part here (pink and orange) might have reminded you of some kind of flower.

Some of you may have said, for example, that the bears looked as if they were climbing up, but it is also very possible that you did not put in that last bit of information. Now is your chance to do so if you want to. If you want to explain to me that the animals you saw looked as if they were stepping from one rock to another, you may add that information now. But perhaps you did *not* see them as if they were stepping. Fine! That is just as important. Perhaps they looked to you as if they were some kind of animal on a heraldic design and you may have already said so. In that case you will not need to give any more information.

Let us suppose that you not only saw cushions here but saw *blue satin* cushions. In this case you would again amplify your answer because it is important for me to know whether you got the impression of the satiny or silky feel of the cushion, and whether you were impressed by its blueness. Again this area may have reminded you of a flower because it was the color of the sweet peas in your back yard. If it was the color that attracted your attention and made you think of those sweet peas, then add this information by writing in the word, 'color.' "

After the instructions have been given and after any pertinent questions have been answered, the slides may be projected again in the usual order, each being shown for approximately two minutes. The word "approximately" is used here because it was easy for the examiner standing in front of the group to see when the subjects had finished this phase of their task. On some slides it was not necessary to wait for a full two minutes to elapse before going on to the next. During this period the lights in the room were on, allowing for accurate delineations of the areas, although the slides themselves were still clearly visible though perhaps not quite as brilliant as before.

Discussion of the Location of Responses in the Group Test

The location of responses by the subject, after full explanations and illustrations have been given, and after he has been allowed to ask questions, seems to us one of the most important features of the group method. It is impossible to score accurately without knowing the correct location of the area employed in the perception. Moreover, this second phase of the test gives us, in addition, further information about the subject and his ability to carry out instructions carefully and accurately which should be utilized to the full. Actually in this procedure we have something analogous to the graphic Rorschach described by Rochlin and Levine (4), a source of additional information over and above that derived from the responses *per se*.

It will be noticed in leafing through records from "normal" or unselected subjects that there is considerable variation in the accuracy with which one and the same location is indicated. Some individuals are content with careless lines, others seem to be much more concerned with a faithful delineation. Where as many as ten answers have been given to one card, we sometimes find a maze of pencil lines which are difficult to disentangle. In other cases with a similar number of answers we will have no difficulty for the subject has spontaneously resorted to the use of different colored leads, if he happens to have them, or to different kinds of lines in order to demarcate the areas clearly.

Among abnormal subjects, psychotics and psychopathic personalities, an even more interesting range of performance is found. Examples of some of the varied attempts found among abnormal subjects together with the more usual forms which the delineation takes are given in Figures 2 and 3.

There is, for example, the ridiculously punctilious individual who outlines each little indentation of the blot, even for whole responses like bat or butterfly to card V, and as in the illustration the "thoracic picture" to card IV (see Figure 3 d). Then there is the individual who superimposes his impressions by drawing in lines as in the "Springfield 38" and the details added in the heel of the boot, when there is nothing in the blot to suggest these particular features (Figure 3 c). There is the individual who gives perfectly good answers (if not "popular" at least well-recognized as occurring frequently in average records), but who is unable to locate them at all, merely placing numbers by the side of the blot and making a few tentative and rambling lines over the surface of the diagram (Figure 3 b). There is also the individual who introduces many quite unhelpful lines and words onto his diagram, lines which are, shall we say, the graphic counterpart of his verbal answer. Just as his answer is both hesitant and unnecessarily verbose ("This appears slightly to resemble segments of a physical geography map showing mountains and lowlands") so his frequent repetition of the word "lowlands" on the diagram seems to illustrate the same trait (Figure 3 a).

We have included the clinical diagnoses with these particular cases, but it should not be assumed that all persons with a similar diagnosis would make identical drawings. In an unselected group, however, the appearance of this unusual method of locating responses has proved of value in screening.

Discussion of the Inquiry to Elicit Further Information Regarding the Determinants

We have utilized two types of booklets in regard to this phase of the test. One edition of the booklet contains the words, *Shape, Color, Movement,* and *Texture* as will be seen in Figure 4 A. Where this edition is used the instructions are for the subject to put *the number of the answer under the headings which are pertinent.* For example, if "blue satin cushions" was his third answer to card VIII, a number 3 would have been put under *color, shape,* and *texture.*

In the alternative form of the booklet the diagram of the card is also given, but no statements are included in regard to the inquiry. When such booklets are used the subjects are asked to *amplify their answers*

Responses

1. Butterfly
2. Man with bowler hat
3. A leg

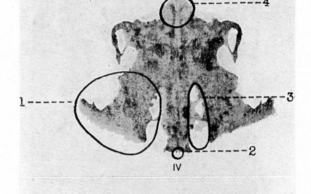

Responses

1. Boots
2. Little feet
3. A profile in white
4. A flower at the top

Responses

1. Clown
2. Scotties

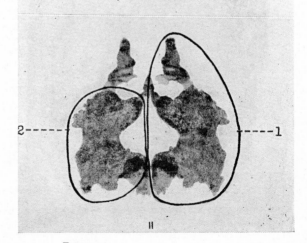

FIGURE 2

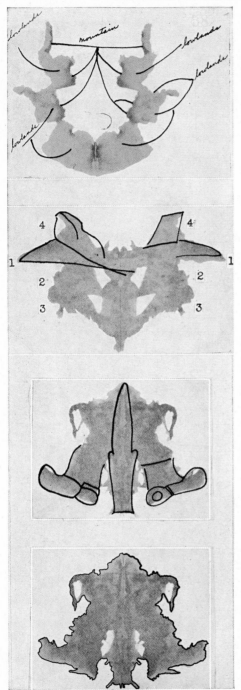

a.

Answer to Card VII

This appears slightly to resemble segments of a physical geography map showing mountains and lowlands.

Illustration of somewhat complicated demarcation.

Clinical diagnosis: Schizophrenia.

b.

Answers to Card I

1. Bat
2. Bell
3. Hour glass
4. Two dancers

Illustration of numbering without demarcating areas.

Clinical diagnosis: Psychosis with mental deficiency.

c.

Answers to Card IV

Springfield 38 cartridge.

Men's boots kicking out.

Illustrations of added details at variance with outline of blot which nonetheless enhance the concept.

Clinical diagnosis: Schizophrenia with paranoid trend.

d.

Answer to Card IV

Such as a thoracic picture.

Illustration of careful and painstaking delineation which is in no way necessary to the task at hand.

Clinical diagnosis: Schizophrenia.

FIGURE 3

in their own way in order to give us as much information as possible about what it is they see (Figure 4 B).

Sometimes this amplification involves merely the statement "color" or "blue" or "alive" or "walking" written by the side of the answer. Sometimes quite lengthy descriptions are added.

SAMPLE PAGE FROM BOOKLET CONTAINING SPECIFIC INQUIRY

This space is to help you describe your answers more fully. Put the number of your answer under any of these words if by so doing you can amplify it in the way just discussed. Add additional words if you need to use them.	*Answers*
	1. A coat of arms.
	2. A sweet pea.
	3. Crossed flags.
	4. Animals.

Shape   Color   Movement   Texture
  1   1
  2   2
  3   3   3
                     4

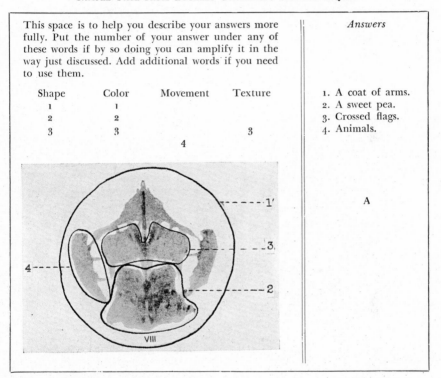

A

FIGURE 4A.

The final published form of the Booklet contains both these possibilities, so that the examiner may use whichever form of the inquiry he prefers, instructing the subjects accordingly.

The exact form which the inquiry should take or what kind of recording blanks should be used has been discussed by Hertz (2) and Sender (3). Our method which contains the use of specific determinants printed in the booklets (see Figure 4 A) has been called "modified inquiry" by Sender, and the "specific factor method" by Hertz. The procedure which allowed the subject to amplify his own answers without these specific suggestions (Figure 4 B) is referred to as the "free inquiry" by Hertz and the "minimum prodding method" by Sender and Klopfer.

From our own experience with both methods it would appear that each has its value. The best will depend to a large extent on the type of subjects who are taking the test, the amount of time which can be devoted to the study of each record and the reason for which

SAMPLE PAGE FROM BOOKLET ASKING FOR AMPLIFICATION OF ANSWERS

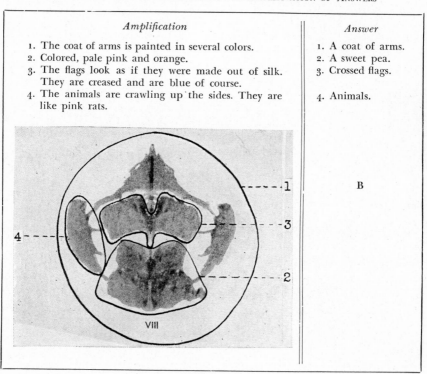

Amplification	Answer
1. The coat of arms is painted in several colors.	1. A coat of arms.
2. Colored, pale pink and orange.	2. A sweet pea.
3. The flags look as if they were made out of silk. They are creased and are blue of course.	3. Crossed flags.
4. The animals are crawling up the sides. They are like pink rats.	4. Animals.

FIGURE 4B.

a record is taken. Hertz has also found both methods useful as the following quotations show. On the one hand she finds:

"The technique of identifying the specific factors that determine responses by questions as to Form, Movement, Color and Shading, is reliably more successful than the Free Inquiry in all groups studied, substantiating this part of Harrower's procedure. This procedure is easy for all subjects whether they have had previous experience with the test or not. For the more intelligent subjects, however, either procedure is adequate for accurate description of responses given."

On the other hand she states: "Although the results show that the Specific Factor method is a reliably better technique for eliciting necessary information concerning the responses given, where subjects are capable of expressing themselves in a Free Inquiry, the information gleaned is of more value than the more restricted enumeration of specific factors. No doubt use of the Free Inquiry should be restricted to the more intelligent subject or to certain subjects who are recalled for additional information."

Hertz's final conclusions, however, are in favor of the specific factor method which she includes in her *Directions for large scale application of the Rorschach method*. While the following instructions do not differ in essence from those which we used originally, they have been added to show how different examiners may need to reword the same information for use with any particular group of subjects:

"While you are locating your responses, we want you to fill in the narrow right hand margin headed 'Factors' by indicating which of these four factors, *Form, Movement, Color, Shading,* was influential in suggesting the responses to you. Ask yourself, was it Form of the blot, or the Movement in it, or the Color or the Shading or a combination of two or more of these? You may use the symbols F, M, C, and Sh in giving these factors. Write these symbols in the last column opposite your responses, numbering them to correspond to the number of the response to which they refer.

"Look at the example. In the Factor column, these symbols are indicated and numbered to show the responses to which they refer.

"Where two or more of these factors were involved in the response they are indicated in order of importance.

"Thus in the example, for Response 2, *Color and Form* determined the answer. C and F are therefore indicated which means that color was more influential and form, too, helped in the determination of the response.

"Write these words at the top of your page so that you will remember them, underlining the F, M, C, and Sh, the symbols.

"If you care to add any descriptive words or remarks you may do so in the blank space which is provided for the purpose.

"If you care to add any response or make any comments you may do so in the empty space.

"Now if you understand your two-fold task, we will show the blots to you again, one by one. Start locating your responses on the outlines and indicate in the last column by letters F, M, C, and Sh, or any two or more of these, what determined your answers" (2).

Sender's conclusions favor the use of the minimum prodding technique:

"Thus the results of this study cannot be assumed to indicate that the Modified Inquiry Method would not be adequate for use with highly selective groups by examiners who have had wide experience with the Rorschach Method. However, this study *does* indicate that in applying the Group Method to heterogeneous groups, the Minimum Prodding Technique is more efficient because it elicits no misleading information but calls forth descriptive and informative explanations and elaborations which are helpful in the scoring of the records, contribute toward a more accurate qualitative interpretation, reduce the time for scoring, and make possible the use of less experienced workers for scoring of group records" (3).

Other methods of eliciting information in order that records may be more accurately scored may be briefly mentioned. Hertzman (5) has asked for amplification of responses, without giving examples to illustrate the form which such an amplification might take. This has been referred to as the "minimal inquiry." Lindner and Chapman (6) have suggested a "tutorial inquiry," which is, in effect, an individual inquiry to be given after the records have been taken by the group procedure. As we reported originally (7), utilization of an individual inquiry is quite satisfactory, provided the group under consideration is not too large. We have also advocated that an individual inquiry should be used by every examiner, for at least the first twenty records which he takes under group conditions, regardless of what type of group inquiry he is using.

Buckle and Cook (8) have reported that they rely solely on the location of responses for information in the inquiry and do not include the phase which deals with the determinants. This raises the question of when a record can be taken at its face value and scored only in terms of the original and spontaneously recorded responses.

After considerable experience with various and varied groups we have come to the conclusion that for extremely rapid *screening purposes,* for spotting of grossly abnormal personalities, and only the grossly abnormal, an inquiry is not imperative.

In dealing with college students or with equivalent groups, however, we have made it a practice always to include some form of inquiry. There are unquestionably debatable points in scoring which *can* be solved when the individual's additional remarks are taken into account. We found also that the failure to recognize and acknowledge an obvious component in the response was in itself indicative of certain personality characteristics.

As a larger body of material from students was accumulated, it became clear that failure to understand the instructions for the inquiry in the time allowed was an extremely rare occurrence. If an individual fails in this part of the task it provides important information about him. In the same way we gain an insight into the behavior of the individual who takes the inquiry so seriously and labors over it with such pains that he asks to take the record home in order to be able to do the job more efficiently, or the individual who asks permission to stay on after the other students have left in order to be quite sure he has done everything he should.

Then, much can be gained from a study of *how* each student records the information asked for in the inquiry. Many are satisfied to follow the specific suggestions given, namely, to put the number of the answer under the various headings where it belongs, or to add a brief amplification, but others *without any encouragement* spontaneously record more elaborate additions to their original answers.

In contrast to the *college age* group we have felt that an inquiry is counterindicated among certain other subjects. We have not used this phase of the inquiry with high school students under 16 years of age, nor with groups of predominantly low intelligence, nor with groups where the span of attention was more circumscribed than normal as, for example, certain types of psychotic patients. Where groups contain varied intelligence levels (even if amongst them are those of subnormal intelligence) *an inquiry may sharpen the difference between some of the subjects,* namely, between those who can and those who cannot follow the instructions. An inquiry is, therefore, of value if a blind diagnosis is to be made in which we must include as much information as possible about the status, intellectual and emotional, of the subject.

An interesting suggestion by Ross may be included at this point. In a short report (9) he advocated the use of half scores when for some reason or other the inquiry has not yielded sufficient information concerning the proper determinant by which a response should be scored.

"In the application of the Rorschach group test to a military purpose, where it has been desirable to obtain scores which could be treated in a statistical manner, the difficulty has been encountered that many of the subjects have failed to supply information adequate for confident scoring of the determinants. This difficulty occurred whether or not booklets were used with headings for the designation of the determinants. In many cases the subjects omitted to acknowledge a determinant which is known commonly to play a part in the particular response in question, e.g., the use of shading in an animal skin for IV or VI or the presence of movement in the side animals in VIII. When individual inquiries have been done on some of these subjects, it has been found that in some cases the subject was taking the usual determinant so much for granted that he forgot to mention it; but in other cases it was found that the subject would not recognize the determinant in question. With individual inquiries out of the question in the examination of large groups, there is the danger of scoring these responses in one of two arbitrary fashions: either according to the most commonly used determinant for that response or according to an assumption that responses not elaborated further are F responses.

"To reduce this dilemma to a consistent quantitative figure which will give some benefit of doubt to the inarticulate subject and yet penalize him for failure to elaborate more adequately, we have tried out a system of half scores. Where there is reasonable doubt between an F and an FM, an F and an Fc, or an Fc and a cF, etc., one-half response is scored for each of these. This half point system has also been extended to additional responses, secondary determinants, tendencies to another determinant and to a few other scoring items. The latter include F/C, scored as one-half FC, C/F as one-half CF, restricted movement or poses, scoring (M) or (FM) as one-half M or one-half FM. In the case of secondaries, or F/Cs (M)s, etc., within additional responses, the scores may be reduced to 1/4 or even 1/8. The system of one-half scores has been applied before to some of the responses excluding those involving percentage estimation but we have not been aware of its application to all additionals and to these special cases. There seems considerable merit in using it in this way insofar as the subjects who present additional responses during the inquiry should receive recognition of these in any statistical treatment of their results, including their total number of responses. Similarly, should the secondary features receive such cognizance although not to the full weight of primary locations and determinants.

"These modifications in group scoring procedure are submitted for consideration as a means of reducing secondary and doubtful scores to a quantitative expression which will aid in the statistical treatment of the data. It is recognized that something is lost in crowding these various nuances into the simplicity of half scores but it is believed at the same time that validity is added to the statistically treatable scores which are derived. This should facilitate the validation of the method for large scale screening purposes."

References

1. Personal communication.
2. Hertz, Marguerite: Modification of the Rorschach inkblot test for large scale application. *J. Orthopsy., 13:* 2:191-211, 1943.
3. Sender, Sadie: The influence of variations in the Rorschach group method administration upon the scorability of the records. *Rorschach Res. Exch.,* 7:54-69, 1943.
4. Rochlin, Gregory, and Levine, Kate: The graphic Rorschach test. *Arch. Neurol. Psychiat., 47:*438-448, 1942.
5. Hertzman, Max: Recent research on the group Rorschach test. *Rorschach Res. Exch.,* 7:1-6, 1943.
6. Lindner, R. M., and Chapman, K.: An eclectic group method. *Rorschach Res. Exch., 6:*139-146, 1942.
7. Harrower, M. R., and Steiner, M. E.: Modification of the Rorschach method for use as a group test. *Rorschach Res. Exch.,* 5:130-144, 1941. Also in: *J. Genet. Psychol., 62:*119-133, 1943.
8. Buckle, D. F., and Cook, P. H.: Group Rorschach method: *Technique. Rorschach Res. Exch.,* 7:159 ff, 1943.
9. Ross, W. D.: A contribution to the objectification of group Rorschach scoring. *Rorschach Res. Exch.,* 7:70, 1943.

Scoring Group Rorschach Records

W E NOTED in the introduction that we would make no attempt to explain the scoring principles involved in the Rorschach. In the examples which follow in this chapter, therefore, we are not attempting to show why responses are scored in this way but have only collected together under the headings of the various determinants responses which are clearly akin to those obtained in the individual method.

The procedure which we advocate in scoring is to first read through the whole booklet of responses and then to score these responses slide by slide *without reference to any additional information* that might be given by the subject himself. When this is done, the inquiry flap for each answer may be turned, and a comparison made between the information given by the subject with the scoring we have arrived at by direct inspection of the answers. As we have previously stated, we gave a group of 40 of our 110 subjects an "individual inquiry" on the answers obtained in the group test, and feel it is well for every examiner to do this for some 20 cases in order to see for himself how much may be taken at its face value in the written records.

Perhaps the best way to illustrate what one is confronted with in scoring is to quote from some of the actual records. The ease with which answers can be scored varies considerably. There are, for instance, those answers which are extremely explicitly stated by the subject in the spontaneous recording. On the other hand there are answers which have to be taken at their face value—those to which conclusions have to be reached without additional evidence. There are also responses which the subject cannot or does not bother to amplify; for example, "cat" (to Card I) with the whole area delineated, which means, as a matter of fact, a cat's face.

In the following pages we have taken examples to illustrate the kind of responses which we scored under various determinants developed by Klopfer from Rorschach's original list.

a. M. In general it must be said that M is not difficult to determine. Almost all human figure responses include explicit references to movement or posture. For example:

Card III

"Two little men in old-fashioned evening clothes dancing or whirling around the floor opposite each other." (In this case both movement and color were indicated by the subject.)

"Two servants carrying a container full of fuel for the fire in the background." (Our scoring with M and an additional CF on this answer was verified in the individual inquiry.)

Card II

"An oriental dance; two masked, robed figures clapping one hand and stamping their feet in unison." (Both movement and color were indicated by the subject and in the individual inquiry the color was revealed as relating to the caps. Our scoring on the basis of the Group-test alone had been *M* with an additional *FC*.)

Again on *II* we have such answers as: "Two witches doing a pat-a-cake dance around the fire." (Fire, lower red. An *M, CF* scoring was indicated by the subject and was verified in the individual inquiry.)

b. FM. Examples of *FM* are as follows:

"A bat flying through the air."
"A bat gasping for breath."
"A bat about to stretch its wings."
"A bat poised for flight."

Innumerable other examples could be given:

"Worms crawling" (in *X*).
"A couple of mice clinging to part of an ancient skeleton" (*VIII*).
"Two little animals trying to crawl on to a bough" (*VIII*).

Less explicit but also verifiable on individual inquiry are such answers as "chameleons" with movement and color marked, the Individual inquiry revealing that the animals were "climbing up the side."

c. m. Movement of inanimate objects, expressions, and "atmospheric impressions" were all found amongst our records. We scored as *m* or additional *m* such answers as:

Card VI

"Impression one might get of a rocket ship taking off from landing."

Card IV

"Torpedo leaving gun over black oily water."

Card IX

"Circular motion."

Card I

"Some threatening evil spirit."

Card V

"A strong but untrustworthy man's face" (*de*).

d. k. Good examples of this type of response have already been given. The repeated reference to x-rays called for a scoring of this kind. Similarly the well-known geographical answers, topographical and relief maps, were frequently found.

e. K. The majority of these answers were found in the cards *IX* and *VII*. They included clouds of all varieties, colored and uncolored, and were usually recorded by the subjects themselves as having been prompted by texture, or by texture and color.

Card IX

"Clouds in a sunset."

"Something poured into odd shaped bowls, comes out at the other end and gives off a colored vapor." (Movement, color, texture recorded.)

"Some sort of water jet with water spouting up in the middle."

"A volcano, it seems to be bubbling and boiling all around and the steam is just beginning to gush up. Suggests fire in its color. The center part seems quite thick." (Movement, color, and texture were all recorded.)

f. FK. As will be seen in Figure 4, Section II, we did not include "vista" amongst the words on the flap in the booklet. It seemed to us, after the first trial booklet had been in use that this was unnecessary, for vista responses were as a rule stated explicitly. We record a few examples:

Card II

"Corridor leading to a throne with a canopy over the top" (a *drs* response).

Card III

"The red section in the middle resembles a corridor leading down to a door at the end."

Card VII

"I can practically see a long steamship passing through a very narrow canal" (a *d* response).

(All these responses were given by the same subject.)

The following examples are taken from another record:

Card IV

"A scene taken from a plane showing houses, hills, churches, ruins, lakes."

Card VI

"A tower built on a hill." (This answer, given again in the individual record and investigated in the inquiry, confirmed the expectation of the vista element.)

g. F. This category can be illustrated by such *de* answers as: "a face," "a man's profile," "an Indian's head," "a man's leg" and many other human details. There are also the "bat" responses where movement is explicitly denied or shape indicated as the only determinant, and many other objects which in the opinion of both the subject and the examiner are determined by shape alone.

h. Fc and c. Perhaps the categories concerning which there is most likelihood of confusion are the *Fc* and *c* scores. In the author's experience, however, these frequently present difficulties in Individual tests also. Some out and out *c* responses are not hard to determine, for example: "pelt," "hide," "skin" (to Cards *VI* and *IV* with texture alone recorded). Or again, "an open sore" (a *di* in *VI*), "a fungus growth" or "sponge" (Card *I*) or "dress material, some sort of soft goods" (Card *VIII*).

Nor are certain *Fc* responses difficult: "A thick twisted old Chinese pine tree" (to Card *IV*, texture and shape), "tabby cat's paw," "a lamb's tail," and "a turtle with its neck out and feathers around it."

However, "a leopard skin hung on the wall with some kind of totem pole in the middle" was scored as *W Fc* on the basis of the group-test information, but the individual inquiry in this case led us to re-score this in terms of two separate responses, *c* and *Fc*. A number of minor corrections of this kind could be referred to. Perhaps we can epitomize this by saying that while there seems to be no difficulty in discovering if shading was utilized, the weight that should be given to it is more difficult to assess in some cases in the Group method.

i. C'. The scoring of *C'* caused relatively few problems. Many subjects spontaneously utilized the word "color" on the inquiry flap, putting in brackets "black" in order to convey their impressions. For example:

Card I

"German imperial emblem" (marked for both movement and "black").

Card IV

"A black bearskin rug."

Card V

"A black bat."

Card VII

"A bright image between the mountains." (This was a white space response and was scored as "color" by the subject.)

There are also responses where "black" is not recorded but can easily be deduced as for example: "a cloud of smoke in the sky." Color is not recorded by the subject in regard to this answer but the individual inquiry confirmed our suspicions that there was a C' element involved. Also scorable as C' are such answers as: "a central line and black and gray splash."

j. FC. While *CF*'s were probably one of the easiest determinants to score accurately in the Group method, *FC*'s presented at first somewhat of a problem. We hesitated to score an answer *FC* in the first 40 records taken by the Group method until Individual inquiry had reinforced our original expectations. We soon found, however, that frequently the record in its entirety gave a clue to an answer which in itself might have been questionable. For example, in Card *II* Subject *RU* responds with "butterfly," giving the determinant as color. How is this to be scored? The answers of this subject to *VIII, IX,* and *X* give us useful information, for in these she shows herself capable of genuine *FC*'s which can be distinguished from her *CF*'s. Her answer to *VIII* is, for example, "a bowl with a plant in it, the two animals being a decorative part of the bowl" (*W*). In her opinion color was the most important determinant, but the form element is plainly visible. In the same way in *IX* and *X* she delineates areas as "a cactus leaf" and "a bloom" (the yellow in *X*). These same answers when repeated in the Individual records gave unmistakable evidence of the utilization of form.

There is no reason, therefore, to doubt that the form of the red butterfly was not accurately seen in *II*, thereby justifying an *FC* score. Neither is there any reason to suppose that *FC* is not the appropriate scoring for "two small caterpillars" (in *X*), nor for "a very majestic pine tree" (in *VIII*), "butterfly" (in the lower portion of *VIII*), and such answers as "the cross section of a red tulip upside-down" (in *X*), "lobsters" (in *IX*), when color is claimed as significant by the subject.

k. CF. There were certainly no dearth of *CF* responses in our records. Here are some of the many examples:

Card II

"Red at the bottom looks like the disintegration of a comet."
"Coals in a lighted fire."

"Fire starting at the bottom."
"Picture of a bomb explosion."

Card VIII

"A forest fire."
"Lower part looks like the inside of a beef steak done rare."
"The colors remind me of the diagrams in biology of the circulatory system."
"A map, colors not shape."

Card IX

"Flames in a fireplace."
"Clouds in a sunset."
"Crude oil burning."
"Colorful chemical experiment."
"Surrealist art."

Card X

"An afghan."
"A colorful rock garden."
"A beautiful garden in Japan."

For all these responses the subjects themselves recorded the importance of color.

l. C. Color naming, color symbolism, and color comments also featured in the records.

Card IX

"Orange, then green with pinkish mass at the bottom."

Card II

"Two headless men kneeling before an altar, giving praise to some phenomenon, the color of which is red."

Color comment.

Card IX

"Something unpleasant; I don't like orange."

Card II

"Combination of two colors I don't like. I don't know why, though."

Card VIII

"The shade of blue and rose gives me a pleasant feeling. Reminds me of spring."

Color and Shading Shock

How will color and shading shock manifest themselves under the new conditions? At first sight it might seem that these important indices would be lost in the new procedure. The following examples, however, will serve to show that, far from being obscured by the new method, they stand out as clearly as before.

  1. *Failure on colored and shaded cards*
Example: Nothing written on page, or "This does not remind me of anything."
  2. *Delay before answering*
Example: "After the longest time I decided this might be a rug" (response to slide VI).
  3. *Color comment preceding response*
Example: "Red, black and white" (on slide II) "Blue, pink and orange" (on slide VIII).
  4. *Comment and no response*
Example: 1. "There are two similar shaped blots on each side with one red blot joining them below. And a red blot above each side at the top. At the top the black blotches go forward to a point" (slide II).
        2. "Central gray line and gray splash (slide VI).
  5. *Unjustified anatomical and geographical answers*
Example: "Organs" (response to VIII, IX, and X). "Map of England" (response to VIII).
  6. *Senseless repetition*
Example: "The spinal cavity of a fish, the spinal cavity of a cricket, the spinal cavity of a crawfish, the spinal cavity of a lobster" (response to VIII).
  7. *False starts*
Example: Sentences begun and then crossed out in slide II, occurring nowhere else in the record.
  8. *Noticeably fewer answers on certain cards*
Example: 1. Four or five answers to Card I to be followed by only one answer to Card II.
        2. Three or four answers for each card up to Card VIII with noticeably fewer answers on the last three cards.
        3. Several answers on Cards I to V; only one answer on Card VI.

The number of answers which may be expected from any given card in percentage terms will be seen in Part II, Section XI, Table VI. Noticeable deviations from the figures found in these tables will therefore be an indication of a disturbance on the card in question.

While these examples of color and shading shock which we have listed are in all probability not the only ones, they do show that in the group method one is certainly not without clear indications of the type of disturbance usually referred to in this way.

Discussion of Research Methods

T HE TASK of evaluating over eight thousand responses from the threefold angle of their location, determinants, and content was quite a formidable one! Consequently the technique which we found to be the simplest and most likely to avoid pitfalls may be briefly described.

TYPE OF CHART USED TO RECORD THE RESPONSES UNDER THEIR SPECIFIC
LOCATION AND WITH THE DETERMANANTS

CONTENT	W	D1	D2	d1	d3	Dr	S
Head of rabbit					F		
Bat	F, F, F, F, F, F, F, F, F, F, F, F, F, F, F, F, F, F, F, F, F, FM, FM, FM, FM, FM, FM, FM, FM, FM, FM						
Butterfly	F, F, F, F, F, FM, FM, FM, FM						
Bird	F, F, F, F, FM, FM, FM, FM FM, FM						
Man			M, M, M, M, M, M, M				
Skinned rabbit	cF, cF, cF						
Forceps				F, F, F			
Mountains	FK, FK					FK	
Head of person (with beard)		F, F, F, Fc, Fc Fc, Fc					

After all the records had been scored and tabulated in the usual way; that is, when the psychograms had been made, and, in the case of the college age group, when reports concerning the particular student in question had been written, we ceased to be interested in any single individual's performance per se and became interested only in the *card by card* performance of the group to which he belonged.

For example, the 632 answers to Card I given by the college age group were recorded on a single large chart. Each response was listed under the heading *content* and its main determinant was placed *in the column for the specific location* in which it occurred. We used large charts of the kind indicated on page 53. Since we were dealing with eight groups (the college age subjects were divided into five separate units) we had 80 such charts, one for each card. The responses were read off, record by record, just in the order in which they were given, by one investigator, and recorded on the chart by the other.

Thus as can be seen on page 53 "head of a rabbit" seen in area d3 was scored as an F on the record, and so recorded on the chart. "Bat," "butterfly" and "bird" were all given by many subjects. The location of these responses was always the same; they involved the whole blot. But the determinants needed to score them were sometimes different, an F in some cases, an FM in others; consequently the different determinants were recorded under the W location.

When computing the graphs and tables for the locations which are presented in the following pages, we had only to add up all items in any given column W, D1, d1 and so on. In computing the graphs for the determinants the whole page was scanned for the determinant in question. These figures were then expressed in percentages of the total number of answers to that card.

Diagrams of Areas Into Which the Rorschach Inkblots Have Been Divided

T HE ILLUSTRATIONS in this section are designed to show at a glance the areas into which each of the 10 inkblots has been divided. Verbal descriptions such as "the central part of the lower left protuberance" may be quite accurate, but are apt to be confusing to persons not well acquainted with the blots. Moreover, some areas defy verbal description. When studying the accompanying graphs, therefore, the reader can refer back quickly and easily to these diagrams and refresh his memory. Or, being interested, let us say, in some response in a record which he has obtained himself under group conditions, he can consult these diagrams, find the number of the area in question, and then refer to the graph to see with what frequency such an area occurs as the location of a response.

We have used as our frame of reference in making these diagrams the areas outlined by Klopfer in the Rorschach Research Exchange (1) and in his book (2). We have, however, made a few changes and, where necessary, have added additional areas. That is, we have taken Klopfer's series of D's and d's, and designated, with the number following that with which Klopfer's series terminated, any area with a frequency higher than, or equal to the lowest in Klopfer's series. For example, in Card I, Klopfer's D 3 was utilized as the location in only .6% of the responses. Other areas, however, which we designated as D7, D8, D9, D10, and D11, were used in .6%, 1.2%, .6%, .9% and 3.3% of the cases respectively. We followed this same procedure for all cards, and for d responses as well.

Since it is sometimes difficult to determine the exact location used, a dotted line has been added in some cases to indicate the additional extension which was occasionally included in the area in question. That this occurs in individual records as well as in those taken by the group procedure may be seen in Klopfer's statement: "Very few subjects delineate their areas, particularly in the achromatic cards, so sharply that the examiner can always be sure of the area with which the subject is concerned" (2).

There are, however, one or two questions which it seems to us are not taken care of in Klopfer's convenient system. For example, there is the matter of treating as perceptually equivalent, responses which involve both halves of the blot and those which involve only one half. In card VII, for instance, Klopfer's D1 is "the entire bottom portion, sometimes each half separate;" or again, in Card VI, D1 is the "entire lower portion, animal skin, or half of the lower portion, king's head." It has seemed misleading to record both of these as D1 in that there is no similarity whatsoever between experiences of the larger area when seen as "a skin," and the smaller, half area, when seen as a "king's head." In this particular instance we have designated the entire lower portion as a W', in contradistinction to $D1$ which we reserved for the one half of the same area. Klopfer's policy in regard to this however, is not entirely consistent for in Card III when two human figures are seen, they are scored as W', and when only one figure is seen it is scored as $D8$. Similarly in Card II, two dogs or bears are scored as a W', one dog or bear is $D3$. We feel that the latter procedure is preferable, and have used it wherever possible.

REFERENCES

1. Klopfer, Bruno, et al.: The technique of Rorschach scoring and tabulation. *Rorschach Res. Exch.*, 4:75-83, 1940.
2. Klopfer, Bruno, and Kelley, D. M.: *The Rorschach technique.* New York, World Book Co., 1942, viii+436 pp.

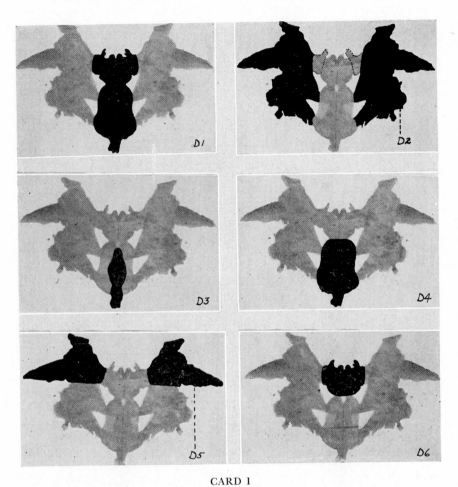

CARD 1

Card 1.—All of Klopfer's large D's and small d's were used here, but D7, D8, D9, D10 and D11 were added. D11 was virtually always used in combination with S.

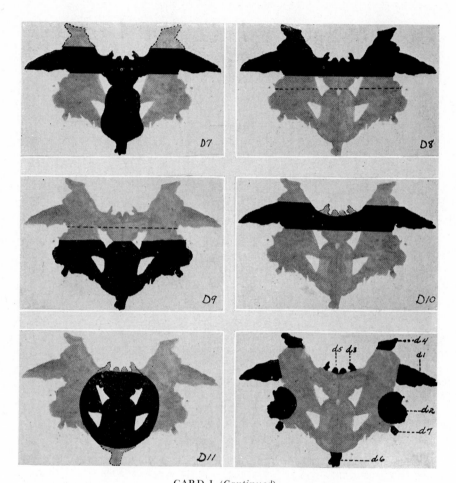

CARD I (*Continued*)

CARD II

⇛ →

Card II.—All of Klopfer's areas were used. The two black figures (dogs) were scored W'.

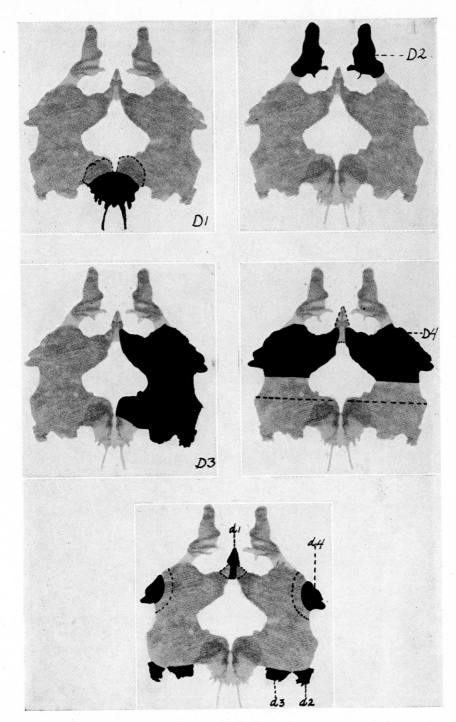

CARD II

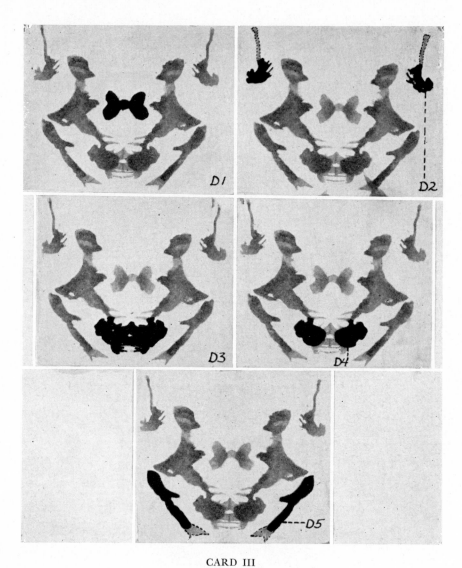

CARD III

Card III.—Klopfer's areas were used, and the two human figures in III were scored W'.

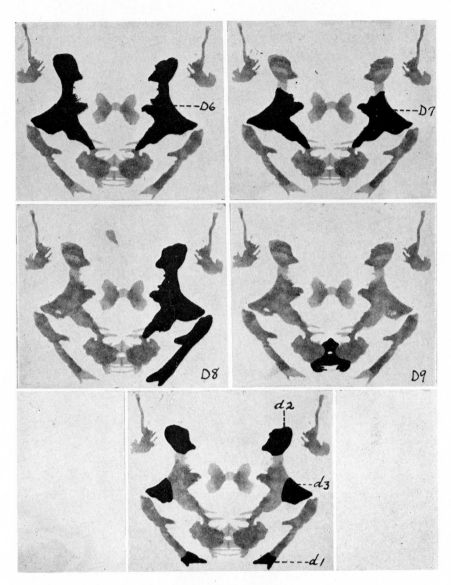

CARD III (*Continued*)

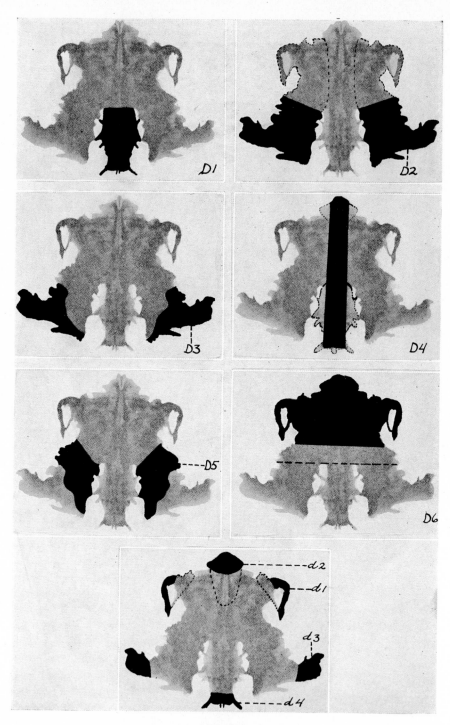

CARD IV

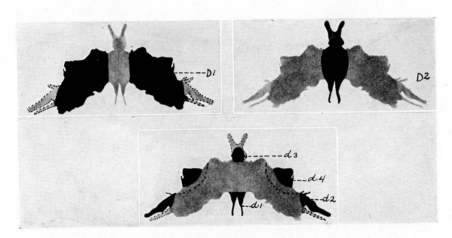

CARD V

Card V.—Klopfer's areas were used and none were added.

←▦

CARD IV

Card IV.—All of Klopfer's areas were used here. In addition D6, the upper half of the blot, was added.

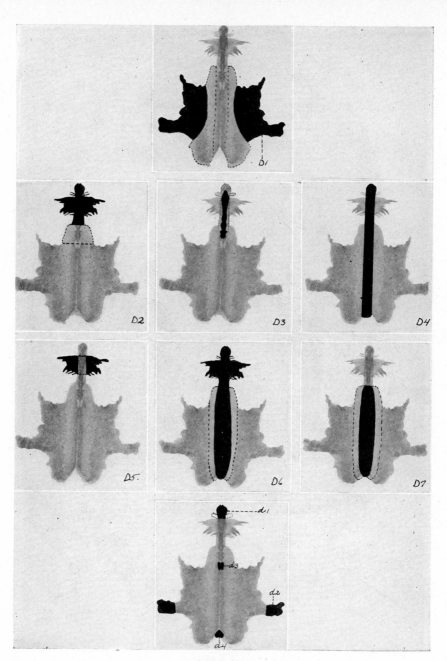

CARD VI

Card VI.—The lower half of this blot was scored W' and D1 was reserved for the side portions. D6 and D7 were added.

CARD VII

⟶

Card VII.—Although one half of this blot was seldom used, it was called D5 rather than **Dr**. Small d4 was added.

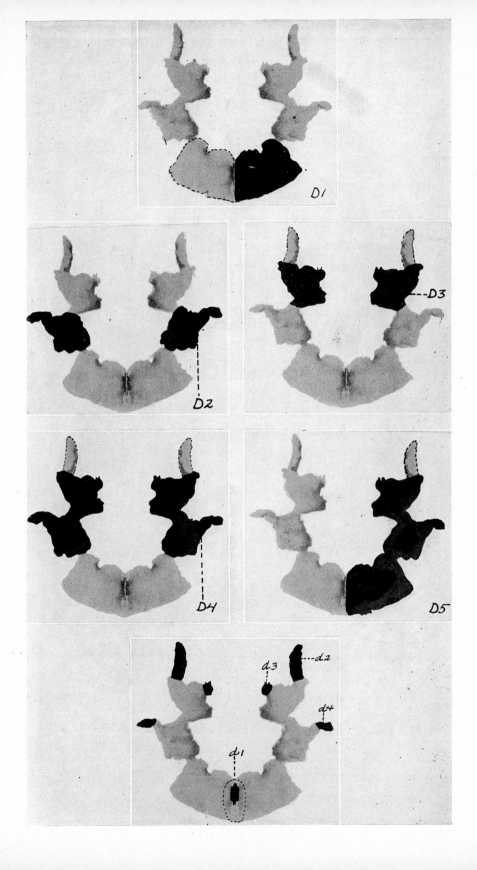

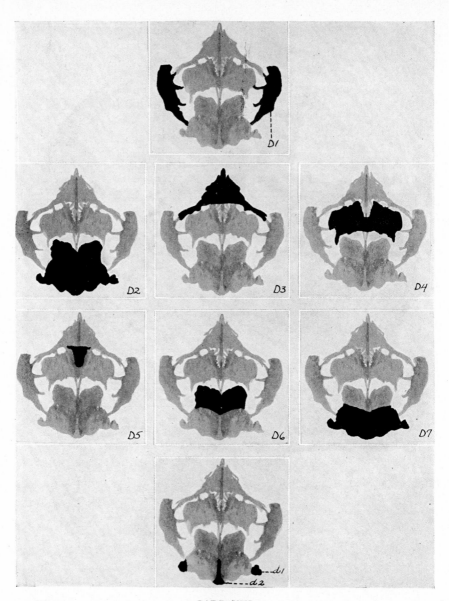

CARD VIII

Card VIII.—"The top gray portion" when taken alone was called D3 and when this was used in combination with other areas we indicated it in the following way: D3+D4+D5. Since we were unable to separate the white portion from the "rib-like figure in the upper center," this small white area was included in D5. Small d2 was added.

Card IX.—Our areas in this follow Klopfer's scoring in the Rorschach Research Exchange (1) where 8 large D's were listed. The area "center portion between lateral greens" was not mentioned here and consequently we added it as D9. In Klopfer's book, however, this area appears in seventh place since the order of the D areas was slightly changed.

D10 which is the area between the green and orange portions has perhaps been scored S by some

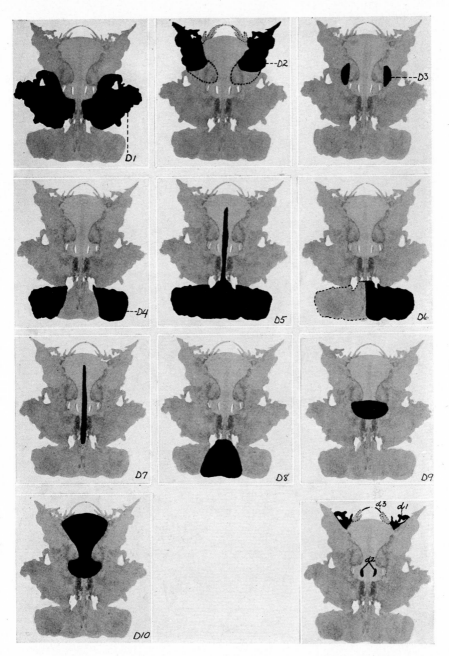

CARD IX

examiners. However, Klopfer says: (2, p. 106): "The situation is somewhat more complicated in Card IX where the greater part of the inner space between the green and orange portions is filled in with rather faint colors and shadings. If the total inside area, frequently interpreted as a violin or cello or vase, is used as a concept area it may not be assumed that a complete reversal of figure and ground prevails; this is predominantly a D response which includes some additional white space areas." Furthermore since D9 is included in this area, it seems a little inconsistent to call one half of the area S and the other half D.

The dotted area on the small d chart might be part of d1 as well as d3.

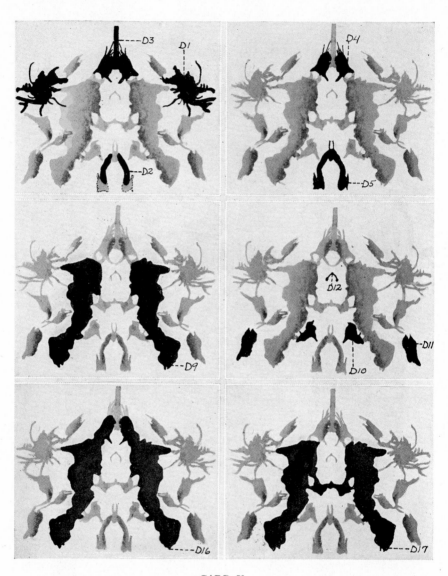

CARD X

Card X.—Our D16 included only D9 and D4, not D9 and D3 as did Klopfer's. D18 was added.

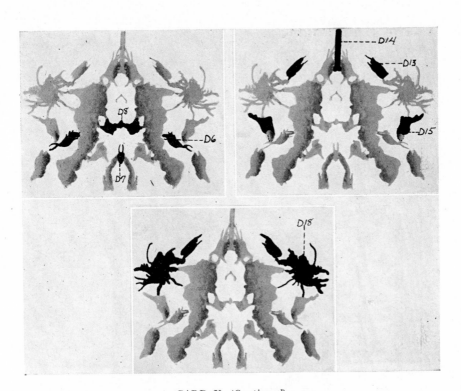

CARD X (*Continued*)

Composite Graphs of the Distribution of Responses According to Location

IT IS CUSTOMARY to epitomize certain aspects of scored Rorschach records graphically in order that one may see at a glance the over-emphasis or lack of emphasis on various ingredients of the personality expressed in Rorschach terms.

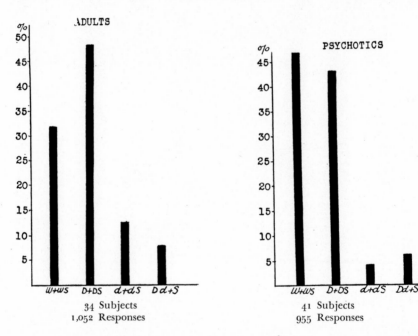

34 Subjects
1,052 Responses

41 Subjects
955 Responses

In our original study we adopted a similar means to express the characteristics, not of our subjects, but of each of the ten Rorschach inkblots when these were considered from the point of view of the various areas utilized by the subjects in the formation of their responses. Seen in this light each of the inkblots had an identifying profile in regard to its whole-part characteristics. This profile was maintained, in essence, regardless from which group of subjects one took the responses.

In this revision, however, only a composite graph for each group of subjects showing the percentage of responses falling into the four location areas is presented, while similar graphs for the determinants will be found in Section VI. Of the 5,806 responses given by the College Age group to all ten cards, for example, 42% involved the whole blot or a combination of the whole blot with white space; 46%, the large details; 6%, the small details and 7%, the rare details.

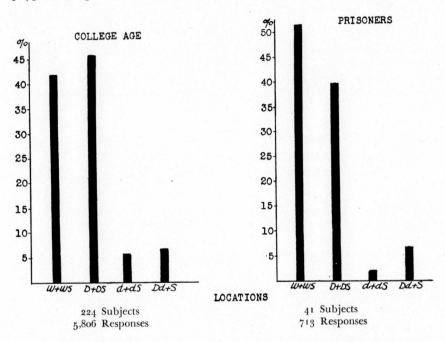

LOCATIONS

224 Subjects
5,806 Responses

41 Subjects
713 Responses

Percentage Tables of the Distribution of Responses According to Location

DISCUSSION OF PRECEDING GRAPHS AND TABLES

In considering the material epitomized in the preceding Graphs and in Tables I and II, it is well to have in mind the main question

TABLE I

SUMMARY OF DISTRIBUTION OF RESPONSES ACCORDING TO LOCATION:
FOUR MAIN GROUPS OF SUBJECTS

LOCATION	224 COLLEGE AGE % RESPONSES	34 ADULTS % RESPONSES	41 PRISONERS % RESPONSES	41 PSYCHOTICS AND PSYCHOPATHIC PERSONALITIES % RESPONSES
W	28.4	23.9	41.4	41.2
W'	11.9	7.0	9.5	5.7
W + W'	40.3	30.9	50.9	46.9
WS + W'S	1.4	.9	.7	.4
Total	41.7	31.8	51.6	47.3
D	44.3	46.1	39.4	41.0
D + S	1.4	2.0	.3	2.0
Total	45.7	48.1	39.7	43.0
d	5.7	12.7	2.2	3.7
d + S	.2	.1	0	0
Total	5.9	12.8	2.2	3.7
dd	.7	.8	.4	0
de	.4	.7	1.3	.7
di	.5	.1	0	.2
dr	3.1	2.5	2.1	2.7
dr + S	.3	1.0	.4	.6
S	1.9	2.4	2.2	1.8
Total	6.9	7.5	6.4	6.0

which motivated this study. Namely, to what extent do these figures correspond to figures already derived from the individual procedure? Or, how closely do records taken by the group method approximate those taken by the individual, when the question of the location of responses is considered?

For the composite graphs and tables there already exist well recognized norms, first postulated by Rorschach and later substantiated by other writers. For example, Klopfer considers that when "the subject follows the Gestalt qualities of the cards without any predilections for one type of area or another" (1) that the following percentages

TABLE II

SUMMARY OF DISTRIBUTION OF RESPONSES ACCORDING TO LOCATION:
COLLEGE AGE GROUPS
(Percentages)

LOCATION	GROUP 1	GROUP 2	GROUP 3	GROUP 4	GROUP 5
W	25.9	32.0	38.6	21.6	20.4
W'	10.2	16.3	13.8	10.3	11.7
W + W'	36.1	48.3	52.4	31.9	32.1
WS + W'S	.9	2.1	2.8	.6	.9
Total	37.0	50.4	55.2	32.5	33.0
D	45.9	40.0	35.8	53.6	53.4
D + S	1.2	1.8	1.2	1.0	2.8
Total	47.1	41.8	37.0	54.6	56.2
d	7.5	3.5	2.7	4.8	5.6
d + S	.1	.2	.3	.2	.3
Total	7.6	3.7	3.0	5.0	5.9
dd	.9	.3	.3	.4	.9
de	.3	0	.1	2.2	.3
di	.8	0	0	0	.9
dr	3.9	2.4	2.6	1.2	1.2
dr + S	.3	.5	.3	.8	0
S	2.1	.9	1.4	3.2	1.5
Total	8.3	4.1	4.7	7.8	4.8

Group   I. Medical Students (108)
Group II. Nurses (40)
Group III. Aviation Cadets (45)
Group IV. Male Arts Students (19)
Group V. Female Arts Students (12)

hold: W 20-30, D 45-55, d 5-15, DdS less than 10. As will be seen in Table I, percentages derived from the Adult group of subjects *fall almost exactly into this distribution:* W 31.8, D 48.1, d 12.8 and DdS 7.5.

The other three groups in Table I show, to a greater or lesser degree, an overemphasis of the W responses; particularly, in the case of the Prisoners, at the expense of the d areas.

When the College Age group is split up into its five sub-groups (Table II) it will be seen that the somewhat increased W% of the total group is derived from sub-groups 2 and 3, whereas sub-groups 4 and 5 more closely approximate the "unemphasized" distribution.

Hertzman has raised the question (2) of whether W responses are not more frequently given in the group test. He comes to the conclusion that, since the absolute number is the same in records taken under both conditions, the higher W% which he found was due to the fact that his group of subjects gave fewer responses under group conditions. He found a W% of 38.1 for 100 college students which is very close to the 41.7 of our 224 college subjects.

In view of the closeness of the percentages of the Adult group (and two of the sub-groups) to the norms for the individual method, we do not feel that the group method per se must always be considered responsible for higher W percentages. The vague and undifferentiated quality of many of the W responses in the Prisoners and Psychotic patients, with the corresponding lack of sharply perceived d areas, seems to us to be characteristic of these groups, in contradistinction to the Adult subjects. This same difference is reflected in the choice of popular answers, as will be seen in Section XI.

REFERENCES

1. Klopfer, Bruno; and, Kelley, D. M.: *The Rorschach Technique.* World Book Co., 1942, viii, 436 pp.
2. Hertzman, Max: A comparison of the individual and group Rorschach tests. *Rorschach Res. Exch.,* 6:89-108, 1942.

Discussion of Graphs of the Distribution of Responses According to Determinants

Introduction

WHAT CARD is most likely to produce an M response? Such a question could probably be easily answered without a statistical study, namely Card III. But would one expect the type of subject, or the size of the group under consideration to affect this result?

TABLE 1

CARDS MOST LIKELY TO PRODUCE EACH OF THE GIVEN DETERMINANTS

DETERMINANTS	COLLEGE AGE	ADULTS	PRISONERS	PSYCHOTICS
M	3	3	3	3
FM	8	5, 8	8	8
m	9	3	6	4
k	4	1	4	4
K	9	7	6	6
FK	6	7	6	7
F	1	1	1	5
Fc	6	6	6	6
c	6	6	6	6
C'	6	5	8	4
FC	8	8	8	8
CF	9	9	9	9

Moreover, how about the card least likely to produce an M response? Or again, what is the answer if we substitute each of the other determinants in the place of M?

Such questions prompted the tables which are presented in this section. We are interested now in the potentialities of each of the cards for producing the various types of perceptual experiences, the so-called determinants. It is quite clear, however, that these perceptual potentialities are not independent of the type of subject who is doing the perceiving. At this point our sharply divergent groups of subjects stand us in good stead. When all four of these groups, normals and abnormals, are in agreement, or, put in another way, when a given determinant appears to be clearly dominant in all four groups in a particular card, we have positive evidence of the strength of that determinant in that card. Conversely, when one determinant fails to be elicited in any of the groups in one particular card, we have evidence that this particular card has little to offer towards this way of perceiving. When one of the groups deviates markedly from the other three, we have, on the other hand, information about the subjects which comprise that group with reference to that particular determinant.

Tables I and II are an attempt to epitomize certain aspects of the more detailed tables and graphs which follow. They answer the initial question: *which cards favor the production of each of the determinants* and in which are they *least likely to be perceived.*

TABLE II

CARDS LEAST LIKELY TO PRODUCE EACH OF THE GIVEN DETERMINANTS

DETERMINANTS	COLLEGE AGE	ADULTS	PRISONERS	PSYCHOTICS
M	6	8	6, 8	6, 8
FM	6	3	6	4
m	8, 5	2, 8, 9	3, 9, 10	5
k	5	4, 5, 9	3, 5, 6, 8, 10	3, 5
K	3	3, 4, 8	1, 2, 5, 8, 9, 10	1, 2, 3, 5
FK	3	2, 3, 8, 9	3, 4, 5, 9	8, 5
F	8	6	6	9
Fc	3	10	2, 3, 8, 10	3, 7, 2, 9, 10
c	3	3, 8, 10	3, 8, 9, 10	8, 3
C'	8	8, 9, 10	3, 4, 5, 9	9
FC	2	2	2	2
CF	3	3	3	3

DISCUSSION OF TABLES I AND II

The most striking points of similarity between the results obtained from these widely discrepant groups occur in the M, FC, and CF scores. Here in all cases the same cards evoke both the most frequent, and the least frequent responses involving these determinants. For the M scores, as might be expected, Card III is always in the lead; for FC, Card VIII; and for CF, Card IX. Similarly for the least frequent use of these determinants we find Card VI and/or Card VIII as the most M resistant, Card II as the least likely to evoke an FC response, and Card III as that which is least likely to produce a CF response. The F responses also belong amongst those where there is an essential similarity between the four groups. Card I is by far the most likely to produce an F response in three of the four groups, while the single deviation (Card V) in the psychotic group exceeds the score for Card I by only a very small amount. Again, except for minor discrepancies, the same pattern or constellation of cards evoke the Fc and c responses in all four groups. Card VI is always in the lead, with Cards III, VIII and in some cases Cards X and VII as being least likely to elicit these responses.

The discrepancies between the groups, despite their divergent character, are very scarce. There is only one complete reversal and that is in the case of the k. For the adults this determinant is least likely to appear in Card IV, whereas in all the other groups, Card IV is most likely to produce it.

The only determinant which is highest in a different card for each of the four groups is m. The lowest score received by m also occurs in a variety of cards, in as many as six different ones. On the other hand K seems to occur in rather circumscribed areas; it does not occur at all in any of the cards listed in Table II, that is, in 14 instances.

FK occurs much more frequently in the college age group than it does elsewhere. There are FK responses in every card amongst this group and the total per cent is much greater, whereas, in contrast, four cards have no FK responses at all amongst the adult group and the prison inmates.

The composite graphs of the distribution of responses according to perceptual determinants follow for each of the main groups and sub groups.

Composite Graphs of the Distribution of Responses According to Determinants

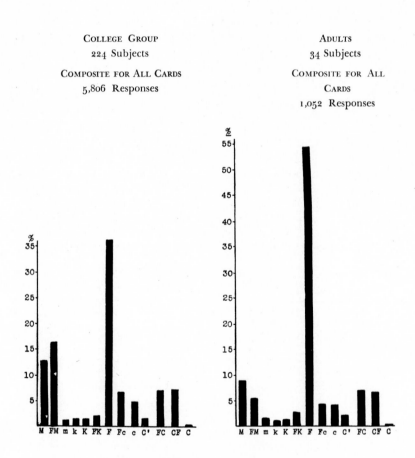

COLLEGE GROUP
224 Subjects

COMPOSITE FOR ALL CARDS
5,806 Responses

ADULTS
34 Subjects

COMPOSITE FOR ALL
CARDS
1,052 Responses

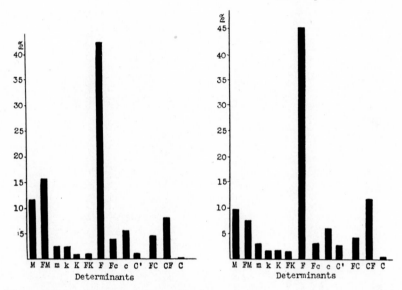

PRISON INMATES
41 Subjects
COMPOSITE FOR ALL CARDS
713 Responses

PSYCHOTICS AND PSYCHOPATHIC
PERSONALITIES
41 Subjects
COMPOSITE FOR ALL CARDS
955 Responses

M FM m k K FK F Fc c C' FC CF C
Determinants

M FM m k K FK F Fc c C' FC CF C
Determinants

The composite graph epitomizes the differences between the groups. As characteristic of the Adult group we find the highest F% (slightly on the constricted side). The M:FM ratio is correct, as is also the FC:CF and the Fc:c. Characteristic of the College age group is the fact that FM is greater than M, the F% is the lowest of the four groups, and the extrovertial relationships are in the correct direction or equal. The prison inmates show FM greater than M, c greater than Fc, CF greater than FC. All normal ratios are reversed. The psychotics also show a reversal of the extrovertial ratios, even to a more marked degree, but the M:FM relationship is in the correct direction. There are characteristic and distinguishing features in all four groups, therefore.

79

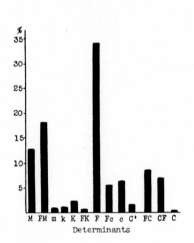

MEDICAL STUDENTS
(College Sub-group 1)
108 Subjects

COMPOSITE FOR ALL CARDS
3,055 Responses

NAVAL AVIATION CADETS IN TRAINING
(College Sub-group 3)
45 Subjects

COMPOSITE FOR ALL CARDS
966 Responses

MALE STUDENTS
(College Sub-group 4)
19 Subjects

COMPOSITE FOR ALL CARDS
496 Responses

FEMALE STUDENTS
(College Sub-group 5)
12 Subjects

COMPOSITE FOR ALL CARDS
324 Responses

COMPOSITE PSYCHOGRAM

CF dominates FC in the aviation cadets. FM is greater than M in all groups except one where the difference is negligible.

Percentage Tables of the Distribution of Responses According to Determinants

TABLE I

SUMMARY OF DISTRIBUTION OF RESPONSES ACCORDING TO DETERMINANTS:
COMPOSITE FOR ALL CARDS
(Percentages)

DETERMI-NANTS	COLLEGE GROUP	ADULTS	PRISON INMATES	PSYCHOTICS AND PSYCHOPATHIC PERSONALITIES
M	12.7	9.1	11.7	9.9
FM	16.3	5.5	15.7	7.7
m	1.3	1.8	2.5	3.0
k	1.6	1.1	2.4	1.8
K	1.6	1.4	.8	1.9
FK	2.1	2.7	1.0	1.7
F	36.2	54.3	42.3	45.3
Fc	6.6	4.2	4.0	3.3
c	4.8	4.1	5.7	6.0
c′	1.8	2.1	1.1	2.7
FC	7.2	7.0	4.5	4.2
CF	7.4	6.5	8.1	11.9
C	.3	.2	.1	.5

TABLE II

CARD BY CARD
DISTRIBUTION OF RESPONSES ACCORDING TO DETERMINANTS:
COLLEGE AGE GROUP
(Percentages)

DETERMINANTS	CARDS									
	I	II	III	IV	V	VI	VII	VIII	IX	X
M	6.7	20.3	41.3	6.6	12.3	.9	26.1	1.8	9.9	5.9
FM	14.7	20.5	11.3	8.3	27.3	5.5	8.8	30.8	8.0	24.6
m	.3	2.6	.5	2.0	.2	2.2	2.1	.2	3.5	.3
k	3.0	.7	1.0	4.6	.4	1.5	1.9	1.1	.9	1.2
K	.3	.7	0	2.8	.8	1.5	4.5	.3	5.8	.4
FK	1.3	3.9	.3	1.4	1.2	6.0	3.3	.7	.5	2.6
F	67.4	29.0	26.3	40.6	45.9	29.2	39.3	22.6	31.5	31.7
Fc	2.1	1.8	.8	16.0	6.7	28.4	8.4	1.8	1.9	.9
c	2.7	.9	.2	15.8	3.0	20.3	4.1	1.3	.7	.4
C′	1.4	4.2	1.3	2.0	2.2	4.4	1.4	.3	.4	.9
FC		4.4	13.2					22.9	8.1	17.2
CF		10.1	3.0					15.5	28.0	13.8
C		.7	.7					.7	.7	.3

TABLE III

CARD BY CARD
DISTRIBUTION OF RESPONSES ACCORDING TO DETERMINANTS
ADULTS
(Percentages)

DETERMINANTS	CARDS									
	I	II	III	IV	V	VI	VII	VIII	IX	X
M	.8	24.5	26.4	10.7	8.2	1.0	10.2	0	2.5	2.9
FM	3.4	9.4	.8	2.7	11.3	2.9	8.2	11.2	5.1	3.6
m	3.4	0	4.0	1.8	1.0	3.8	2.0	0	0	.7
k	4.2	.9	.8	0	0	1.0	1.0	1.1	0	1.4
K	.8	1.9	0	0	1.0	1.0	5.1	0	3.8	1.4
FK	.8	0	0	1.8	2.1	7.7	12.2	0	0	2.9
F	80.5	42.5	44.0	63.4	69.1	34.6	50.0	37.1	53.2	62.1
Fc	.8	.9	.8	10.7	1.0	20.2	5.1	2.2	1.3	0
c	1.7	.9	0	8.0	1.0	23.1	4.1	0	3.8	0
C'	3.4	3.8	.8	.9	5.2	4.8	2.0	0	0	0
FC		3.8	17.6					36.0	8.9	7.1
CF		11.3	4.8					12.4	21.5	16.4
C		0	0					0	0	1.4

TABLE IV

CARD BY CARD
DISTRIBUTION OF RESPONSES ACCORDING TO DETERMINANTS
PRISON INMATES
(Percentages)

DETERMINANTS	CARDS									
	I	II	III	IV	V	VI	VII	VIII	IX	X
M	3.3	14.1	50.	7.5	10.	0	25.9	0	5.1	5.9
FM	11.0	28.2	11.4	7.5	18.6	1.6	10.3	37.7	10.2	17.8
m	1.1	5.6	0	4.5	1.4	8.1	5.2	1.4	0	0
k	2.2	1.4	0	13.4	0	0	3.4	0	5.1	0
K	0	0	1.4	1.5	0	4.8	1.7	0	0	0
FK	1.1	1.4	0	0	0	3.2	1.7	1.4	0	1.0
F	75.8	35.2	21.4	41.8	64.3	17.7	41.4	23.2	45.8	43.6
Fc	1.1	0	0	10.4	1.4	22.6	8.6	0	1.7	0
c	2.2	1.4	0	13.4	4.3	40.3	1.7	0	0	0
C'	2.2	2.8	0	0	0	1.6	0	2.9	0	1.0
FC		0	11.4					13.0	3.4	12.9
CF		9.9	4.3					20.3	28.8	16.8
C		0	0					0	0	1.0

TABLE V

CARD BY CARD
DISTRIBUTION OF RESPONSES ACCORDING TO DETERMINANTS
PSYCHOTICS AND PSYCHOPATHIC PERSONALITIES
(Percentages)

DETERMINANTS	CARDS									
	I	II	III	IV	V	VI	VII	VIII	IX	X
M	6.7	21.3	36.1	2.3	6.5	0	6.8	0	12.0	6.1
FM	2.5	11.1	4.1	2.3	13.0	6.0	6.8	14.3	4.3	11.5
m	4.2	2.8	1.0	6.8	0	4.8	2.7	.9	4.3	2.3
k	2.5	.9	0	6.8	0	1.2	4.1	1.8	1.1	.8
K	0	0	0	3.4	0	6.0	2.7	.9	5.4	2.3
FK	.8	3.7	1.0	2.3	0	3.6	5.4	0	1.1	.8
F	68.1	38.9	35.1	43.2	74.0	31.0	62.2	40.2	25.0	40.5
Fc	5.9	0	0	4.5	1.3	20.2	0	2.7	0	0
c	5.9	1.9	0	21.6	2.6	23.8	6.8	0	3.3	.8
C′	3.4	2.8	3.1	6.8	2.6	3.6	2.7	1.8	0	1.5
FC		2.8	8.2					12.5	5.4	9.2
CF		14.8	11.3					23.2	34.8	24.4
C		0	0					1.8	3.3	0

TABLE VI

SUMMARY OF DISTRIBUTION OF RESPONSES ACCORDING TO DETERMINANTS:
COMPOSITE FOR ALL CARDS,
COLLEGE AGE SUB-GROUPS
(Percentages)

DETERMINANTS	GROUP 1	GROUP 2	GROUP 3	GROUP 4	GROUP 5
M	11.1	16.6	12.6	14.3	12.8
FM	14.0	20.3	20.5	12.9	18.3
m	1.4	1.5	1.2	.8	.9
k	1.1	2.4	3.0	.8	1.2
K	1.5	1.6	1.9	1.0	2.4
FK	1.6	3.8	2.6	2.2	.6
F	39.9	26.9	32.4	40.4	34.1
Fc	8.0	5.6	5.3	3.4	5.5
c	4.6	5.1	5.1	4.0	6.4
C′	1.5	1.8	1.3	4.8	1.8
FC	8.3	5.6	4.3	8.6	8.5
CF	6.7	8.2	9.5	6.6	7.0
C	.3	.5	.2	.2	.3

TABLE VII

CARD BY CARD

DISTRIBUTION OF RESPONSES ACCORDING TO DETERMINANTS:

MEDICAL STUDENTS

(Sub-group 1)

(Percentages)

DETERMINANTS	CARDS									
	I	II	III	IV	V	VI	VII	VIII	IX	X
M	4.1	17.0	36.1	6.1	12.7	1.6	24.4	1.6	7.8	4.4
FM	10.0	21.5	10.6	8.2	20.8	3.9	9.1	29.8	6.8	18.1
m	.6	3.1	.3	2.4	.4	1.6	1.7	0	4.2	.2
k	1.9	0	.6	4.4	.4	1.9	.4	1.0	.3	.5
K	.3	.3	0	4.4	.8	1.3	4.1	0	4.9	.2
FK	.6	2.4	0	2.0	1.2	4.5	2.1	1.0	0	2.0
F	76.2	34.9	29.6	38.1	49.8	29.8	43.4	25.6	34.7	38.7
Fc	3.4	2.1	1.2	19.0	8.5	31.4	9.9	2.9	3.2	1.5
c	1.9	1.0	0	13.9	4.2	19.4	4.1	1.6	1.0	.2
C'	.9	3.8	.6	1.4	1.2	4.5	.8	.3	0	1.2
FC		5.5	16.5					23.3	8.1	21.6
CF		8.0	3.4					12.3	28.2	11.0
C		.3	.9					.6	.6	.2

TABLE VIII

CARD BY CARD

DISTRIBUTION OF RESPONSES ACCORDING TO DETERMINANTS

NURSES IN TRAINING (GROUP RECORDS)

(Sub-group 2)

(Percentages)

DETERMINANTS	CARDS									
	I	II	III	IV	V	VI	VII	VIII	IX	X
M	10.9	30.4	57.0	2.2	9.4	0	30	3.8	22.4	7.9
FM	23.6	18.5	11.8	12.1	40.0	4.8	12.2	32.1	4.7	37.3
m	0	1.1	2.2	3.3	0	3.8	3.3	.9	1.2	0
k	6.4	0	1.1	6.6	1.2	1.9	1.1	.9	2.4	2.4
K	0	1.1	0	2.2	1.2	1.9	3.3	0	7.1	.8
FK	2.7	9.8	2.2	1.1	2.4	7.6	6.7	.9	0	4.0
F	51.8	13.0	17.2	41.8	36.5	28.6	32.2	15.1	21.2	13.5
Fc	0	2.2	0	14.2	3.5	26.7	7.8	1.9	0	0
c	3.6	1.1	0	16.5	3.5	21.9	2.2	.9	1.2	0
C'	.9	6.5	3.2	0	2.4	2.9	1 1	0	2.4	0
FC		1.1	5.4					20.8	8.2	15.9
CF		13.0	0					21.7	28.2	17.5
C		2.1	0					.9	1.2	.8

TABLE IX

CARD BY CARD
DISTRIBUTION OF RESPONSES ACCORDING TO DETERMINANTS
NAVAL AVIATION CADETS IN TRAINING
(Sub-group 3)
(Percentages)

DETERMINANTS	CARDS									
	I	II	III	IV	V	VI	VII	VIII	IX	X
M	5.8	16.3	46.5	11.7	13.6	0	23.5	1.0	4.4	6.3
FM	19.2	20.9	13.9	8.5	36.4	9.5	7.1	35.6	14.3	35.7
m	0	3.5	0	0	0	1.1	2.4	0	5.5	.9
k	3.3	4.7	3.0	5.3	0	1.1	5.9	1.9	2.2	2.7
K	.8	2.3	0	0	0	2.1	7.1	1.0	6.6	.9
FK	1.7	4.7	0	0	0	6.3	4.7	0	3.3	5.4
F	62.5	20.9	23.8	34.0	46.6	31.6	36.5	21.2	24.2	18.8
Fc	1.7	0	1.0	17.0	2.3	26.3	5.9	0	0	.9
c	1.7	1.2	1.0	21.3	0	20.0	7.1	1.0	0	0
C'	3.3	4.7	0	2.1	1.1	2.1	0	0	0	0
FC		4.7	5.0					20.2	5.5	6.3
CF		16.3	5.0					18.3	33.0	22.3
C		0	1.0					0	1.1	0

TABLE X

CARD BY CARD
DISTRIBUTION. OF RESPONSES ACCORDING TO DETERMINANTS
MALE COLLEGE STUDENTS
(Sub-group 4)
(Percentages)

DETERMINANTS	CARDS									
	I	II	III	IV	V	VI	VII	VIII	IX	X
M	12.2	22.4	40.4	8.0	13.5	0	26.2	1.9	11.8	12.0
FM	18.4	18.4	4.3	2.0	27.0	8.2	2.4	22.6	7.8	17.3
m	0	0	0	2.0	0	4.1	2.4	0	0	0
k	2.0	0	0	4.0	0	0	2.4	0	0	0
K	0	0	0	0	0	0	2.4	1.9	5.9	0
FK	2.0	2.0	0	2.0	2.7	12.2	0	0	0	1.3
F	61.2	34.7	25.5	56.0	43.2	22.4	50.0	20.8	43.1	46.7
Fc	0	4.1	0	6.0	2.7	18.4	4.8	0	0	0
c	2.0	0	0	12.0	0	22.4	2.4	0	0	1.3
C'	2.0	2.0	6.4	8.0	10.8	12.2	7.1	0	0	2.7
FC		6.1	19.1					35.8	11.8	8.0
CF		8.2	4.3					17.0	19.6	10.7
C		2.0	0					0	0	0

TABLE XI

CARD BY CARD
DISTRIBUTION OF RESPONSES ACCORDING TO DETERMINANTS
FEMALE COLLEGE STUDENTS
(*Sub-group 5*)
(Percentages)

DETERMINANTS	CARDS									
	I	II	III	IV	V	VI	VII	VIII	IX	X
M	14.3	30.8	32.3	5.7	11.5	0	37.0	0	10.0	3.4
FM	7.1	19.2	19.4	8.6	19.2	7.4	11.1	33.3	10.0	30.5
m	0	3.8	0	0	0	3.7	0	0	3.3	0
k	3.6	0	0	0	0	0	3.7	2.6	0	1.7
K	0	0	0	2.9	3.8	3.7	7.4	0	10.0	0
FK	0	0	0	0	0	3.7	3.7	0	0	0
F	60.7	34.6	29.0	54.3	38.5	29.6	18.5	25.6	30.0	27.1
Fc	0	0	0	5.7	19.2	25.9	11.1	0	3.3	0
c	14.3	0	0	20.0	3.8	22.2	3.7	2.6	0	1.7
C'	0	3.8	0	2.9	3.8	3.7	3.7	2.6	0	0
FC		0	19.4					15.4	10.0	22.0
CF		7.7	0					15.4	23.3	13.6
C		0	0					2.6	0	0

Discussion of Content Categories

IN CHOOSING the categories into which our content was to be divided we tried as far as possible to retain those already in common usage. Eleven of those which we employed are, therefore, the same as those used by Klopfer and Davidson in the latest edition of the *Individual Record Blank* (1). These are: human figures, human details, animal figures, animal details, animal objects, sex, objects, plants, art, architecture, and fire. Several others were only slight modifications of those described by Klopfer; for example, we have used Symbolism in presumably a similar manner to the way in which he used Abstract. Our Natural Objects may be considered the equivalent of Nature except that we also included in it diffuse and formless natural objects such as "smoke," "clouds,' "mist," etc. Our Anatomy was divided into Anatomy (animal), Anatomy (embryological), and Anatomy (human). Vista responses when they involved buildings were included under Architecture. In place of Geography we introduced Maps, Charts, Slides, and Photographs. Coastlines, Islands, etc. which were not *seen as maps* were placed with the Natural Objects. X-rays were introduced as a separate category because the frequency of their occurrence in certain groups seemed significant. Signs and Symbols, Color, and Miscellaneous completed our list.

Any list of content categories is bound to be somewhat arbitrary. In analyzing the 8,526 responses from this angle we were frequently struck by the fact that a given item might equally well have appeared under either of two headings. Animal Detail, Animal Anatomy, and Animal Object, for example, very frequently laid claim to one and the same item. There were times when we wished for a much more differentiated series particularly when we did not do justice to the Anatomical responses of high scientific caliber by putting them in with others of a vague and hazy sort. However, since our aim was to see how the responses were distributed over these areas of different interests, too many small divisions would have defeated our purpose and made comparison between the groups of subjects too complicated and painstaking a task for the reader.

The graphs and tables of the distribution of content follow in

Sections IX and X. The actual responses, listed under their correct locations, and accompanied by figures expressing their frequency, will be found in Part V for the College Age group only.

CONTENT CATEGORIES

Anatomy (animal)
Anatomy (embryological)
Anatomy (human)
Animals
  Winged
  Other than winged
Animal details
Animal objects
Architecture (also involving perspective, including bridges, stairways, entrances, corridors, steps, etc.)
Art
Color
Fire (including flames, explosions, etc.)
Human beings (including caricatures, mythological or fantastic beings, etc.)
Human details
Maps (including charts, photographs, slides)
Natural objects (including diffuse and formless objects—smoke, clouds, mist, shadows, gas, vapor, steam, incense, light, snow, dust, dirt, mud, decay, smudge, smear, geographical concepts, vista, fountains, geysers, water, lakes, waterfalls, landscapes, oil wells, etc.)
Objects (including food, masks, emblems, paint, ink, metal, etc.)
Plants (including fruits, vegetables, etc.)
Sex
Signs and symbols
Symbolism
X-ray
Miscellaneous

REFERENCES

1. Klopfer, Bruno; and, Kelley, D. M.: *The Rorschach Technique.* New York, World Book Co., 1942, viii+436 pp.

Graphs of the Distribution of Responses in Terms of Content

DISTRIBUTION OF RESPONSES ACCORDING TO CONTENT

COMPOSITE FOR ALL CARDS

COLLEGE AGE GROUP

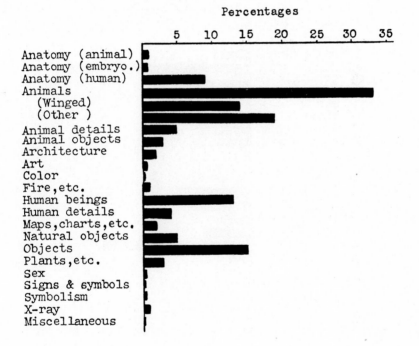

Percentages

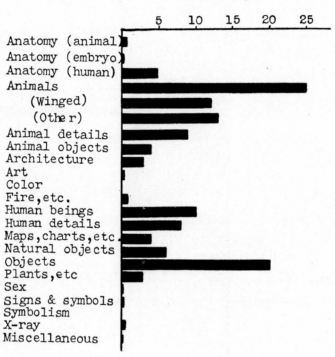

Percentages

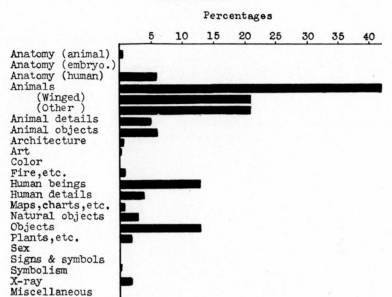

PSYCHOTICS AND PSYCHOPATHIC PERSONALITIES

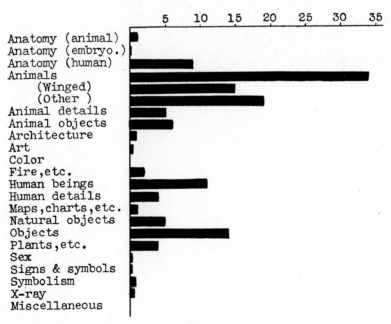

Percentage Tables of the Distribution of Responses in Terms of Content

Table I

SUMMARY OF DISTRIBUTION OF RESPONSES ACCORDING TO CONTENT
COMPOSITE FOR ALL CARDS
(Percentages)

CONTENT	COLLEGE AGE GROUP	ADULTS	PRISON INMATES	PSYCHOTICS AND PSYCHOPATHS
Anatomy (animal)	1	.6	.5	1
Anatomy embryological)	.6	.2	0	.1
Anatomy (human)	9	5	6	9
Animals	33	25	42	34
Winged	14	12	21	15
Other than winged	19	13	21	19
Animal details	5	9	5	5
Animal objects	3	4	6	6
Architecture	2	3	.7	.9
Art	.5	.3	.2	.4
Color	.2	0	0	0
Fire, etc.	1	.9	1	2
Human beings	13	10	13	11
Human details	4	8	4	4
Maps, charts, etc.	2	4	1	1
Natural objects	5	6	3	5
Objects	15	20	13	14
Plants, etc.	3	3	3	4
Sex	.2	.1	0	.2
Signs and symbols	.1	.2	0	.2
Symbolism	.2	0	.1	.8
X-ray	.7	.5	2	.7
Miscellaneous	.1	.1	0	0

TABLE II

CARD BY CARD
DISTRIBUTION OF RESPONSES ACCORDING TO CONTENT
COLLEGE AGE GROUP
(Percentages)

CONTENT	CARDS									
	I	II	III	IV	V	VI	VII	VIII	IX	X
Anatomy (animal)	.7	.1	.6	2	0	1	.2	3	1	.8
Anatomy (embryo.)	0	.3	.3	2	0	2	.2	.8	1	.3
Anatomy (human)	23	5	9	6	3	4	6	7	15	8
Animals	36	32	29	22	57	16	11	44	18	52
Winged	28	8	19	8	48	6	3	6	1	11
Other than winged	8	24	9	15	9	10	8	38	17	41
Animal details	7	3	3	12	9	5	5	3	7	2
Animal objects	.6	.5	0	12	.8	17	.6	.9	.5	2
Architecture	.1	4	.3	.8	.4	4	.8	2	.3	4
Art	0	.1	.3	0	0	.1	.4	.9	1	2
Color	0	.9	0	0	0	.1	0	.4	.1	.2
Fire, etc.	.1	4	.7	.3	0	.5	0	.6	6	.1
Human beings	8	21	42	7	12	1	26	2	11	7
Human details	2	7	2	5	6	3	11	2	7	2
Maps, etc.	2	2	.5	2	.2	1	3	4	3	2
Natural objects	3	4	.6	4	3	10	14	3	8	4
Objects	15	14	10	15	7	30	20	17	12	7
Plants, etc.	.4	.5	.8	4	1	4	.8	6	6	5
Sex	.1	.9	.3	.3	0	.3	.4	0	.1	.1
Signs & Symbols	.1	0	.3	0	1	0	0	0	.5	0
Symbolism	0	.3	.5	0	0	0	0	.4	.7	.3
X-ray	.7	.1	.5	3	.2	.3	.2	.6	.3	.6
Miscellaneous	0	.1	0	.1	.4	.7	0	0	.1	.1

TABLE III

CARD BY CARD

DISTRIBUTION OF RESPONSES ACCORDING TO CONTENT

ADULTS

(Percentages)

CONTENT	CARDS									
	I	II	III	IV	V	VI	VII	VIII	IX	X
Anatomy (animal)	0	0	0	.9	0	0	0	6	1	0
Anatomy (embryo.)	0	0	0	0	0	.9	0	0	1	.7
Anatomy (human)	15	3	10	4	1	0	3	7	8	4
Animals	32	10	27	9	40	13	8	50	15	40
Winged	26	4	19	5	32	6	4	17	1	3
Other than winged	6	6	8	5	7	7	4	33	14	37
Animal details	12	5	4	19	23	6	4	1	19	3
Animal objects	2	2	0	8	3	21	1	1	1	2
Architecture	0	4	0	2	1	7	6	0	0	8
Art	0	0	0	0	0	0	2	1	0	.7
Color	0	0	0	0	0	0	0	0	1	0
Fire, etc.	0	3	0	.9	1	2	1	0	1	.7
Human beings	2	27	28	11	8	.9	8	0	3	4
Human details	6	17	6	14	3	4	17	2	5	2
Maps, etc.	3	3	3	5	2	0	10	2	5	9
Natural objects	6	4	0	0	8	9	19	0	5	9
Objects	20	22	21	25	8	25	19	18	31	14
Plants, etc.	0	2	0	2	0	7	1	10	4	4
Sex	0	0	0	0	0	2	0	0	0	0
Signs & symbols	0	0	0	0	1	.9	0	1	0	0
Symbolism	0	0	0	0	0	0	0	0	0	0
X-ray	3	0	.8	0	0	.9	0	1	0	0
Miscellaneous	0	0	0	0	0	.9	0	0	0	0

TABLE IV

CARD BY CARD
DISTRIBUTION OF RESPONSES ACCORDING TO CONTENT
PRISON INMATES
(Percentages)

CONTENT	CARDS									
	I	II	III	IV	V	VI	VII	VIII	IX	X
Anatomy (animal)	0	0	0	2	0	0	0	3	0	1
Anatomy (embryo.)	0	0	0	0	0	0	0	0	0	0
Anatomy (human)	5	4	4	6	3	0	2	12	12	9
Animals	72	38	31	20	77	10	14	60	19	51
Winged	58	6	29	6	66	5	3	4	2	12
Other than winged	14	32	3	14	11	5	10	56	17	39
Animal details	2	6	1	15	1	2	12	1	8	3
Animal objects	1	0	1	14	0	42	2	0	0	5
Architecture	0	3	0	0	0	3	0	0	0	1
Art	0	0	0	0	0	2	0	0	2	0
Color	0	0	0	0	0	0	0	0	0	0
Fire, etc.	0	6	0	0	0	2	0	1	5	0
Human beings	5	16	50	8	10	0	28	0	7	7
Human details	2	6	3	3	4	2	14	1	12	2
Maps	0	0	0	0	0	0	7	0	5	3
Natural objects	1	1	1	2	1	5	5	3	7	2
Objects	10	20	7	15	3	32	17	12	17	7
Plants, etc.	0	0	0	6	0	0	0	6	2	8
Sex	0	0	0	0	0	0	0	0	0	0
Signs & symbols	0	0	0	0	0	0	0	0	0	0
Symbolism	0	0	0	0	0	0	0	0	0	1
X-ray	1	1	0	11	0	0	0	0	5	0
Miscellaneous	0	0	0	0	0	0	0	0	0	0

TABLE V

CARD BY CARD
DISTRIBUTION OF RESPONSES ACCORDING TO CONTENT
PSYCHOTICS AND PSYCHOPATHIC PERSONALITIES
(Percentages)

CONTENT	CARDS									
	I	II	III	IV	V	VI	VII	VIII	IX	X
Anatomy (animal)	3	0	2	1	0	0	1	3	0	.7
Anatomy (embryo.)	0	0	0	0	0	0	0	.9	0	0
Anatomy (human)	7	7	10	9	7	7	4	16	16	8
Animals	41	27	28	28	62	21	14	40	21	46
Winged	30	5	15	11	54	12	6	8	3	8
Other than winged	11	23	12	17	8	10	9	31	18	38
Animal details	7	5	3	10	9	2	4	3	4	2
Animal objects	6	2	0	22	3	20	4	3	2	3
Architecture	0	2	0	1	0	0	1	.9	0	3
Art	0	0	2	0	0	0	0	0	2	0
Color	0	0	0	0	0	0	0	0	0	0
Fire, etc.	0	5	2	0	0	1	0	0	5	.7
Human beings	7	21	36	2	7	2	10	.9	11	8
Human details	3	5	3	2	7	2	16	.9	5	0
Maps, etc.	3	2	0	0	0	2	6	.9	1	.7
Natural objects	4	5	1	5	3	8	13	.9	9	7
Objects	15	15	10	12	4	29	23	16	9	13
Plants, etc.	4	.9	2	4	0	1	0	10	11	5
Sex	0	.9	0	0	0	1	0	0	0	0
Signs & symbols	0	0	0	0	0	0	0	.9	0	.7
Symbolism	0	0	0	0	0	0	1	2	1	3
X-ray	.9	.9	0	2	0	1	0	.9	1	0
Miscellaneous	0	0	0	0	0	0	0	0	0	0

Lists of Popular Answers, Rejections, Distribution of Anatomical Answers, and Percentage Distribution of Answers to Each Card

POPULAR ANSWERS DEFINED

THE FOUR lists of responses that follow which we have designated as *"populars"* were derived in the following way: The number of answers from any one content category given to any one location has been expressed as a percentage of the number of persons in the group concerned. In dealing with any one location an answer has been considered *popular* when it was given in 25% of the cases or over. This means that the lists include responses given by one out of every four subjects in that particular group and have been subdivided

TABLE I

POPULAR RESPONSES:
COLLEGE AGE GROUP

	CARD	LOCATION	RESPONSE	No. GIVING RESPONSE	% GROUP GIVING RESPONSE
(1 in 2)	V	W	Winged animal	219	98
	III	W′	Human beings	194	87
	VIII*	D1	Animals	179	80
	I	W	Winged animal	115	51
(1 in 3)	X**	D1	Animals	104	46
	I	W	Human anatomy	86	38
	II	W	Human beings	86	38
	II	W′	Animals	84	38
	VII	W	Human beings	7·1	33
(1 in 4)	VI	D2	Object	67	30
	IV	W	Animal object	61	27
	VI	W′	Animal object	59	26

* Winged animals have been omitted.
** Winged animals have been included.

TABLE II

POPULAR RESPONSES
ADULTS

	CARD	LOCATION	RESPONSE	No. GIVING RESPONSE	% GROUP GIVING RESPONSE
(1 in 2)	V	W	Winged animal	29	85
	II	W	Human beings	23	68
	III	W'	Human beings	23	68
	VIII*	D1	Animals	23	68
	I	W	Winged animal	17	50
	III	D1	Winged animal	17	50
	X**	D18	Animals	17	50
(1 in 3)	VI	W'	Animal object	15	44
	I	W	Object	13	38
	IV	D2	Object	13	38
	II	S	Object	12	35
	IV	D1	Animal detail	12	35
(1 in 4)	VII	D3	Human detail	11	32
	X	D1	Animals	11	32
	III	W	Human beings	10	29
	IV	W	Human being	10	29
	VIII	W	Object	10	29
	II	d4	Human detail	9	26
	IV	W	Animal object	9	26
	VIII	D2	Winged animal	9	26
	IX	W	Object	9	26

* Winged animals have been omitted.
** Winged animals have been included.

TABLE III

POPULAR RESPONSES
PRISON INMATES

	CARD	LOCATION	RESPONSE	No. GIVING RESPONSE	% GROUP GIVING RESPONSE
(1 in 2)	V	W	Winged animal	45	110
	I	W	Winged animal	40	98
	VIII	D1	Animals	26	63
	X**	D1	Animals	23	56
(1 in 3)	III	W'	Human beings	20	49
	VI	W'	Animal object	16	39
	III	W	Human beings	14	34
(1 in 4)	III	D1	Butterfly	13	32
	II	W'	Animals	12	29

** Winged animals have been included.

to show the answers given by one out of every three subjects and those given by one out of every two subjects.[1]

Although the same criterion was used to derive each of these four lists, it is interesting to notice to what extent they vary. For example, the list for the adult group is twice as long as that for the psychotics and that for the prison inmates. Moreover, it contains a much greater

TABLE IV

POPULAR RESPONSES
PSYCHOTICS AND PSYCHOPATHIC PERSONALITIES

	CARD	LOCATION	RESPONSE	No. GIVING RESPONSE	% GROUP GIVING RESPONSE
	V	W	Winged animal	41	100
	I	W	Winged animal	30	73
(1 in 2)	VIII*	D1	Animals	28	68
	III	W	Human beings	24	59
	X	D1	Animals	21	51
	II	W	Human beings	20	49
(1 in 3)	IV	W	Animal object	18	46
	VI	W	Animal object	14	34
(1 in 4)	IV	W	Animal	11	27

* Winged animals have been omitted.

variety of locations, including even one d and one S area. Since the records of this adult group when considered as individual performances were unquestionably superior, characterized by the large number of original responses and the high quality of the form perception, it is interesting to see that such a group also tends to extend the range of its popular responses rather than concentrating them in the larger and more obvious areas.

In the college age group, of which approximately 50% were medical students, we find that the Human Anatomy responses in Card I exceed in frequency some responses usually considered as *popular* among all classes of subjects.

It is also worthy of note that there are only three answers which are given in over 50% of the cases in all four groups. *Popular* answers, therefore, must be considered as less universal in character than one might have supposed, and to vary for the different subjects examined.

---

[1] There is one case in which the figure is over 100%. This means that one or two individuals have given more than one popular answer to this location. (In Card I, "bat" and "butterfly" may have been given by some subjects.)

REJECTED CARDS

The graphs below show the number of failures to any one card expressed as a percentage of the number of persons in the group; that is, the number of persons potentially able to respond to that card.

This brings us at long last to some very striking differences between

Distribution of Failures in the Various Cards

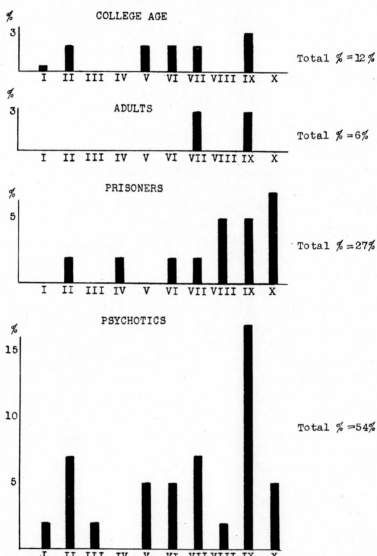

The total scores indicate that failures were found in the records of 12, 6, 27 and 54% of the groups respectively.

the performance of the individuals in the four groups. With the exception of the differences in number and kind of the popular responses, we have, till now, only been able to point to minor discrepancies between our subjects—slight differences in the distribution of the location of responses, slight differences in the use of the various determinants. But, by and large, our four groups of subjects have not appeared very different one from the other. Rather what has been shown are the characteristics of the cards per se which emerge despite the differences in the personalities of the subjects.

Considering the failures, or the rejections on the various cards, however, we can draw different conclusions. The much greater incidence of failures in the psychotic group is all the more striking in view of the essential similarity of their performance, card for card, to the other groups when locations and determinants are considered.

We cannot say that such a distribution of failures is in any way characteristic of psychotic patients as no comparable data as derived by the individual method exists for comparison. We can say, however, that the distribution is unlike that which we have found among a large group of psychoneurotic patients,* particularly in the fact that Cards VI and IV, which are often rejected by the neurotics are among the less frequently rejected cards by the psychotics, Card IV as it happens being the only card on which no failure occurred in this group.

The concentration of failures in the last three colored cards among the prison inmates is interesting, particularly in view of the fact that neither Card VIII nor Card X shows any failures in the normal groups. A comparable study to ours reported by Lindner and Chapman (1) would show a similar tendency in the prison inmates whose group records these authors analyzed from this angle. Their findings if expressed in a comparable way to ours would show that Cards IX and X are second only to Card VII in the frequency of their rejections.

In conformity with their generally superior performance the number of failures in the Adult group is very small. There are failures in only 6% of the cases. The college age group is also relatively free of rejections.

Considering the rejections in terms of the individual cards, rather than the groups of subjects, it can be seen that Card IX is most likely to be rejected by all groups. At the other extreme stands Card IV with surprisingly infrequent failures.

---

* Unpublished study by authors.

The Distribution of Anatomical Answers

Table V illustrates certain points of interest in regard to the anatomical answers given by the college age group. It will be seen in column one that certain cards are more likely to produce anatomical responses than others, Card I, in particular, yielding many such responses while cards V, II, and VII produce few.

In the second and third columns of this table the percentages of these anatomical responses found in the records of the medical stu-

TABLE V

DISTRIBUTION OF ANATOMICAL ANSWERS IN THE TEN CARDS
(MEDICAL STUDENTS AND NON-MEDICAL STUDENTS)

CARD	TOTAL NO. OF ANATOMICAL ANSWERS GIVEN BY COLLEGE AGE GROUP (224 SUBJECTS)	% OF ANATOMICAL ANSWERS DERIVED FROM RECORDS OF MEDICAL STUDENTS (108 SUBJECTS)	% OF ANATOMICAL ANSWERS DERIVED FROM RECORDS OF ALL OTHER SUBJECTS (116 SUBJECTS)
I	152	75.0	25.0
II	30	63.3	36.7
III	61	75.4	24.6
IV	56	66.1	33.9
V	15	80.0	20.0
VI	37	75.7	24.3
VII	30	80.0	20.0
VIII	69	55.1	44.9
IX	94	66.0	34.0
X	65	62.7	37.3

dents (108 subjects) are compared with those found in the records of the remainder of the group (116 subjects). Provided no additional factor influenced the results, we might expect an equal distribution in each of these columns. That some factor is at work can be seen at a glance. Only in Card VIII do the figures even approximate what would have been expected on a purely arbitrary division. In all other cases one sees preponderance of anatomical answers in the records of the medical students. It would seem clear that familiarity with anatomical concepts and structures, and interest in anatomy courses which are taken during the year clearly leave their mark on the responses given to the ink-blots.

For some reason, however, there has been a reluctance among Rorschach workers to assume such a vocational or training factor. They have tended to interpret anatomical answers in the same way regardless of the background of the individual in whose record they appear. These results indicate that one must expect a higher anatomical percentage in the records of persons in whom anatomy is a field of study, and must not attribute to them neurotic or anxiety-indicating features. Hertz in an unpublished study* in 1932 makes a similar

TABLE VI

PERCENTAGE OF TOTAL NUMBER OF RESPONSES
DERIVED FROM EACH CARD: FOUR MAIN GROUPS

COLLEGE GROUP (5806 RESPONSES)		ADULTS (1052 RESPONSES)		PRISON INMATES (713 RESPONSES)		PSYCHOTICS AND PSYCHOPATHIC PERSONALITIES (955 RESPONSES)	
CARD	%	CARD	%	CARD	%	CARD	%
X	13.6	X	13.1	X	14.0	X	13.9
I	10.9	III	11.6	I	12.9	II	11.5
VIII	10.5	I	11.0	II	10.0	I	11.3
III	10.2	IV	10.5	{ III	9.8	VIII	11.1
VI	9.7	II	10.0	{ V	9.8	III	10.2
IV	9.6	VI	9.6	VIII	9.5	IX	9.5
IX	9.5	{ V	9.1	IV	9.3	VI	8.8
II	9.3	{ VII	9.1	{ IX	8.3	IV	8.5
V	8.4	VIII	8.6	{ VI	8.3	V	8.0
VII	8.3	IX	7.4	VII	8.1	VII	7.2

PERCENTAGE OF TOTAL NUMBER OF RESPONSES
COLLEGE SUB-GROUPS

MEDICAL STUDENTS		NURSES		NAVAL CADETS		MALE STUDENTS		FEMALE STUDENTS	
CARD	%	CARD	%	CARD	%	CARD	%	CARD	%
X	13.8	X	12.6	I	12.5	X	15.1	X	18.2
III	10.6	I	11.5	X	11.6	VIII	10.7	VIII	11.4
I	10.5	VIII	11.2	VIII	10.5	{ II	10.1	IV	10.8
VIII	10.1	VI	10.6	III	10.4	{ IX	10.1	III	9.6
IX	9.8	III	9.4	IV	9.8	I	9.9	IX	9.3
VI	9.8	{ II	9.1	VI	9.5	{ VI	9.5	I	9.0
{ II	9.5	{ IV	9.1	V	9.1	{ III	9.5	V	8.0
{ IV	9.5	VII	9.0	{ II	8.9	{ IV	9.5	{ VI	8.0
V	8.4	IX	8.8	{ VII	8.9	VII	8.9	{ VII	8.0
VII	7.8	V	8.6	IX	8.8	V	6.9	II	7.7

observation: "Medical students gave by far the largest number of anatomical terms," and she also concludes that "medical students and nurses show the effect of their specialized education."

RELATIVE PRODUCTIVITY ON EACH OF THE TEN CARDS

A few remarks may be made about the cards most likely to produce the greatest and least number of responses as recorded in Table VI.

---

* Personal communication.

Card X it will be seen leads in the four main groups of subjects with Card I in second and third place. At the other end of the scale Card VII is the card which gives rise to the fewest responses in three of the four groups, and is also low in the list of the fourth group. In view of the relative productivity which occurred in Card II in three of the four groups, the fact that it is low in the college age group would lead us to wonder whether color shock was more pronounced in this group than in the others. This supposition has been borne out in a number of ways.

REFERENCE

1. Lindner, R. M.: A further contribution to the group Rorschach. *Rorschach Res. Exch.*, 7:7-15, 1943.

Analysis of the Effect of Repetition and Change of Method on Performance

A T THE TIME of our initial presentation of the group Rorschach considerable interest was shown in the difference in the records which might be expected to occur as a result of the new mode of administration. As the method has come into wider usage, however, and has demonstrated its effectiveness as a tool in its own right, much less importance has been attached to these detailed comparative studies.

As we mentioned earlier (Section I), such comparisons can only be made by either repeating the test on the same subjects, each time using a different method, or by equating two groups of subjects and administering the test to each group in a different way. In the first case we have to disentangle the effect of repetition per se; in the second, there is always the possibility that the two groups are not as similar in personality or temperament as they appear to be in background, education, intelligence, and the like.

In this section we are presenting comparative material derived from our earlier investigations. In these investigations we separated the two factors of repetition, and change of method, by having four groups of subjects: the control groups repeated the test without change of method; the experimental groups repeated the test with a change of method in the second administration. Referring to Table I it will be seen that group A repeated the individual test; B repeated the group test; while C took the individual test first, and repeated with the group procedure; D took the group test first, and repeated with the individual procedure.

In Table I it will be seen that there is a consistent shift in the selection of locations. All second, or repeat performances, show a decrease in the whole percentage and a corresponding rise in the other locations. This shift occurs independently of a change of method, and occurs in the same direction, regardless of which method of administration occurs in the second place. Greater preoccupation with the smaller areas in the blots is first and foremost, then, a result of repeating the test.

To some extent it may be said that the individual procedure tends to work in the same direction as repetition; or otherwise stated, that one is apt to get a greater number of whole responses in the group procedure, since a comparison of C and D shows that a more marked shift occurs (in D) when the individual test is in second place. But the factor of repeating the test is unquestionably the strongest influence.

TABLE I

THE EFFECT OF REPETITION AND CHANGE OF METHOD ON THE
DISTRIBUTION OF ANSWERS ACCORDING TO LOCATION
SUBJECTS TAKING INDIVIDUAL TEST BOTH TIMES
(20 Subjects)

	LOCATION	% RESPONSES FIRST TIME	% RESPONSES SECOND TIME	% DIFFERENCE
	W	44.8	34.6	—10.2
	D	49.3	52.9	3.6
	d	2.4	4.2	1.8
A.	Dd + S	3.5	8.3	4.8
	dd	0	1.3	1.3
	de	.2	.7	.5
	di	.2	.4	.2
	dr	1.2	2.8	1.6
	S	1.9	3.1	1.2

SUBJECTS TAKING GROUP TEST BOTH TIMES
(20 Subjects)

	W	32.2	19.6	—12.6
	D	54.4	57.8	3.4
	d	4.8	6.5	1.7
B.	Dd + S	8.6	16.1	7.5
	dd	.4	2.5	2.1
	de	2.1	4.7	2.6
	di	0	.7	.7
	dr	1.1	2.2	1.1
	S	5.0	5.9	.9

REPETITION AND CHANGE OF METHOD
SUBJECTS TAKING INDIVIDUAL TEST FIRST, GROUP TEST SECOND
(20 Subjects)

	LOCATION	% RESPONSES INDIVIDUAL	% RESPONSES GROUP	% DIFFERENCE
	W	26.6	20.5	—6.1
	D	51.2	52.6	1.4
	d	9.6	11.0	1.4
C.	Dd + S	12.6	15.9	3.3
	dd	3.4	2.7	—.7
	de	.6	1.7	1.1
	di	1.6	.9	—.7
	dr	4.4	5.7	1.3
	S	2.6	4.9	2.3

TABLE I (*Continued*)

SUBJECTS TAKING GROUP TEST FIRST, INDIVIDUAL TEST SECOND
(40 Subjects)

	LOCATION	% RESPONSES GROUP	% RESPONSES INDIVIDUAL	% DIFFERENCE
	W	50.4	35.1	—15.3
	D	40	50.4	10.4
	d	3.5	6.5	3.0
D.	Dd + S	6.1	8.0	1.9
	dd	.3	1.3	1.0
	de	0	.6	.6
	di	0	.1	.1
	dr	2.4	2.6	.2
	S	3.4	3.4	0

Table II makes a similar comparison possible between our four groups. In this case the determinants are considered. The outstanding impression from scanning this table, however, is the remarkable similarity between all four groups on first and second performances. Unlike the findings in regard to the locations there is no striking and consistent difference that appears as a result of repetition, except perhaps a slight decrease in CF and FM responses on the second performance. One cannot help but be struck on the other hand by the number of instances in which there is no difference, or virtually no difference, between the figures for the various determinants.

TABLE II

THE EFFECT OF REPETITION AND CHANGE OF METHOD ON THE
DISTRIBUTION OF ANSWERS ACCORDING TO DETERMINANTS
(Percentages)

DETER-MINANTS	REPETITION ONLY						REPETITION AND CHANGE OF METHOD					
	INDIVIDUAL			GROUP			IND. GROUP			GROUP IND.		
	1st.	2nd.	Diff.	1st.	2nd.	Diff.	1st.	2nd.	Diff.	1st.	2nd.	Diff.
M	15.8	16.0	.2	14.4	11.5	—2.9	10.1	10.5	.4	16.6	14.5	—2.1
FM	23.3	22.3	—1.0	14.4	12.4	—2.0	15.7	15.3	— .4	20.3	17.4	—2.9
m	.5	.4	— .1	.8	.3	— .5	.5	.5	0	1.5	2.4	.9
k	.9	.9	0	.8	.9	.1	2.1	1.4	— .7	2.4	1.0	—1.4
K	.7	.7	0	.9	.7	— .2	1.3	1.5	.2	1.6	2.8	1.2
FK	1.7	1.3	— .4	2.1	3.9	1.8	.8	.8	0	3.8	3.8	0
F	27.8	28.4	.6	39.4	41.9	2.5	41.9	39.6	—2.3	26.9	31.2	4.3
Fc	6.4	6.6	.2	3.8	7.7	3.9	6.2	7.0	.8	5.6	5.1	— .5
c	3.5	3.3	— .2	3.8	2.6	—1.2	4.4	4.0	— .4	5.1	5.1	0
C′	3.1	2.9	— .2	4.5	4.7	.2	2.9	4.4	1.5	1.8	3.5	1.7
FC	7.5	9.2	1.7	8.3	8.3	0	6.2	7.8	1.6	5.6	6.6	1.0
CF	8.0	7.4	— .6	6.4	4.4	—2.0	7.3	6.8	— .5	8.2	6.4	—1.8
C	.7	.6	— .1	.4	.6	.2	.6	.4	— .2	.5	.3	— .2

CARD BY CARD COMPARISON OF DISTRIBUTION OF DETERMINANTS IN
GROUP AND INDIVIDUAL TESTS. 40 NURSES IN TRAINING
(COLLEGE AGE SUB-GROUP 2)

In the eleven pairs of graphs which follow, a card by card comparison of the 40 subjects in Group D (group test first, followed by the
individual) is made. The composite graphs (on page 113) with all
the determinants for all the cards, are extremely similar. Only in a
few instances do certain cards reveal slightly different profiles under
the two conditions.

CARD I

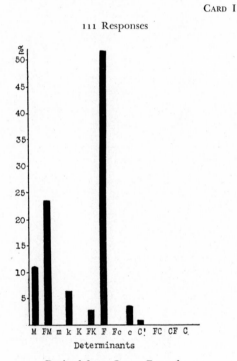

111 Responses

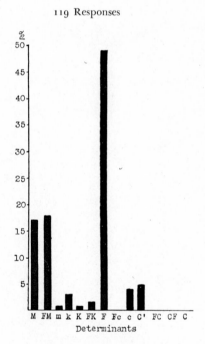

119 Responses

Derived from Group Records
First Performance

Derived from Individual Records
Repeat Performance

88 Responses

98 Responses

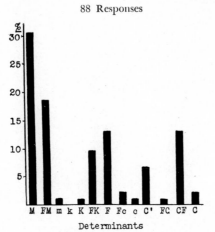

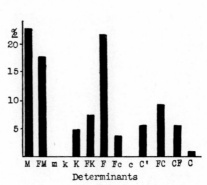

Derived from Group Records
First Performance

Derived from Individual Records
Repeat Performance

91 Responses

105 Responses

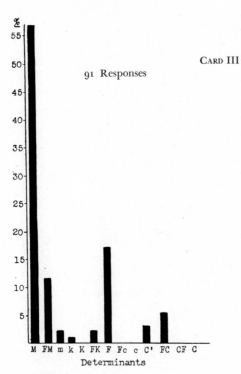

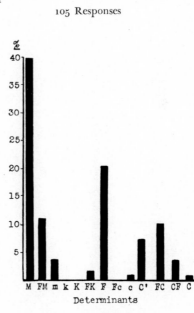

Derived from Group Records
First Performance

Derived from Individual Records
Repeat Performance

88 Responses

96 Responses

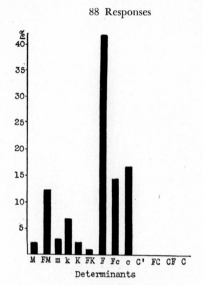

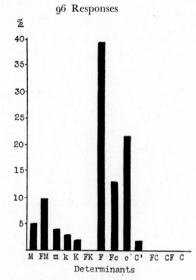

Derived from Group Records
First Performance

Derived from Individual Records
Repeat Performance

CARD V

83 Responses

95 Responses

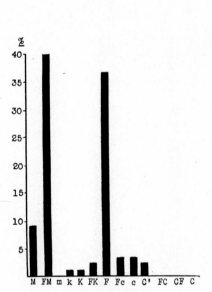

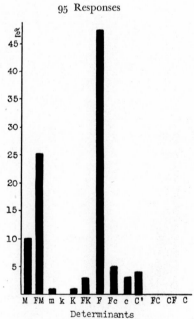

Derived from Group Records
First Performance

Derived from Individual Records
Repeat Performance

102 Responses

110 Responses

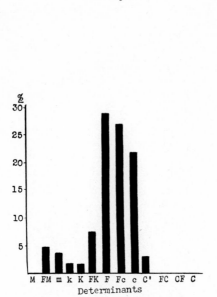

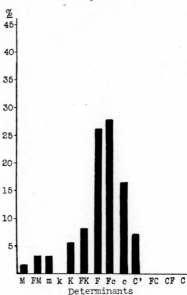

Derived from Group Records
First Performance

Derived from Individual Records
Repeat Performance

CARD VII

87 Responses

101 Responses

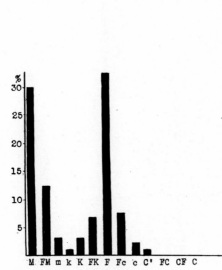

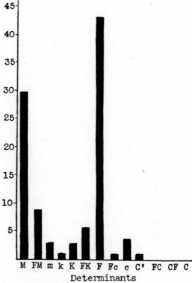

Derived from Group Records
First Performance

Derived from Individual Records
Repeat Performance

CARD VIII

108 Responses

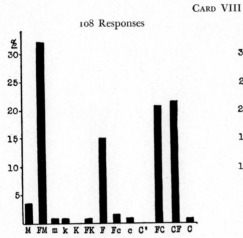

Determinants
Derived from Group Records
First Performance

112 Responses

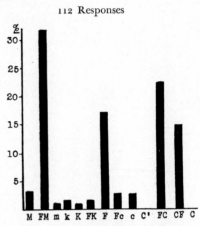

Determinants
Derived from Individual Records
Repeat Performance

CARD IX

85 Responses

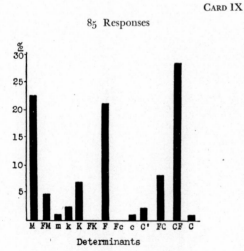

Determinants
Derived from Group Records
First Performance

107 Responses

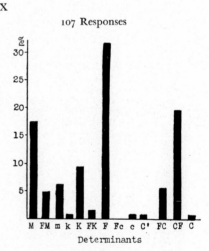

Determinants
Derived from Individual Records
Repeat Performance

CARD X

122 Responses

177 Responses

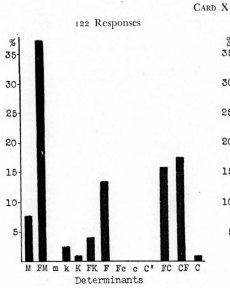

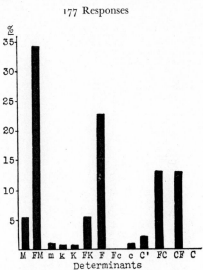

Derived from Group Records
First Performance

Derived from Individual Records
Repeat Performance

COMPOSITE FOR ALL CARDS

965 Responses

1120 Responses

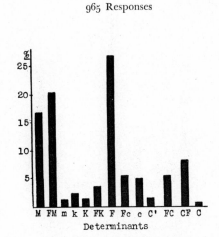

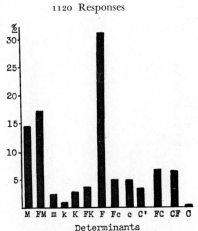

Derived from Group Records
First Performance

Derived from Individual Records
Repeat Performance

TABLE III

Tables III and IV summarize the material presented in the graphs on the preceding pages.

DISTRIBUTION OF RESPONSES ACCORDING TO DETERMINANTS:
NURSES IN TRAINING, FIRST PERFORMANCE, GROUP RECORDS

DETERMINANTS	CARDS									
	I	II	III	IV	V	VI	VII	VIII	IX	X
M	10.9	30.4	57.0	2.2	9.4	0	30	3.8	22.4	7.9
FM	23.6	18.5	11.8	12.1	40.0	4.8	12.2	32.1	4.7	37.3
m	0	1.1	2.2	3.3	0	3.8	3.3	.9	1.2	0
k	6.4	0	1.1	6.6	1.2	1.9	1.1	.9	2.4	2.4
K	0	1.1	0	2.2	1.2	1.9	3.3	0	7.1	.8
FK	2.7	9.8	2.2	1.1	2.4	7.6	6.7	.9	0	4.0
F	51.8	13.0	17.2	41.8	36.5	28.6	32.2	15.1	21.2	13.5
Fc	0	2.2	0	14.2	3.5	26.7	7.8	1.9	0	0
c	3.6	1.1	0	16.5	3.5	21.9	2.2	.9	1.2	0
C'	.9	6.5	3.2	0	2.4	2.9	1.1	0	2.4	0
FC		1.1	5.4					20.8	8.2	15.9
CF		13.0	0					21.7	28.2	17.5
C		2.1	0					.9	1.2	.8

TABLE IV

DISTRIBUTION OF RESPONSES ACCORDING TO DETERMINANTS:
NURSES IN TRAINING, REPEAT PERFORMANCE, INDIVIDUAL RECORDS

DETERMINANTS	CARDS									
	I	II	III	IV	V	VI	VII	VIII	IX	X
M	17.2	22.6	39.8	5.0	10.1	1.6	29.8	3.4	17.5	5.5
FM	18.0	17.9	11.1	9.9	25.3	3.3	8.7	31.9	4.8	34.3
m	.8	0	3.7	4.0	1.0	3.3	2.9	.9	6.3	1.1
k	3.3	0	0	3.0	0	0	1.0	1.7	.8	.6
K	.8	4.7	0	2.0	1.0	5.7	2.9	.9	9.5	.6
FK	1.6	7.5	2.8	0	3.0	8.2	5.8	1.7	1.6	5.5
F	49.2	21.7	20.4	39.6	47.5	26.2	43.3	17.2	31.7	22.7
Fc	0	3.8	0	12.9	5.1	27.9	1.0	2.6	0	0
c	4.1	0	.9	21.8	3.0	16.4	3.8	2.6	.8	1.1
C'	4.9	5.7	7.4	2.0	4.0	7.4	1.0	0	.8	2.2
FC		9.4	10.2					22.4	5.6	13.3
CF		5.7	3.7					14.7	19.8	13.3
C		.9	.9					0	.8	0

PART III

A MULTIPLE CHOICE TEST
FOR SCREENING PURPOSES

The Development of the Multiple Choice Test for Screening Purposes

W E STATED in Section I, Part I, that the *group Rorschach* originated in an attempt to reduce the time required for administration of a valuable clinical method in order to extend the sphere of its usefulness. It was, undoubtedly, a beginning in the right direction but it soon became clear as we developed this new method that we had not gone nearly far enough in our attempt to shorten and simplify the procedure.

Moreover, we had not circumvented the most important obstacle to its widespread usage, namely the fact that skilled Rorschach workers were needed to score and evaluate the group records even if untrained persons could administer the test, while the complicated scoring system still defied any attempt to handle results in a mechanical fashion. The Rorschach, therefore, remained a method requiring its own specialists and could not be considered a psychological test in the usual sense of the word.

In the multiple choice test, which we present in this chapter, we have cut the *Gordian Knot*. We have departed so far in fact from the essence of what Rorschach intended in the spontaneous unimpeded recording of responses that it is probably fairest to all concerned to consider it as an entirely different procedure rather than a further modification of the original method. For quite clearly a test which can be given and evaluated in a few minutes cannot hope to achieve the type of detailed analysis of the individual's personality which the Rorschach method achieves in the hands of a specialist. In the last analysis, however, in any program of screening out of the unfit, we are much less interested in knowing in detail why the individual is unfit, provided we can spot him.

The use of multiple choice answers with ink blots is not new. Terman (1) in 1936 utilized four alternative answers with a small series of ink spots to determine dominant interests with reference to masculine and feminine traits. Our original procedure, therefore, was somewhat similar to his. On receiving the Rorschach card, or

1

☐ An army or navy emblem
☐ Mud and dirt
☐ A bat
☐ Nothing at all
☐ Two people
☐ A pelvis
☐ An x-ray picture
☐ Pincers of a crab
☐ A dirty mess
☐ Part of my body
☐ Something other than the above:—

2

☐ A bug somebody stepped on
☐ Nothing at all
☐ Two scottie dogs
☐ Little faces on the sides
☐ A bloody spinal column
☐ A white top
☐ A bursting bomb
☐ Two elephants
☐ Two clowns
☐ Black and red
☐ Something other than the above:—

3

☐ Two birds
☐ Meat in a butcher shop
☐ Two men
☐ Part of my body
☐ Red and black
☐ A colored butterfly
☐ Spots of blood or paint
☐ Monkeys hanging by their tails
☐ A red bow-tie
☐ Nothing at all
☐ Something other than the above:—

4

☐ Head of an animal
☐ Lungs and chest
☐ A nasty mess
☐ A pair of boots
☐ Black smoke and dirt
☐ Nothing at all
☐ A man in a fur coat
☐ An animal skin
☐ A big gorilla
☐ An x-ray picture
☐ Something other than the above:—

5

☐ Nothing at all
☐ An alligator's head
☐ A smashed body
☐ A fan dancer
☐ An x-ray picture
☐ Legs
☐ A bat or butterfly
☐ Lungs and chest
☐ Black clouds
☐ A pair of pliers
☐ Something other than the above:—

6

☐ Two kings' heads with crowns
☐ An x-ray picture
☐ Sex organs
☐ A totem pole
☐ A fur rug
☐ Mud and water
☐ A polished post
☐ Nothing at all
☐ A turtle
☐ A gray smudge
☐ Something other than the above:—

7

☐ Smoke or clouds
☐ Two women talking
☐ Part of my body
☐ Animals or animal heads
☐ Nothing at all
☐ A map
☐ Dirty ice and snow
☐ Lambs' tails, or feathers
☐ An x-ray picture
☐ Bookends
☐ Something other than the above:—

8

☐ Flowers or leaves
☐ An x-ray picture
☐ Nothing at all
☐ Pink, blue, and orange
☐ A horseshoe crab
☐ A colored coat of arms
☐ Fire and ice, life and death
☐ Two animals
☐ Blue flags
☐ Parts of my body
☐ Something other than the above:—

9

☐ Red, green, and orange
☐ Sea horses, or lobsters
☐ Flowers or underwater vegetation
☐ Parts of my body
☐ Smoke, flames, or an explosion
☐ Deer or horns of a deer
☐ Nothing at all
☐ Two people-witches or Santa Clauses
☐ Bloody clouds
☐ A candle
☐ Something other than the above:—

10

☐ Two people
☐ Spilt paint
☐ A Chinese print
☐ An x-ray picture
☐ Red, blue, and green
☐ Spiders, caterpillars, crabs and insects
☐ Parts of my insides
☐ A colored chart or map
☐ Nothing at all
☐ A flower garden or gay tropical fish
☐ Something other than the above:—

looking at a slide of the blot, the individual was presented with ten alternative answers and asked to pick that one which in his opinion was the best description of the blot or any part of the blot. Five of these 10 answers were chosen from the records given by healthy normal individuals, the remaining five from the records of persons with various types of psychological disturbances. They were selected after we had studied over 1,000 records, clinical and otherwise, taken individually and accumulated by the writers during the course of several years.

The underlying assumption has been that those individuals most likely to give certain types of responses when responding freely in the Rorschach method will pick such responses when confronted with them in a multiple choice situation.

In scoring the test the key given in Section X was consulted.* Answers from normal records received the numbers 1, 2, 3, 4, and 5, while answers occurring more frequently in abnormal records were scored 6, 7, 8, 9, and 10. The score, therefore, was recorded in a series of 10 digits since one answer represented by one number was selected from each list of the 10 cards. Each of these numbers in addition to representing the good and poor answers for each card had significance so far as Rorschach scoring was concerned; that is, it had been chosen so that the important determinants or elements in Rorschach's scoring system were presented as systematically as possible. For example, a number 1 always stood for a human movement (the M) response (except in Card VIII where no M's were listed). Number 2 stood for the popular response to the card—in many cases an FM response. Good color responses, FC, another essential ingredient, were represented by 3 and 4 in the colored cards. Number 6 indicated anatomical answers. Number 7 in many cases represented answers depicting anxiety. Numbers 8 and 9 represented various types of disturbed answers. Number 10 signified failure. This, it would appear, might eventually lay the basis for at least some kind of differential diagnosis (see Section III and VII).

Answers given as *"something other than the above,"* i.e., written in by the subject in the blank space, were scored *A or alternate answers,* except when the difference was a purely verbal one, i.e., when the answer clearly belonged in the same category as one of the given suggestions. That is the only point where the trained Rorschach worker

---

* The Key in Section X is the key for the amplified version of the Multiple Choice test. It *includes* the key for the original form discussed here which has 100 choices.

had an advantage. He did not need to use the "alternate" classification so often and hence avoided false positives. When the test was used by untrained Rorschach workers, the alternate answers had to be considered deviations and counted in with the poor answers, so that if the total of poor *and* alternate answers together reached four or more than four, the individual was placed in the questionable group. If the test was scored by an individual with Rorschach experience, it was found a very simple matter to score alternates as A+ and A— respectively. Original answers with good form were scored alternate plus, and were not counted as a deviation from the normal. Bizarre alternate answers, and those with poor form, were considered alternate minus answers and were counted in with the poor answers.

ADMINISTRATION

The test could be given in three ways: as a group test to large numbers of persons, as an individual test, and even as a self-administering test. The *group test procedure* took approximately 20 minutes when over 200 individuals were involved. First, the written instructions on the test form were read aloud while the subjects read them too. Then each ink blot was projected for *30 seconds in a completely darkened room*. After this time the lights were put on for an additional 30 seconds (*or a full minute if necessary*) to allow for the recording of the responses. The blot remained in full view on the screen during the period of recording but was naturally a little dimmer when the lights were on. Since the last three colored blots could not be seen well with room lighting, they were exposed a second time for a few seconds after the recording period to allow for a final check.

As each slide was exposed, *its number was called out by the examiner* and the subjects' attention was directed to the fact that they must be sure to look at the *list pertaining to this particular slide*. There was almost always one individual in a large group of subjects who, despite the heavy lines on the page, and the initial instructions, checked his answers under the wrong inkblot and consequently invalidated his record! It was of the utmost importance that the slides were presented in the correct order and correct orientation. While this would not constitute a problem for persons who had had experience in the Rorschach method, it might well present a difficulty in the hands of an untrained technician. All slides were clearly marked, therefore, with the number of the blot which they represented, and the correct manner of inserting them was indicated.

Directions for Administering the First Multiple Choice Test to groups read as follows:

Procedure*

"Issue the record forms saying in effect, 'Do not turn this form over until so directed. Put your name and the other data in the space provided here,' (demonstrate on blank form). Now I will read over the instructions with you:

"You will be shown a series of 10 inkblot pictures. First you will take a good look at each picture as it is shown and see whether it or any part of it, reminds you of anything or resembles something you have seen. Then you will read through a list of suggested replies to see which of these is the best description of the blot. Put a cross in the little box beside the suggestion that *you* think is the best description of the blot. If you see two things, put a 2 in the square corresponding to your second choice. If you see nothing, put a cross by the word 'Nothing.' If you see something that is not listed and is quite unlike anything that has been suggested, put down what you see on the blank line at the bottom of the column.

"Each figure will be shown about half a minute with the room rather dark, and then lights will be turned on, to enable you to write your answers, for another half-minute before the next slide is shown. Each time a new slide is shown, I will call out its number, 1, 2, 3, and so on. Notice that the numbers run across the page like this . . . (demonstrate with blank form). Is that all perfectly clear? Now turn the page, slide number one.

"The changing of light and slides will ordinarily be difficult for a single examiner. With two, one examiner can easily work the projector while the other regulates the lights. The slides should be left exposed while the light is on, the room being again darkened for the initial exposure of each new slide. Call its number as each new slide is exposed.

Scoring

"When the records have been collected, the examiner must:

1) Give the rank number of each response
2) Add up the number of 'minus' responses (those of rank 6 and over)
3) List the number of alternates
4) Epitomize the subject's record in such a way as:

> 0 poor answers, or
> 1 poor answer plus 3 alternates, or
> 6 poor answers, or
> 8 poor answers

as the score demands."

INDIVIDUAL PRESENTATION

When a *single individual* was examined the test took approximately five minutes. The same instructions were given except that the individual was not asked to mark the blank. He was asked to tell the examiner his first and second choices and the examiner marked these two choices on the test blank as each card was responded to. The indi-

---

* The authors are indebted to Dr. F. L. Wells for this concise formulation of the directions.

vidual, for example, was presented with the Rorschach picture and a card on which were written the ten suggestions for that inkblot. He selected, let us say, "a bat" on Card 1 as his first choice and "pelvis" as his second. The examiner, however, did not write "bat" or "pelvis" but marked these answers on the test form and simultaneously, or subsequently, transcribed the numbers in the space at the lower right of the test blank (see page 121) and so on for each of the 10 answers. If the subject was unable to read easily, the examiner read out the list to him while he looked at the card.

A third manner of administration was simply to hand an individual a series of the inkblots in their correct order and orientation and let him administer the test to himself, taking his own time and marking the blank himself.

SCORING

For transcribing the scores subsequent to the group administration, we found that if the key was known by heart, transcribing ten digits was an affair of seconds. At the most a minute was allowed for each record blank. Whether first choices were to be given equal weight, or even whether third or fourth choices were to be asked for depended on the purpose to which the test was to be put. If the roughest, quickest screening was desired, then first answers alone were sufficient to indicate gross disturbance. However, a remarkably full analysis was possible if the subject was asked to pick out and mark in order of preference "all those answers that he could see in the blot." This, however, required evaluation by persons with some Rorschach training (Sections III and VII).

In the usual procedure where two answers were requested (see Procedure on page 121), most weight was given to first answers. They constituted the ten digit score, but important information could be derived from second answers in questionable cases. For example, attention to second answers might differentiate between the more seriously disturbed individuals with four poor answers and those who were less disturbed. Moreover, as Washburne and Jacobs* have found, certain types of difficulties might be shown in second rather than in first choices. The absence of second choices on certain cards was also significant, indicating a greater difficulty with the card in question. Sometimes "nothing at all" was given as second choice despite the fact that an answer had already been selected in the first place, indicating a hesitancy about committing oneself on that particular card,

---

* Personal communication.

Table I shows the subjects who took part in our initial experiment.

TABLE I

THE SUBJECTS IN OUR INITIAL EXPERIMENT

SUBJECTS	TYPE OF INFORMATION AVAILABLE FOR COMPARISON AND VALIDATION OF PERFORMANCE ON TEST
33 Superior adults (m. & f.) 31 Unselected adults (m. & f.) 48 Student nurses (f.)	Correlations with impressions on psychiatric interview and with "Washburne Social-Adjustment Inventory" and "Aptitude Test for Nursing." Comparison with performance during training, supervisor's rating, etc.
217 Women in Service	Comparison with performance during intensive training period, ability to adjust to new conditions, occurrence of functional disorders, etc.
Total 329	
225 Prisoners at Waupun Prison (m.) (Age 18-38)	Information from Warden and Deputy Warden, opinion of Board of Public Welfare.
53 Students referred by college psychiatrists (m. & f.)	Clinical diagnoses and follow-up studies by Drs. Washburne and Jacobs.
29 Patients from Hospital for Criminally Insane, Waupun (m.)	Clinical histories, diagnoses, discussion with physician in charge, Dr. Klepfer.
43 Patients from neuropsychiatric wards, Wisconsin General Hospital (m. & f.)	Clinical histories, diagnoses, by Drs. Reese, Kant, Masten, Haynes.
71 Patients from Mendota State Hospital (m. & f.)	Diagnoses from attending physicians, Drs. Sauthoff, Ware.
Total 143	

RESULTS OF INITIAL EXPERIMENTS

What differences did we find in the selection of answers in terms of our digit system between the normal and abnormal subjects? Did the normals select fewer poor answers? That is, did we find more 1, 2, 3, 4, 5's and fewer 6, 7, 8, 9, 10's in the normal group? The answer was emphatically "yes." There was a very striking difference between the scores of the normal and abnormal subjects which could be seen in a variety of ways.

The accompanying graph, page 124, presents the answer in the clearest and most simple form. Expressed in these columns in percentage terms is the number of persons in each group whose score includes four or more than four poor answers. At the one extreme we have the 6% to 16% of the normal groups; at the other the 73%

to 79% of the institutionalized patients and neuropsychiatric cases; the prisoners, and the students referred by the psychiatrist showing intermediate positions.

There was nothing absolute or final about the choice of four poor answers as the score at which to become suspicious of an individual's performance. We selected this point empirically since it seemed to be the one which caught the maximum number of persons who showed some significant disturbance in the particular groups that

PERCENTAGE OF EACH GROUP WITH FOUR OR MORE THAN FOUR POOR ANSWERS

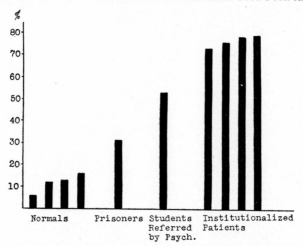

we tested. However, if only the most disturbed individuals were to be screened out, then five poor answers, or even six might be taken as the criterion. Similarly, if exceptionally well balanced and inte- grated individuals were to be selected, picking these on the basis of their having no poor answers, or only one poor answer, might be useful. On page 125 it may be seen that, whereas chance would decree that only .09% of the individuals in a group might be expected to have ten good answers (no poor answers), in the superior adult group 55% fall in this area. And the whole distribution of the curve is quite at variance with what would be expected on a chance basis.*

Table II breaks down the results epitomized above, so that we see the different distributions within the groups in four classifications: those with none, one and two poor answers, which we consider good records, those with three poor answers, those with four, and those with more than four. It is interesting to note, among other things, that the prisoners have a relatively small percentage of persons with

_____

* See footnote on page 125.

more than four poor answers, i.e. they are much closer to the normal distribution than to that of the psychiatric patients, but at the same time they have a much smaller percentage of persons with outstandingly good records (with none, one, and two poor answers) when compared with the superior adults, the women in service and the student nurses.

In Section II the actual scores of some of our subjects will be found. For example, 48 student nurses may be compared with 41 female patients from a state hospital. Similarly the scores of 33 superior normals* can be contrasted with the scores of 33 patients from the

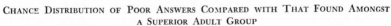

CHANCE DISTRIBUTION OF POOR ANSWERS COMPARED WITH THAT FOUND AMONGST A SUPERIOR ADULT GROUP

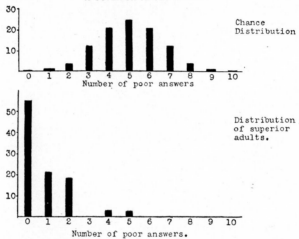

neuropsychiatric wards. The ten digit score is recorded horizontally in each case, with a final column epitomizing the number of poor answers together with the number of alternate answers. All poor answers are bracketed so that they stand out in the score more clearly. *The line drawn across the page separates those with four or more than four poor answers from the rest.* It will be noticed that "four or more than four poor answers" includes alternate answers; for example, subject 43 amongst the student nurses has two poor answers and two alternate answers. While in all probability this record shows nowhere near the disturbance that four poor answers would show, in order not to involve any qualitative estimate of the answers at this point, such a subject is placed below the line.

---

* Mann and Archibald (2) published figures for two groups of subjects in England. Their superior adult group shows 4% of the individuals with four or more poor answers, their group of factory workers shows 25%.

Unquestionably then, a striking difference can be demonstrated quantitatively between the groups. But what can we say about the exceptions? That small percentage of persons who do well in the abnormal group, and that small percentage who do badly in the normal group. Here some of the most interesting features of the whole study appear. For example, subject 35 among the superior adults was the only one in the group to have more than four poor answers. This individual, it subsequently transpired, had been hos-

TABLE II % POOR ANSWERS

	0, 1, 2	3	4	MORE THAN 4
Superior adults	94	0	3	3
Unselected adults	77	6	13	3
Student nurses	80	8	8	4
Women in Service	73	14	9	4
Prisoners at Waupun	44	24	16	15
Students referred by college psychiatrist	33	13	23	30
Patients from Hospital for Criminally Insane, Waupun	14	10	24	52
Patients from neuro-psych. wards Wisconsin General Hospital	9	12	9	70
Patients from Mendota State Hospital (female)	10	12	15	63
Patients from Mendota State Hospital (male)	20	7	10	63

pitalized for manic depressive psychosis. The only individual with as many as eight poor answers among the women in service was at that time "deaf," unable to hear the code, and was subsequently diagnosed as conversion hysteria.

Four of the six individuals who fell below the line in the nurses group received low ratings on the psychiatric interview (3 D's and a C). In addition, those with the D ratings also did badly on both other psychological tests, the Washburne Social Adjustment and the Nursing Aptitude test.

There are, however, records which must be considered *false positives, i.e.,* records of well-adjusted persons who fall below the line of demarcation because of technical defects in the scoring system at the present time. Such cases, as a matter of fact, occur most frequently in members of the medical profession or medical students. They are the result of a professional or occupational attitude which is carried over into the test, particularly in the first two cards so that anatomical answers are selected. While other occupational interests are not penalized, anatomical answers must receive high numbers (actually six and seven in the scoring system because of the significance which anatomical answers have in the records of many neurotic patients. Two anatomical answers, however, may be sufficient to place a well-adjusted individual with *medical interests* into the group with four poor answers, if he has in addition two poor answers which would *not* otherwise have been significant. We do not feel that this need constitute a grave obstacle, however. A medical background is something that is usually known about the individual who is taking the test, and when a sufficient number of medical students have been tested it will be easy to know which answers to score differently in such cases. We can make this statement with confidence, in view of the analysis of the group Rorschach records of the 108 medical students where a striking difference in the percentage of anatomical answers was demonstrated when contrasted with other students (Part II, Section XI).

On the other side of the picture some patients did well from the neuropsychiatric and institutionalized groups. For some of these exceptions, but not all, there is an understandable explanation. For example, several manic patients in the State Hospital were specifically reported as being in a good condition at the time of examination. Number 26 in the neuropsychiatric group, a soldier, with only one poor answer, was not felt to be psychoneurotic on clinical examination although referred with that diagnosis. Number 14 in the same group had a pituitary tumor and regular Rorschach examination had failed to reveal personality changes in many of these cases. There still remained, however, a small group of cases whom we missed if four or more than four poor answers was to be taken as the only point of departure for questioning the subject's psychological condition. These cases, however, would have decreased considerably if some *qualitative estimate* of the poor answers was allowed. For example, most Rorschach experts would have agreed that *three failures,* or three 10's in a record probably indicated greater psychological difficulties than some constellations of four poor answers.

REFERENCES

1. Terman, L. M., and Miles, C. C.: *Sex and Personality.* New York, McGraw-Hill, 1936, xi+600 pp.
2. Mann, Ida, and Archibald, Dorothy: A study of a selected group of women employed on extremely fine work. *Brit. Med. J., 1*:387, 1944.

SECTION II

Scores Obtained from "Unselected" and Clinical Subjects on the Multiple Choice Test

TABLE I

33 SUPERIOR NORMALS

SUBJECTS	CARDS										NO. OF POOR ANSWERS
	I	II	III	IV	V	VI	VII	VIII	IX	X	
1	1	1	1	1	1	4	1	2	1	1	0
2	1	2	1	2	1	A	1	2	1	1	0 + 1A
3	1	1	1	2	A	1	1	1	1	1	0 + 1A
4	1	1	1	1	2	1	1	1	1	1	0
5	2	2	1	5	2	1	1	2	4	4	0
6	2	2	1	2	2	1	1	1	5	4	0
7	2	1	1	2	2	1	1	2	3	2	0
8	2	2	1	4	2	1	1	2	3	A	0 + 1A
9	A	2	1	2	2	5	A	2	A	2	0 + 3A
10	3	2	1	4	3	1	1	2	5	2	0
11	2	2	1	4	2	1	1	2	3	2	0
12	2	1	1	2	1	1	1	2	1	2	0
13	1	1	1	2	2	1	1	2	1	2	0
14	2	1	1	1	2	2	1	2	1	2	0
15	2	2	1	2	2	2	1	2	A	1	0 + 1A
16	2	1	1	2	1	1	1	2	1	1	0
17	1	1	1	1	2	1	5	1	4	4	0
18	2	2	1	4	1	1	1	2	3	2	0
19	1	1	(8)	5	2	3	1	1	4	4	1
20	2	2	4	(7)	2	3	1	2	1	2	1
21	3	4	1	2	2	1	5	4	(6)	2	1
22	2	2	1	1	1	2	1	1	(7)	4	1
23	(6)	1	1	2	2	1	3	2	3	2	1
24	2	3	1	2	A	5	1	2	(6)	2	1 + 1A
25	2	2	1	4	2	1	2	2	(7)	2	1
26	(6)	2	1	2	2	1	1	(6)	4	2	2
27	2	2	1	4	2	5	1	(6)	(8)	2	2
28	2	1	1	2	2	(6)	1	4	(7)	2	2
29	(7)	1	4	1	2	(7)	1	1	4	5	2
30	1	1	1	4	2	2	1	(8)	(8)	4	2
31	(6)	2	1	(7)	1	1	5	4	3	2	2
32	(6)	2	A	2	2	1	5	(8)	A	2	2 + 2A
33*	(6)	(7)	(6)	A	2	1	(7)	4	(8)	2	5 + 1A

* Twice hospitalized for M.D.I.
A stands for alternate answer.

TABLE I

33 PATIENTS FROM NEUROPSYCHIATRIC WARDS

SUBJECTS	CARDS										No. of Poor Answers
	I	II	III	IV	V	VI	VII	VIII	IX	X	
Psychoneurotic	2	1	1	(7)	2	5	5	2	3	5	1
Pituitary adenoma, reactive depression	3	1	1	2	2	5	(Fa)	2	(8)	3	2
Involutional	(6)	(7)	1	2	3	1	1	2	3	2	2
Psychoneurotic, anxiety type	1	1	1	2	(7)	1	5	1	(7)	(Fa)	3
Psychoneurotic	3	(7)	1	4	2	1	1	2	(8)	(8)	3
Post-traumatic headache, anxiety neurosis	2	2	1	2	2	1	2	(6)	(8)	(8)	3
Schizophrenia	2	2	(8)	2	2	5	(7)	4	(6)	A	3 + 1A
Hysteria?	A	2	1	2	2	1	1	(8)	(8)	(Fa)	3 + 1A
Psychopathic personality	(6)	2	1	2	2	1	(8)	(8)	(Fa)	2	4
Schizophrenia	2	(Fa)	A	2	2	(Fa)	5	(6)	(Fa)	3	4 + 1A
Paranoid involutional	A	(Fa)	1	(8)	2	1	1	(8)	3	(Fa)	4 + 1A
Psychoneurotic, epileptic	2	(7)	(Fa)	2	2	1	A	(8)	(8)	2	4 + 1A
Behavior problem	A	A	(6)	4	3	3	1	(8)	(8)	(8)	4 + 2A
Behavior problem or schizophrenia?	(Fa)	2	(Fa)	(Fa)	2	1	(Fa)	A	A	2	4 + 2A
Psychasthenia, lead poisoning	(7)	(8)	3	(Fa)	A	A	(7)	2	2	A	4 + 3A
Diagnosis deferred	(6)	(7)	(6)	A	2	1	5	(6)	A	A	4 + 3A
Hysteria	A	A	(Fa)	A	(Fa)	A	A	(6)	(Fa)	A	4 + 6A
Tuberous sclerosis	2	(7)	2	(7)	2	(7)	(6)	2	(7)	5	5
Epileptic	2	(Fa)	2	(7)	(Fa)	3	5	(8)	(8)	5	5
Anxiety state, schizophrenic type	(6)	2	(6)	2	2	1	(6)	2	(8)	(Fa)	5
Epileptic	2	(Fa)	(Fa)	(Fa)	2	3	1	(8)	(8)	2	5
Epileptic	5	(6)	3	(7)	(Fa)	(7)	5	3	5	(Fa)	5
Neurasthenia	A	1	1	(Fa)	2	(Fa)	1	(8)	(8)	(Fa)	5 + 1A
Diagnosis deferred	(6)	(Fa)	(8)	(7)	2	1	(7)	2	4	(Fa)	6
Diagnosis deferred	(6)	2	3	(Fa)	2	(7)	(Fa)	2	(Fa)	(7)	6
Schizophrenia	(6)	(7)	(Fa)	2	2	(Fa)	(Fa)	2	2	(Fa)	6
Psychoneurotic	(6)	(6)	1	(7)	2	5	(Fa)	(8)	(8)	2	6
Diagnosis deferred	(8)	(7)	1	4	2	(7)	(8)	(8)	A	(7)	6 + 1A
Schizophrenia	(7)	(8)	1	2	2	(7)	(7)	(8)	(8)	(8)	7
Hysteria	(6)	(7)	(6)	(6)	2	1	(8)	(8)	(8)	(7)	8
Schizophrenia	(Fa)	(Fa)	(8)	(Fa)	(Fa)	1	(Fa)	(7)	(8)	A	8 + 1A
Schizophrenia	(8)	(7)	(6)	(7)	A	(7)	(8)	(6)	(8)	(7)	9 + 1A
Epileptic	(6)	(7)	(6)	(7)	(7)	(7)	(Fa)	(8)	(8)	(8)	10

A stands for alternate answer.

TABLE II

41 SUPERIOR NORMAL SUBJECTS

SUBJECT	CARDS										NO. OF POOR ANSWERS
	I	II	III	IV	V	VI	VII	VIII	IX	X	
1	2	2	1	2	2	2	1	2	4	2	0
2	2	1	1	4	2	2	1	2	1	2	0
3	2	3	1	4	2	2	1	2	4	1	0
4	1	3	1	2	1	2	1	2	4	4	0
5	2	1	1	4	2	2	1	2	1	2	0
6	3	3	1	2	2	2	1	2	3	2	0
7	1	1	1	1	1	2	1	2	1	2	0
8	1	3	1	3	2	2	1	2	1	2	0
9	1	1	1	4	2	2	1	2	3	1	0
10	2	2	1	2	2	2	1	2	4	2	0
11	5	3	1	2	2	2	1	2	1	3	0
12	5	1	1	2	2	1	1	1	2	4	0
13	5	1	1	2	2	1	1	2	1	2	0
14	5	3	1	4	2	2	1	2	4	2	0
15	5	1	1	4	1	3	1	2	1	1	0
16	5	2	1	2	2	3	2	2	5	3	0
17	2	1	1	4	1	2	1	A	4	2	0 + 1A
18	2	3	A	4	2	2	1	2	4	2	0 + 1A
19	A	2	1	2	2	2	1	1	4	1	0 + 1A
20	2	3	1	5	2	2	A	1	1	2	0 + 1A
21	2	1	1	2	2	2	4	1	A	4	0 + 1A
22	A	1	1	2	2	4	1	2	3	2	0 + 1A
23	5	2	1	(6)	2	2	1	2	1	2	1
24	2	2	1	2	2	(Fa)	2	2	1	2	1
25	2	3	1	5	2	2	1	2	(7)	2	1
26	2	1	1	2	2	(6)	1	2	3	2	1
27	3	(7)	1	4	2	5	1	1	4	3	1
28	3	2	1	4	2	(Fa)	1	1	4	3	1
29	3	3	3	4	2	2	4	1	(9)	3	1
30	3	2	1	(Fa)	2	3	1	1	(7)	3	2
31	2	2	1	5	2	2	(6)	(6)	4	2	2
32	3	1	1	2	2	(7)	5	2	1	(8)	2
33	2	(6)	1	5	2	2	1	2	(7)	2	2
34	2	(7)	1	2	2	4	(8)	1	4	2	2
35	2	(7)	1	2	2	2	5	2	4	(6)	2
36	2	2	1	4	2	2	(Fa)	4	(9)	2	2
37	5	1	1	2	2	(6)	5	1	(7)	2	2
38	5	3	1	(7)	2	2	(6)	1	4	2	2
39	1	1	1	2	1	(8)	1	2	A	A	1 + 2A
40	5	1	(6)	(6)	2	2	(6)	1	3	2	3
41	A	(Fa)	(6)	4	2	4	1	A	4	2	2 + 2A

TABLE II

SUBJECT	I	II	III	IV	V	VI	VII	VIII	IX	X	No. of Poor Answers
Psychoneurosis	5	3	1	2	2	2	1	2	4	(7)	1
Benign depression or psychoneurosis	(6)	3	1	2	2	2	1	2	4	(9)	2
Psychoneurosis	5	3	1	5	2	3	(8)	(6)	1	3	2
Agitated depression	3	2	1	(7)	2	1	(9)	5	4	5	2
Manic-depressive	2	3	(8)	4	2	1	(8)	4	(9)	1	3
Neurasthenic type	3	2	1	4	2	(6)	1	(6)	(7)	2	3
Conversion hysteria	3	(6)	(6)	4	2	2	(9)	2	4	2	3
Involutional depression	(6)	3	1	4	2	4	(8)	2	(9)	3	3
Schizophrenia	2	1	1	(6)	2	4	2	(9)	(Fa)	1	3
?	2	3	1	5	2	4	(8)	1	(7)	(9)	3
Mental deficiency with psychosis	1	3	1	5	2	1	(8)	(7)	4	(8)	3
Manic depressive	(6)	1	1	(7)	2	1	1	(9)	3	(8)	4
Pre-frontal lobotomy (Schizophrenic)	2	(9)	1	2	2	2	5	(6)	(6)	(6)	4
Mental deficiency	(Fa)	(7)	1	2	2	(9)	1	(8)	1	2	4
Subnormal intelligence with pathological intoxication	2	1	1	4	2	2	(Fa)	(6)	(6)	(6)	4
Psychoneurosis	(Fa)	2	1	2	2	2	(8)	(9)	(9)	2	4
Mental deficiency, tension state	5	(9)	(9)	2	2	4	5	5	(9)	(9)	4
?	A	(7)	A	2	2	(Fa)	4	A	2	2	2 + 3A
Simple schizophrenia	5	(9)	1	4	A	2	A	2	(9)	(6)	3 + 2A
Epilepsy	3	2	1	(7)	2	A	(Fa)	(7)	A	3	3 + 2A
Involutional	2	2	1	(6)	2	A	(6)	(6)	(9)	2	4 + 1A
?	(6)	3	(8)	2	2	(9)	(8)	5	3	A	4 + 1A
Schizoid personality	4	(8)	4	(7)	2	(7)	(7)	2	(6)	2	5
Incest	3	(9)	4	5	2	(9)	(Fa)	(9)	(8)	5	5
Jacksonian epilepsy	1	(7)	1	4	2	2	(Fa)	(9)	(9)	(8)	5
Postencephalitis	(Fa)	2	1	(6)	2	4	1	(9)	(9)	(8)	5
Psychoneurosis	(6)	(9)	1	3	2	2	(7)	(9)	(6)	2	5
Psychoneurosis	(Fa)	(9)	(Fa)	4	2	2	1	(9)	(9)	2	5
Psychoneurotic features	(7)	(6)	4	(7)	2	2	(9)	(7)	A	2	5 + 1A
Behavior problem, encephalitis	2	(9)	(9)	5	2	(7)	(7)	(7)	(9)	4	6
Acute schizophrenia	A	(7)	A	A	A	(7)	4	A	3	3	2 + 5A
Psychoneurosis, panic state	(6)	1	(6)	4	2	(9)	(6)	(6)	(6)	(6)	7
Agitated depressive	(8)	3	(6)	(6)	(9)	5	(Fa)	(Fa)	3	(Fa)	7
Early schizophrenia	2	(6)	(9)	(7)	4	4	(7)	(6)	(6)	(6)	7
Recurrent depression	2	(9)	(6)	(6)	2	(7)	(6)	(9)	(9)	2	7
Schizophrenia	A	(8)	1	(Fa)	2	A	A	A	(9)	(9)	4 + 4A
Psychoneurosis	(6)	(9)	(9)	(7)	2	(9)	(Fa)	(9)	(9)	(9)	9
Schizophrenia	(7)	3	(Fa)	(7)	(7)	(7)	(Fa)	(Fa)	(Fa)	(Fa)	9
?	(6)	(Fa)	(Fa)	(Fa)	2	(Fa)	(Fa)	(Fa)	(Fa)	(Fa)	9
Schizophrenia, paranoid type	(8)	(Fa)	(Fa)	(Fa)	(Fa)	(Fa)	(Fa)	(Fa)	A	(Fa)	9 + 1A
Immature personality, sexual psychopathic trends	(Fa)	(7)	(Fa)	(Fa)	(Fa)	(6)	(6)	(6)	(6)	(6)	10

TABLE III

41 FEMALE PATIENTS FROM A STATE HOSPITAL

SUBJECTS	CARDS										NO. OF POOR ANSWERS
	I	II	III	IV	V	VI	VII	VIII	IX	X	
Manic	2	1	1	3	2	2	1	4	3	2	0
Praecox, paranoid	3	3	2	4	2	2	3	A	1	1	0 + 1A
Manic	2	3	(6)	2	2	4	4	2	1	2	1
Praecox	2	(9)	1	4	2	(9)	1	1	1	3	2
Psychoneurosis, hys.	2	3	1	(9)	2	4	(8)	A	1	2	2 + 1A
Involutional?	(7)	1	1	A	2	2	(8)	4	1	3	2 + 1A
Manic	2	3	(Fa)	4	2	4	(8)	2	(Fa)	2	3
Manic	(6)	3	2	(6)	2	2	4	(9)	3	1	3
Praecox	4	(6)	1	1	2	(6)	1	4	(7)	1	3
Praecox	2	3	(6)	3	2	2	(7)	A	(8)	2	3 + 1A
Mixed manic	A	(9)	3	5	4	4	(8)	4	4	(8)	3 + 1A
Manic	5	1	3	(7)	(6)	A	3	(8)	3	2	3 + 1A
Involutional	5	(6)	4	5	A	(Fa)	(8)	2	3	A	3 + 2A
Epileptic	1	(6)	2	(6)	5	(Fa)	(8)	2	3	3	4
Praecox (simple)	2	3	1	(7)	2	(Fa)	1	(7)	(7)	5	4
Praecox (hebephrenia)	2	(6)	3	2	2	4	(8)	(6)	4	(8)	4
Praecox (old)	2	2	A	(6)	2	2	1	(9)	(9)	(9)	4 + 1A
Manic (depressed)	3	A	(Fa)	(7)	(Fa)	4	(8)	4	1	3	4 + 1A
Praecox (simple)	2	3	2	(Fa)	2	4	A	(9)	(9)	(Fa)	4 + 1A
Praecox	2	(7)	1	4	5	3	(9)	(7)	(9)	A	4 + 1A
Manic	(6)	(7)	4	2	2	(7)	(9)	1	(9)	3	5
Manic	(6)	(8)	(6)	4	2	5	(6)	3	(9)	A	5 + 1A
Praecox (simple)	2	(7)	2	(6)	2	(7)	(8)	4	(6)	5	5
Praecox	2	(9)	(8)	(9)	2	4	(6)	4	(9)	3	5
Involutional, confused	2	(7)	(6)	(6)	(7)	4	5	(9)	(9)	2	6
Praecox, paranoid	1	(7)	(6)	4	2	(8)	(8)	2	(8)	(7)	6
Praecox, manic type	(6)	3	3	4	2	(Fa)	(Fa)	(Fa)	(Fa)	(Fa)	6
Praecox (simple)	2	3	(Fa)	(7)	2	(7)	5	(9)	(9)	(9)	6
Praecox	(9)	(9)	1	2	2	2	(8)	(6)	(9)	(6)	6
Praecox	5	(8)	(7)	A	(9)	(Fa)	(9)	3	A	(8)	6 + 2A
Praecox (simple)	3	3	(6)	(7)	2	(6)	(6)	(6)	(6)	(7)	7
Involutional	(6)	(9)	(8)	2	2	2	(Fa)	(9)	(9)	(9)	7
Deteriorated paretic	A	3	A	A	A	4	A	2	A	A	0 + 7A
Paresis, deteriorated	2	(Fa)	(Fa)	(Fa)	(Fa)	2	(8)	(9)	(9)	(9)	8
Involutional	(6)	(9)	(Fa)	(Fa)	2	3	(9)	(9)	(9)	(9)	8
Praecox, manic type	(8)	3	(6)	(7)	2	(Fa)	(7)	(9)	(9)	(Fa)	8
Epileptic	2	(7)	(Fa)	(7)	2	(8)	(Fa)	(7)	(6)	(Fa)	8
Manic	(8)	(6)	(9)	(6)	2	4	(6)	(7)	(6)	(6)	8
Praecox	(Fa)	(9)	(9)	(Fa)	(8)	(9)	(9)	(Fa)	(Fa)	(9)	10
Involutional	(Fa)	(9)	(9)	(Fa)	(Fa)	(Fa)	(Fa)	(Fa)	(Fa)	(Fa)	10
Paranoid	(7)	(6)	(6)	(6)	(6)	(7)	(7)	(7)	(6)	(7)	10

A stands for alternate answer.

TABLE III

48 STUDENT NURSES

SUBJECTS	CARDS										NO. OF POOR ANSWERS
	I	II	III	IV	V	VI	VII	VIII	IX	X	
1	4	2	1	A	2	A	1	1	A	4	0 + 3A
2	2	2	1	2	2	1	1	2	1	1	0
3	1	1	1	2	2	1	1	1	3	2	0
4	2	5	2	1	2	1	1	1	5	2	0
5	2	2	1	2	1	2	1	1	A	2	0 + 1A
6	3	A	2	4	A	5	1	2	A	3	0 + 3A
7	2	3	1	2	2	2	1	1	A	4	0 + 1A
8	2	2	1	2	2	1	1	1	A	2	0 + 1A
9	(6)	1	1	2	2	A	1	1	A	4	1 + 2A
10	2	2	1	2	2	1	1	(8)	A	2	1 + 1A
11	2	1	1	2	2	4	1	1	(Fa)	2	1
12	2	1	1	2	2	(6)	2	5	1	2	1
13	2	2	1	2	2	(8)	1	2	3	3	1
14	2	2	1	4	2	2	1	(8)	5	2	1
15	(6)	2	2	4	4	1	1	1	5	2	1
16	3	4	1	4	2	1	1	(6)	3	2	1
17	(6)	2	1	4	2	2	1	2	5	5	1
18	2	2	1	2	2	2	1	(8)	4	2	1
19	2	1	1	4	2	1	1	(6)	4	5	1
20	2	2	1	4	1	(Fa)	1	1	2	3	1
21	2	5	1	4	2	A	1	1	(6)	5	1 + 1A
22	(6)	2	4	1	2	2	1	2	2	2	1
23	2	(7)	1	4	2	3	1	2	5	5	1
24	2	1	1	2	2	(Fa)	1	1	3	2	1
25	1	1	1	(8)	2	5	1	1	5	1	1
26	2	1	1	(7)	1	1	1	2	A	3	1 + 1A
27	2	2	1	5	2	(6)	1	2	1	2	1
28	2	2	2	2	2	(6)	A	2	1	4	1 + 1A
29	2	2	1	4	1	1	1	(8)	1	3	1
30	1	2	1	2	2	1	1	1	(Fa)	4	1
31	3	1	1	2	2	1	(Fa)	(8)	3	3	2
32	(6)	2	1	2	2	5	1	(6)	3	5	2
33	3	2	1	(7)	2	2	1	(6)	3	2	2
34	2	1	1	(7)	2	1	1	(8)	3	5	2
35	3	2	1	1	2	1	1	2	(8)	(8)	2
36	2	1	1	2	2	(6)	1	1	(Fa)	A	2 + 1A
37	2	2	1	2	2	2	1	(8)	(8)	2	2
38	(6)	2	1	2	2	1	1	(8)	A	2	2 + 1A
39	(6)	2	2	(7)	2	1	1	1	(Fa)	4	3
40	(6)	(7)	1	4	2	5	1	(7)	3	2	3
41	2	(7)	2	2	2	(6)	4	(8)	3	3	3
42	2	1	1	2	2	(Fa)	(Fa)	2	(6)	2	3
43	(6)	A	1	2	2	1	5	(6)	4	A	2 + 2A
44	A	(7)	1	2	A	(Fa)	1	(6)	(8)	2	4 + 2A
45	(6)	2	1	(7)	2	1	1	(6)	(6)	1	4
46	1	1	A	A	2	A	2	1	A	4	0 + 4A
47	(6)	(7)	1	2	2	(6)	5	(6)	(6)	A	5 + 1A
48	2	(7)	(8)	2	2	(8)	(8)	(6)	(6)	2	6

A stands for alternate answer.

TABLE IV

217 WOMEN IN SERVICE

SUBJECT	CARDS										NO. OF POOR ANSWERS
	I	II	III	IV	V	VI	VII	VIII	IX	X	
1	2	2	1	2	2	2	1	1	5	2	0
2	2	2	1	2	2	1	1	4	4	2	0
3	2	1	1	4	2	2	1	2	4	2	0
4	2	2	1	2	2	3	1	1	3	3	0
5	3	1	1	2	1	2	1	1	5	2	0
6	2	1	1	4	2	4	1	1	1	2	0
7	2	2	1	5	1	5	5	1	2	2	0
8	2	2	1	4	1	2	1	2	5	3	0
9	2	2	1	4	1	1	1	1	5	2	0
10	2	1	1	2	1	1	1	2	5	2	0
11	3	2	1	2	2	5	1	1	3	3	0
12	2	1	1	4	2	1	1	1	3	1	0
13	4	1	1	4	2	4	1	2	5	1	0
14	2	2	1	2	2	2	1	2	3	2	0
15	3	2	1	4	2	1	1	1	4	2	0
16	2	1	1	2	4	4	2	4	3	2	0
17	1	2	1	4	1	2	1	2	5	2	0
18	2	1	1	2	2	1	1	1	5	2	0
19	2	2	1	4	2	1	1	1	4	3	0
20	2	1	1	2	2	1	1	1	A	2	0 + 1A
21	2	1	1	2	2	2	A	1	4	3	0 + 1A
22	2	1	1	1	1	1	5	2	A	3	0 + 1A
23	2	1	1	A	2	1	1	1	3	3	0 + 1A
24	4	1	A	4	1	3	1	1	5	2	0 + 1A
25	2	2	1	4	2	5	1	A	3	1	0 + 1A
26	2	1	1	2	2	1	2	1	A	2	0 + 1A
27	2	2	1	2	2	2	2	A	5	1	0 + 1A
28	2	2	1	1	1	1	1	A	5	1	0 + 1A
29	A	1	1	4	2	A	1	4	3	1	0 + 2A
30	2	2	1	A	2	2	1	1	A	1	0 + 2A
31	1	2	1	4	1	2	1	A	A	2	0 + 2A
32	2	1	A	4	2	A	1	1	4	3	0 + 2A
33	A	2	1	2	2	4	2	5	A	A	0 + 3A
34	A	2	1	5	2	1	A	4	4	A	0 + 3A
35	A	1	1	4	2	2	1	A	A	1	0 + 3A
36	A	1	1	2	2	A	1	4	A	1	0 + 3A
37	2	1	1	4	1	1	1	1	(Fa)	2	1
38	4	1	1	4	2	1	1	(8)	1	2	1
39	(6)	2	1	2	1	1	1	1	4	2	1
40	2	2	1	4	1	2	1	1	(8)	1	1
41	2	2	1	4	1	1	1	1	(8)	2	1
42	2	2	1	5	2	1	1	1	(6)	2	1
43	2	2	1	2	2	(Fa)	1	2	5	2	1
44	(6)	2	1	2	2	5	1	4	4	1	1
45	2	1	1	2	2	2	1	(6)	4	2	1
46	5	1	3	2	2	(8)	2	4	5	3	1
47	2	2	1	4	2	1	1	4	(8)	2	1
48	2	2	1	2	4	1	2	1	(8)	2	1
49	2	1	1	2	2	2	1	1	(8)	2	1

TABLE IV—*continued*

217 WOMEN IN SERVICE

SUBJECT	CARDS										NO. OF POOR ANSWERS
	I	II	III	IV	V	VI	VII	VIII	IX	X	
50	2	2	1	2	2	1	2	(8)	3	2	1
51	2	1	1	3	2	(Fa)	1	1	4	2	1
52	2	1	5	2	2	2	4	(8)	2	1	1
53	2	1	1	4	1	(8)	1	2	5	2	1
54	1	1	1	4	2	1	1	1	(8)	4	1
55	2	2	1	2	2	1	1	(8)	2	2	1
56	4	2	1	2	2	1	2	(8)	3	2	1
57	(6)	2	1	4	2	1	1	1	3	2	1
58	2	2	1	2	1	2	5	1	(8)	3	1
59	2	2	1	4	1	4	1	1	(8)	3	1
60	2	1	1	2	2	1	1	(8)	4	3	1
61	(8)	2	1	4	2	2	1	1	5	1	1
62	3	2	1	2	2	(Fa)	1	1	4	3	1
63	(8)	1	1	4	1	1	1	1	4	2	1
64	2	1	1	4	5	1	1	(8)	2	3	1
65	2	2	1	(7)	2	5	1	1	4	3	1
66	3	2	1	4	2	1	1	1	(6)	3	1
67	2	2	1	4	2	1	1	(8)	5	2	1
68	3	1	1	4	2	4	1	1	(6)	2	1
69	2	2	1	2	2	1	1	1	(6)	2	1
70	2	2	1	4	2	1	2	(8)	1	3	1
71	2	2	1	4	2	1	1	1	(8)	2	1
72	2	2	1	4	2	2	1	1	(8)	2	1
73	2	2	1	(7)	2	2	1	2	3	2	1
74	2	2	1	2	2	2	1	4	(8)	2	1
75	2	2	1	4	2	1	3	2	(8)	2	1
76	2	1	1	2	2	(Fa)	1	1	5	1	1
77	2	2	1	4	2	1	1	1	(6)	2	1
78	(6)	2	1	4	2	1	5	1	3	3	1
79	2	1	1	4	2	1	1	4	(8)	3	1
80	2	1	1	2	2	1	(Fa)	1	4	2	1
81	2	2	1	2	2	1	1	1	(8)	2	1
82	2	2	4	4	2	1	(Fa)	1	3	2	1
83	5	1	1	2	2	(8)	5	1	4	3	1
84	4	1	1	2	2	2	1	1	(8)	1	1
85	2	2	1	2	2	1	5	1	(6)	3	1
86	2	2	1	2	2	1	1	A	(8)	3	1 + 1A
87	1	2	1	(6)	2	A	1	2	3	2	1 + 1A
88	A	1	1	1	5	(8)	1	1	1	3	1 + 1A
89	2	1	1	2	2	A	1	4	(8)	2	1 + 1A
90	2	1	1	A	2	1	5	(8)	4	2	1 + 1A
91	2	1	1	(6)	1	2	1	1	A	3	1 + 1A
92	2	1	1	4	2	(Fa)	1	1	A	3	1 + 1A
93	(6)	1	1	4	2	1	1	1	5	A	1 + 1A
94	2	1	1	4	(Fa)	1	4	1	A	2	1 + 1A
95	2	1	1	4	1	A	1	(8)	4	2	1 + 1A
96	3	1	1	2	2	(8)	A	1	5	2	1 + 1A
97	A	2	1	2	2	A	1	1	(8)	3	1 + 2A
98	(8)	2	1	2	2	A	1	3	A	3	1 + 2A

TABLE IV—*continued*

217 WOMEN IN SERVICE

SUBJECT	CARDS										No. OF POOR ANSWERS
	I	II	III	IV	V	VI	VII	VIII	IX	X	
99	(6)	2	1	4	1	1	1	1	(8)	2	2
100	(6)	1	1	2	2	2	2	(8)	4	3	2
101	(6)	2	1	4	2	1	1	(8)	1	3	2
102	(6)	1	1	2	2	2	1	1	(6)	2	2
103	3	1	1	2	2	2	1	(8)	(6)	2	2
104	1	1	1	2	2	(8)	2	(8)	4	2	2
105	2	1	1	2	2	2	2	(8)	(6)	2	2
106	2	1	1	2	1	2	1	(8)	(6)	2	2
107	1	1	1	(7)	2	2	1	4	(6)	2	2
108	2	2	1	4	2	(Fa)	1	4	(6)	2	2
109	(6)	2	1	2	2	2	1	1	(6)	2	2
110	2	2	1	2	2	(Fa)	4	4	(6)	2	2
111	2	1	(6)	2	2	2	1	(6)	3	2	2
112	4	2	1	2	2	4	1	(8)	(8)	3	2
113	2	2	1	(7)	2	2	1	(8)	4	3	2
114	2	1	1	4	2	1	1	(8)	(6)	2	2
115	2	2	1	2	2	(Fa)	1	(8)	3	2	2
116	2	1	1	2	2	2	5	(8)	(6)	2	2
117	2	1	1	2	2	5	1	(8)	(6)	1	2
118	(6)	1	1	4	2	(8)	1	1	4	5	2
119	3	2	1	4	(6)	2	1	1	(6)	3	2
120	2	2	1	2	2	(8)	1	(8)	4	2	2
121	2	2	1	2	2	(8)	5	(8)	3	2	2
122	2	2	1	2	2	(6)	1	(8)	3	3	2
123	2	2	1	2	4	(6)	1	(8)	4	4	2
124	2	2	1	4	2	2	(6)	1	(8)	2	2
125	2	1	3	2	2	(7)	1	4	(8)	3	2
126	2	1	1	2	2	(8)	1	4	(6)	3	2
127	2	2	1	2	1	(8)	1	(8)	2	3	2
128	2	2	1	4	2	1	1	(6)	(6)	2	2
129	2	1	1	4	2	1	(Fa)	(8)	5	2	2
130	3	2	1	4	2	(Fa)	1	1	(Fa)	1	2
131	2	2	1	2	2	2	1	(8)	(8)	2	2
132	2	2	1	4	2	1	2	(8)	(6)	3	2
133	3	2	5	1	2	1	1	(6)	(7)	3	2
134	2	1	1	2	2	(8)	5	1	(8)	2	2
135	3	1	(7)	2	2	2	(7)	1	4	3	2
136	4	2	(6)	2	2	1	1	(8)	3	1	2
137	(8)	2	1	(7)	2	2	1	1	5	2	2
138	2	2	1	2	2	(8)	1	1	(8)	1	2
139	2	2	1	4	(8)	1	1	1	(Fa)	3	2
140	2	1	1	4	2	(8)	1	2	(6)	2	2
141	1	1	1	4	2	1	1	(8)	(6)	2	2
142	2	2	(7)	4	2	2	1	1	(6)	3	2
143	2	2	1	4	1	1	A	(8)	(6)	3	2 + 1A
144	4	2	(7)	2	2	1	2	(6)	A	2	2 + 1A
145	A	2	1	2	1	(Fa)	1	1	(6)	2	2 + 1A
146	2	2	1	4	A	2	1	(Fa)	(6)	2	2 + 1A
147	2	2	1	2	2	(Fa)	(7)	1	A	2	2 + 1A
148	(Fa)	2	1	2	A	2	1	(6)	4	3	2 + 1A

TABLE IV—*continued*

217 WOMEN IN SERVICE

| SUBJECT | CARDS | | | | | | | | | | NO. OF POOR ANSWERS |
	I	II	III	IV	V	VI	VII	VIII	IX	X	
149	2	1	1	4	2	1	A	(8)	(8)	3	2 + 1A
150	(6)	2	1	A	2	1	1	1	(8)	3	2 + 1A
151	1	2	1	2	2	(Fa)	1	(8)	A	2	2 + 1A
152	(8)	1	1	2	2	A	5	2	(8)	2	2 + 1A
153	(6)	2	1	5	2	A	5	(8)	3	4	2 + 1A
154	2	1	1	5	2	(Fa)	(7)	4	A	2	2 + 1A
155	2	2	1	2	2	(8)	(Fa)	A	5	3	2 + 1A
156	2	1	1	4	(Fa)	1	A	1	(8)	2	2 + 1A
157	(6)	1	1	2	2	(8)	1	(6)	4	2	3
158	3	1	(6)	2	2	(Fa)	1	(8)	5	2	3
159	2	2	(6)	2	2	(8)	5	1	(8)	2	3
160	2	1	4	4	2	5	(7)	(6)	(8)	2	3
161	2	2	1	4	2	(8)	1	(8)	(Fa)	2	3
162	(6)	2	1	4	2	2	1	(8)	(Fa)	3	3
163	3	2	1	5	2	(8)	(7)	1	3	(Fa)	3
164	2	(8)	1	4	2	1	3	(8)	(8)	3	3
165	(6)	1	1	2	2	(8)	1	(8)	4	3	3
166	(6)	1	1	4	2	(8)	1	(8)	4	3	3
167	3	2	1	2	2	(8)	(7)	2	(8)	3	3
168	2	(8)	1	(7)	2	2	(6)	1	3	3	3
169	2	(Fa)	1	4	2	1	1	(8)	3	(Fa)	3
170	2	(7)	1	2	2	(Fa)	1	4	(6)	2	3
171	2	1	1	4	2	(6)	1	(8)	(8)	1	3
172	(8)	2	1	2	2	(8)	1	1	(7)	3	3
173	(7)	2	1	4	2	1	1	(6)	(6)	2	3
174	2	1	1	4	2	(Fa)	2	1	(8)	(Fa)	3
175	2	1	1	4	2	(Fa)	1	(Fa)	(8)	2	3
176	2	2	1	2	2	(8)	1	(8)	(8)	2	3
177	3	2	1	2	2	(7)	1	(8)	(8)	3	3
178	(6)	1	1	4	2	(7)	1	1	(6)	3	3
179	2	2	1	4	2	(Fa)	1	(8)	(8)	2	3
180	2	2	1	2	2	(7)	1	(8)	(8)	3	3
181	2	2	1	4	2	(8)	1	(8)	(6)	3	3
182	2	(Fa)	1	2	2	(8)	1	(8)	4	3	3
183	(6)	2	1	2	2	1	1	(8)	(8)	2	3
184	3	1	1	2	2	(8)	1	(8)	(6)	2	3
185	2	1	1	2	2	(8)	(7)	(8)	4	2	3
186	(6)	2	1	2	1	2	1	(8)	(Fa)	2	3
187	(Fa)	2	1	4	2	(7)	1	(8)	A	4	3 + 1A
188	A	1	1	5	2	(8)	(8)	1	(8)	2	3 + 1A
189	(8)	2	1	4	2	A	1	(8)	(Fa)	2	3 + 1A
190	A	2	1	2	2	(8)	1	(6)	(8)	1	3 + 1A
191	2	(7)	A	(6)	2	1	1	2	(6)	3	3 + 1A
192	2	1	1	A	(7)	(8)	A	1	(8)	3	3 + 2A
193	2	(8)	1	2	1	(8)	A	(8)	4	A	3 + 2A
194	A	2	1	A	2	1	1	A	A	2	0 + 4A
195	A	2	1	4	2	A	(7)	1	A	3	1 + 3A
196	2	1	1	(Fa)	2	A	1	(8)	A	3	2 + 2A

TABLE IV—continued

217 WOMEN IN SERVICE

SUBJECT	CARDS										NO. OF POOR ANSWERS
	I	II	III	IV	V	VI	VII	VIII	IX	X	
197	A	2	1	1	2	(8)	1	(8)	A	4	2 + 2A
198	2	1	1	(7)	2	(8)	(Fa)	1	(6)	2	4
199	2	(8)	(6)	(7)	2	(Fa)	1	4	5	5	4
200	(6)	1	1	(8)	2	(Fa)	1	1	(6)	1	4
201	2	(Fa)	1	2	2	(Fa)	5	(8)	(6)	2	4
202	(6)	(Fa)	1	2	2	(8)	5	(8)	4	2	4
203	(6)	1	1	2	2	2	(6)	(8)	(6)	2	4
204	(8)	4	1	2	2	(8)	1	(8)	(6)	2	4
205	(6)	2	1	1	2	1	(Fa)	(8)	(8)	2	4
206	2	1	1	2	2	(8)	(7)	(8)	(6)	2	4
207	(6)	2	1	2	1	(Fa)	1	(8)	(6)	1	4
208	2	(7)	1	(7)	2	1	(6)	1	(6)	2	4
209	3	1	1	2	A	A	1	A	A	A	0 + 5A
210	(8)	1	1	5	2	(8)	(7)	(8)	(8)	3	5
211	(6)	(7)	1	2	(Fa)	(8)	2	(8)	4	2	5
212	(6)	2	1	2	2	(8)	(Fa)	(8)	(8)	2	5
213	2	1	(6)	2	(Fa)	(Fa)	(7)	(8)	3	3	5
214	(6)	2	(6)	2	2	1	(7)	(6)	(8)	2	5
215	3	(7)	(6)	2	2	(8)	(7)	(8)	(8)	(7)	7
216	(7)	(8)	(8)	(7)	2	(7)	(7)	(8)	(6)	2	8**
217	(Fa)	(Fa)	?	2	?	?	?	?	?	?	9

** Diagnosed as conversion hysteria.

TABLE V

225 PRISONERS IN STATE PRISON

SUBJECT	CARDS										NO. OF POOR ANSWERS
	I	II	III	IV	V	VI	VII	VIII	IX	X	
1	3	1	1	4	2	4	1	1	1	2	0
2	3	1	1	2	2	4	1	1	3	2	0
3	2	1	1	2	2	2	1	2	1	2	0
4	2	1	1	2	2	2	5	2	1	2	0
5	2	1	1	2	2	2	5	2	1	2	0
6	2	1	2	2	2	1	1	2	1	4	0
7	3	2	1	3	2	1	1	1	1	4	0
8	3	1	1	4	2	1	1	1	1	2	0
9	2	3	1	4	2	2	1	1	3	2	0
10	2	3	1	2	2	2	1	4	1	2	0
11	3	1	2	2	2	5	1	2	4	1	0
12	3	2	3	4	2	3	1	4	1	3	0

TABLE V—*continued*

225 PRISONERS IN STATE PRISON

SUBJECT	CARDS										NO. OF POOR ANSWERS
	I	II	III	IV	V	VI	VII	VIII	IX	X	
13	4	4	1	2	2	4	2	2	3	2	0
14	2	1	1	2	2	3	1	1	4	2	0
15	2	1	1	2	2	3	1	1	4	2	0
16	2	3	1	4	1	A	5	2	1	3	0 + 1
17	3	3	1	2	2	2	1	(9)	4	2	1
18	(6)	3	1	3	2	1	1	1	4	2	1
19	2	1	1	4	2	2	(8)	2	3	2	1
20	2	1	1	2	2	2	(6)	1	1	1	1
21	2	1	1	2	2	3	1	(6)	4	2	1
22	2	1	1	4	2	(9)	1	2	4	2	1
23	3	1	3	4	2	2	(8)	2	4	4	1
24	3	(Fa)	3	4	2	3	1	2	4	2	1
25	3	1	1	4	2	4	(Fa)	1	1	2	1
26	2	1	1	5	2	(6)	1	1	4	3	1
27	3	2	1	3	2	4	(6)	1	3	2	1
28	3	(7)	3	2	4	2	5	3	1	3	1
29	2	1	1	2	2	2	1	3	(6)	4	1
30	3	2	1	3	2	4	(6)	1	3	2	1
31	3	1	(6)	2	2	4	1	1	4	5	1
32	2	3	1	3	2	2	4	(9)	1	5	1
33	(7)	1	1	4	2	2	1	4	1	3	1
34	(6)	1	1	1	2	2	1	1	1	1	1
35	2	3	1	2	2	(Fa)	5	1	3	1	1
36	3	1	1	4	2	1	(6)	1	3	2	1
37	(9)	3	1	2	2	2	1	1	4	3	1
38	2	1	3	4	2	2	1	(7)	2	1	1
39	3	1	1	4	2	(8)	2	4	1	2	1
40	2	1	2	4	2	2	1	1	(6)	3	1
41	3	1	1	4	2	4	(6)	1	1	2	1
42	3	1	1	4	2	(6)	1	1	2	4	1
43	3	1	2	4	2	(6)	2	1	3	2	1
44	5	4	1	5	2	(6)	2	1	4	2	1
45	3	2	(8)	4	2	2	2	1	4	1	1
46	(6)	3	1	4	2	2	1	2	1	5	1
47	3	1	1	3	1	3	(8)	1	3	4	1
48	2	2	3	4	2	4	4	5	(9)	2	1
49	A	3	1	2	1	A	1	2	1	4	0 + 2A
50	3	3	1	4	2	A	1	1	1	A	0 + 2A
51	A	1	1	4	2	(9)	1	1	1	3	1 + 1A
52	2	1	1	A	2	(8)	2	1	4	4	1 + 1A
53	3	1	(Fa)	3	1	2	2	A	4	3	1 + 1A
54	2	(9)	1	4	2	(9)	5	2	3	1	2
55	5	1	3	4	2	2	(8)	1	3	(7)	2
56	(9)	2	1	2	2	4	(9)	4	1	2	2
57	3	4	1	2	2	(Fa)	(8)	1	3	3	2
58	5	3	1	4	2	(9)	(8)	1	4	3	2
59	2	2	1	2	2	2	(8)	4	(Fa)	2	2
60	2	1	1	4	2	(Fa)	(9)	2	3	2	2

TABLE V—*continued*

225 PRISONERS IN STATE PRISON

SUBJECT	CARDS										NO. OF POOR ANSWERS
	I	II	III	IV	V	VI	VII	VIII	IX	X	
61	3	4	3	2	2	(6)	(6)	1	3	2	2
62	3	1	1	2	2	(7)	2	1	1	(8)	2
63	5	1	1	3	2	4	2	(7)	3	(Fa)	2
64	(6)	1	1	4	2	2	1	(7)	1	1	2
65	2	1	1	4	2	(Fa)	1	(6)	4	2	2
66	3	1	1	2	2	(7)	(9)	1	4	1	2
67	5	(6)	(9)	2	2	1	1	2	4	2	2
68	2	2	3	4	2	2	4	(6)	(9)	2	2
69	(6)	1	1	4	2	2	(6)	4	1	3	2
70	(9)	(9)	3	4	2	2	1	2	4	2	2
71	3	(6)	1	4	2	2	1	(6)	1	3	2
72	(7)	1	2	4	2	(6)	1	3	4	3	2
73	5	4	1	5	2	(6)	(6)	1	4	2	2
74	3	1	1	4	2	(7)	(8)	1	1	2	2
75	2	3	1	2	2	(6)	1	(Fa)	2	2	2
76	3	1	1	4	2	4	(6)	2	(7)	2	2
77	3	1	1	4	2	4	(6)	2	(7)	2	2
78	3	(6)	1	2	2	2	(6)	1	1	3	2
79	3	(6)	1	1	2	2	(6)	1	1	3	2
80	3	2	1	2	2	2	(6)	2	(7)	2	2
81	2	3	(8)	2	2	2	1	1	(6)	3	2
82	(6)	1	1	2	2	2	1	1	(6)	3	2
83	3	(9)	3	3	(8)	3	2	1	4	3	2
84	(7)	4	2	2	2	4	(7)	1	4	2	2
85	3	2	1	4	2	(6)	1	1	(6)	2	2
86	3	1	1	2	2	(Fa)	1	(6)	1	3	2
87	3	(9)	1	4	2	3	1	4	(9)	1	2
88	3	(9)	1	4	2	2	1	(9)	4	3	2
89	2	1	1	(Fa)	2	2	5	(6)	1	2	2
90	3	3	1	4	2	2	(8)	(7)	1	3	2
91	(6)	1	1	2	2	(7)	1	1	1	4	2
92	3	1	2	2	2	2	(8)	(7)	1	3	2
93	2	3	1	4	2	3	(9)	1	(6)	2	2
94	(7)	2	(6)	2	2	5	5	1	1	3	2
95	2	2	(6)	4	2	(Fa)	1	2	4	1	2
96	2	1	(8)	2	2	(Fa)	2	2	1	5	2
97	2	1	1	4	2	2	(6)	(6)	4	3	2
98	3	1	1	2	2	(Fa)	(6)	1	4	3	2
99	(6)	2	1	2	2	1	1	1	A	(8)	2 + 1A
100	5	2	A	4	2	(7)	(6)	1	1	5	2 + 1A
101	3	2	A	4	2	(8)	(9)	1	4	2	2 + 1A
102	2	2	1	2	2	A	(9)	1	(Fa)	3	2 + 1A
103	2	(7)	1	2	2	(7)	5	1	(6)	2	3
104	2	(9)	1	4	2	5	(6)	1	(9)	2	3
105	3	3	(8)	2	2	1	(8)	(7)	4	2	3
106	2	(9)	1	4	2	2	2	(6)	(6)	2	3
107	(8)	1	1	4	2	2	1	(6)	(Fa)	3	3
108	2	3	2	3	2	2	(Fa)	(6)	(Fa)	2	3
109	2	1	(8)	4	2	(9)	(8)	3	1	2	3

TABLE V—*continued*

225 PRISONERS IN STATE PRISON

SUBJECT	CARDS										No. of Poor Answers
	I	II	III	IV	V	VI	VII	VIII	IX	X	
110	(6)	4	1	2	2	(8)	(9)	1	4	3	3
111	3	4	1	1	2	(6)	1	(9)	(9)	3	3
112	(6)	1	3	2	2	2	(9)	(6)	1	3	3
113	(6)	2	1	(9)	2	2	1	2	(7)	2	3
114	3	(9)	(8)	4	2	1	3	2	(9)	2	3
115	2	(9)	(6)	1	2	3	(6)	1	1	3	3
116	2	2	1	2	2	(6)	(Fa)	1	(9)	2	3
117	1	(9)	2	2	(9)	3	(8)	2	1	3	3
118	2	(9)	1	4	2	2	2	(6)	(6)	2	3
119	(6)	(9)	3	4	2	3	(8)	4	1	2	3
120	(7)	(7)	1	2	2	2	1	1	(6)	2	3
121	3	1	1	4	2	(6)	1	(Fa)	(6)	4	3
122	3	1	1	(9)	2	(6)	1	1	(6)	4	3
123	2	(9)	1	2	2	(8)	1	1	2	(9)	3
124	3	1	1	4	2	(7)	(8)	1	(6)	2	3
125	2	1	1	2	2	(6)	(6)	3	(7)	2	3
126	(7)	1	(8)	4	2	3	(9)	2	1	2	3
127	3	(9)	3	5	2	(6)	(7)	4	1	1	3
128	(9)	(9)	3	2	2	2	(Fa)	1	1	1	3
129	(6)	3	3	2	2	4	2	(9)	(7)	2	3
130	2	(7)	(6)	2	2	(9)	4	1	1	2	3
131	2	(9)	3	2	2	3	(8)	(9)	3	4	3
132	2	(9)	2	2	2	2	(8)	(9)	3	4	3
133	3	1	(6)	2	2	(7)	5	1	1	(6)	3
134	2	(7)	3	4	2	5	(8)	2	(Fa)	1	3
135	5	(6)	(7)	(6)	2	3	5	4	1	1	3
136	(8)	(Fa)	1	2	2	2	(7)	4	1	8	3
137	2	(9)	1	2	2	(9)	(6)	1	4	1	3
138	2	1	3	2	2	(9)	(6)	(9)	4	2	3
139	5	1	1	4	2	(Fa)	(9)	1	(6)	2	3
140	(9)	(9)	1	4	5	(6)	1	4	4	2	3
141	(6)	1	1	4	2	(6)	(9)	1	4	2	3
142	(6)	1	3	2	2	3	5	(7)	(6)	2	3
143	2	(7)	(6)	2	2	2	(9)	4	1	2	3
144	(7)	4	1	4	2	4	(6)	2	3	(8)	3
145	2	1	1	(7)	2	2	(6)	(7)	4	4	3
146	2	1	1	3	2	(9)	(6)	(7)	4	2	3
147	3	1	1	4	2	(7)	(6)	1	(9)	1	3
148	3	1	1	4	2	(7)	(7)	(6)	3	1	3
149	3	2	1	4	2	2	(Fa)	1	(9)	(9)	3
150	(6)	1	1	2	2	(9)	(9)	1	1	2	3
151	2	1	1	5	A	A	1	2	A	A	0 + 4A
152	A	1	(6)	A	2	A	1	2	4	4	1 + 3A
153	(6)	1	1	4	1	A	(Fa)	2	(7)	5	3 + 1A
154	A	1	1	5	(8)	(6)	1	(9)	1	4	3 + 1A
155	A	3	(6)	2	2	2	(6)	4	1	(8)	3 + 1A
156	(6)	3	1	4	2	(Fa)	5	(6)	(6)	1	4
157	2	(7)	5	(8)	2	2	(7)	4	(6)	2	4
158	(6)	1	1	2	2	(Fa)	(6)	1	(9)	3	4

TABLE V—*continued*

225 PRISONERS IN STATE PRISON

SUBJECT	CARDS										NO. OF POOR ANSWERS
	I	II	III	IV	V	VI	VII	VIII	IX	X	
159	1	1	(Fa)	3	2	2	(Fa)	(Fa)	(6)	2	4
160	2	1	(6)	(7)	2	2	(9)	1	(6)	3	4
161	2	(9)	(9)	2	2	2	5	(9)	(8)	2	4
162	(9)	1	1	2	2	(6)	(9)	1	(6)	2	4
163	2	(9)	3	2	2	(9)	1	(9)	(9)	3	4
164	2	2	1	4	2	(9)	1	(6)	(Fa)	(9)	4
165	(6)	(9)	3	4	2	3	(8)	4	(7)	5	4
166	(6)	3	3	4	2	(8)	(9)	4	(7)	2	4
167	(6)	3	(9)	4	2	(7)	(8)	1	3	4	4
168	(7)	1	1	2	2	1	(Fa)	(6)	(Fa)	3	4
169	(9)	(7)	1	2	2	2	(Fa)	1	(9)	2	4
170	2	(9)	3	2	2	3	(8)	(6)	(7)	2	4
171	2	(9)	3	4	2	5	(8)	(6)	(Fa)	1	4
172	1	(9)	3	1	2	(6)	(9)	(9)	3	4	4
173	2	(6)	1	2	2	(6)	(6)	(6)	4	2	4
174	(7)	1	1	2	2	(Fa)	(6)	(9)	4	3	4
175	(6)	3	(6)	2	(9)	4	(6)	2	4	3	4
176	(6)	1	(5)	2	2	(6)	(8)	1	4	2	4
177	(7)	(7)	(6)	2	2	2	(9)	1	1	2	4
178	2	4	1	2	2	(Fa)	(8)	4	(6)	(8)	4
179	3	(9)	2	(8)	2	(8)	(6)	4	4	3	4
180	2	1	(9)	2	2	(7)	(8)	1	(6)	1	4
181	2	2	(6)	2	2	(Fa)	(8)	(9)	3	5	4
182	2	(9)	4	2	2	2	(Fa)	(7)	(6)	3	4
183	2	(9)	(7)	2	2	2	(Fa)	(7)	1	2	4
184	(7)	(9)	1	2	2	(Fa)	5	1	(6)	2	4
185	2	(9)	1	4	2	(6)	(8)	(6)	4	2	4
186	2	1	1	(6)	2	(6)	(8)	(6)	4	2	4
187	3	4	(6)	4	2	(8)	(9)	1	(6)	1	4
188	3	4	(6)	4	2	(8)	(7)	1	(6)	2	4
189	3	1	1	4	2	(7)	(7)	(6)	(8)	1	4
190	(7)	3	1	(6)	2	5	(6)	1	(6)	1	4
191	A	4	(Fa)	4	(6)	2	(6)	1	(Fa)	2	4 + 1A
192	(6)	2	A	5	2	2	(6)	2	(6)	(6)	4 + 1A
193	(7)	1	(8)	4	2	(7)	(6)	(9)	4	2	5
194	2	(9)	1	4	2	(9)	(Fa)	(6)	(6)	1	5
195	(Fa)	1	(8)	3	2	(6)	(8)	(8)	3	2	5
196	3	(9)	(8)	2	2	(6)	1	(7)	(9)	2	5
197	(6)	1	(Fa)	2	2	(7)	1	2	(6)	(9)	5
198	3	(9)	1	3	2	3	(Fa)	(7)	(9)	(9)	5
199	(Fa)	(9)	(6)	2	2	5	(8)	(6)	3	2	5
200	(6)	2	1	(7)	2	(6)	(6)	2	(6)	3	5
201	(7)	1	(6)	2	2	(8)	(6)	(6)	4	2	5
202	3	4	(6)	4	2	(8)	(9)	(7)	(6)	1	5
203	(6)	3	1	4	2	(7)	(6)	(7)	(Fa)	1	5
204	(6)	1	(Fa)	2	2	(Fa)	(Fa)	1	(6)	2	5
205	(Fa)	(Fa)	(Fa)	2	2	(Fa)	A	(Fa)	2	1	5 + 1A
206	(6)	1	(6)	2	2	(6)	(6)	A	(6)	3	5 + 1A

TABLE V—*continued*

225 PRISONERS IN STATE PRISON

SUBJECT	CARDS										NO. OF POOR ANSWERS
	I	II	III	IV	V	VI	VII	VIII	IX	X	
207	3	A	(Fa)	3	2	(6)	(6)	(6)	(6)	2	5 + 1A
208	3	(9)	(9)	(7)	2	(Fa)	(Fa)	(6)	1	3	6
209	(7)	(Fa)	(9)	2	2	(Fa)	(6)	(6)	4	3	6
210	(6)	(9)	(9)	2	2	(9)	4	(6)	(6)	3	6
211	2	2	(8)	(Fa)	2	(7)	(6)	(6)	(6)	2	6
212	3	3	1	(8)	(6)	(7)	(8)	(9)	(9)	4	6
213	(9)	(9)	(9)	2	2	(9)	(9)	4	1	(8)	6
214	(6)	(9)	1	2	2	5	(9)	(6)	(6)	(6)	6
215	(9)	(9)	(9)	2	2	(9)	(9)	4	4	(8)	6
216	2	(9)	(9)	2	2	(7)	(9)	(6)	1	(8)	6
217	5	(7)	1	(9)	2	(9)	(6)	(7)	1	(8)	6
218	(Fa)	(9)	1	1	(9)	(7)	2	(6)	(9)	4	6
219	(7)	(8)	1	2	2	(8)	(8)	1	(6)	(9)	6
220	(7)	4	(9)	(7)	2	A	(Fa)	(Fa)	A	3	5 + 2A
221	2	(9)	(6)	(9)	2	3	(8)	(7)	(9)	(8)	7
222	(6)	(Fa)	(Fa)	2	2	(6)	(6)	(6)	1	(8)	7
223	(6)	(6)	(6)	(7)	2	(7)	(6)	(6)	(6)	3	8
224	2	1	(6)	(6)	(7)	(6)	(8)	(6)	(9)	(8)	8
225	(7)	(6)	(6)	(8)	2	(6)	(6)	(6)	(6)	(6)	9

TABLE VI

36 STUDENTS FROM ELEMENTARY SCHOOL

SUBJECT	AGE	CARDS										NO. OF POOR ANSWERS
		I	II	III	IV	V	VI	VII	VIII	IX	X	
1	12	3	1	1	1	2	2	1	2	2	2	0
2	11	2	1	1	4	2	5	3	2	5	4	0
3	11	4	2	1	5	2	4	1	1	1	2	0
4	10	3	3	1(4)	4	2	1	2	2(6)	4	2	0 + 1
5	10	A	3	1	4	2	1	1	2	1	2	0 + 1A
6	10	3	3	1	2	1	A	1	2	2	2	0 + 1A
7	10	3	5	5	A	2	A	4	1	3	3	0 + 2A
8	10	A	4	4	4	A	1	1	A	3	4	0 + 2A
9	12	2	3	1	(8)	2	2	1	5	3	2	1
10	10	3	2	1	3	2	1	1	(7)	4	2	1
11	11	2	3	4	2	2	2	1	(6)	4	2	1
12	11	2	2	1	4	2	(A)	1	(7)	3	2	1 + 1A
13	13	2	2	1	4	2	(Fa)	1	A	3	2	1 + 1A
14	12	A	1	3	4	2	2	1	(7)	3	3	1 + 1A
15	10	(7)	3	4	5	2	A	1	2	4	2	1 + 1A
16	10	A	2	1	1	2	A	3	5	(7)	2	1 + 2A
17	12	2	2	(6)	2	2	2	1	(7)	3	2	2
18	11	3	3	5	(7)	2	(Fa)	1	4	1	2	2
19	11	3	2	1	(6)	1	3	1	5	(7)	2	2
20	11	2	2	1	3	2	4	1	(6)	(9)	2	2
21	10	2	3	1	(7)	2	(Fa)	1	4	3	2	2
22	11	3	4	5	5	2	3	(8)	(6)	4	3	2
23	11	2	2	5	2	2	A	4	(6)	(7)	2	2 + 1A
24	10	3	3	3	(7)	2	(Fa)	1	A	4	2	2 + 1A
25	10	1	(7)	1	4	2	4	1	(7)	(6)	2	3
26	12	3	(7)	4	(7)	2	4	3	3	(6)	3	3
27	11	3	1	(6)	2	(Fa)	3	4	(6)	1	4	3
28	11	(6)	2	1	2	2	2	(9)	5	(6)	2	3
29	11	3	3	1	(7)	(6)	4	(8)	A	1	2	3 + 1A
30	10	A	3	1	2	(Fa)	A	1	(7)	(9)	A	3 + 3A
31	11	3	2	1	2	2	(6)	1	(6)	(6)	(8)	4
32	11	3	3	(9)	2	2	(9)	3	(9)	(9)	3	4
33	11	3	2	1	2	2	(9)	(8)	(9)	(7)	2	4
34	11	2	1	1	2	(Fa)	3	A	(6)	(Fa)	(Fa)	4 + 1A
35	12	(7)	2	(8)	2	2	(9)	4	(9)	(9)	3	5
36	11	3	(9)	(6)	(6)	2	(6)	A	(6)	(6)	3	6 + 1A

NOTE: Five of the eight children below the line were reported as problems by their teachers.

Expanded Multiple Choice Records

A somewhat different use can be made of the Multiple Choice Test if it is in the hands of experienced Rorschach workers, and if slightly different instructions are given to the subject.

The examiner asks the subject, for instance, to check in order of preference, *all the answers to any card which he finds acceptable,* or can see in the blot. This will result in from 20-35 responses being given. These can then be scored in the traditional Rorschach manner, or if technicians are employed, a chart with all the regular scoring symbols can be consulted, and a psychogram made which can give added information, in the traditional Rorschach terms, about the individual who has taken the test.

We have included here a few sample records, with their psychograms, four from unselected normal individuals (see page 000) and four from clinical cases (see page 000). The amazing variety that can be obtained even with this framework is striking.

Once the records have been scored in the traditional Rorschach manner they are, of course, technically amenable to the usual kind of interpretative principles. Although many validating studies will have to be made before one can be sure that these interpretative principles still hold under the new conditions of testing, it is worth contrasting some of the findings from our normal and psychotic subjects.

For instance, the summary of the determinants for Subject 1 (page 146) and Patient 1 (page 150) present very different Rorschach pictures. These two individuals are equally different behaviorally. Subject 1 is an unusually productive and well adjusted individual, combining successful creative work with social availability and friendliness. The M:C ratio, although essentially introversive, reflects this dual facet of personality. The lack of F— answers, and the F% (24%) show intellectual integrity and control without undue constriction. The FM answers, and their subordination to the M score, is another feature indicating this subject's maturity. On the other hand Patient 1 shows in the lack of FC answers in the high C', CF and C scores, in the F-answers, and lack of FM responses some of the abnormal features which characterize him clinically.

In Sections VI and VII Due, Wright and Wright have demonstrated the practical application and further use of these suggestions.

TABLE I

EXPANDED MULTIPLE CHOICE RECORD
SUBJECT NO. 1

CARD	LOCATION	DETERMINANT	CONTENT
I	W	F	Obj.
	D	M	H
II	W	M	H
	S	F	Obj.
III	W'	M	H
	D	FC	Obj.
IV	W	M	H
	W'	cF	Aobj.
	D	F	Obj.
	W	FM, Fc	A
V	W	M	H
	W	F	A
	d	F	Hd
	d	F	Obj.
VI	D	Fc	Obj.
	W'	cF	Aobj.
VII	W	M	H
	W	K	Cl.
	W	k	Geog.
	W	F	Obj.
VIII	W	FC	Emb.
	D	FM	A
	D	FC	Obj.
IX	D	FC	A
	W	CF, K, m	Explosion
	D	M	H
X	D	M	H
	W	FC	Obj.
	W	FM	A

	R 29	M 8	Multiple Choice Summary
	W 17	FM 3	Number of poor answers: 2
	D 9	m + 1	Per cent poor answers: 7
	d 2	k 1	
	S 1	K 1 + 1	
		F 7	
		Fc 1 + 1	
		c 2	
		FC 5	
		CF 1	

TABLE II

EXPANDED MULTIPLE CHOICE RECORD
SUBJECT NO. 2

CARD	LOCATION	DETERMINANT	CONTENT
I	W	F	Emb.
	W	F	A
II	W	CF	At.
	W'	FM	A
III	W	F—	At.
	D	FM	A
	D	FC	Obj.
IV	W	cF	Aobj.
	D	F	Ad
V	W	M	H
	d	F	Hd
	W	F	A
	d	F	Obj.
VI	D	Fc	Obj.
	W'	cF	Aobj.
VII	W	M	H
	D	F	A
	W	F	Geog.
VIII	W	CF	At.
	W	FC	Emb.
IX	D	FC	A
	D	F	Obj.
	W	FC	Pl.
X	D	FM	A
	R 24	M 2	Multiple Choice Summary
	W 14	FM 3	Number of poor answers: 3
	D 8	F 9	Per cent poor answers: 13
	d 2	F— 1	
		Fc 1	
		c 2	
		FC 4	
		CF 2	

TABLE III

EXPANDED MULTIPLE CHOICE RECORD
SUBJECT No. 3

CARD	LOCATION	DETERMINANT	CONTENT
I	W	F	At.
	W	F	A
II	W'	FM	A
	W	CF	At.
III	W'	M	H
IV	W	FM, Fc	A
	W	cF	Aobj.
V	W	F	A
	d	F	Hd
	W	M	H
VI	D	F	Hd
	W'	cF	Aobj.
VII	W	M	H
VIII	W	F—	X-ray
	D	FM	A
IX	W	FC	Pl.
	D	F	Obj.
X	W	FM	A
	W	FC	Pl.
	R 19	M 3	Multiple Choice Summary
	W 15	FM 4	Number of poor answers: 2
	D 3	F 6	Per cent poor answers: 10
	d 1	F— 1	
		Fc + 1	
		cF 2	
		FC 2	
		CF 1	

TABLE IV

EXPANDED MULTIPLE CHOICE RECORD
SUBJECT NO. 4

CARD	LOCATION	DETERMINANT	CONTENT
I	W	F	A
	W	F	Emb.
II	W	M	H
	W'	FM	A
III	W'	FM	A
	D	FC	Obj.
	D	CF	Paint
IV	D	F	Ad
	D	F	Obj.
V	W	F	A
VI	W'	cF	Aobj.
VII	W	F	Geog.
	W	M	H
	W	F	Obj.
VIII	W	FC	Pl.
	D	FM	A
	D	FC	Obj.
	W	FC	Emb.
IX	D	FC	A
	W	CF	At.
X	W	FM	A
	R 21	M 2	Multiple Choice Summary
	W 14	FM 4	Number of poor answers: 2
	D 7	F 7	Per cent poor answers: 10
		c 1	
		FC 5	
		CF 2	

TABLE V

EXPANDED MULTIPLE CHOICE RECORD
PATIENT NO. 1

CARD	LOCATION	DETERMINANT	CONTENT
I	W	C', c	Mud and dirt
	W	F	A
II	W	CF	At.
	S	F	Obj.
III	W'	M	H
	W	F—	At.
	W	C	Color
	D	CF	Paint
IV	W	C', c	Mess
	W	C', K, c	Smoke and dirt
V	W	F	A
	W	F—	At.
VI	W	k	X-ray
	W'	cF	Aobj.
	W'	C', K, c	Mud and water
	W	C'	Smudge
VII	W	M	H
	W	C', c	Ice and snow
VIII	W	C	Color
	W	CF	At.
IX	W	C	Color
X	Failure		
	R 21	M 2	Multiple Choice Summary
	W 19	k 1	Number of poor answers: 15
	D 1	K + 2	Per cent poor answers: 71
	S 1	F 3	
		F— 2	
		c 1 + 5	
		C' 6	
		CF 3	
		C 3	

TABLE VI

EXPANDED MULTIPLE CHOICE RECORD
PATIENT NO. 2

CARD	LOCATION	DETERMINANT	CONTENT
I	W	F—	At.
II	W	CF	At.
	W	CF, m	Bomb
III	W'	M	H
	W	F—	At.
	W	C	Color
IV	W	C', c	Mess
	D	F	Obj.
	W	k	X-ray
V	d	F	Ad
	W	k	X-ray
	W	F	A
VI	W	k	X-ray
	D	Fc	Obj.
VII	W	K	Cl.
	W	k	Map
VIII	W	FC	Pl.
	D	FM	A
IX	W	CF, K, m	Explosion
X	W	FM	A
	R 20	M 1	Multiple Choice Summary
	W 16	FM 2	Number of poor answers: 11
	D 3	m + 2	Per cent poor answers: 55
	d 1	k 4	
		K 1 + 1	
		F 3	
		F— 2	
		Fc 1	
		c + 1	
		C' 1	
		FC 1	
		CF 3	
		C 1	

TABLE VII

EXPANDED MULTIPLE CHOICE RECORD
PATIENT No. 3

CARD	LOCATION	DETERMINANT	CONTENT
I	D	M	H
	W	k	X-ray
	W	F	A
II	Failure		
III	W′	M	H
IV	W	F—	At.
	W	cF	Aobj.
V	W	F	A
VI	W′	cF	Aobj.
VII	d	Fc	Ad
	W	K	Cl.
VIII	W	F—	X-ray
	W	CF	At.
IX	W	CF	At.
	W	CF, K, m	Explosion
X	W	F—	X-ray
	W	CF	At.

	R 16	M 2	Multiple Choice Summary
	W 14	m + 1	Number of poor answers: 9
	D 1	k 1	Per cent poor answers: 56
	d 1	K 1 + 1	
		F 2	
		F— 3	
		Fc 1	
		c 2	
		CF 4	

TABLE VIII

EXPANDED MULTIPLE CHOICE RECORD
PATIENT No. 4

CARD	LOCATION	DETERMINANT	CONTENT
I	W	F—	At.
II	W'	FM	A
III	W	F—	At.
	W'	FM	A
IV	Failure		
V	d	F	Hd.
	W	C', K	Cl.
VI	D	Fc	Totem
VII	W	k	X-ray
	W	M	H
VIII	W	CF	At.
	D	FM	A
IX	D	F	Ad
X	W	FM	A

	R 13	M 1	Multiple Choice Summary
	W 9	FM 4	Number of poor answers: 6
	D 3	k 1	Per cent poor answers: 46
	d 1	K + 1	
		F 2	
		F— 2	
		Fc 1	
		C' 1	
		CF 1	

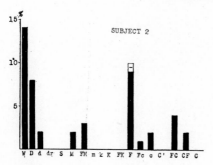

SUBJECT 2

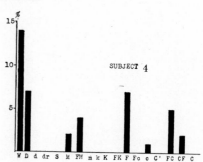

SUBJECT 4

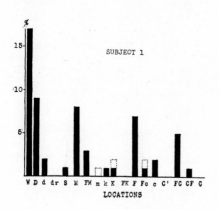

SUBJECT 1

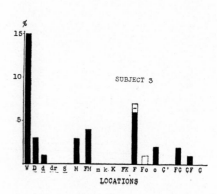

SUBJECT 3

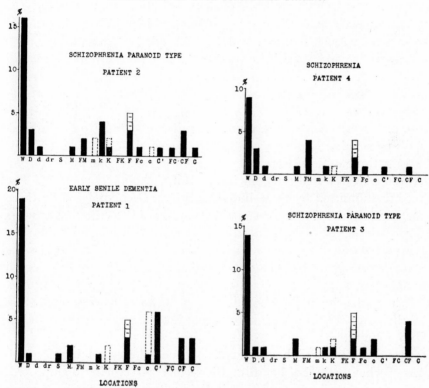

The Effect of Repetition on Multiple Choice Test Scores

A QUESTION which naturally comes to mind in connection with the Multiple Choice Test is that of its reliability. Will an individual who gives a good record, let us say, with only one poor answer, give an equally good record if he repeats the test after a short interval of time?

To answer this question we have recorded here the results of 113 subjects who were retested at short intervals, intervals which we can presume were "neutral" in that no significant change to the individual's personality structure could have occurred.

Fifty-three subjects were retested after a period of one hour (Group A); 60 were retested after an interval of 24 hours (Group B). The records submitted by these individuals have been analyzed by three methods. In the first we have paid attention only to the first answers recorded; that is, we have considered a record "unchanged" when the score of the first answers remained the same on both tests. In the second method we have taken second answers into account: a record is unchanged only if all 20 answers remain the same on the two tests. Method 3 has included alternate answers as poor answers (regardless of their quality) in addition to taking both first and second choices into account.

Results from these short intervals of time are very striking. Regardless of what method of handling the records and scoring is employed, only a very small percentage of individuals shows a change of more than two places, that is, of more than two poor answers appearing in one record and not in the other. In the group repeating the test after one hour, only 2% of the records change in this way (4% in methods 2 and 3). In those repeating the test after one day, 7% show such a change. It should also be noticed that the changes occur both in the direction of an improvement and in the direction of a less good record. In marked contrast to this are the results obtained from certain experimental groups in which the interval has not been a "neutral" one but has, for instance, included the taking of some drug. In these experimental groups it has been found that as many as 72% of the individuals show a change of more than two places and, moreover, that the change, in the particular groups under consideration, has been only in terms of an improvement in the records. Jacobs (1) has reported one such series with regression neuroses when the drug used was combined amphetamine sulfate and belladonna alkaloid. Table II on page 160 taken from his test epitomizes his results concerning which he writes:

"All of the patients, except case 1, received this before therapy was commenced. All except cases 4 and 8 gave over four abnormal responses at that time. These subjects exhibited only two. The former's record, at present, shows only normal responses, as do those of cases 3, 5, and 6. Those of cases 2, 7, and 8 show 1 abnormal response; case 1 shows 3 abnormal responses. Of especial interest are the tests performed upon case 7. Before therapy he gave seven pathological answers. Three days after combined amphetamine sulfate and belladonna medication was instituted, six such responses occurred. Five days later, he scored '4;' after eight days, '3;' after ten days, '2.' This score remained unchanged for fifteen days, notwithstanding symptomatic improvement. At that time belladonna was withheld and amphetamine sulfate continued for four days. At the end of this period, during which there was an increase in symptoms, his test produced three abnormal responses. Belladonna was again added and in three days the score had dropped to '2.' Within one week, this had decreased to '1,' at which point it has remained. At no time did this patient receive active psychotherapy or an explanation of the purpose of the tests. He was merely asked to return regularly to the clinic, 'in order that his medication could be regulated.' "

REFERENCE

1. JACOBS, JAMES S. L.: Combined amphetamine sulfate and belladonna alkaloid therapy of the regression neuroses. *Psychosomatic Medicine, 6:2,* 132-140, 1944.

TABLE Ia

THE EFFECT OF REPETITION ON MULTIPLE CHOICE TEST SCORES
Method 1—A weight of 1 given to first poor answers;
second poor answers and alternates disregarded.

GROUP A	GROUP B
53 Subjects repeating test after an hour's interval	60 Subjects repeating test after a day's interval
No change................ 53%	No change................ 37%
1 change in the direction of a better record.............. 19% ⎫ 32% 1 change in the direction of a worse record.............. 13% ⎭	1 change in the direction of a better record.............. 28% ⎫ 41% 1 change in the direction of a worse record.............. 13% ⎭
2 changes in the direction of a better record.............. 6% ⎫ 14% 2 changes in the direction of a worse record.............. 8% ⎭	2 changes in the direction of a better record.............. 10% ⎫ 15% 2 changes in the direction of a worse record.............. 5% ⎭
More than 2 changes in the direction of a better record.... 2% ⎫ 2% More than 2 changes in the direction of a worse record.... 0% ⎭	More than 2 changes in the direction of a better record.... 0% ⎫ 7% More than 2 changes in the direction of a worse record.... 7% ⎭

TABLE Ib

Method 2—A weight of 1 given to first poor answers; .5 to
second poor answers and alternates disregarded.

Group A	Group B
No change................ 30%	No change................ 28%
.5 change in the direction of a better record............... 11% ⎫ ⎬20% .5 change in the direction of a worse record............... 9% ⎭	.5 change in the direction of a better record............... 8% ⎫ ⎬16% .5 change in the direction of a worse record............... 8% ⎭
No change plus .5 change.... 50%	No change plus .5 change.... 44%
1 change in the direction of a better record...... 19% ⎫ ⎬36% 1 change in the direction of a worse record...... 17% ⎭ ⎫ ⎬42% 1.5 change in the direction of a better record.. 6% ⎫ ⎬6% 1.5 change in the direction of a worse record.. 0% ⎭	1 change in the direction of a better record..... 23% ⎫ ⎬30% 1 change in the direction of a worse record...... 7% ⎭ ⎫ ⎬34% 1.5 change in the direction of a better record.. 2% ⎫ ⎬4% 1.5 change in the direction of a worse record.. 2% ⎭
2 changes in the direction of a better record............... 2% ⎫ ⎬4% 2 changes in the direction of a worse record............... 2% ⎭	2 changes in the direction of a better record............... 10% ⎫ ⎬15% 2 changes in the direction of a worse record............... 5% ⎭
More than 2 changes in the direction of a better record.. 4% ⎫ ⎬4% More than 2 changes in the direction of a worse record 0% ⎭	More than 2 changes in the direction of a better record... 2% ⎫ ⎬7% More than 2 changes in the direction of a worse record... 5% ⎭

TABLE Ic

Method 3—A weight of 1 given to first poor answers; .5 to second poor answers; .5 to first and second alternates.

GROUP A		GROUP B	
No change.................. 32%		No change.................. 25%	
.5 change in the direction of a better record............... 13%	} 24%	.5 change in the direction of a better record............... 13%	} 21%
.5 change in the direction of a worse record............... 11%		.5 change in the direction of a worse record............... 8%	
No change plus .5 change..... 56%		No change plus .5 change...... 46%	
1 change in the direction of a better record...... 13%	} 28%	1 change in the direction of a better record...... 18%	} 26%
1 change in the direction of a worse record....... 15%		1 change in the direction of a worse record...... 8%	
1.5 change in the direction of a better record... 8%	} 8% (36%)	1.5 change in the direction of a better record... 2%	} 4% (30%)
1.5 change in the direction of a worse record... 0%		1.5 change in the direction of a worse record.... 2%	
2 changes in the direction of a better record............... 2%	} 4%	2 changes in the direction of a better record............... 10%	} 17%
2 changes in the direction of a worse record............... 2%		2 changes in the direction of a worse record............... 7%	
More than 2 changes in the direction of a better record.... 4%	} 4%	More than 2 changes in the direction of the better record... 2%	} 7%
More than 2 changes in the direction of a worse record... 0%		More than 2 changes in the direction of a worse record... 5%	

TABLE II

THE MULTIPLE CHOICE TEST SCORES BEFORE AND AFTER TREATMENT WITH COMBINED AMPHETAMINE SULFATE AND BELLADONNA ALKALOID
(Taken from Jacobs)

CASE	BEFORE TREATMENT	AFTER TREATMENT
1	Not tested	3
2	5	1
3	8	0
4	2	0
5	8	0
6	6	0
7	7	1
8	2	1

The Multiple Choice Rorschach Test in Military Psychiatric Differentiation: The Use of Statistical Criteria *

Floyd O. Due, M.D.
M. Erik Wright, Ph.D.
Beatrice A. Wright, Ph.D.

Problems of Military Psychiatric Screening

THE SPECIAL demands of the military program have led psychiatrists and psychologists in the armed forces to place emphasis on the diagnostic and prognostic functions of the psychiatric interview. It is particularly important for group morale, group safety, economic and military reasons, that those individuals who will most probably fail to make an adequate adjustment to the military way of life be separated from the military services as early as possible. This means that a psychiatric evaluation as to probable future behavior must be made of individuals about whom relatively little is known.

If well staffed teams including psychiatrists, psychologists and social workers were able to make a study of each individual, it is quite likely that most future neuropsychiatric casualties would be screened out. Unfortunately, the trained personnel charged with the responsibilities of screening are very few in number, and the demands upon their judgment tremendous. The time available for each individual interview is to be counted in minutes rather than hours. Thus, any objective instrument which enables the military psychiatric worker to give

* This article has been released for publication by the Division of Publications of the Bureau of Medicine and Surgery of the United States Navy. The opinions and views set forth in this article are those of the writers and are not to be considered as reflecting the policies of the Navy Department.

Appreciation is expressed to Capt. Hook, (M.C.), U.S.N., Commanding Officer of the hospital at which time this data was gathered, for his interest and cooperation in making this study possible.

Thanks are expressed to Lt. J. W. Lyons, (M.C.), U.S.N., for his assistance in collecting many of the clinical summaries. The authors feel indebted to C. F. Ritcher, Phm2c, for his conscientious administration of the tests to both the patients and normals.

more time to those men who may find difficulty in adjusting to military life by separating them from those who are likely to adjust adequately is worth serious study in a classification and screening program.

A supplementary screening test for this purpose must fulfill certain requirements: 1) Individuals with even a limited educational background should be able to comprehend the instructions, 2) elaborate apparatus should not be required, 3) the test should be administrable to large groups at the same time, 4) the test should not take more than half an hour of the recruit's time, 5) highly trained assistants should not be required to administer the test, 6) the immediate situation should have little effect on the results, and 7) the validity should be sufficiently high.

The Multiple Choice Test was developed with these considerations in mind, and the reports which have already appeared on it are sufficiently encouraging to warrant more intensive study. The research to be reported in these sections deals with possible contributions of this test to the military psychiatric program.

ORIENTATION OF STUDY

Our initial purpose was to explore the validity of certain objective criteria in differentiating neuropsychiatric patients from normal individuals in order to determine the extent to which untrained clerical assignments can be used in military psychiatric screening and classification.

The procedure suggested by Harrower was followed in all essential details. The slides of the Rorschach ink-blot pictures were projected in a darkened room for the normal subjects. A cleared space on the ward had to be used for the patients. The average size of a group tested was about 45. After the test blanks had been distributed, the printed directions were projected on the screen and a sample answer shown. The subjects were then told not to write anything on their papers until directed by the examiner. The picture was exposed for 30 seconds, after which an overhead light was turned on and the subjects given a minute to make their responses, the picture remaining exposed all the time.

SUBJECTS

There were 731 patients in the experimental group. These were randomly selected from the new admissions to the psychiatric service over a three month period. A large proportion of the patients had long periods of overseas duty, some in severe combat areas. Many of these men had also sustained wounds, malaria, filariasis and other infectious diseases. Upon removal from the combat zone, many men showed clinically observable signs of recovery, although at the time of this study they were still hospitalized.

The control group was composed of men who were still in the recruit phase of their Navy experience. Few had had overseas duty, and the service history of most was under six months. A large proportion were assigned to duty they had not chosen. Many, in fact, actively resented their assignment. A sampling of opinion among those officers who have frequent contact with this group led to estimates ranging from 20% to 30% of this group as showing moderate to severe maladjustment. However, at the time of the study, this maladjustment had not reached a stage severe enough to warrant hospitalization. Unfortunately, the conditions were not suitable for the selection of a group which could be designated as "well-adjusted" without qualification. However, it was felt that in spite of the degree of overlap, this group was substantially more normal than the patient group, and that a study of the performance of the two groups might reveal some differentiating statistical criteria which could later be validated under optimal conditions.

AGE AND EDUCATION

In general the patients included an older group of men than did the normals, the average age of the patients being 27 years as contrasted with a mean of 20 years for the control group.

The educational achievements (based on the individual's own report of last grade completed) of the two groups also showed some differences. The majority (62%) of the patient group claimed to have broken off their education before completing high school; whereas, most of the normal group (79%) finished high school or went even further with their education.

Part of the explanation for both the lower age and higher educational levels among the normals may be found in the selective factors which placed them in the particular work which they were doing. Moreover, the patients, as a group, had been in the Navy for a longer period of time than the normal group.

TEST SCORE AS A CRITERION

By adding the scoring values given to the first choice for each blot, it is possible to get a total score which reflects something of the qualitative character of the performance.* Unfortunately, low scores do not necessarily mean good adjustment. For example, a score of 10 (all M responses), the lowest obtainable, is as indicative of a maladjustment as one of 80 or 90, although the type of psychological difficulty thus described may be different. The former would be more often associated with an introversive, obsessive, emotionally repressed personality structure, whereas a score of 80 or 90 would be found in persons with outgoing, emotionally labile, explosive, disorganized patterns of behavior. Thus the total score is a complex score which was investigated for its possible contributions to a set of screening criteria.

The distribution of the total score on the Multiple Choice Test by the patients and normals is shown in Table I.

TABLE I

DISTRIBUTION OF TOTAL SCORES ON THE MULTIPLE CHOICE RORSCHACH
TEST BY PATIENTS AND NORMALS

SCORE	PATIENTS		NORMALS	
	N	%	N	%
18— 23	18	3	13	4
24— 29	59	8	55	15
30— 35	83	11	59	16
36— 41	114	16	69	19
42— 47	121	17	62	17
48— 53	108	15	42	11
54— 59	82	11	28	8
60— 65	54	7	18	5
66— 71	40	6	16	4
72— 77	15	2	4	1
78— 83	16	2	3	1
84— 89	6	1	—	—
90— 95	9	1	—	—
96—100	6	1	—	—
	731		369	

The patients showed a wider distribution of scores, especially on the high or "poorly adjusted" end of the scale. This is consistent with the objective fact that these patients are more seriously disturbed and should show more extreme deviation in the direction of maladjustment. When the central tendencies of the groups are compared we find that the patient group has a mean total score of 48.3; whereas, the normal group has a mean total score of 42.0. This difference

---

* Throughout the discussion to follow only the first choices were used, since many of the subjects revealed that they did not understand the directions to permit further choices (a difficulty which was corrected in later administrations by the use of the sample slide).

yielded a critical ratio of 7.2. This means that there is little doubt that the two groups show a statistically significant difference in their reaction to the test (as measured by the total score). However, it is more significant to note that this statistical difference is of little value in screening the given individual on the basis of total score because of the large overlap of the two groups.

On the basis of previous information as to the probable degree of maladjustment existing among the normals, it seems safe to infer that a total score of 54 or more is very likely to be associated with moderate to severe maladjustments. Such a dividing line would focus attention on about 31% of the patient group and about 19% of the normals. Unfortunately there is no way of validating whether the 19% of the normals so designated would be the ones who had been judged to be adjusting with great difficulty by their superior officers. However, subsequent experience with this test at an embarkation center has strongly validated this inference.

What, then, can be said about the use of the total score in screening? It is not a very sharp criterion for pruning away the borderline group of psychiatric problems and it would, of course, be far more satisfying if a larger proportion of potential psychiatric casualties could be screened out by their total score. Nonetheless, the positive contributions of this criterion should not be overlooked. A reasonably positive identification of 30% of the psychiatric unfits represents a considerable saving of available military psychiatric manpower, as well as assisting in the evaluation of the individual thus brought to the fore.

NUMBER OF NEGATIVES AS A CRITERION

Harrower used the number of negative responses to differentiate between well-adjusted and maladjusted individuals rather than the total score. She found that about 75% of various groups of patients with neuropsychiatric diagnosis gave four or more than four negative responses, while only 6% to 16% of the normals were screened out by this technique. In Table II we have grouped the number of negative and positive answers given by the patients and the normals in our study.

These results are less differentiating between the normal and patient groups than those reported by Harrower as holding for superior normals and institutionalized psychotics. Although the mean number of negative responses for the patients, 3.93, is significantly greater than that for normals, 2.96, there seems to be far too much overlap in the distribution for the two groups to use this as the sole screening criterion. If a more rigorous criterion of five negative responses is taken, we find that it selects 37% of our patients and 23% of our normals. In the light of our previous discussion about the normals, this criterion (five or more poor answers) seems to be more fruitful as an indication of severe maladjustment for the groups included in this study. Clinical experience with the test has repeatedly demonstrated to the authors that an individual with five negative responses

TABLE II

FREQUENCY OF NEGATIVE RESPONSES IN THE RECORDS OF PATIENTS
AND NORMALS

NUMBER OF NEGATIVES	PATIENTS		NORMALS	
	N	%	N	%
0, 1, or 2	224	31	176	48
3	114	16	66	18
4	124	17	41	11
5 or more	393	37	127	23

shows marked behavior disturbance. This difficulty is almost always of a sufficient degree to prove disabling for military service.

THE INDIVIDUAL RESPONSES IN INTERPRETATIVE DIAGNOSIS

Thus far the discussion has been confined primarily to quantitative expressions of the individual's performance on the Multiple Choice Test, neglecting the important contribution which a trained Rorschach worker could make towards evaluating the personality by an interpretation of the individual responses. We will now deal with some differences between patients and normals on specific responses, and attempt an interpretation of these differences in terms of the Rorschach factors involved.

According to the underlying principles of choosing the responses which Harrower followed, a number 1 stands for a human movement response (the M) on each card except the eighth card where no M was available and a form-color response substituted. Number 2 was the designation of the popular, and very often an animal movement (FM) response. Good form-color responses (FC), straight regard for form, and moderate use of shading were scored 3 or 4. The scoring of 5 was reserved for responses which were found in normal records but tended to be somewhat unusual. Small details, white space usage, and other borderline projections which had passable form quality were given this rating. Number 6 was used to indicate anatomical

answers, generally with poor form. The last four scorings all suggested progressive lowering of the intellectual control and the rising
dominance of disturbed emotionality. The number 7 responses in
many cases reflect the anxiety implied in Fk and K responses. Numbers 8 and 9 represent various types of disturbed answers, including
factors suggesting anxiety, phobic reactions, inanimate movement,
and negative effect. The number 10 was indicative of either a failure
or a rejection of the given card.

On the first slide the normals showed a significantly higher proportion of responses to number 5, "a pelvis," than did the patients (34%
vs. 18%).* The result may be, in part, conditioned by the medical
orientation of the normal group. Inasmuch as the use of one's vocational background as a source of projection is frequently indicative
of evasiveness, fear of exposing the self, and insecurity, this choice
may imply a more cautious, suspicious, and conservative approach to
the test by the normals than by the patients. That is, the patients
more readily became involved in the task; whereas, the normals attempted to dissociate themselves from deep involvement. The difference may also imply a tendency for the normals to be somewhat more
concerned over their own body functions or self-image. Such attitudes
are rather characteristic of adolescent groups, and the data on age
levels revealed that more of the normals than the patients fell in this
age group.

Slides II and III revealed no significant differences between normals and patients on the individual choices. The fourth slide, however, showed several marked differences between the two groups.
Only 5% of the normals chose response number 2, "an animal skin"
whereas 34% of the patients selected this answer. Significantly more
of the normals chose the third response, "a big gorilla" (23% vs.
11%), and the fourth response "a pair of boots" (48% vs. 21%).
Response 2 emphasizes the factor of surface texture and shading (Fc)
more than the form considerations (F). This Fc determinant is clinically related to a contactual-nonaesthetic reactivity to environmental
changes. Responses three and four have their primary determinants,
animal movement (FM) and form (F). The differences may be interpreted to mean that the patient group tends to show a greater sensitivity to environmental changes (Fc) than the normals, especially
those having to do with social relationships. On the other hand the

* Whenever a difference is cited, it has been statistically evaluated and found to have a
critical ratio (C.R.) of at least 2.45. Exceptions to this will be especially noted in the
discussion.

normal group tends to present a more vigorous expression of its inner drives (FM), as well as to demonstrate more control on the intellectual level (F). There is also the suggestion that the normal group may tend to show more adolescent behavior, as the lower social sensitivity and the more unrepressed inner drives are frequent expressions of this transition period.

The fifth slide probably presents the easiest of all the projections, especially response 2, "A bat or butterfly." The normal group shows a significantly higher frequency for this choice than the patients (92% vs. 84%). In view of the fact that both groups choose this response so frequently, failure to project this popular response, or the production of a negative response on Slide V is especially significant of a loss of intellectual control and, possibly, of a decrease of the sense of personal integrity.

Both groups show a significant rise in the proportion of failure responses on the sixth slide. This blot offered the greatest difficulty for concept formation of any blot in the series. The physical characteristics of the blot are sharp and well defined with many possibilities for either whole or detail projections. It seems reasonable to infer that much of the failure or rejection of the card lies not in the form characteristics of the blot, but in the emotional disturbance it tends to arouse. When sufficient time is given, most subjects achieve some sort of response. The time limit and the emotional blocking may account for the high failure. The patient group showed a higher incidence of failure on this card than did the normal group, (20% vs. 14%). This card has often been referred to as the "sex" card. This reference tends to be corroborated by the fact that the choice "sex organs" was the most frequently chosen response by both the patients and the normals.

On Slide VII, the normal group chose response 1, "two women talking," significantly more frequently than the patients (36% vs. 23%). The patients, on the other hand, had a higher frequency for the choice, "mud and water" (24% vs. 13%), and for the failure response, than did the normal group. The normals thus tended to show more human movement, implying a readier identification with people as well as a more stable inner life than that of the patients. They also showed less of the rejection and dysphoric content, with its suggestion of anxiety and negative effect, than the patient group. The use of the shading factors (Fc and cF) in this card again suggests that the patient group tended to be relatively more sensitive to the social and physical environment, a trend previously noted on Slide IV.

There is a strong coloring of negative affect associated with this social awareness, implying either inadequacy in such relations or fear of being involved.

The eighth slide re-introduces the element of color which in the Rorschach frame of reference has come to mean an added emotional stimulus. The new stimulating factor seemed to affect the patient group more than it did the normals, for the former had a significantly higher proportion of negative responses than the normals (56% vs. 41%). The same unfavorable balance persisted on all three colored cards, with the patients showing more negative responses. There are several indications that the normals are more mature and adjusted in the emotional sphere. This is revealed by the incidence of form-color responses, the lower frequency of anxiety and failure responses, and the tendency to project integrated wholes. For example, on Slide X, the patients tend to avoid the color response by choosing "spiders, caterpillars, and insects" (47% vs. 28%); whereas, the normals meet the color issue squarely with the response "a Chinese print" (50% vs. 4%). In these two responses we see the expression of the inner drives (possible FM) with the suggestion of emotional immaturity and of unintegrated tendencies within the personality structure and an avoidance of the use of the color on the part of the patients. The failure to use color tends to corroborate the influence of a fear of emotional involvement with people on new situations, a kind of neurotic inadequacy in social situations.

There were several other differences in which the criterion of statistical significance was satisfied, but where the difference did not seem large enough to warrant a psychological differentiation. The purpose of the above discussion was to show how the differences between the two groups on specific responses has more than statistical significance when the Rorschach factors implied in the response are analyzed. It further suggests that a refined system of weighting the differences on specific items found between the two groups when added to the criteria of total score and number of negative responses, may provide a more adequate set of objective criteria for screening potential psychiatric casualties.

SUMMARY AND CONCLUSIONS

The Multiple Choice Test was administered to a group of 731 patients on the neuropsychiatric service of a Naval Hospital and to 369 "normals" who were living under comparable conditions. The following are the main findings:

1. A comparison of the patients and the normals showed:
    a. A statistically significant lower average total score for the normals than for the patients (42.0 vs. 48.3).
    b. Significantly fewer negative responses, on the average, given by the normals than the patients (2.96 vs. 3.93). Thus, on the basis of these two criteria, the normal group showed more adequate adjustment than the patient group.

2. For purposes of screening out the potential psychiatric casualty, the use of four negative responses does not provide a sharp enough differentiation to warrant its usage by untrained personnel. Use of this criterion alone would have screened only a third of the neuropsychiatric casualties, with the possibility of some false positives having been included.

3. Analysis of the differences between the patient and the normal group on the individual responses suggests a number of criteria which might be included in setting up a weighted scoring system that might be more effective in screening out the probable psychiatric casualty.

4. The application of Rorschach principles of interpretation to the response differences between the normals and patients indicates wide possibilities of the Multiple Choice Test for screening uses.

5. It seems probable that as the Multiple Choice Test is improved and more adequate objective criteria formulated, this instrument will become one of the most valuable techniques for objectively isolating the probable psychiatric casualty. This conclusion is based on clinical experience with a modified form of the original test as well as the implications of series of studies.

The Multiple Choice Rorschach Test in Military Psychiatric Differentiation: The Validity and Reliability of Interpretative Analysis

Floyd O. Due, M.D.
M. Erik Wright, Ph.D.
Beatrice A. Wright, Ph.D.

T HE PRESENT study is concerned with evaluating the Multiple Choice Test as an aid in clinical diagnosis. To this end the responses on the test were used in two ways: First, a description of the subject's personality was inferred from the Rorschach factors implicit in the Multiple Choice responses, utilizing principles of interpretation found to be valid with the individual Rorschach. Experience with the Multiple Choice Test led to various modifications in the application of these principles. Secondly, from this personality structure, a judgment as to degree of maladjustment was made.

SUBJECTS

The subjects were 200 men selected at random from the groups of neuropsychiatric patients. The men ranged in age from 17 to 49 years with an average of 26 years. Fifty per cent were below the age of 24.

The average education was the tenth grade.

PROBLEMS OF VALIDATION

Differential diagnosis: Evaluations of these 200 subjects were written by various psychiatrists in the normal hospital procedure of case treatment. Each of the 200 Multiple Choice records was analyzed independently and a blind description of the personality made.

In view of the various considerations not dealt with here, it was decided to express the agreement between the clinical and Rorschach psychiatric findings in terms of four degrees as follows:

1. *Complete agreement:* This rating was given to those cases where the personality structure of the individual revealed by the Rorschach resembled in its main features the picture represented in the clinical evaluation. Case No. 185 (age 34) serves as an example:

Clinical Evaluation	Evaluation from Multiple Choice Test
Had "nervous breakdown" for six months in 1939 in which was nervous, depressed, could not sleep, neglected his business which failed. Psychiatric findings are: listless, slightly depressed, tense, hypochondriacal, and complains of headache, palpitation and is chronically tired. Insight and judgment superficial. He has shown no improvement. Diagnosis: Psychoneurosis, neurasthenia.	Psychoneurosis with anxiety and tension state. Propensity for psychosomatic symptoms and hypochondriacal preoccupation. Tends to react strongly to emotional stimuli, but is unable to integrate and sublimate. Tends to withdraw and rationalize without insight. Diagnosis: Maladjusted. Psychoneuroses, anxiety, and hypochondriasis.

This individual is shown to be first, tense and depressed; secondly, hypochondriacal; and thirdly, poor in judgment and insight. Each of these characteristics is revealed in the Multiple Choice record.*

2. *Essential agreement:* This rating was given to those cases in which the clinical and Multiple Choice findings agreed in the most significant characteristics of the personality but where some less pronounced aspects of the personality revealed in only one of the two evaluations tended to modify the total personality impression. Case No. 37 (age 18) is an example:

Clinical Evaluation	Evaluation from Multiple Choice Test
Always shy, sensitive, nervous, seclusive and subject to depressions. Raised on a farm and came from a broken home. Psychiatric findings show a schizoid personality requiring close supervision for two weeks because of confusion and disorientation, hearing bells and his mother's voice calling him at night. Believed reached former emotional state of seclusiveness, fatigability	Evidence of withdrawal from the environment with bodily overconcern producing hypochondriasis. Possible schizoid trends. Diagnosis: Probable maladjustment. Question of schizophrenic trends.

---

* There are some elaborations which appear in only one of the summaries. For example, Multiple Choice findings state that the individual tends to react strongly to emotional stimuli. This, however, does not modify the total personality impression revealed by the clinical findings. Consequently a rating of complete agreement is appropriate.

Clinical Evaluation (continued) moderate depression and loss of interest in his work.

Diagnosis: Constitutional psychopath, schizoid personality.

Evaluation from Multiple Choice Test (Continued)

The main characteristics of this individual, his schizoid personality, is also revealed in the Multiple Choice record. However, the Multiple Choice summary more moderately portrays this factor and introduces a hypochondriacal feature. Because of this a rating of essential agreement rather than complete agreement was made.

3. *Partial agreement:* This rating was given to cases in which the Multiple Choice record either revealed only part of the important characteristics of the personality or contributed additional features which rather markedly altered the personality picture. Case No. 137 (age 34) may serve as an example:

Clinical Evaluation

Enuretic until 15. Had nightmares and occasional bouts of somnambulism as a child. No symptoms referable to present trouble prior to enlistment. At this hospital limps continually and complains of back pain and headache, has numerous dizzy spells and becomes startled quite easily. Has a stocking anaesthesia in legs. Complaints are considered hysterical conversions.

Diagnosis: Psychoneurosis, hysteria.

Evaluation from Multiple Choice Test

Probably withdrawn individual with difficulty in making adjustment to the environment. Underlying emotional instability is probably covered up. There is a breakdown indicating a possible schizoid trend.

Diagnosis: Maladjusted. Probably schizoid personality.

The clinical summary reveals an individual with a history of enuresis and somnambulism who at the present time is easily startled. These findings are reflected in the Multiple Choice description of the individual as emotionally unstable and having difficulty in adjusting to the environment. The second important characteristic of this patient, his hysterical symptoms, does not appear in the Multiple Choice record. Instead the Multiple Choice record stresses more a schizoid type of personality. It is for this reason that a rating of partial agreement was made.

4. *Disagreement:* Where the clinical and Multiple Choice summaries indicated two different personality structures having no important features in common, a judgment of disagreement was made. Case No. 83 (age 18) is an example.

Clinical Evaluation

For many years had recurrent precardial pains similar to those of which he now complains. In South Pacific but no combat duty. Psychiatric examination shows immature in intellect, judgment, and general behavior. Emotional reaction is unstable, and lack of inhibition has made him a disciplinary problem. No psychosis is present. His symptoms are considered the result of an inadequate individual who finds himself in a difficult situation from which no escape is evident.

Diagnosis: Psychoneurosis, situational.

Evaluation from Multiple Choice Test

No maladjustment is evident.

The disagreement between these two evaluations is clearly evident, the clinical picture revealing an unstable, inadequate personality whereas the Multiple Choice Test gives no evidence of maladjustment.

DEGREE OF MALADJUSTMENT

In addition to examining the Multiple Choice record for a differential diagnosis, it was possible to judge the resulting personality picture from the point of view of *degree of maladjustment*. In order to validate such ratings, they could be compared with similar ratings of the clinical findings. There was some question as to whether degree of maladjustment should be expressed in terms of adjustment to military life or general personality organization. After some consideration, it was seen that these two orientations would not conflict but would supplement each other if the clinical and Multiple Choice evaluations were rated according to the following criteria:

1. *Very little or no maladjustment.* This rating was reserved for Multiple Choice and clinical personality descriptions in which, at most, only slight maladjustment was evident. Such cases ought to be good risks for military service.

2. *Mild to moderate maladjustment.* This rating was given to those personality descriptions which indicated a definite maladjustment but where the difficulty did not lead to a general disablement of the personality. Such individuals could be expected to make a fairly satisfactory adjustment in ordinary situations, but would be question-

able as far as military service was concerned. Here the differential diagnosis and further psychiatric investigation could help decide the disposition of the case to military or civilian life.

3. *Severe maladjustment.* This rating was given to personality descriptions which revealed a disabling personality defect. These cases showed marked intellectual and emotional disturbances which would make them unfit for military service.

These judgments of agreement between the clinical and Multiple Choice evaluations and between degree of maladjustment as evidenced clinically and by the test, were made by three raters independently.

DIFFERENTIAL DIAGNOSIS CAN BE MADE FROM MULTIPLE CHOICE RECORDS

The essential data bearing on this point are shown in Table I.

When the judgments of the three raters are combined, A, B, and C, 90% of the cases show at least partial agreement between the clinical

TABLE I

AGREEMENT BETWEEN CLINICAL AND MULTIPLE CHOICE EVALUATIONS

DEGREE OF AGREEMENT	PERCENTAGE OF CASES FOR RATERS			
	A	B	C	A + B + C
Complete	33	33	48	38
Essential	35	27	25	30
Partial	21	28	18	22
Disagreement	11	11	8	10

evaluation of the individual and his Multiple Choice interpretation. Almost 70% show essential or complete agreement and only 10% show disagreement. Chance alone would place twenty-five per cent of the cases in the disagreement category.*

The extent of agreement between the clinical and Multiple Choice evaluations is about the same for each of the three raters. The reliability, however, is better expressed in terms of agreement between the raters for individual cases as is shown in Table II.

When pairs of raters are compared with each other, they show

---

* The question may be raised as to whether such high agreement would be obtained in a population which included a larger proportion of normals. It may be, for example, that many normals on the Multiple Choice would give abnormal responses so that while it is easy to detect the truly pathological, one would also include many so-called false positives. Though the data as yet have not been statistically evaluated, we venture to predict, on the basis of further use with the test, that the validity of the Multiple Choice when applied to normals would not be impaired.

"complete agreement" in more than half the cases as to the correspondence between the clinical and Multiple Choice evaluations, i.e., both raters made judgments of complete, essential, or partial agreement or disagreement. About 90% of the cases show either complete agreement or agreement within one step, and less than one-tenth

TABLE II

AGREEMENT OF RATERS AS TO CORRESPONDENCE BETWEEN CLINICAL AND
MULTIPLE CHOICE EVALUATIONS

JUDGMENTS MADE BY RATERS	DEGREE OF AGREEMENT BETWEEN RATERS	PERCENTAGE OF CASES FOR RATERS		
		A + B	A + C	B + C
Complete—Complete Essential—Essential Partial—Partial Disagree—Disagree	Complete agreement	52	55	55
Complete—Essential Essential—Partial Partial—Disagree	Agreement within one step	46	39	36
Complete—Partial Essential—Disagree	Agreement within two steps	3	7	9
Complete—Disagree	Agreement within three steps	1	1	0

of the cases show a disagreement between the raters of more than one step.

DEGREE OF MALADJUSTMENT REVEALED BY TEST

Once the clinical and Multiple Choice evaluations were rated for degree of maladjustment, it was very simple to determine the agreement between such judgments. Complete agreement refers to cases in which the clinical and Multiple Choice evaluations were given the same rating of degree of maladjustment; partial agreement to cases where a difference of one degree on the ratings was obtained (e.g., severe maladjustment on Multiple Choice interpretation and moderate maladjustment on clinical), and disagreement to cases where one of the summaries was rated as severe and the other as little or no maladjustment. These results are summarized in Table III.

It is seen that in about seventy per cent of the cases the Multiple Choice Test is able to reflect very accurately the extent of the individual's maladjustment. In only 5% of the cases does the Multiple Choice picture present an individual who differs markedly as to degree of maladjustment from the clinical picture. The same question regarding the ability of the Multiple Choice Test to single out normals with respect to degree of maladjustment holds here. Preliminary evidence of current research is pointing to an affirmative answer to this question.

Tables I and II may be compared for an appraisal of the relative validity of the two uses of the Multiple Choice evaluations. As one

TABLE III

AGREEMENT BETWEEN CLINICAL AND MULTIPLE CHOICE EVALUATIONS
AS TO DEGREE OF MALADJUSTMENT

AGREEMENT	PERCENTAGE OF CASES FOR RATERS			
	A	B	C	A + B + C
Complete agreement	67	72	68	70
Partial agreement	29	24	26	27
Disagreement	5	5	7	5

would expect, judgments of degree of maladjustment as revealed in the Multiple Choice picture may be made with somewhat higher validity than judgments as to differential diagnosis. In the former instance, 5% of the cases disagree with the clinical evaluation, whereas in the latter, 10% showed disagreement.

The reliability of the ratings is shown in Table IV:

TABLE IV

AGREEMENT BETWEEN RATERS AS TO JUDGMENTS OF DEGREE OF MALADJUSTMENT

DEGREE OF AGREEMENT BETWEEN RATERS*	MULTIPLE CHOICE EVALUATION			CLINICAL EVALUATION		
	A + B	A + C	B + C	A + B	A + C	B + C
Complete agreement	86	79	81	84	73	82
Partial agreement	15	22	19	16	26	18
Disagreement	0	0	0	1	1	1

APPLICATION OF THE MULTIPLE CHOICE TEST

The results of this study clearly indicate that the application of Rorschach principles of interpretation to the Multiple Choice Test permits a relatively accurate description of the personality as well as of the degree of maladjustment. When one considers the economy of

---

* The classifications of complete agreement, partial agreement and disagreement have the same connotations as described for the data in Table III. The reliability of the judgments for both the clinical and Rorschach evaluations is shown to be very high. In only 1% of the cases is there disagreement between the raters as to degree of maladjustment expressed in the clinical valuation. The slight tendency for the Rorschach ratings to show a higher reliability is due to the occasional statements of degree of maladjustment which the individual making the blind analysis incorporated into the report.

time involved in administering and analyzing the test, the results are truly striking. This feature, combined with the validity of the test, makes the Multiple Choice Test particularly useful in a wide variety of fields.

In the military situation the test can be used to great advantage at the induction centers for screening purposes. Neuropsychiatric departments in service hospitals can also develop the use of this test in several ways. A brief summary of the personality structure of each patient at the time of admission may be of considerable help in arriving at a more accurate diagnostic description of the case in a shorter period of time. This preliminary evaluation can direct the observation of the therapist to at least some of the significant difficulties of the patient. Experience with the test has shown that it may be useful in estimating the relative amenability or resistance of the patient to psychotherapeutic treatment. It is quite probable that the test can also be used as an objective evaluation of therapeutic progress.

Personnel selection in the field of industry offers many opportunities for the application of this test. Where a position requires an aggressive personality, or an introversive personality, or one with high emotional stability, etc., the data from the Multiple Choice Test could be of considerable help in the selection.

Finally, the test could very usefully be used for research purposes, as in problems of psychiatric trends with prolongation of war, or personality features of those engaged in volunteer services, and so on.

It is appropriate here to stress two important cautions. First, the results and conclusions presented above are not to be construed that the test can in any way be regarded as a substitute for more intensive clinical evaluation. Those individuals who are selected by the test as having certain characteristics can in each case be interviewed and followed through for final appraisal. The second important point is that the use of the Multiple Choice Test for differential diagnosis presupposes an extensive training and experience in the Rorschach method and in clinical psychology. Since there are only a limited number of individuals having this training, the possibilities of this new method are thus restricted. This points to the serious need for providing more training facilities for psychiatrists, psychologists, social workers, and others who are concerned with diagnostic and therapeutic efforts.

SUMMARY AND CONCLUSIONS

The Multiple Choice Test records of 200 patients (94% of whom were suffering from some neuropsychiatric difficulty) were analyzed "blind" in order to evaluate the validity of this test for differential diagnosis. The main results may be summarized as follows:

1. Ninety per cent of the cases show at least partial agreement between clinical evaluation of the individual and the interpretation from his Multiple Choice Test. Almost 70% show essential or complete agreement and only 10% show disagreement.

2. The Multiple Choice and clinical evaluations were also rated for degree of maladjustment. This use of the Multiple Choice Test even more accurately classifies the individual, only 5% of the cases showing disagreement between the clinical and Multiple Choice pictures. Complete agreement was obtained in 70% of the cases.

3. These results have led to the conclusion that the Multiple Choice Test can be used by personnel trained in the Rorschach method for a wide variety of purposes.

The Multiple Choice Rorschach Test in Military Psychiatric Differentiation: Application of Interpretative Principles in Differential Diagnosis *

Floyd O. Due, M.D.

M. Erik Wright, Ph.D.

Beatrice A. Wright, Ph.D.

O UR STATISTICAL analysis in Section V demonstrated that the quantitative criteria of total score and number of "bad" answers in the Multiple Choice Rorschach Test are of only limited value in military psychiatric screening. Although we are not as pessimistic as Wittson, Hunt and Older (9) we agree that in the present development of the test, these criteria are not sufficiently valid to warrant its usage by untrained personnel. The degree of overlap in our statistics indicated that such usage would segregate more than fifty per cent of the prospective neuropsychiatric casualties, but that there would be also included a large number of false positives who adjust satisfactorily despite evidences of conflicts on a deeper level. Therefore, it would seem that the test is likely to be even too sensitive by placing these men on an equal footing with those whose maladjustment precludes adaptability to the military milieu.

Because of this defect in operation of the test, a need was felt for exploration in the field of differential diagnosis to discern whether or not a reasonably adequate personality description and diagnosis could be inferred from interpretation of the response patterns given by different psychiatric groups on the test. As there was no precedent for such procedure, the blind analyses were made from the interpre-

---

* This article has been released for publication by the Division of Publication of the Bureau of Medicine and Surgery of the United States Navy. The opinions and views set forth in this article are those of the writers and are not to be considered as reflecting the policies of the Navy Department.

tative principles of the individual Rorschach combined with subjective clinical hunches. Section VI contains a résumé of the results of the blind analyses done on this basis. These results, in our opinion, are imposing enough to warrant optimism that differential diagnostic descriptions can be made by trained Rorschach personnel utilizing the Multiple Choice Test. Although this development does not enable the use of the test by untrained personnel, it does constitute an important instrument with which any trained worker can increase manifold the number of personality diagnoses possible in a limited period. As such, it offers at least a partial answer to the need for large scale evaluations today.

In this section we shall attempt to elucidate the methodology by which our interpretations and blind analyses were made. In the discussion of the psychoneuroses, a brief summary of the interpretative principles involved in the individual Rorschach will be outlined. Then, an analysis of the application of these principles to the Multiple Choice Test will be stated. The records from representative cases in each diagnostic category of the psychoneuroses will be presented along with a detailed step by step analysis of the responses to demonstrate how the interpretations and diagnoses are performed.

Other diagnostic groups will be illustrated by response records and brief summaries of the interpretations and predictions. A comparison of these records will demonstrate well-marked differences in the response patterns of the various diagnostic groups. Unfortunately, the present material does not include enough records from major functional psychoses to warrant their inclusion in this paper. However, subsequent clinical experience by one of us confirms the impression that a majority of this group can be segregated by the test. This is particularly true of the schizophrenic psychoses, but experience with the manic-depressive group is too limited for generalization.

THE PSYCHONEUROSES

There is little written concerning the differentiation of the various diagnostic sub-groups of the psychoneuroses by means of the individual Rorschach test. However, the different descriptive manifestations such as anxiety, depression, compulsiveness, obsessional rumination, and tendencies toward psychosomatic organ dysfunction can be discerned and evaluated in terms of the personality as a whole.

The psychoneurotic states, in general, tend to show a limited number of responses on the individual Rorschach, usually less than 25 (2).

There are disturbances on the "complex stimulating" cards (blots eliciting responses particularly relevant to emotional complexes), as Cards IV, VI, VII, and the colored cards, II, VIII, and IX. In the latter group, "color shock" may be manifested by rejection, delay, and deviation in form and content. Animal and animal-derived responses usually exceed human projections, this being reflected in the preponderance of animal movement over human movement. A high percentage of pure form $(F\%)$ and animal answers $(A\%)$ demonstrate a rigidity of personality in which there is a lack of free emotional expression. In other words the whole personality function is damaged by an excessive super-ego and ego control. The appearance of one of the "complex" cards may produce so much disturbance that the card is rejected entirely. The reaction to color is inhibited or evaded to a great extent, but those reactions which break through demonstrate a poor ability to integrate social and adaptive control in emotional relationships with the environment. This is evidenced by the over-weighting of pure color and color-form responses over those in which form is well integrated with color. Free-floating anxiety (6) is often indicated by the predilection for shading responses, particularly where the shading is not utilized as part of a surface object. Dysphoric use of achromatic color along with inanimate movement will often point toward anxious and depressed states. The nature of the content also points toward areas of the body of particular interest to the subject, especially when this content is of the anatomical variety.

PSYCHONEUROSIS, HYSTERIA, AND HYSTERICAL PERSONALITIES

In the individual Rorschach, hysterics and hysterical personalities generally follow the above principles in their reactions to the inkblots. However, there are some fairly specific findings in this subgroup which are important enough for special attention. The intellectual approach is usually marked by an overemphasis of easy and undifferentiated whole responses, with some attention to the large details and infrequent reaction to small or rare details. This indicates a personality in which the environment is viewed from a superficial standpoint rather than subjected to a careful analysis. That this is symptomatic of the immaturity of the hysteric is suggested by the similarity of the approach to that of six year old normal children (4), whereas eight year old children begin to be responsive to details, a trend which increases into the adolescent period. Intellectual integrity is maintained, however, as indicated by the appearance of popular responses, particularly on the non-complex cards, and by general coherence throughout the test.

The hysteric is not as likely to reject cards as some of the other diagnostic groups; but, if this should occur, it is limited to the "complex" cards where disturbance has been stimulated. The lack of human movement suggests that adequate identifications with parental figures have been impossible, producing an experiential level of immaturity conflicting with the demands of an adult environment. This is further emphasized by the preponderance of animal movement which suggests that the instinctive drives (6) are incompletely repressed, but are not acceptable because of their infantile and immature character. The accompanying sexual immaturity is productive of strong conflict and confusion of sensual and contactual relationships to the environment. This may be especially shown in the disturbed reactions to the sixth and seventh cards.

Emotional reactivity to the environment is strongly egocentric and immature with impulsive emotionality exceeding the intellectually controlled reactions of the more normal personality. This is evidenced by the preponderance of color-form responses over the more intellectualized form-color choices. Because of the ease of emotional reactivity, in which the expressions are behaviorally on the infantile level, and because of the ease of symptom-formation, very little anxiety is experienced in the more purely hysterical cases. Thus the projection of anxiety responses, such as inanimate movement (m), diffuse shading (K), and dimensional shading (k) (6), is not likely to occur. The lack of self-evaluation and capacity for insight is also suggested by the infrequency of perspective responses (FK). Because of the passive-dependent nature of the hysterical personality, all movement is likely to be of the passive "bowing" quality rather than dynamic forces "pulling," "fighting," "exploding," or other kinaesthetic responses of aggression in an outward sense.

In the Multiple Choice Test, only a brief sampling of the subject's total behavior to the test is possible as compared with the individual test. However, the hysterical personality, with the type of reactivity described above, is likely to produce a fairly recognizable pattern in the Multiple Choice Test. For instance, the first card is likely to be responded to with a popular, easy whole response, more likely animal than human, such as "a bat." Occasionally other "good" whole responses are utilized, such as "an army or navy emblem" or a "pelvis."

In line with the limited number of responses, the hysteric is not likely to bother with second and third choices on any of the blots. Furthermore, in accordance with the intactness of intellectual integrity, the first card is not likely to produce a "bad" response. In view of the lack of discriminatory powers in dealing with the environment, responses to the small detail, "pincers of a crab" is not expected. In discussing this possible choice, it might also be said that the hysteric lacks the compulsiveness, deep-seated anxiety and constriction of personality that goes along with undue attention to small details.

The second card, to the contrary, is productive of profound emotional stimulation. The patient may either reject the card or respond in a poorly integrated manner. In the Multiple Choice Test, we do not have the element of hesitation and delay as an indication of "color shock" to help us.* However, the state of confusion will often be revealed by the choice of one of the bad responses, particularly one in which an undifferentiated reaction to color is a factor. Frequently, the hysteric will be able to recover and choose one of the animal responses, but for reasons stated before, seldom accepts the human projection, "two clowns."

On the third card there is a tendency toward recovery, the best chance of producing a human response, occurring here, although the percentage of hysterics doing so is less than any group except the convulsive states. The inadequacy in human identifications and lack of maturity of drives often lead to the choice of an animal response, "two birds," rather than "two men," the object for the projections being essentially identical. In keeping with intellectual integrity, there is little tendency to choose from one of the grossly pathological responses on this card.

The fourth and fifth blots are likely to stimulate popular responses which are animal or animal-derived. In the fourth card, the normal group leaned heavily toward the response, "a pair of boots," but this did not hold true for the hysterical group whose choice was predominantly an "animal skin." The choice of a strongly pathological response on either of these blots is evidence against a purely hysterical condition.

The recurrence of acute disturbance on the sixth card is evidenced by the frequency of "bad" answers. The sexual and sensual stimulation is likely to produce an anatomical response, but other bad responses occur frequently. Occasionally a more non-committal response

---

* This is much less true of the amplified version (see Section VIII).

is given such as "a fur rug" or "a turtle." Continuation of the disturbance is shown by frequent "bad" responses on the seventh card such
as "dirty ice and snow" or "smoke and clouds" rather than anatomical projections. This indicates conflict in contactual relationships with
the environment. A limited percentage is able to accept the feminine
figures, "two women talking" for one of the rare human movement
responses.

The eighth card again introduces color which is reacted to in either
an undifferentiated fashion with the color-naming response, "pink,
blue, and orange," the color-predominant response, "flowers and
leaves" or else evaded with retreat to the animal movement response,
"two animals." The same statement holds for Cards IX and X where
similar responses are given. It is interesting that hysterics are not particularly prone to project anatomical responses into the last three
cards, this being more frequent in convulsive states and mixed psychoneurotics.

An example of the above analysis is shown by Case No. 309 who
gave the following responses:

Card	I	"A bat"
Card	II	"Black and red"
Card	III	"Two men"
Card	IV	"An animal skin"
Card	V	"A bat or butterfly"
Card	VI	"Nothing at all"
Card	VII	"Dirty ice and snow"
Card	VIII	"Pink, blue, and orange"
Card	IX	"Red, green, and orange"
Card	X	"A flower garden or gay tropical fish"

In this record is seen the intellectual factors pointed out in the general analysis. Briefly, the intellectual approach is without drive, in
that there is a preponderance of easy, undifferentiated whole responses with no attempt to analyze or carefully to discriminate the
blots either in parts or as a whole. Not a single detail response is
chosen. The subject does not take the trouble to respond more than
once to each blot, nor does he demonstrate any originality by writing
in alternative responses. That he exhibits intellectual integrity is
suggested by the fact that there are no failures or bad responses in
the non-complex cards. Only one human movement response appears,
there being three animal or animal-derived choices. Emotional disturbance is first evidenced when colors are presented in the second
blot, which arouses too much confusion and disturbance to allow an

intellectual recovery. That the color stimulus is strongly perceived and responsible for this disturbance is shown by his choice of the "color-naming" response which does not have the same serious import as in the individual Rorschach. Here, the very fact that this response is printed in line with other possible responses gives it the permissive aspect of being adequate for a response. Thus, the choice here would seem to be the easy way out of the situation.

The next area of disturbance begins with the stimulation of the sensual aspects of the personality by the appearance of the texture and symbolism of the sixth card. This arouses so much anxiety that the only rejection in the test occurs. The pained affective state resulting is further shown on the seventh card where the response "dirty ice and snow" is chosen. This combination indicates sexual maladjustment and when further correlated with the responses on all the color cards suggests an impaired ability of the individual to integrate himself satisfactorily in contactual relationships with the environment. The emotional stimulation of Cards VIII and IX is again handled as in Card II, but on the last card some recovery occurs with a better, but still undifferentiated whole, color-form response.

Interpretively, one derives the impression of an immature individual with emotional lability. The lack of drive and absence of oppositional or of aggressive movements suggests a passive-dependent status in which there is little tendency to try to cope with disturbances or to aggressively overcome handicaps. In line with the latter tendencies, conflicting situations are more likely to be met by symptom formation than behaviorally acted out on the environment. A hysterical pattern is therefore predicted with probable symptom-formation under stress leading to personality inadequacy.

Case History: No. 309; Age 20; Completed 11th grade; Clinical Diagnosis, Psychoneurosis, hysteria.

This patient was a parachute trooper who had made twelve practice jumps in the field, but had not yet experienced combat. Following a minor blow on the head in his last jump, he complained of nervousness and tremors which prevented further performance of his duties. The pressure of resumption of training was met by a variety of somatic complaints, including headache which seemed to increase in degree as demands were made upon him. He was admitted to the sick list where physical, neurological and laboratory studies were normal. Psychiatric observation showed him to be emotionally unstable, poorly able to tolerate monotony and restriction, and incapable of exercising adequate judgment and control when emotionally stimulated. He failed to improve under treatment, with exacerbation of his complaints when faced with the possibility of returning to duty. He finally was discharged from the service.

THE ANXIETY STATES

The psychoneurotic whose manifest clinical symptoms involve anxiety which is subjectively felt as such, and objectively demonstrated by tension, restlessness, and over-stimulation of the sympathetic nervous system, will present a slightly different pattern than the above. Often a more introversive pattern is shown by the appearance of human movement. Color produces a violent reaction which often leads to rejection or evasion with very little use of the color itself. Frequently, however, these cards will stimulate explosive and bombastic effects which are expressed particularly on the second and ninth cards. Furthermore, the strongly shaded cards produce disturbance in which the responses are dysphorically and sometimes depressively toned with relatively untrammeled use of the shading nuances. Thus, x-rays and anatomical responses are frequent on the fourth and sixth cards. The seventh card is likely to stimulate a diffuse shading response such as smoke or clouds. The intellectual approach is similar to that of the hysteric in that there is very little tendency to analyze carefully the component parts of the blots, although an occasional obvious large detail is chosen.

A fair sampling of this behavior to the blots is obtained in the Multiple Choice Test. The subject with an anxiety state is more likely to respond more than once to a blot than is the hysteric, but even so not all cards elicit a second response. In a similar fashion more large details are seen, but the record as a whole is characterized by undifferentiated whole responses. In our sub-group statistics, the anxiety neurotics were more likely to reject cards and give anatomical responses than any of the other psychoneurotic groups. Pained affective responses to shading were demonstrated by the higher incidence of responses such as "a dirty mess" to the first card, "a nasty mess" to the fourth card, and frank rejection to the sixth card. In the seventh card this sub-group showed the highest number of "smoke and clouds" responses as well as a fairly high percentage of "dirty ice and snow" choices. The incidence of the color-naming response was very high on the eighth and ninth cards whereas recovery almost universally occurred on the tenth card with the selection of the animal (non-color) choice of "spiders, caterpillars. crabs and insects."

An example is afforded by case No. 70, who produced the following record: (Responses are recorded in order of choice)

Card	I	"A pelvis"
		"A bat"
Card	II	"A bursting bomb"
Card	III	"A red bow-tie"
		"Two men"
Card	IV	"An x-ray picture"
Card	V	"A bat or butterfly"
Card	VI	"A totem pole"
Card	VII	"Dirty ice and snow"
Card	VIII	"An x-ray picture"
		"Pink, blue and orange"
Card	IX	"Parts of my body"
Card	X	"Spiders, caterpillars, crabs and insects"

This record is seen to be quite similar in many respects to case No. 309 in which a hysterical personality was predicted. However, there are several differences which become apparent. On three cards, there are second choices; and also on three cards, there are prominent or large details chosen. It is to be noted, in contradistinction to obsessionals and those with psychosomatic organ dysfunction, that there are no additional or original responses nor are there any small or rare details.

On the first card, the response, "A pelvis" occurring among non-medical personnel may be significant of an anxiously toned response in which the anxiety is referred to a specific area of the body. Recovery is attained adequately on the second choice, "a bat," which is of course a popular response.

The emotional stimulation of the second card produces the explosive response, "A bursting bomb" which may express the feeling tone of the individual, who is so full of tension and inner driving force that he is about to explode. Proceeding to the third card, we find that the patient has made an almost remarkable recovery from this outburst to choose two good responses, "a red bow-tie" and "two men," which suggests that the subject is able to pull himself together in favorable circumstances and handle reality in a satisfactory manner. However, the advent of the massive and dark shading of the fourth card again creates acute disturbance as illustrated by the response, "an x-ray picture." This supports our early impression of anxiety and tension derived from the second card. Intellectual integrity is demonstrated by the choice, "a bat or butterfly" on the fifth card. The choice "totem pole" does not reveal the depth of disturbance usually evoked by the sixth card in the anxiety group. Instead, it reflects a tendency to intellectualize and rationalize the approach to sexual problems. The pained effect created by the continuance of the shaded cards is apparent again in the response "dirty ice and snow" to the seventh card.

The recurrence of color stimulation in the eighth card creates a violent reaction which is poorly handled by the patient in the responses, "an x-ray picture" and "pink, blue and orange." This emotional confusion is carried over into the ninth card and refers to anxiety concerning his own somatic function in the response, "parts of my body." This suggests that in face of prolonged stress with emotional stimulation, he becomes concerned about his own body function and, therefore, possibly hypochondriacal. It might also be speculated that there is a pattern established in which prolonged anxiety produces secondary physiological dysfunction which focuses the attention of the patient on his somatic symptoms. In the last card, the patient again demonstrates his capacity for recovery and responds with the popular, "spiders, caterpillars, crabs and insects" which also evades the issue of color and further undue stimulation.

In summary we find that this patient has fulfilled the criteria for anxiety states, with intellectual integrity evidenced by an adequate number of popular responses, and by breakdown only on the "complex" cards. The lack of intellectual impairment is an indication that we are probably not dealing with a psychotic reaction. The intellectual approach is primarily superficial, and lacks the drive of the more compulsive picture. Such an intellectual approach suggests that the man is fixated upon an immature emotional level. In practically all of the disturbed responses he demonstrated overt anxiety and tension with a tendency for body over-concern and hypochondriasis, in conjunction with the anxiety. Furthermore, his responses to the colored cards indicates emotional instability and explosiveness in the face of pronounced stimulation and environmental stress. A diagnosis is therefore predicted of psychoneurosis, anxiety state with hypochondriasis and undue emotional instability. Although capable of holding himself together in favorable circumstances, he is probably unable to adjust adequately to situations of stress, particularly where complicated and perhaps dangerous demands are made upon him. In other words, the combination of external sources of anxiety, with the already strong potential of anxiety from internal sources, dooms the man to failure in the multiple adjustments, dangers and reality anxieties manifest in a military situation.

Case History: No. 70; Slc; Age 22; Completed 7th grade; Duration of service, 10 months; Clinical Diagnosis, Psychoneurosis, Anxiety Neurosis.

This man was admitted to the sick list, overseas, because of difficult breathing, pressure in the head, insomnia, nervous chills, poor vision, poor hearing and palpitation. Pre-enlistment history revealed that he had "chorea" at the ages of 14 to 18 because of "nervousness." During this period he was under medical treatment and attended one special school which he soon left because he was unable to "stand it." The psychiatrist's summary follows: "Psychiatric examination shows him to be restless, hypochondriacal, egocentric and subject to a multiplicity of physical complaints. Trivial difficulties reduce him to a state of nervousness and inadequacy in which he is quite incapable of exercising mature judgment or initiative. Emotional reaction is markedly unstable. No psychosis is present." He was discharged from the service.

THE OBSESSIVE-COMPULSIVE STATES

The records of the obsessive-compulsive states in the individual Rorschach often differ from the general picture for the neuroses described before. In contrast to the limited number of responses, this group may, in compulsive need for perfection and fear of inadequacy, project many responses into the blots. Some of the highest response totals in the individual Rorschach come from this general group. The intellectual approach, instead of being superficial with easy whole responses, is likely to show an emphasis on small and rare details, indicating meticulousness, thoroughness, and perhaps even anxiety in broad generalizations because of the doubts and indecision that haunt these characters. The compulsive character can feel more secure in his ability to give an accurate perception in the small detail of the blot. It should be noted, however, that broad generalizations are not impossible for this group, as there will occasionally be good organizational whole responses in which details are constructed into meaningful concepts.

Occasionally, compulsives will present a record of a limited number of responses, for instance, one response per card, in which the "whole percentage" is quite high. The explanation of this phenomenon is not clear, but it is possible that the subject feels it necessary to utilize the whole blot in each response and that his energy is all used up in this single effort. This pattern may also reflect the ambivalence of the compulsive in which there is a need to submit to environmental demands because of the fear of the consequences should he refuse, as opposed to the negativistic attitudes derived from the childhood frustration of his own needs for individuality and ego expression. Thus the single response to each blot satisfies the former and the refusal to proceed despite his obvious ability to do so is a reaction to the latter. At any rate, this type of record is usually distinguishable from the superficial approach of the hysteric by the presence of original and combinatory whole responses.

The intellectual approach of the obsessive-compulsive in general indicates the existence of a higher potential of drive, which though distorted and wasted in many side issues and substitutions, is not blocked and paralyzed as was demonstrated in the hysterical and anxious subject.

Not infrequently, perfectionism and indecision leads to rejection of a blot in which there is a popular response such as a winged animal in the fifth card. The reason for these rejections is often stated, "the form isn't perfect enough." Frequently responses are given reluctantly and timidly with many self-qualifications and denials, for instance, "It might be a bat, but it doesn't look like one," or the protest, "This takes a lot of imagination, but it could be a butterfly." The compulsive need to give detailed evidence that the projection is justified (1) is further illustration of the doubt, indecision and distrust of self that exists in these personalities.

Examination of the psychogram of the obsessive-compulsive reveals first of all an emphasis on form which is likely to be of the unmodified and undifferentiated sort, the "unrefined control" described by Klopfer (6). Thus a high F% with painful accuracy (very high percentage of F, or pure and good form) is characteristic of this group. The treatment accorded this determinant by the compulsive indicates the intellectualized and conscious control exerted over personality reactions in order to avoid the threats perceived to be a consequence of a more relaxed and free emotional expression. This control reduces the percentages of movement and color responses appearing in the psychogram. The ratio of movement to color (M:C) is usually said to approach equality. However, it has been our clinical observation that the compulsive who acts out his rituals on the environment is more likely to show an excess of color responsiveness; whereas, the obsessional whose final reaction is on a psychic plane, rather than a skeletal muscular one, demonstrates an introversive pattern with an emphasis of movement over color. In either, these color responses that are given are not likely to be adaptive and controlled in type, but are usually of the impulsive and sometimes bombastic and violent sort, indicating the fountainhead of aggressiveness and general emotional reactiveness that the obsessive-compulsive is continually holding in check.

The content of responses is another item of differentiation. It will be recalled that the hysteric is seldom wont to project human responses into the blots, the emphasis being almost entirely on animals, and animal-derived objects. Anxiety states also demonstrate this tendency with the addition of anatomy and shading responses. The obsessive-compulsive, and particularly the obsessional on the contrary is likely to project a relatively large percentage of human responses. The latter responses, however, may reflect hostilities and ambivalences in the inability of the subject to identify himself freely with the complete human form. This may be seen in the perseveration of human details (parts of humans) or by the devaluation of the human projection, *i.e.,* "ghosts." The character of the human movement invested in the human responses is often indicative of the degree of inner tension, indecisiveness and conflict in the individual. An example of this is the response, "two men pulling."

Again there is sufficient sampling of the above behavior in the Multiple Choice Test to allow identification of the compulsive character, with inferential diagnostic predictions regarding the degree and form of his neurosis. An over-all survey of the Multiple Choice records from this sub-group reveals several important factors. There may be many choices to each blot; or as stated above, there may be only a single response. Those records showing a single choice per card can be differentiated from other neurotic subgroups by the coincidence of human movement, small details, rejections and alternative responses. Whereas, rejection was more likely to occur on the "complex" cards in the hysterical and anxiety groups, compulsives may reject Card I, Card V, and Card X. These rejections are incompatible with the level of performance on the other cards. The phenomenon of alternative responses introduces the element of added drive for performance as well as perfectionism and perhaps the oppositionalism of the compulsive individual. Other evidences of perfectionism such as alteration of the record by crossing out part of the printed response may aid in differentiation. For instance, the "or butterfly" may be crossed out of the choice, "a bat or butterfly." White spaces are often utilized, particularly in the combinatory whole responses.

Other compulsives will give as many as four or five choices per card in some instances. Small details such as "pincers of a crab" may be included among large details. The appearance of human responses along with immature and occasionally violent color responses complete the picture.

An example is afforded by Case No. 692: ("Alternative" refers to the fact that the answer was written in the space marked, "Something other than the above" by the subject).

Card	I	"Ghost behind a window" (Alternative)
Card	II	"Kids playing pat-a-cake" (Alternative)
Card	III	"Two men"
Card	IV	"A giant" (Alternative)
Card	V	"An x-ray picture"
Card	VI	"A turtle"
Card	VII	"I don't know" (Alternative)
Card	VIII	"Two animals"
Card	IX	"Cross section of an erupting volcano" (Alternative)
Card	X	"I don't know" (Alternative)

A general survey of this record reveals several outstanding facts. This subject has accepted only four of the suggested responses, and in the place of four others has written in alternative responses. In two others he has rejected the blots, but instead of checking "Nothing at all," has written in the space, "Something other than the above," the words, "I don't know." This treatment of the test situation appears to have meaning in revealing the personality techniques of this individual. The first impression regards the patient's degree of suggestibility. Certainly, he lacks the ordinary degree of this phenomenon, and on the contrary, demonstrates a strong degree of oppositionalism and negativism to stimuli from the environment. The previously mentioned trait of giving one whole response per card is noted here, probably indicating compulsiveness when correlated with this constellation of factors. It is also noted that human and human-like responses are more frequent than animal responses. Only one color response is present, a violent color-form response involving inanimate movement.

The alternative response to the first card is very interesting and revealing. The projection of "ghost behind the window" infers the use of shading in an anxious and dysphoric sense. The use of white spaces indicates oppositional trends. Furthermore, the projection of a devaluated human figure, "ghost," one invested with ideas of death and at the same time of fear-producing qualities, is indicative of inner feelings of dread, despair and depression. Another factor is the concept of a figure behind the window which strongly suggests a potentially persecutory figure. Already, then, from just one response, we are able to speculate the following psychological phenomena in this individual. He is anxious, depressed and projective with a potential paranoid reaction. The projection of his inner self as a ghost in connection with the white spaces indicates that he is at great conflict with forces from within, and that these inner drives are unacceptable, foreign in character, disturbing, and, therefore, must be opposed and further projected. This response gives rise to the fear of a potential break with reality which suggests the possibility of a psychosis.

The response to the second card is almost astounding in its change of affect from the projection discussed above. "Kids playing pat-a-cake" is a good human movement response with none of the despair and anxiety displayed in the first card. This seems to express a regressive need to return to some of the happier aspects of his childhood, perhaps the positive part of his relationship to his mother. The response to the third card, "Two men," is another human movement response and we must now note that the continuation of this trend indicates strong introversive factors along with average or better than average intelligence.

The projection, "giant," to the fourth card again brings up material of probable psychodynamic importance, i.e., the unreal proportions and distortions which the body image has for this individual. Our experience with this card suggests that the use of the choices, "giant" and "a big gorilla" is frequently indicative of a disturbed relationship with the father. It suggests, in view of the previous projections, that the individual has a negative attitude toward a domineering, criticizing and overwhelming type of father figure. To speculate further, a need to prevent fear and annihilation has led to introjection of the ambivalently regarded father as a super-ego figure which now operates in his own personality as a criticizing and devaluating force against his own drives and strivings to be an individual. The extent of the inner disturbances wrought by this card may be reflected in the bad response, "an x-ray picture" to the next or fifth blot which is an evidence of shading shock and anxiety referred to his own anatomy. The failure here to choose the popular response, "a bat or butterfly," is also significant in its possible inference that the subject does not think along conventional lines and that the force of his inner conflicts is productive of thinking disturbances. This implication is particularly important when correlated with the possibility of a break with reality speculated in the response to the first card.

The response to the sixth or "sex" card is rather surprising, "a turtle," being a non-committal response adequate to the stimulus. However, the first failure comes in the next card which indicates the degree of disturbance that continued exposure to shading and texture arouses. One concludes that he is very sensitive to stimuli arising from the environment, is sensually stimulated, but becomes disturbed and retreats into a withdrawn and self-contained type of adjustment. The technique that he utilizes in rejecting this card is also revealing in that he fails to become positive enough to check the suggested response, "Nothing at all," but prefers to write in "I don't know." This is indicative of doubt, indecisiveness and fear of being wrong. He would rather admit a failure from a negative aspect than be caught in error exerting a positive attitude. This psychological technique is an important component in the perfectionism of compulsive characters.

The emotional stimulation of color again seems to bring about a degree of recovery in the response, "Two animals," in the eighth card. Thus, although he can meet new stimulations and changes in the environment with a temporary adequate adjustment, this breaks down under prolonged stimulation as is evidenced by the response, "Cross section of an erupting volcano" to the ninth card. This response is clearly indicative of a strong feeling tone that has been aroused by the colors. A violent emotional outburst with rage and destructiveness is seen to threaten this individual should he relax the rigidity of control and the dynamics of repression. That the emotional confusion and fear of inability to recover is overwhelming, is demonstrated by the rejection of the infrequently failed tenth card, still in the indecisive manner of "I don't know."

To summarize, this is an over-all picture of an obsessive compulsive personality with strong anxiety and depression. He is perfectionistic, but haunted by doubts, indecision and fear of inadequacy. Inasmuch as he is primarily introversive, it is likely that the primary scene of conflict lies in the sphere of psychic reactivity rather than acted out through skeletal muscle function. It may be predicted that he is an obsessional neurotic, with the potentiality of a schizoid breakdown, possibly a paranoid reaction.

Case Summary: No. 692; Age 22; Finished first college year; Clinical Diagnosis, Psychoneurosis, Obsessive-Compulsive Type with Anxiety and Depression.

This man consulted a psychiatrist because of nervousness, headaches, feelings of inferiority and "blue spells." During the interview, he divulged that he has indulged in compulsive counting of people and objects throughout his lifetime. He has a compulsion to make things balance and is continually obsessed regarding the aspects of "large and small." He worries about the future and is generally disturbed when anticipating new things. He can't stand the lack of routine and doesn't like military life. He feels uncomfortable in the presence of strangers. His past history reveals that he experienced nail-biting, stuttering, thumb-sucking, nightmares, headaches, nervousness and enuresis in childhood. He is married to a girl three years older than himself. In this general examination, he shows anxiety, tension, rigidity and continuous nail-biting.

In retrospect, the obsession regarding "large and small" may be somewhat enlightened by the responses of "Giant" and "Kids" playing pat-a-cake, *i.e.,* that the whole struggle for power between the father and the little child has been introjected and is being continually waged within the patient. The regressive aspect of the "pat-a-cake" response may also be borne out clinically by the marriage to an older girl, an effort to re-establish the pleasant aspects of the mother-child relationship. Unfortunately, history of the inter-personal relationships was not recorded so that these speculations must remain in the field of conjecture.

PSYCHOSOMATIC ORGAN DYSFUNCTION

The differentiation of psychosomatic organ dysfunction such as irritable bowel syndromes, peptic ulcer, asthma, and others should not be expected as such by a test of this sort. Usually, in the individual Rorschach, these disorders are found to exist in neurotic personality patterns, and the type of dysfunction cannot always be predicted. However, much could be saved in military hospitalization if those with strong predilection for such disorders could be screened out. Although there is not enough data in our collection to be specific, it is our present experience that these personalities show enough evidence of maladjustment on the Multiple Choice Test to warrant further psychiatric history and evaluation.

Our present collection of cases are too mixed for generalization although there is a trend toward a compulsive and perfectionistic pattern with attention to small details and an occasional bad response. A frequent occurrence is the presence of one or two good responses alongside of a bad response on the same card. This may occur in most of the blots so that the final result may show 10-15 good answers and 4-8 bad answers. Intellectual integrity is maintained as shown by appearance of popular responses and general coherence throughout the test. Anatomical and x-ray responses are fairly frequent.

Case No. 637 is an example of psychosomatic organ dysfunction. Responses are given in order of the patient's choice.

Card	I	"Pincers of a crab"
		"A pelvis"
Card	II	"Black and red"
Card	III	"Red and black"
		"A red bow-tie"
Card	IV	"Lungs and chest"
		"A pair of boots"
		"An x-ray picture"
Card	V	"A bat or butterfly"
Card	VI	"Sex organs"
Card	VII	"Nothing at all"
		"Dirty ice and snow"
Card	VIII	"Pink, blue and orange"
		"A colored coat of arms"
Card	IX	"Parts of my body"
		"Red, green and orange"
Card	X	"Red, blue and green"
		"Spiders, caterpillars, crabs and insects"
		"Parts of my insides"

This record actually is indicative of a severe psychoneurosis with anxiety, body overconcern, hypochondriasis, and emotional lability and instability. One would expect a very abnormal life history with neurasthenic attitudes amounting in degree to an inadequate personality.

Case History: No. 637; PhM3c; Age 23; Completed 10th grade; Clinical Diagnosis, Pylorospasm.

This patient was admitted to the sick list with the diagnosis of Constitutional Psychopathic State, Inadequate Personality, because of persistent complaints of epigastric pain, bloating, vomiting, nausea, constipation, nervousness and easy fatigue. He had been hospitalized many times for this group of symptoms since enlistment in the Navy, and to be specific, had spent 126 days on the sick list in the five months prior to the present entry. Past history revealed that he had suffered the same symptoms since the age of 14. The physical and neurological examinations were normal.

X-ray examination of the stomach showed pylorospasm with delayed emptying time. A psychiatrist described the man as being emotionally unstable, hypochondriacal, unsettled personality. The diagnosis was changed to pylorospasm and the man was invalided from the service.

It is common experience of military medicine to have severe psychoneurotics spending long terms of hospitalization under physical diagnoses, because one of the end reactions of their total disturbance is dysfunction of some visceral organ. If these men could be screened out, tremendous savings of time and hospitalization could be made. It is our belief that the Multiple Choice Rorschach Test offers promise of a relative degree of success in this direction.

Organic and Convulsive States

Organic and convulsive states are pooled in this discussion inasmuch as they are indistinguishable, interpretively, in the Multiple Choice Test. In our sub-group analysis, convulsive states demonstrated the most abnormal records in terms of number of bad responses and in terms of qualitative analysis. This is an important finding as epileptics are often "negative malingerers" and in their desire to get into the service often conceal the history of their abnormality. A group test showing uniform abnormality in this category should be successful in bringing such recruits to a more detailed questioning and investigation. In our experience, such men are not persistent in their denials if the matter is pressed and there is threat of further investigation. It is therefore of great interest and importance that their responses to the Multiple Choice Test are so universally bad.

The Rorschach characteristics of organic reaction types have been well-covered in previous publications and will not be repeated here (3) (6) (8). In the Multiple Choice Test, convulsives show more rejections than any diagnostic group except psychopathic personalities. Surprisingly, they demonstrate more anatomical responses than any group except the anxiety neuroses. They show the least percentage of human movement responses of all groups. In general, organics and epileptics show intellectual inconsistencies in failure to get popular responses to an adequate number of the cards in which popular percentages are relatively high. The significance of this popular failure is often enhanced by the appearance of bad answers on the easier cards, such as I, II, V and X. Occasionally, a perseverative trend is noted, for instance, the choice of three to six x-ray responses throughout the test. Such a phenomenon, particularly on single choice per card records, is likely to indicate intellectual dysfunction rather than anxiety. Pure color choices, such as "spots of blood and paint" on Card III and "spilt paint" on Card X, are often found in organic records along with other poorly controlled color responses such as the color-naming variety. Responses indicating inner explosiveness, hostility and aggression are often present, especially in the convulsive group. Strongly pathological responses such as "meat in a butcher shop" on Card III and "smashed body" on Card V may occur, indicating a rather severe breakdown of intellectual control.

In summary, it can be said that organics and convulsives of various types are poorly differentiated from each other in the Multiple Choice Test, but that the degree of abnormality shown by them on the test sets them apart for further attention and evaluation.

Three case records will be cited to illustrate this group, one with grand mal epilepsy and two cases demonstrating psychiatric evidences of organic intellectual impairment, one with post-traumatic encephalopathy and the other having central nervous system syphilis with paresis.

Case No. 25

Card	I	"An x-ray picture"
Card	II	"Black and red"
Card	III	"Something other than the above," but the patient failed to write in the response.
Card	IV	"Nothing at all"
Card	V	"Nothing at all"
Card	VI	"Nothing at all"
Card	VII	"Nothing at all"
Card	VIII	"Pink, blue, and orange"
Card	IX	"Red, green, and orange"
Card	X	"Nothing at all"

This record is obviously abnormal with six failures and no popular responses. Not a single blot was successful in stimulating a good response. Such a record would seem to come from an individual in whom there is profound intellectual disorder. Although no diagnostic impression is possible from the record itself, the color-naming responses in such a constellation might suggest an organic brain condition in which emotional lability is prominent. One is loath to accredit the interpretation of anxiety to the x-ray choice in such an abnormal record, but if it should be valid in a descriptive sense, it is certainly only a secondary factor.

Case History: No. 25; SF3c; Age 24; Clinical Diagnosis, Epilepsy.

This man was admitted to the sick list, overseas, after one year of service, because of convulsive seizures. History revealed that he had experienced convulsive seizures with aura, unconsciousness, urinary incontinence, and post-seizure confusion for at least six years prior to enlistment. He was enuretic until the age of 8, had frequent and severe nightmares, persistent finger-nail biting and nervousness with restlessness. Physical and neurological examinations and skull x-rays were normal. Electroencephalogram demonstrated a dysrhythmia compatible with grand mal epilepsy. He was invalided from the service.

Case No. 74

Card	I	"Nothing at all"
Card	II	"Black and red"
Card	III	"Spots of blood or paint"
Card	IV	"Nothing at all"
Card	V	"A bat or butterfly"
Card	VI	"A turtle"
Card	VII	"Smoke or clouds"
Card	VIII	"Pink, blue and orange"
Card	IX	"Red, green and orange"
Card	X	"Spilt paint"

A perusal of this record reveals eight bad responses with only one popular choice. The outstanding emphasis is on color with color naming and pure color responses suggesting emotional lability. This subject lacks enough responses indicating intellectual control and human movement to exert a dampening influence upon this emotional reactivity. In our diagnostic prediction, an organic brain condition with emotional lability seems to be the most likely possibility, but we are unable to specify further.

Case History: No. 74; BK3c; Age 33; Clinical Diagnosis, Post-traumatic Encephalopathy with Post-traumatic Personality Disorder, Emotional Lability and Instability, and Intellectual Impairment.

This man sustained a severe head injury, several years before enlistment, during which he was unconscious for 27 days and was subject to a trephine operation. Subsequently, he had experienced symptoms characteristic of a post-traumatic syndrome, with headaches, dizziness, faintness on postural change, intolerance of heat, emotional irritability and forgetfulness. He had been discharged from several jobs as a baker because of intolerance of heat and the frequent disturbances while bending over. A continuation of the above symptoms after enlistment led to his entry to the sick list. Physical and neurological examinations were negative except for a large cranial defect in the right temporal area which pulsated and bulged upon jugular compression. During phychiatric examination, he demonstrated emotional irritability, lability and explosiveness with quick mood changes from anger to tears. Intellectual impairment was evident upon gross testing with routine clinical tests.

Case No. 468 is an example of generalized brain disorder.

Card	I	"A pelvis"
Card	II	"A bloody spinal column"
Card	III	"Part of my body"
Card	IV	"A nasty mess"
Card	V	"A bat or butterfly"
Card	VI	"An x-ray picture"
Card	VII	"Smoke or clouds"
Card	VIII	"Fire, and ice, life and death"
Card	IX	"Red, green and orange"
Card	X	"Nothing at all"
		"Red, blue and green"

This is another record in which there are eight bad responses. Again there is but one popular response and there are no responses in which human movement could be predicted. The lack of direction and patterning of responses suggest intellectual dysfunction. Responses to shading and color are uncontrolled and indicate emotional lability. The most likely prediction would seem to involve an organic brain condition with intellectual disturbance.

Case History: No. 468; ACMM (AA); Age 38; Diagnosis, Dementia Paralytica.

This man was admitted to the sick list because a routine spinal fluid showed a $4+$ Kahn and a gold curve of 555432100. Psychiatric examination revealed emotional lability and evidence of intellectual impairment. The Shipley Scale for Intellectual Impairment demonstrated vocabulary evidence of average original intelligence with strong evidence of acquired impairment when compared to his conceptual level (Conceptual Quotient, 59). He was not psychotic.

The above cases demonstrate the sensitivity of the Multiple Choice Test for organic brain cases. Many other cases could be cited showing this sensitivity. Although the test does not identify types of organic reaction or even in many instances differentiate them from the convulsive states, the degree of abnormality shown on the test would be effective in selecting such cases for special investigation in screening activities.

PSYCHOPATHIC PERSONALITIES

The lack of Rorschach literature on diagnosis and classification of the psychopathic personalities is but a reflection of the lack of clarity and cohesion in the classification and understanding of these disorders generally. The heterogeneity of the group is perhaps the most prominent handicap in the clarification of this status. A promising development in the field is the work by Lindner (7) which suggests that the Rorschach test can be used to aid in our understanding of the group as a whole.

To expect the Multiple Choice Test to be able to distinguish such a heterogenous group is to hope for an impossible fulfillment. However, the test will often "spot" the emotionally unstable, the chronic offenders, the potentially criminal, and the sexual and schizoid psychopathies. Any means to eliminate a fair percentage of these men would be of great value in military selection as the psychopath is often the bane of existence of officers and fellow enlisted men. Checks of brig populations usually reveal large percentage of "regular customers" or men who are continually breaking regulations. These men are not only of little value in a military set-up as a whole, but are frequently a distinct liability from the standpoint of morale. Examination of our records show that many of these men could have been isolated by the Multiple Choice test for further psychiatric and historical check despite the lack of diagnostic specifity.

In the search for some approximation of group characteristics a tendency is found to combine an occasional human movement response with an organic type of reaction to the colored cards. Popular responses are more likely to occur than in organics, but these exist side by side with grossly pathological responses, pure color responses, and evidence of hostility and aggression. Early experience with a revised form of the Multiple Choice in which there is included some "fighting" responses has proved a definite aid in segregating these characters. It is noteworthy that the highest percentage of card rejection of all diagnostic groups occurred in the psychopathic group indicating an oppositionalism and negativism to environmental demands. Frequently, a highly colored original response with strong sado-masochistic content will point out a psychopathological substratum. A combination of hostile-aggressive, sado-masochistic and undifferentiated color response is indicative of the tendency to act out aggressions against the environment that is so characteristically demonstrated by chronic offenders. Uncontrolled shading responses suggesting disturbances in affective relationships with the environment are also prominent in many cases.

Suggestions of homosexual trends were often noted in the blind analysis of the overt homosexual group of the sexual psychopaths. This group gives responses suggesting confusion in the body image in regards to the sex role and utilizes objects of primarily feminine interest. Elucidation of these trends is to be accomplished in a forth-coming publication emphasizing the frequent occurrence of certain content in the records of overt homosexuals.

Schizoid personalities often show little or no utilization of color with a heavy emphasis of movement responses.

Case No. 8 is a demonstration of psychopathic personality of mixed type in which schizoid elements were prominent.

Card	I	"Nothing at all"
Card	II	"Two clowns"
Card	III	"Monkeys hanging by their tails"
Card	IV	"A dead dog" (Alternative)
Card	V	"A fan dancer"
Card	VI	"Nothing at all"
Card	VII	"A Map"
Card	VIII	"Inside of a volcano" (Alternative)
Card	IX	"Sea horses, or lobsters"
Card	X	"Spilt paint"

This record reflects a severe degree of maladjustment with popular failure, rejections, and inclusion of human movement indicating in-tellectual inconsistency, failure to think along common lines and social adaptability. His reactions to the color cards suggest a marked degree of emotional instability with capability of violent and explo-sive reactions, perhaps of an aggressive character, against the environ-ment. Strong internal conflict pervades his whole ego damaging the structure and function of his personality. A sado-masochistic response to the fourth card brings out interesting speculations. It seems here to reflect more a resentful and aggressive component than depressive feeling tone. Anxiety, evasiveness and negativism are also inferred. The combination of good human movement responses with popular failure and very bad responses brings up the possibility of a schizo-phrenic state, but the emotional reactivity to the environment impells one to reject this as a diagnosis and predict a psychopathic personality with schizoid trends.

Case History: No. 8; S2c; Age 18; Completed the tenth grade; Clinical Diagnosis, Constitutional Psychopathic State, Schizoid Personality.

This man was referred for psychiatric evaluation because of repeated violations, being A.W.O.L. three times, 24, 18, and 12 days respectively.

History from a reliable source revealed that he had been the ward of a social agency for years, being a constant problem from the standpoint of home placement. Following the death of his father, the child had been "given away" by the mother at the age of three. He has always been bashful, seclusive, and has feared crowds and cities. Since his enlistment, he has located his real mother and his periods of over-leave have been spent in pursuing and trying to remain with her. To psychiatric examination, he was quiet, inoffensive in appearance, childish in manner, and unsociable. Mild ideas of reference and persecution were present; "Everyone is against me." No delusions, or hallucinations were elicited. He was discharged from the service.

Case No. 84 is further illustrative of the mixed picture in the psychopathies.

Card	I	"An x-ray picture"
Card	II	"Kidneys" (Alternative)
Card	III	"Two men"
Card	IV	"An animal skin"
Card	V	"A bat or butterfly"
Card	VI	"Nothing at all"
Card	VII	"Dirty ice and snow"
Card	VIII	"Two animals in a cave of lava" (Alternative)
Card	IX	"Two people-witches or Santa Clauses"
Card	X	"Hobgoblins" (Alternative)

This record is again indicative of severe maladjustment with a mixture of anxiety, sexual maladjustment, difficulty in dealing with the environment, and emotional instability. The peculiar aspects of the original responses may also reflect a schizoid trend. The alternative response, "Kidneys" to the second card is interesting in the light of the observations of Jacob (5) that enuretics and stutterers are likely to project urogenital organs, water and sea animals into the blots. A brief survey of our material tends to corroborate this clinical observation with the addition of fire or fire-like projections. Furthermore, convulsives also show a predilection for this content.

Case History: No. 184; Age 19; Completed tenth grade; Clinical Diagnosis, Constitutional Psychopathic State, Inadequate Personality.

This patient was admitted to the sick list with a tentative diagnosis of psychoneurosis, Anxiety Neurosis, because of anxiety symptoms rendering him unfit for duty as a hospital corpsman. He had completed hospital corps school only three months prior to admission. Past history revealed that he has always been seclusive, indifferent and apathetic in his habits. Nail-biting has persisted throughout his lifetime and he was enuretic until the age of 16. He had run away from home three times for "a change" and was frequently truant from school. His mother had stated that he was so nervous at home that it was improbable that he would be able to stand the service. The clinical psychiatric findings were those of constitutional psychopathy with periodic anxiety, restlessness and irritability. The personality integration was considered to be inadequate with willfulness and stubbornness. He was discharged from the service.

MENTAL DEFICIENCY

The Multiple Choice Rorschach response patterns tend to break down in mental defectives from the interpretive standpoint. Some of our most glaring errors in predictions have occurred in this group. However, practically all of the mental defectives demonstrate pathological records from the consideration of number of bad responses. They will, therefore, be segregated for further investigation in the process of screening even though specific diagnostic prediction is incorrect. Case No. 664 is illustrative of this point.

Case No. 664

Card	I	"A bat"
Card	II	"Two scottie dogs"
Card	III	"Meat in a butcher shop"
Card	IV	"A nasty mess"
Card	V	"Nothing at all"
Card	VI	"Mud and water"
Card	VII	"Smoke and clouds"
Card	VIII	"Two animals"
Card	IX	"Red, green and orange"
Card	X	"Spilt paint"

Although this record is definitely abnormal with seven bad responses, it is difficult to categorize from the standpoint of differential diagnosis. It does not suggest a diagnosis of mental deficiency, but rather emotional immaturity, instability, anxiety, and disturbance in dealing with the environment with likelihood of aggressive behavior. Thus the prediction is more in line with a personality disorder with emotional instability and probable behavioral disturbance.

Case History: No. 664; Age 17; Completed sixth grade; Clinical Diagnosis,
    Mental Deficiency, Moron.

Admitted to the sick list following a panic state with confusion, excitement and fear of impending harm following ingestion of a moderate amount of alcohol. Past history revealed that he had been unable to learn in school after the third grade, having repeated the third, fourth and fifth grades. He reached the sixth grade at the age of 16. Following enlistment, he had engaged in several fights because others had called him "stupe."

Physical examination revealed microcephaly. The Wechsler-Bellevue test gave an intelligence quotient of 66. He was discharged from the service.

SUMMARY AND CONCLUSIONS

The possibilities of success in differential diagnosis by utilization of the Multiple Choice Test have been explored in 200 neuropsychiatric cases. Interpretive principles in common usage with the individual Rorschach have been applied as far as feasible in addition to other factors which arise from a radical change in the testing situation. Significant correlations were obtained between the blind analyses and clinical summaries of the cases in this study.

A methodology of interpretation for use with the Multiple Choice Tests has been outlined with illustrations demonstrating its application. Representative cases have been presented from various diagnostic groups with a discussion of the psychodynamics and psychological techniques which underlie the response patterns on the Multiple Choice. A comparison of these records demonstrated well-marked differences in pattern among the diagnostic groups. These differences permit relatively successful classifications as to diagnostic category, prediction of personality structure and degree of maladjustment.

The most accurate inferences of form and degree of maladjustment are possible in the psychoneurotic sub-groups. Organic and convulsive states can be differentiated from other diagnostic categories in a large percentage of cases, but are less accurately specified within the group. Psychopathic personalities can often be recognized by their response patterns. Mental defectives show very abnormal response records, but are not accurately discriminated by this modification of the Rorschach Test.

REFERENCES

1. Goldfarb, W.: A Definition and Validation of Obsessional Trends in the Rorschach Examinations of Adolescents. *Rorschach Res. Exch.,* 7:81-108, 1943.
2. Harrower, M. R.: Diagnosis of Psychogenic Factors in Disease by Means of the Rorschach Method. *Psychiatric Quar.,* 17:57-67, 1943.
3. Harrower, M. R.: Personality Changes Accompanying Cerebral Lesions. I. Rorschach Studies of Patients with Cerebral Tumors. *Arch. Neurol. and Psychiat.,* 43:859-890, 1940.
4. Hertz, M. R., and Ebert, E. H.: The Mental Procedure of 6 and 8 year old Children as Revealed by the Rorschach Inkblot Method. *Rorschach Res. Exch.,* 8:1; 10-30, 1944.
5. Jacob, Zoltan: Some Suggestions on the Use of Content Symbolism. *Rorschach Res. Exch.,* 8:1; 41-42, 1944.

6. Klopfer, B., and Kelley, D. M.: *The Rorschach Technique,* Yonkers-on-Hudson, New York, World Book Company, 1942.
7. Lindner, R. M.: The Rorschach Test and the Diagnosis of Psychopathic Personality. *Journal of Criminal Psychopathology, 5*:69-93, 1943.
8. Piotrowski, Z.: The Rorschach Inkblot Method in Organic Disturbances of the Central Nervous System. *Journal of Nervous and Mental Dis., 86*:5, 1937.
9. Wittson, C. L.; Hunt, W. A.; and, Older, T. J.: The Use of the Multiple Choice Group Rorschach Test in Military Screening. *J. Psychol., 17*:91-95, 1944.

Modification of the Multiple Choice Test in the Light of Recent Investigation

THE AMPLIFIED form of the Multiple Choice Test* (see Section X) resulted from a study of the results obtained over a period of one year with the original version presented and discussed in the preceding sections.

More than 300 investigators worked with this original test blank and many were willing to discuss and share their findings with us and to report the difficulties which they encountered in their investigations so that we were able to take steps to modify the material and procedure.

We found from these informal reports that the test was used for a wide variety of problems, under various conditions and by persons fully trained in the Rorschach method as well as by those who knew nothing about it. More than 50,000 test blanks were utilized and norms, derived from the study of various groups of subjects, were submitted to us. While it is quite impossible to mention all these numerous investigations, we may say that as far as the military application of the test is concerned, it was applied in Induction, Rehabilitation, and Classification centers, and in a large number of neuropsychiatric divisions of station hospitals in this country. Reports were also received from psychologists and psychiatrists using the procedure overseas. Schools, colleges, industrial organizations, state hospitals, guidance clinics, and placement bureaus were among the civilian agencies interested in its use.

In the course of the year we were much interested to notice that the primary emphasis shifted away from the use of the test as essentially a mechanical screening device and was placed upon the infor-

---

* Dr. Frank Fremont-Smith is responsible for many ideas which are epitomized in this new version of the test. We are also indebted to Lt. (j.g.) Floyd Due, Ensign Erik Wright and Dr. B. Wright for submitting items which they had found to be of special significance, also to Mrs. F. R. Miale for helpful suggestions.

mation which could be derived from it concerning the individual's personality make-up.

In the light of this rather extensive experimental period several alterations were made in the form of the test and in the manner of handling results which we shall enumerate and discuss here.

ALTERNATE ANSWERS

The inclusion of the space for an alternative answer, "Something other than the above," of the original test form, proved to be more confusing than helpful, since such answers in order to be handled properly, necessitated the knowledge of Rorschach scoring principles. Our initial instructions, that all alternate answers were to be classified as poor answers, were definitely misleading and resulted in the increase of false positives among normal subjects in a number of cases.

It is true that when the investigator was cognizant of Rorschach principles, much helpful information about the testee was derived (see Section VII). It is also true that in some cases, even without knowledge of Rorschach principles, the alternative answers proved helpful. For example, several examiners reported that it was essentially a compulsive type of individual who insisted on writing in his own answers instead of checking very similar ones already listed. Others reported that frequently the content of the alternative answer was a good lead to follow in the psychiatric interview since it frequently revealed some peculiarly personal problem.

For statistical handling of results, however, and for comparative purposes, the alternative answers were not helpful, introducing as they did one source of ambiguity and lack of uniformity between the results of different investigators. The revised form of the test blank, therefore, has eliminated the choice, reading "Something other than the above."

PLACING THE CUTTING POINT AT FOUR "POOR" ANSWERS

In deciding which point on the scale should be considered as the critical one for separating the suspect from any group, it is necessary, as Mittelmann has pointed out, to have clearly in mind what one wishes to accomplish through the use of the test: "One may aim at either of two goals: a) to devise and score tests so as to detect only those who are unquestionably unfit, emotionally, for military service. In this case, the number of those rejected by the test may be a relatively small percentage, e.g., 8% and many of the unfit will not be caught by the test; or, b) to devise and score tests to separate all those unfit for military service. In this case, the separated group will inevitably include many of those who are fit for service. It is then the task for the examining psychiatrist to determine the status of those marked as questionable by the test. In this case, the percentage of men referred for interview will be higher, *e.g.*, 33% (1).

In our original experiment we contrasted the performance of psychotics and severe psychoneurotics with groups of normal subjects who, with the exception of the prisoner group, came from rather superior backgrounds. It was clear that, in this particular comparison, we caught more of the patients and correspondingly misjudged fewer normals when the cutting point was placed at four poor answers. Our sample, however, was not, statistically speaking, a large one. The groups had not been accurately equated for the factor of intelligence,* nor had we dealt with a large enough group of psychoneurotics as distinct from the institutionalized psychotics. It is not surprising to find, therefore, that our first rather arbitrary suggestion as to the point where the screening out of cases should take place was not adequate in all groups and was actually misleading in some others.

Although it is possible with certain types of subjects to get worthwhile results with a cutting point of four poor answers, the degree of overlap between the normal and the maladjusted, or psychoneurotic recruit, has been shown to be too great to make this the sole criterion for screening in investigations with military personnel.

The study of Wittson, Hunt, and Older (2) illustrated this clearly. They found that in order to detect (with a cutting point of four poor answers) 59% of the group of recruits subsequently unfit for service, 44% of a group who were accepted for service would also be suspect. They conclude therefore, that "The Multiple Choice Test has not been developed to a stage where it is a serviceable instrument for military selection."

Similarly Due, Wright, and Wright report that "the degree of overlap in our statistics indicate that a cutting point of four would segregate more than 50% of the prospective neuropsychiatric casualties, but that it would also include a large number of false positives who adjust satisfactorily despite evidences of conflicts on a deeper level" (see

---

Eysenck at the Mill Hill Emergency Hospital in London has commented on this fact and writes: "We are going to give the test to all our incoming patients for a while, and I hope to be able to get a normal control group from various . . . places in the neighborhood. I propose to use a rather different form of recording and scoring which will give a wider spread than your own, *and we are going to devote special attention to the influence of intelligence on responses. I am also rather interested in the question of sex differences as far as they may effect this test.*" (Italics ours.)

Section VII). These same investigators have also shown that with an alternative, but also purely quantitative scoring, they would detect "31% of the patient group, but would also single out 19% of the normal subjects." However, and this is the interesting point, they felt that "subsequent experimentation with the test at embarkation centers has strongly validated the inference that the 19% so designated are the ones who have been judged to be adjusting with difficulty" (see Section V).

In other words while the inadequacy of this cutting point as a sole criterion cannot be overlooked, neither can the possibility that the "normals" screened out at this point, are not those who subsequently show maladjustment.

PLACING THE CUTTING POINT AT FIVE "POOR" ANSWERS

Several investigations would seem to indicate that a cutting point of five poor answers is a useful one. Due, Wright, and Wright (see Section V) report "Clinical experience with the test has repeatedly demonstrated to the authors that an individual with five negative responses shows marked behavior disturbance. This difficulty is almost always of a sufficient degree to prove disabling for military service."

An investigation (3) with a student population may be quoted in this connection. Three hundred and eight entering summer school students (ages 16 to 45 years) were examined by the Multiple Choice Test as part of their physical health examination. With a cutting point of five poor answers 90 students or 29% of this group were screened out.* These 90 students were then given a psychiatric examination, and of these, 40 were considered by the psychiatrists to show some psychopathology. During the psychiatric interview the Multiple Choice Test was repeated, this time as an individual test. The diagnoses given subsequent to the psychiatric interview for these 40 subjects are listed here:

Incipient schizophrenia	3
Anxiety tension state	19
Narcissistic regression pattern	1
Adolescent reaction	5
Psychopathic personality	5
Fatigue neurosis	1
Menopausal syndrome	1
Compulsive obsessive neurosis	1
Mentally dull	1
Diagnosis deferred	3

---

* These figures were erroneously given as 79 and 26% in (3).

It is clear that in order to spot these 40 individuals, another 50 persons, with only minor worries and anxieties, had been picked out. On the other hand some cases which would not otherwise have come to the psychiatrist's notice were made available for *immediate* treatment. This initial screening test also made possible *continued* psychotherapeutic treatment throughout the summer school period which was considered important.

As a result of this study the authors have pointed out several facts which may be helpful in the handling of similar groups. For example, it was felt that repetition of the Multiple Choice Test, with individuals who had been screened out was valuable. Of those who *repeated* their poor scores on the second test, 95% showed some psychopathology, while amongst those subjects who improved on the second presentation of the cards only 33% were considered to be disturbed.

Various reasons for the appearance of "false positives" were also listed. For example, since the test was given at the same time as the physical examination it "tended to engender anxiety in the minds of those with physical disabilities. Amongst those later considered as false positives was a student who had undergone a pulmonary lobectomy, and another whose history showed a recent cerebral hematoma." These students were apprehensive lest their physical disabilities might bar them from summer school.

Amongst other factors which tended to produce false positives were: the misunderstanding of the instructions with regard to alternate answers, the inability to see the slides clearly owing to refractive errors, and an erroneous assumption or "mental set" that, since this was a medical examination, the slides were biological or anatomical in nature.

A similar investigation from another university (4) shows an interesting contrast between the freshmen and senior groups in medical school. Amongst the freshman class 29% of the members showed records with five or more poor answers, indicating some degree of maladjustment, while amongst the seniors, from whose ranks it is to be assumed the weaklings had already dropped by the wayside, only 4% were found to show a similar score. Moreover, of the six individuals who comprised this 4% of the senior class, three were already known to be under psychiatric guidance.

PLACING THE CUTTING POINT AT SIX "POOR" ANSWERS

In certain cases an even higher cutting point may be advocated; for example, if it is the examiner's desire to earmark only those with some disturbance and to exclude false positives. A report from an army camp (5) shows that with a cutting point of six poor answers, in contrasting 100 "normal" soldiers with 113 who have failed to adjust, 7% of the former group was screened out as opposed to 37% of the latter. With a cutting point of seven only 1% of the normal group was included as opposed to 25% of those who had failed to adjust. For this type of subject, therefore, in order to detect with certainty 25% of those who would not adjust and in order not to include any of those who would adjust, a cutting point of seven poor answers is clearly indicated.

In the revised form of the test blank, therefore, 60% poor answers is suggested as probably the best cutting point, with the cases falling between 40% and 60% being considered as borderline, or questionable, and investigated in the light of other criteria.

The Weighting of Scores

We were aware in our initial experiments that in all probability the poor answers should not be considered of equal weight. We felt that after large numbers of subjects had been investigated, certain poor answers would turn out to be considerably "worse" than others. It was impossible, however, to do more than guess from our small sample as to which answers would turn out to be the most significant.

Several investigators have now analyzed their data to determine which answers were most significant for the purpose of discriminating between the adjusted and maladjusted individual. Three independent investigations all point to the same conclusions; namely, answer #10, failure to give any answer, is considerably more important than any other type of poor answer. When one remembers the extent to which failures show up among the psychotic patients in the group Rorschach (see page 000) this result is not surprising. At the other extreme answers #6 and #7 (anatomical answers and the x-ray answers), unless present in great quantities in a record, are hardly diagnostic at all. In fact, they sometimes occur more frequently in the well-adjusted than in the poorly adjusted group!

Consideration of results from one Induction center may illustrate this point. Answer #10, for example, is given on an average of .1 and .2 times per record in two control groups; but in a group of equal size of persons diagnosed as schizoid personalities, answer #10 occurs 1.6 times per record. On the other hand for these same groups, answer #6 appears .6 and 1.0 times per record amongst the two control groups, and 1.1 times per record amongst the schizoid personalities.

Clearly, then, for this type of subject, the normal inductee, answer #6 is not a poor answer at all and is not diagnostically significant in any way. In the amplified version of the test, therefore, answers #6 and #7 are scored as only one half; or two such answers are required to be present before they are scored as one poor answer. This means that it would require ten such answers in a record before an individual would be screened out in terms of these answers alone. We might also recommend at this point that the weighting of twice the number of poor answers be given to each score of #10, although this had not been adopted to date.

Answers Given as Second and Third Choices

One of the main difficulties which arose in the original form of the Multiple Choice Test was the scoring of second (often third and fourth) choices. Were these to be given equal weight with the first choices? How severely was an obviously productive individual, who had added many additional choices, to be penalized if his additionals contained poor choices? Some investigators reported cases where the first answers were good but where second choices were markedly poor and that the picture presented by the second choices was closer to the clinical estimate. Other investigators were inclined to disregard second choices entirely either as insignificant or because no uniform policies had been outlined for their scoring.

A clearer understanding of the relationship of a first choice to an additional one was obviously necessary and as the new instructions show, has been explicitly dealt with in the revised form of the test. In the new form of the test the subject is asked to underline the one answer in each of three groups of answers which he thinks is the best description of the inkblot or any of its parts. Then, when he has done this, he is asked to put a check beside any other answer in any of the three groups which he also feels is a good description of the inkblot or any of its parts (see Section X). By these instructions we have not only tried to obtain one answer from each of three groups of ten answers for each inkblot (*i.e.,* three answers for each inkblot), but also to elicit as many other answers as possible which the subject cares to give.

Suggestions for Scoring

In the scoring of these answers we suggest that, first of all, a percentage is obtained of the number of poor answers in the record as a whole regardless of whether or not they are given as first or additional choices. When a score of over 60% is obtained in this way, the record can be considered as suspect. Records with a total score of from 40% to 60% should be considered borderline and re-examined in the light of the scores obtained from the first and the additional answers, separately. They should also be considered in the light of the total number of responses given to the test as a whole. By and large the individual who gives several additional answers to each card, and whose total number of responses is therefore over 50, is probably less disturbed, even with the *same percentage* of poor answers, than the individual whose total number of responses is 30 or less. Or again, the individual who shows most of his poor answers in his first choices, particularly if these contain the choice "Nothing at all," is probably less adequately equipped psychologically than the individual who, with good first answers, adds "Nothing at all" amongst the additional ones.

We are unwilling, however, at this point to be too insistent on the significance of the relationship of poor answers in first and additional choices. We feel that the more productive individual is much better able to do himself justice in this new version of the test than he was in the original one, and that in a great many cases the person screened out at a cutting of four, five, or even six when first answers alone are considered, will not be screened out when the test gives him the opportunity to add as many answers as he wishes and when these answers are considered as equally indicative of his performance as a single choice would have been.

Thus the three hundred choices offered in the revised form of the test afford the opportunity for a richer and more detailed record to be obtained from the productive individual, *i.e.*, the individual whose productivity, if allowed to register, will cancel out the detrimental aspects of the poor answers. Records obtained from this version of the blank lend themselves to fuller interpretation along orthodox Rorschach lines, and at the same time borderline cases may be somewhat better understood by the investigator without knowledge of Rorschach principles.

THE "DEPTH" OF A GIVEN DISTURBANCE

A similar problem to that of the additional answers presents itself in the question of how serious is the disturbance, or blocking, revealed in any poor answer.

"Color shock" for example, was frequently revealed by a failure on

Card II or by the choice of the answer "Red and Black" on the original form. In the orthodox Rorschach record we are interested in the "depth" or extent of this inability of the subject to respond to the colored cards. Can he, for instance, recover his balance quickly or will he be unable to respond to the card no matter how long he is allowed to look at it?

The revised form of the test has aimed at showing something of the degree of a given disturbance. The three groups of answers (see Section X), from each of which a choice is required, allow of two additional "approaches" to the blot to be made. An individual who continues to give "Nothing at all" in all three groups of answers is clearly more disturbed by it than is the individual who can recover from his "Nothing at all" answer in group A, giving good answers in both groups B and C. In this way many cases, which on the original form would have been screened out by virtue of their one "Nothing at all," will not necessarily be screened out in the longer version. The "recovery" will be registered and the scores (now in percentage terms) of first and additional answers will demonstrate or take this recovery into account.

THE USE OF THE MULTIPLE CHOICE TEST IN CONNECTION WITH OTHER TESTS

A number of investigators have reported the use of the Multiple Choice Test as part of a battery of psychological tests. This, we feel, is the most advantageous way of using it, and we may mention here one or two constellations in which it has appeared.

A frequent partner has been the Cornell Selectee Index (6). In this connection the results as described by Mittelmann seem to have been upheld in subsequent investigations. Mittelmann (1) reported: "The Selectee Index has shown itself to be most effective in detecting the presence of anxiety states, hypochondriasis, asocial trends, convulsive disorders, and psychosomatic syndrome. It is less effective in the screening of those likely to exhibit the so-called monosymptomatic disturbance, i.e., hysterical palsies, etc. It is also limited in detecting obsessive states and pre-psychotic states. In comparison the Multiple Choice Test does best on psychoses and less well on psychoneuroses. It is possible that the best results will be arrived at through a combined administration of both tests." A similar report has been made from one of the Induction Centers: "The Multiple Choice Test appears to have an advantage with schizoid personalities, to do less well with psychoneurotics, and to rate as abnormal about the same proportion of normal subjects as does the Selectee Index. The data also suggest that the Multiple Choice Test may be superior with psychopathic personalities" (7).

A comparison of the Multiple Choice findings with the Thurstone Personality Inventory seems to indicate that these two tests may be valuable when given in conjunction, since they may provide supplementary information to each other. Comparison with the Minnesota Multiphasic Test (8) has been undertaken by several investigators and their results should be available shortly.

In an investigation aimed at the selection of officer candidates in one of the women's services, the Multiple Choice Test was "administered and scored early in the battery of tests in order that the scores could be known to the interviewer and Military Testing Officer. Any candidate scoring more than four poor answers on this test was given a modified form of the Thematic Apperception Test" (9). The interest in this investigation centered primarily on those with exceptionally good records on the Multiple Choice Test. Comparison of Multiple Choice scores with other findings indicated that for one group thus examined 78% with no poor answers were considered as unquestionably acceptable candidates by the Selection Board on the basis of the interview and their performance on the other tests in the battery (9).

An important investigation to discover the *degree of literacy* necessary to make the findings of the Multiple Choice Test valid was undertaken by Smith (10). Seventy-five subjects rating seven, eight and nine (out of a possible 17) on the Army Qualification Test, which is primarily a literacy test, were also examined by the Multiple Choice Test. Upon completing this, they were asked: "Was there anything about this that you did not understand? Was there anything that bothered you?" It was found that 53 subjects did not know five or more than five words or phrases. It was felt, therefore, that possibly the Multiple Choice Test was not valid for these groups. However, even with these gaps in the subjects' understanding, the relation of the Multiple Choice Test scores to the psychiatric finding is still suggestive. Of those with less than four poor answers only one case, or 4%, was rejected for psychiatric reasons; whereas, of these with five or more poor answers 16 cases, or 31% were rejected by the psychiatrist.

REFERENCES

1. Mittelmann, Bela: Proceedings of the military session. *Psychosom. Med.*, 5:359, 1943.

2. Wittson, C. L.; Hunt, W. A.; and, Older, H. J.: The use of the Multiple Choice Group Rorschach Test in Military Screening. *J. of Psychol., 17*:91-94, 1944.
3. Harrower, M. R.; Washburn, A. C.; and, Jacobs, J. S. L.: A preliminary screening test for disturbances in personality. *Bull. Canad. Psychol. A., 4*:4-6, 1944.
4. Personal Communication from Dr. McCulloch.
5. Friedman, Samuel: The Harrower-Erickson Multiple Choice Test in military psychiatry. (Paper read at the Symposium on the Use of the Rorschach Method in the Armed Forces, 1944.)
6. Weider, Arthur; Mittelmann, Bela; Wechsler, David; and, Wolff, Harold: The Cornell Selectee Index. *J. Am. Med. A., 124:4,* 224-228, 1944.
7. Unpublished report.
8. McKinley, J. C.; and, Hathaway, S. R.: The identification and measurement of the psychoneuroses in medical practice. *J. Am. Med. A., 122:3,* 161-167, 1943.
9. Harrower, M. R.: The use of the Multiple Choice Test in the military services. *Proc. Brief Psychotherapy Council,* 1944.
10. Smith, Douglas. (Paper read at the Symposium on the Use of the Rorschach Method in the Armed Forces, 1944.)

Summary of Alterations and Suggestions for Handling Results

1. The number of choices has been increased from 100 to 300.
2. Alternate answers are not mentioned in the instructions nor are they provided for with a space to record "something other than the above."
3. Three choices are required for each inkblot, one to be taken from each of three groups of ten answers. These choices are to be underlined.
4. In addition, any other response which the subject also sees is permitted. These additional choices are marked with a check.
5. The instructions on the new test blank have been rephrased after many attempts to find the shortest and simplest form.*
6. A few items have been omitted from the original version of the test because they give rise to difficulties related to false positives.
7. The record should be scored by consulting the key (see Section X). The number which describes any given answer should be recorded beside the choice on the test blank. When all answers have been scored, the total number of answers from #1 to #5 ("good" answers) and the total number of answers from #6 to #10 ("poor" answers) should be recorded for the underlined answers (first choices) and the checked answers (additional choices) separately.
8. A percentage rather than an absolute number is taken as the cutting point. It is suggested that three percentages be calculated: a) the percentage of poor answers for the record as a whole. In this case no distinction is made between first choices and the additional ones, but consideration should be given to whether or not the total number of choices is large or small; b) the percentage of poor answers in the thirty required choices; and, c) the percentage of poor answers in the unlimited number of additional choices.

---

* We are indebted to Mr. Cassens for help in regard to clarification of the instructions after use of the test in an Induction Center.

9. Since the cutting point of four poor answers (or 40%) is not the most advantageous one, we suggest that if poor answers constitute 60% of the total score, the record should be screened out for more careful study of the individual from other angles by other tests or psychiatric interview. Cases with scores between 40% and 60% should be further investigated in the light of other factors in the test itself before they are considered as records which should be screened out. In these borderline cases the richness or meagreness of the record should be considered.

10. Answers #6 and #7 have recently been shown to be statistically less significant as indications of maladjustment than answers #8, #9 and #10. It is suggested that these answers (#6 and #7) be scored as one half poor answers. Numbers should be rounded off to the nearest digit. For example, three #6 answers would count as only one poor answer. Or, again, two #6 answers and three #7 answers would count as only two "poor" answers and so on. In view of recent findings, it may also be suggested that #10 should be scored as two poor answers.

11. When given as a group test, the amplified version requires *a three minute exposure period* for each slide. The slides should be presented in total darkness for at least *30 seconds,* and should still be clearly visible (even if not so brilliant) when lights, sufficient only for reading the blanks, have been put on in the auditorium.

SECTION X

Amplified Multiple Choice Test Combined With Key Numbers for Examiners' Use

A COMBINATION of the 300 responses offered in the Amplified version of the test, and the key numbers by which these responses are represented, is given in the following pages. *Needless to say these numbers do not appear on the actual blanks which are supplied for the subjects taking the test nor are the poor answers italicized.* It was found however, after several experimental versions of this key had been tried out, that there is less chance of error in scoring if the numbers are listed by the side of the responses, rather than without them.

If the used test blank is folded, so that, as each Inkblot is scored, it is put alongside the equivalent list in these pages, it will be found that the underlined and checked answers can be readily recorded. If a very rapid and undifferentiated scoring is required, then merely counting the *number* of poor answers chosen by the subject is facilitated by the italicized words and by the darker type in which numbers 6, 7, 8, 9, 10 have been set.

The following Instructions are printed on each blank, but in group situations should also be read aloud by the examiner.

INSTRUCTIONS

You are going to see ten inkblot pictures one after another.

Begin by taking a good look at Inkblot I and see if it, or any part of it, reminds you of anything or resembles something you have seen.

Then read through each of the three groups of answers for Inkblot I (A, B, C).

Now underline the one answer in Group A, the one answer in Group B, the one answer in Group C, which you think is the best description of that inkblot or any of its parts. You, therefore, underline three answers for Inkblot I.

When you have done this, if you wish, you may put a check beside any other answer in any of the three groups which you also feel is a good description of the inkblot or any of its parts.

Then do exactly the same thing for each of the other inkblots.

INKBLOT 1	INKBLOT 2

A

3 An army or navy emblem	8 *A bug somebody stepped on*
9 *Crumbling cliffs*	10 *Nothing at all*
2 A bat	2 Two scottie dogs
10 *Nothing at all*	4 Little faces on the sides
1 Two people	6 *A bloody spinal column*
3 A pelvis	5 A white top
7 *An x-ray picture*	8 *A bursting bomb*
4 Pincers of a crab	2 Two elephants
9 *A dirty mess*	1 Two clowns
6 *Part of my body*	9 *Red and black ink*

B

1 A headless figure	7 *An animal skin*
3 Vertebra	2 Two bears rubbing noses
4 Tiny boxing gloves	4 Faces of Indians on the side
9 *Spilt ink*	8 *Blood*
6 *Someone's insides*	10 *Nothing at all*
10 *Nothing at all*	5 A white lamp
2 A butterfly flying	8 *An exploding firecracker*
9 *Lava*	3 A red butterfly
3 A coat of arms	1 Two people playing . . .
7 *An x-ray of the chest*	9 *Red and black splotches*

C

3 A Halloween mask	1 Two witches
7 *Storm clouds*	9 *Black and red paint*
2 A moth	2 Bears' heads
1 Two people . . .	9 *An empty hole*
3 A bell in the center	4 Faces carved in stone
7 *An x-ray picture of the spine*	6 *Lungs and blood*
4 Animal heads on the sides	5 A white sting ray
6 *The stomach*	4 A little temple in the center
10 *Nothing at all*	10 *Nothing at all*
8 *Eyes glaring at me*	8 *An erupting volcano*

(Continued on next page)

INKBLOT 3

A

2 Two birds fighting
8 *Meat in a butcher's shop*
1 Two men pulling . . .
6 *Part of my body*
9 *Just colored blots*
3 A colored butterfly
8 *Spots of blood and paint*
2 Monkeys hanging . . .
3 A red bow tie
10 *Nothing at all*

B

3 A red brooch
6 *A person's insides*
1 Two cannibals
2 Donald Ducks
8 *Fire and smoke*
10 *Nothing at all*
8 *Spilt paint*
1 Two women quarreling
9 *Blood and dirt*
1 Alphonse and Gaston—
"after you"

C

4 Two birds' heads
6 *A bloody stomach*
1 Two waiters bowing
7 *An x-ray picture*
9 *Dirty spots and bloody spots*
3 A colored hair ribbon
8 *Lipstick splotches*
2 Falling cats
10 *Nothing at all*
2 Fish swimming

INKBLOT 4

A

4 Head of an animal
6 *Lungs and chest*
9 *A nasty, dirty mess*
4 A pair of boots
9 *A burnt mass*
10 *Nothing at all*
1 A giant in a fur coat
3 An animal skin
2 A big gorilla
7 *An x-ray picture*

B

4 A little flower on the top
6 *The spine*
9 *Dirty water*
3 Charlie Chaplin's feet
9 *A nightmare*
1 A man sitting down
3 A fur rug
2 Two Scottie dogs
9 *A black smudge*
10 *Nothing at all*

C

7 *Clouds*
2 A bat
1 A man seen from below
10 *Nothing at all*
9 *Something squashed*
9 *A frightening picture*
6 *A person's insides*
4 Two little snakes
3 Big overshoes
3 A cow's head

(Continued on next page)

INKBLOT 5	INKBLOT 6
A	A

4 A bird's beak	3 Two kings' heads . . .
9 *Something squashed*	7 *An x-ray picture*
1 A ballet dancer	6 *Parts of the body*
10 *Nothing at all*	3 A totem pole
7 *A map*	3 A fur rug
4 Sugar tongs	9 *Mud and water*
2 A moth	4 A polished post
6 *Shoulders*	10 *Nothing at all*
7 *Smoke*	2 A turtle
4 A rabbit's head	9 *A landslide*

B	B
3 A man's face	2 A dragonfly
9 *A black mess*	6 *The spinal column*
1 Two men with arms folded	4 A cat's whiskers
7 *An island*	6 *Male and female organs*
1 A policeman	3 An animal skin
2 A bird flying	9 *Dirty water*
6 *A pelvis*	3 A sceptre
9 *Tar and soot*	4 A snake's head
4 Nutcrackers	10 *Nothing at all*
10 *Nothing at all*	9 *A spattered mess*

C	C
4 An alligator's head	2 A butterfly at the top
10 *Nothing at all*	7 *An x-ray of the spine*
9 *A smashed body*	4 Feathers at the top
1 A fan dancer	3 A bear skin
7 *An x-ray picture*	7 *A leaf*
4 Legs	4 A table leg
2 A bat or butterfly	10 *Nothing at all*
6 *Lungs and chest*	9 *Gushing oil*
9 *Black clouds*	1 A little man
4 A pair of pliers	6 *Part of the body*

(Continued on next page)

INKBLOT 7

A

7 *Smoke*
1 Two women talking
6 *Parts of the body*
2 Animals
10 *Nothing at all*
5 A white chandelier
9 *Burning fragments*
4 Lambs' tails
7 *An x-ray picture*
3 Bookends

B

3 Men's faces with big noses
2 A butterfly at the bottom
9 *Dirt from the gutter*
2 Scotties
6 *A pelvis*
1 Indians with feathered caps
10 *Nothing at all*
7 *Clouds*
7 *An x-ray of part of the body*
3 A necklace

C

1 Children playing
6 *The lower part of the body*
7 *Fog or mist*
10 *Nothing at all*
7 *A squashed frog*
3 Statues
9 *A gray mess*
2 A moth
2 Dogs playing
5 A white lamp

INKBLOT 8

A

3 An orange or pink butterfly
6 *Shoulders, lungs, and stomach*
10 *Nothing at all*
9 *Just colors*
3 An emblem
3 A pretty flower
8 *Heaven and Hell*
3 Two blue cushions
2 Two bears climbing
7 *Colored clouds*

B

3 Flowers and leaves
7 *An x-ray picture*
9 *Colored blobs*
3 A horseshoe crab
10 *Nothing at all*
3 Blue flags
2 Two animals climbing
3 A colored coat of arms
8 *Fire and ice*
6 *Parts of the body*

C

3 A Christmas tree
8 *A medical picture*
2 Frogs' heads
8 *Life and Death*
3 A mountain at the top
3 A design for wallpaper
8 *Inside the mouth*
2 Two beavers walking . . .
10 *Nothing at all*
9 *Colored ink splashed on paper*

(Continued on next page)

INKBLOT 9

A

3 Sea horses
9 *Just spilt paint*
3 Flowers
6 *Parts of the body*
8 *Smoke and flames*
2 Deer or horns of deer
10 *Nothing at all*
1 Two witches
8 *Bloody clouds*
3 A candle

B

10 *Nothing at all*
3 A pink jacket
9 *Just colors*
3 Tropical plants
6 *The stomach and intestines*
8 *A forest fire*
2 An animal's head on the side
1 Two gnomes
8 *Bloody hands*
3 A fountain

C

3 A tropical flower or orchid
3 Lobsters
6 *The inside of a person*
8 *An explosion*
3 Men's faces on the sides
10 *Nothing at all*
1 Two Santa Clauses
8 *Storm clouds at sunset*
3 A violin
9 *Messy colors*

INKBLOT 10

A

1 Two people
8 *Spilt paint*
3 A Chinese print
7 *An x-ray picture*
9 *Just colored ink spots*
2 Spiders, caterpillars, insects
6 *Parts of my insides*
3 A colored map of California
10 *Nothing at all*
3 A flower garden

B

3 Undersea pictures
2 Two little dogs sitting up
6 *Stomach and intestines*
9 *A lot of colors*
8 *A medical picture*
3 A design for wallpaper
8 *A child's painting*
1 Two ladies holding hands
10 *Nothing at all*
2 Lots of animals running around

C

3 A blue flower
8 *Colored ink*
3 A picture of spring or fall
6 *Parts of the body*
9 *Just colors*
2 Octopus and crabs
6 *Bones*
3 Coral and seaweed
3 Flowers
10 *Nothing at all*

EXPLANATION OF NUMERICAL VALUES ASSIGNED TO ANSWERS IN TERMS OF RORSCHACH SCORING

\#1 Human movement responses (Rorschach's M).

\#2 Animal responses, either with or without movement, including many "populars."

\#3 Good form answers given relatively frequently by unselected normals. In the colored cards \#3 stands for Form-Color responses. (FC)

\#4 Answer located in the small detail area of the card.

\#5 White space answers.

\#6 Anatomical answers with bad form. (F—)

\#7 X-ray responses, clouds, and a few vague formless whole answers (leaf on Card VI, animal skin on Card II, etc.)

\#8 Answer indicating an explosive response to color. (CF or C answers)

\#9 Completely formless answers in uncolored cards, including those indicative of unpleasant feeling tone in looking at the card (nightmare, etc.). In the colored cards \#9 stands for an evasion of the response, or a mere statement of the colors on the blot.

\#10 Failure, the "nothing at all" answer.

Part IV

RECENT DEVELOPMENTS IN GROUP
TECHNIQUES FOR THE RORSCHACH TEST

Recent Developments: Group Rorschach Test, Multiple Choice Test, Stress Tolerance Test*

IT IS almost 10 years since the first tentative tampering with the sacrosanct Rorschach Method resulted in the Group Rorschach Technique! Since in the course of these years it has become an orthodox and accepted procedure: it is hard to recapture the skepticism, and, in some cases, hostility which greeted its appearance, or to realize the atmosphere which made it necessary for the punctiliously detailed and careful accounting for every step taken in its development, together with the rather rigid standardization of instructions and procedure.

As is now common knowledge, the Group Rorschach involves the presentation of the Rorschach blots in the form of slides in a semi-darkened room which may accommodate, provided all seats are centrally located, as many as several hundred persons. A three-minute time interval is allotted for the presentation of each slide and the subjects write down a full description of the things that they see in the blot. Following the initial presentation, the slides are repeated to allow for various types of *Inquiries* depending on the preferences of the examiner.

As would be expected, the types of responses vary from those which are monosyllabic and without amplification to full-page descriptions of a single percept. Further, as would also be expected, these responses run the gamut of good and poor form, from rich and expressive movement to blatant and undirected use of color and the various reactions to shading. And while many investigators have embarked on this

---

* All material needed for the administration of the Group Rorschach Test and Multiple Choice Test is available from The Psychological Corporation, 522 Fifth Avenue, New York City. This material includes the Rorschach slides which may be obtained in two sizes, the regular lantern slide size and the Kodaslide. Booklets for recording responses in the Group Rorschach and blanks with the 300 multiple choice items are also supplied by the Corporation.

new method with some feelings of misgiving and even skepticism, they have found that in this respect, the Rorschach is foolproof.

If the test is conducted properly, material for diagnostic evaluation will be available.

A detailed account of the instructions for administration, together *with those* for the *Inquiry,* will be found in Part I, Sections II and III. In the light of many years' experience, however, the writer now feels that stereotyped instructions are of very little use and an individual well acquainted with the Rorschach method, who has frequently administered it individually, will find that in presenting it to different groups, he will do much better to address the group spontaneously, explaining the procedure without reference to any published or "correct" instructions. To a large extent, the successful presentation of the group method, as indeed with the individual method, depends on a proper rapport between the experimenter and his subjects, between the psychologist and his patients. The handling of groups is different from handling a single individual, and any given administrator of the Group Technique should think primarily in terms of establishing a good group relationship.

While at this stage it seems clear that considerable leeway should be allowed in terms of the instructions and also, to this writer's way of thinking, in the type of *Inquiry* pursued, a rather rigid standardization has been maintained in regard to the slides which have been available for group presentation. For the last six or seven years, these slides have been made by an expert photographer, Dr. M. E. Diemer. Considering the great difficulties which arose during the war years in getting reliable film, the uniformity and excellence of his production has been extraordinary. With a few exceptions, the sets of slides have not differed one from the other to a greater degree than various editions of the Rorschach cards differ from one another.

While the question of uniformity in the type of booklet used by the subject to record his responses is obviously of much less importance than the standardized slides, we have for the last five years utilized a booklet which had as perhaps its main feature rather unusually detailed and carefully shaded black-white representations of the blots for locating the responses. For convenience, Munroe's excellent check list (1) is included on the back page of this booklet.*

---

* To avoid confusion which still occurs, it might be well to state that neither Dr. Diemer nor the writer is concerned with the sale of slides or booklets, which are handled exclusively by the Psychological Corporation, 522 Fifth Avenue, New York City.

Essentially the same material, then, is available to the examiner as the result of the Group Method of presentation as is available to him through the individual method, if he has conducted his group procedure successfully. With this material he may proceed as with gross screening by merely scanning the record for the most obviously disturbed performances. Or, as Munroe has so ably demonstrated, with her check list, he can introduce an intermediate type of scanning and scoring whereby certain outstanding features of the performance can be rapidly assessed without the mechanics of the complete evaluation. But there is nothing to stop him from scoring the record in the traditional manner, be his orientation directly from Rorschach, Klopfer, or Beck, and proceeding with the differentiated evaluation on the basis of the detailed scoring.

If the Group Rorschach procedure was greeted with raised eyebrows, the introduction of the Multiple Choice Test was greeted with an even colder reception. It is well, therefore, to emphasize here that this is best described not as a variation of the Rorschach technique, but as *a different type of test.* Clearly it would have been better for all concerned if this test could have been put out as a new procedure with an alternative set of inkblots; however, this was not possible at that time.

The Multiple Choice Test can be given in group form or individually. Since our concern here is with group techniques, it will be described as if presented in a group situation. So, in this case, the Rorschach slides are thrown on a screen, but the subject, instead of writing down his various impressions, chooses from a list of thirty possible choices those three which most nearly approximate his own perception of the particular blot. While we have freely admitted that this is not Rorschach's procedure, and while the final form of this test has probably not yet been devised, it nonetheless has certain undeniable advantages, not over and against the Rorschach, *but as a procedure in its own right.*

The obvious difference here between the checking of answers and the recording of spontaneous impressions is to eliminate all detailed Rorschach and psychological knowledge on the part of the mechanical scorer, so that the assessing of several hundreds or even thousands of records becomes a technical possibility, and in a relatively short time. As will be discussed later, various investigators have now reached the point where the Multiple Choice answers have been transposed to IBM scoring sheets, so that we are on the verge of an era where statistically valid handling of age levels, of professional groups, of various psychopathological entities can be collected. It was, of course, under precisely the pressure of screening demands in wartime that this particular test procedure was devised. There was a need for a machine-scored variant of Rorschach's method, and the Multiple Choice, for better or for worse, was offered in this capacity. *Time did not allow the selection of responses by statistical means.* A survey of the records obtained by the writer over a period of several years was utilized to select, for every given card, fifteen answers occurring with noticeable frequency in the records of well-adjusted individuals and fifteen answers drawn from the records of individuals with various types of psychopathology. Thus an individual's score on the test is assessed in terms of the number of times he spontaneously picks choices which have been drawn from "normal" records and the number of times he picks answers which have been drawn from the psychopathological group.

We have suggested as an appropriate cutting point those cases in which more than 40% of responses are equated with those which have been given by various types of disturbed individuals.

It is highly probable that the least valuable aspect of the test is its amenability to machine scoring. As the examiner himself becomes more immersed in the whole principle underlying the projective techniques, he becomes able to utilize at its face value the meaning and significance of any answer or constellation of answers.

To illustrate this, the 30 answers to Rorschach's well-known Card II are listed here:

A

A bug somebody stepped on
Nothing at all
Two scottie dogs
Little faces on the sides
A bloody spinal column
A white top
A bursting bomb
Two elephants
Two clowns
Red and black ink

B

An animal skin
Two bears rubbing noses
Faces of Indians on the side

Blood
Nothing at all
A white lamp
An exploding firecracker
A red butterfly
Two people playing pat-a-cake
Red and black splotches

C

Two witches
Black and red paint
Bears' heads
An empty hole
Faces carved in stone
Lungs and blood
A white sting ray
A little temple in the center
Nothing at all
An erupting volcano

Let us look at three very different choices made by individuals whom we will call A, B, and C. These choices are as follows:

A bursting bomb
Red and black ink
Blood
Black and red paint
An empty hole
Lungs and blood
An erupting volcano

B's choices run:

Nothing at all
Two bears rubbing noses
Two witches

C's choices run:

Two clowns
Two bears rubbing noses
Two people playing pat-a-cake
Two witches
A red butterfly

Individual A was tested by four other psychological techniques, including the full Rorschach, a drawing of the human figures, an analysis of the handwriting, and the Bellevue-Wechsler. A full study of this material indicated an acute psychotic episode. He was diagnosed both through the test battery and by psychiatric interview as an acute schizophrenia, paranoid type. Individual B, on detailed testing, showed initial color shock on the full Rorschach and some neurotic anxiety which, however, was in no way incapacitating. Individual C was a "normal" worker in the clinic with superior scores on the Bellevue-Wechsler and an all-round personality rating on detailed psychological testing of "excellent."

Due, Wright, and Wright, in Part III, Sections VI and VII, have given ample evidence of the extent to which the Multiple Choice Test can be used for differential diagnosis.

The Stress-Tolerance Test (2) is also somewhat of a hybrid procedure utilizing five of Rorschach's original blots, 10 pictures similar to those of Murray's Thematic Apperception Test, and five of the Harrower Alternate Series of Inkblots (3). Also presented as a group test, the blots and pictures are again on slides and the responses of the individual recorded in writing.

Briefly stated, the procedure involves presentation of five of the Rorschach (or Harrower) blots, followed by the ten content pictures which in this instance were rather lurid battle scenes, although highly abstract and symbolic in quality, and as a third stage, the presentation of the Harrower (or Rorschach) blots. The instructions here are for the subject to describe what each inkblot looks like to him and to describe what he sees in the ten pictures which have meaningful content.

In this instance, scoring of the text depends on two different yardsticks: a comparison of the performance in the second inkblot series with the first, and the type of description given to the meaningful pictures. In regard to the first criterion, a poor performance, or one which clearly reflects a temporary state of acute anxiety, would be shown by the individual who, while able to give an answer to each of the five inkblots presented in the initial series, *would, after having experienced the trauma of the intervening war pictures, fail on two, three, four, or even five of the (equated) inkblots which followed.* Further evidence of disturbance was found in five types of answers to the meaningful pictures, which we epitomized as follows:

1. *Failure*
The subject is unable to give any description of the picture presented.

2. *Evasion*

a) Instead of a description some general remark is made as; for example, "Painting," "A war poster," "Good imagination," "A good painting" and the like.

b) The individual would resort to cynicism rather than description; for example, "What a touching scene!" "What a beautiful scene!" "What —no sword?"

c) Minute attention would be given to small details with a complete disregard for the meaning of the picture as a whole; for example, "Parts of a wheel of a plane," "An ax near the ground," "A spot on the man's chest near the heart," "Three spots on the top of the photo," "Enormous teeth and eyes."

3. *Universal or monosyllabic descriptions*

A single word was made to carry the full content of the picture. For example, "Crash," "Dying," "War," "Fire," "Fear."

4. *Personalization*

The individual instead of describing the abstract scene introduced his own personal memories; for example, "This is my co-pilot lying dead," "Reminds me of my own fear," "This might have been me," "Thinking of my brother," "One of my nightmares," "My dreams," "Brings to mind friends who were killed."

5. *Overt expressions of feeling*

For example, "Oh my God I can't stand such pictures," "I hate to think how much of this I have caused."

Answers of the above type were found with significant frequency in the records of patients but did not characterize the records of the control subjects.

A description of the three group techniques having been given, let us now turn to a survey of their various uses in different fields.

THE USE OF GROUP TECHNIQUES IN INDUSTRY

The following quotation from Steiner may serve as an introduction to this section:

"During the last 10 years, industry has become increasingly interested in psychological testing. Though countless opinions, both pro and con, have been expressed concerning the value of testing programs, those experimenting with tests have considered results helpful in supplementing information derived from the interview, the application blank, and other sources. For the most part, industrial testing programs have included personality tests of the questionnaire type, possibly because they are easily administered, quickly scored, and require little specialized training for interpretation. At this time, however, when personnel workers are becoming aware of the shortcomings of most personality tests of the questionnaire type, when periodicals are lauding results obtained by the use of the Rorschach method, and when more psychologists are receiving Rorschach training, occupational investigations utilizing this projective technique comparable in number to those in the clinical field will undoubtedly be forthcoming." (4)

As representative of work in this field, the work of Steiner (5) after a four-year period of experimentation and investigation in the General Electric Company, and that of Cox (6) in Canada will be presented. Steiner's most recent findings, based on an investigation of 920 Group Rorschach records, allow for some interesting comparisons to be made between the different occupational groups which Steiner tested. Contrasting engineers, clerical personnel, advertising copywriters, and commercial artists, she draws the following conclusions from her very adequate sample:

Engineers

"The group records show a high W per cent, emphasizing the more abstract forms of thinking and indicating good synthetic ability. There is also evidenced good analytic ability, and in some instances concern with the more routing features of the task. In general, human movement responses are few, although with the more recent graduates, a greater incidence of M responses has been found. The F per cent is high, though normal, indicating good refined control. Although there are few color answers, the FC to CF ratio is in favor of the form-color type of response, as is found in the college age group of subjects previously investigated."

Clerical Personnel

"The records of the clerical personnel show a low W per cent, a high D and d, and dd plus S. There is a decrease (as compared to the other groups) in the use of human movement responses. FM responses are twice as frequently given as are the M's. Control is high but normal, and there is good emotional responsiveness, FC being equal to CF."

Advertising Copywriters

"Copywriters show an emphasis on the abstract and an average concern with the practical. The most striking characteristic of this group is the high incidence of M's. The originality of the responses, the high productivity, the sensitivity, the tendency towards introspection, and the considerable tension are other features which differentiate this group. The F per cent is lower for this group than for all other occupational groups. There is average responsiveness to the environment."

Commercial Artists

"The outstanding features in the records of the commercial artists are: the great number of responses, many of them original; an emphasis on the W (though not an over-emphasis, as found by other investigators); an average concern with large details, but an over-emphasis on rare details. The F per cent is high but normal; the M's outnumber the FM's; Fc and c responses are plentiful, while—and this is an important deviation from the other groups—CF responses are twice as frequently given as are FC's."

TABLE I

FOLLOW-UP STUDY AFTER ONE YEAR ON JOB: GROUP RORSCHACH

PERSONALITY RATING	NUMBER	SATISFACTORY ADJUSTMENT TO WORK	POOR ADJUSTMENT TO WORK
Excellent Above Average Average	109	97% (106)	3% (3)
Poor	35	29% (10)	71% (25)

Tetrachoric coefficient of correlation .93

Steiner's general conclusions in regard to industrial personnel are summarized as follows:

"A general overall comparison of industrial personnel with non-industrial personnel leads to the conclusion that the former show a strikingly higher level of tension."

In the opinion of the present writer, *such studies emphasize the most valuable use of the Group Rorschach technique.* Where group characteristics are to be elicited, where a minimum disruption in a program is important, and where sufficiently large numbers must be handled in order to give significance to the results, group presentation becomes almost a necessity!

Another project with the group test, also developed by Steiner has been the utilization of the alternative set of blots (4). In this study, changes were revealed in the records of previously disturbed workers who had had time to make satisfactory work adjustments. The subjects in this instance were returning veterans.

Steiner's earlier published findings also deserve comment at this point (4). Group records obtained from 144 clerical subjects and follow-up investigations a year later provide evidence for the type of predictive hypothesis which are possible through the group procedure. On the basis of group records with both the Rorschach and Harrower blots, these subjects were assigned an overall personality rating ranging from excellent to poor. Table I exemplifies the findings in this instance. The tetrachoric coefficient of correlation, not published by Steiner, is .93.

Steiner has also utilized the Multiple Choice Test in the industrial situation with similar kinds of predictive reports and follow-up studies a year later to determine the degree of adjustment. Her findings in this instance are epitomized in Table II. She finds the tendency of a Multiple Choice Test score with less than 50% poor answers to be associated with satisfactory adjustment to work, and a

TABLE II

FOLLOW-UP STUDY AFTER ONE YEAR ON JOB: MULTIPLE CHOICE TEST

PERCENTAGE OF POOR RESPONSES	NUMBER	SATISFACTORY ADJUSTMENT	POOR ADJUSTMENT
Less than 50% poor responses	201	95% (191)	5% (10)
50% or more than 50% poor responses	29	34% (10)	66% (19)

Tetrachoric coefficient of correlation .89

Multiple Choice Test of more than 50% poor responses to be associated with poor adjustment to work. The tetrachoric coefficient of correlation in this instance is $+.89$.

In a paper (6) entitled "The Use of the Harrower Multiple Choice Rorschach in a Selection of Sales Personnel for a Department Store," K. A. Cox writes:

"With the authorization of the management, the personnel department of a large store elicited the services of the author as psychological consultant to carry out a research project to determine what psychological tests or questionnaires could be used to better select salespersons for retail merchandising.

"In setting up the program, sessions were held with the two department managers who had volunteered the use of the staff of their departments in the necessary experimentation. As a result of these interviews, the following tests were selected: (1) Otis Quick-Scoring Mental Ability Test, (2) Harrower Multiple-Choice Rorschach Test, (3) Benge Interest Analysis for Salespersons, (4) Cox Personality Questionnaire.

"The two department managers rated their staff on the basis of sales records as follows: Group A, the upper 25%; Group B, the middle 50%; Group C, the lower 25%.

"Psychological tests were given by members of the Employment Division of the Personnel Department to small groups of sales personnel. These groups were tested in the first period of the morning and in small enough numbers so as not to incapacitate departments. The tests took approximately one and a half hours of the examinees' time, and caused considerable interest. Department managers reported no unfavorable reactions; the Personnel Department staff corroborated this observation.

"The test results were studied and the findings on Group A compared with those of Group C. The results were as follows: the Otis Quick-Scoring Mental Ability Test, with a correlation of .27, *did not differentiate* the A from the C groupings in any department. Some of the A group had a mental age of a little over 11 years, and some of the C group had the mentality of university graduates. Thus general intelligence, as measured by the above, was not a differentiating factor.

"The Benge Interest Analysis for Salespersons, with a correlation of .26, *did not differentiate,* nor did the Cox Questionnaire. Both these questionnaires have proved valuable elsewhere, but in this situation did not give significant results.

"The Harrower Multiple Choice Test gave good results. A number of specific points of discrimination were discovered on item analysis of the Multiple Choice blanks. Eleven of the Multiple Choice responses were discovered which selected the C group from the A group and were thus considered indicators of poorer sales persons. At the same time, nine responses were discovered that selected the A group from the C group. The 11 responses characteristic of the C group were considered negative; those characteristic of the A group, positive.*

"The tests were then rescored, with these results: All those in one department of 36 persons with an A rating, with the exception of one individual, received a positive score. All those in the C group, with the exception of four persons, received a negative score.

"In another department of 72 persons, the results were even better. All those with A ratings received a positive score, whereas only one with a C rating received a positive score. The tetrachoric coefficient of correlation obtained in these instances would be .51 for the first group and .81 for the second."

Cox makes the comment that the coefficient of correlation, .81, is

---

* "The procedure established for making the item analysis of the responses of the A and C groupings was as follows: The responses for each inkblot were classified into groupings using the key number system set out on page 253 to 259 of Harrower and Steiner's book *Large Scale Rorschach Techniques.* Thus there was the possibility of as many as ten categories per inkblot. With this classification made, the A groupings were compared to the C groupings to discover any points of significant difference. To test the significance between the two groupings a method, as yet unpublished, was proposed by Dr. Robert W. B. Jackson which required the squaring and the summing of the classified responses of each person in the two groupings. Means and differences of means were calculated and from these a correlation coefficient could be computed as well as a 'Chi Square.' The 5% and 1% points for the distribution of F could be determined by Snedecor's tables, the n1 degrees of freedom being one and the n2 degrees of freedom being the number of cases compared less unity. Wherever the grouping being compared fell within the 5% category, significance was assumed and a positive or a negative value assigned to the grouping, the signs being determined by whether the mean of the A grouping was greater than the mean of the C grouping and vice versa. If the mean of the A grouping was greater, a positive value was given; and if the mean of the C grouping was greater, a negative value was given. No effort was made to weigh the scores other than positive or negative."

as high as anything yet recorded in the literature of aptitude testing in industry. He summarized his findings as follows:

"It is our belief that the Harrower Multiple Choice Test could be used industrially if criteria were established which would divide employees into the high rating and low rating groups, against which an item analysis could be carried out to discover the items which differentiate. When these items are discovered, one can then build up personality pictures based on the responses as to what type of personalities the high-raters and low-raters possess. Such data should be obtained in terms of local situations, as even within another branch of the same company such test items may not differentiate, since it has been found that tests and questionnaires may work very well in one branch and will not work in another. *This leads one to believe that tests must be set up in terms of a specific branch of the company, a phenomenon which warrants further investigation by those trained in social psychology and familiar with the industrial setting.*"

As will be discussed in another section (page 261), some of the discrepancy in the findings of investigators who have used the Multiple Choice in its original form may be related to this factor. Lawshe and Forster (7) have called attention to the fact that significant sex differences in score distribution and item selection reveal the need for different male and female scoring keys!

The use of the projective techniques in industry is quite clearly only in its infancy. The studies by Steiner and Cox are undoubtedly the forerunners of many and expensive investigations. The challenge which industry offers is enormous. Some of the areas of much needed research have been highlighted by Williams (8) in the following statement:

"Personalities are more complicated than materials and products, more intricate than the most complex machine ever constructed. To discover how that complicated personality, with its delicate interplay of intellectual and emotional factors will react to a given job situation with its unique strains and stresses requires much serious research.

"Probably the most successful attack on the problem would be through a cooperative research project financed by a number of industries with the research being undertaken by the staff of some university interested in industrial research. Through such cooperation, a comprehensive job of research could be accomplished which would benefit many industries and would investigate all aspects of the problem from the angles of both job and worker. Such research would embrace (1) the requirements of the job itself, (2) the stresses and strains peculiar to the job, (3) the qualifications needed by the worker to meet the requirement of the job, to withstand its unique stresses and strains, (4) the satisfactions which the job situation could offer to the worker, (5) the satisfactions which the worker would need to meet his own problems adequately. The results of such research applied to selection and hiring would benefit industries vastly by bringing the right people with the right attitude into the right job."

The Use of Group Techniques in the Hospital or Clinical Setting

The average hospital or clinical setting affords fewer opportunities for group administration of projective techniques than does, for example, the industrial or educational field. Nonetheless, it has

TABLE III

MEAN SCORES ON MULTIPLE CHOICE RORSCHACH FOR DIFFERENT TYPES OF SUBJECTS

TYPE OF SUBJECT	NUMBER CASES	NUMBER PATHOLOGICAL RESPONSES MEAN SCORES
1. Extramural controls	1156	2.5
2. Paranoid behavior reactions	307	3.1
3. Patients without psychosis	386	3.6
4. Organic behavior reactions	450	3.8
5. Affective behavior reactions	264	4.0
6. Constitutional behavior reactions	86	4.2
7. Schizophrenic behavior reactions	641	5.8

seemed pertinent here to include the results of large scale investigations, particularly that of Wittman (9), for while in this instance the patients were tested individually, the number of her subjects, which were over 4,000, renders her results highly significant.

Wittman's study is based on 3,150 psychotic patients, 883 attendants, 172 professional adults, and 100 teen-age girl scouts. A brief summary of her findings is given in Table III.

A more detailed analysis, with a breakdown for each sub-group, is given in Table IV.

Discussing Table III, Wittman says:

"The schizophrenic patients have the poorest showing and hence rank at the bottom of the list. Then come the constitutional and affective behavior reactions, followed by the organic and the patients without psychosis, the paranoid, and the extramural subjects in that order. Certainly the most significant finding is the position of one of the psychotic groups, the paranoid, ranking in one of the top positions and superior to the group of patients diagnosed as those without psychosis. Another important finding is the definitely poor level of the schizophrenic group.

We have found these extremely different types of reactions for the schizo-phrenic and paranoid groups to be of definite value in diagnostic aid."

TABLE IV

PERCENTAGE OF SUBJECTS IN EACH SUB-GROUP WITH PATHOLOGICALLY
SIGNIFICANT SCORES

	NUMBER OF CASES	PER CENT PATHOLOGICALLY SIGNIFICANT
Schizophrenic behavior reactions:		
Hebephrenia	111	91.5
Simple	63	84.0
Catatonic	136	71.5
Undetermined	331	65.3
Paranoid behavior reactions:		
Paranoid (dementia praecox)	197	34.1
Paranoid state	110	31.3
Affective behavior reactions:		
Manic	112	46.9
Depressive	98	56.3
Mixed	54	73.7
Organic behavior reactions:		
Syphilitic meningo encephalitic	193	55.6
Senile and cerebral arteriosclerotics	143	29.2
Organic brain diseases	78	46.7
Epileptics	36	71.9
Primary constitutional behavior reactions:		
Feebleminded	24	81.9
Psychopathic personalities	62	54.0
Patients classified without psychosis:		
Psychoneurotics	217	58.9
Adult Maladjustments	57	61.3
Chronic alcoholics	72	26.6
Extramural controls:		
Hospital attendants	884	27.1
High school girl scouts	100	25.0
Professional adults	172	16.6

Concerning Table IV, Wittman writes:

"The hebephrenic praecox do by far the poorest of any of the groups, with 91.5 per cent answers of pathological significance. The simple praecox also do poorly as a group. The catatonic and undetermined types have relatively poor scores, although not so poor as the feebleminded cases that are classified in the group of constitutional behavior reactions . . . these rather inconclusive findings for the catatonic and undetermined types are possibly merely a reflection of the lack of homogeneity among the cases so classified, resulting from the indefiniteness and looseness of these diagnostic concepts. The so-called paranoid schizophrenics stand out from the other schizophrenics in dramatic fashion."

Wittman's discussion and conclusions in relation to this large study are perhaps the most thoughtful contribution to the whole problem of what it is that actually is measured by the Multiple Choice Test. Her suggestion is that the test measures "a type of inner-adjustment which might be labeled personality integration." Her suggestions are given here in full:

"There are differences shown on the Multiple Choice Test* between psychotic and non-psychotic subjects, but even more between certain psychotic types. This suggests that the scale does measure some psychological factor or component. However, since there are greater differences between psychotic types than the difference between psychotic and 'normal' non-institutionalized controls, the primary factor differentiated by the scale is not the presence or absence of psychopathology. Analysis of the data does give evidence, however, that the scale may be a valid instrument for measuring type rather than degree of adjustment. Those patients with a passive or regressive type of adjustment, extreme enough to be considered pathological, do very poorly. On the other hand, those subjects making psychologically a compensatory type of adjustment, are not differentiated from the 'normal' or non-psychotic subject on the basis of the scale results. Observation of the present levels of adjustment of both intra and extramural groups and study of social service histories of the intramural groups has suggested that this type of inner-adjustment evaluated by the Multiple Choice Test is something that might be labeled 'personality integration.'

"The term personality integration, as we use it, implies an intrapersonal harmony of those components making up the personality as it affects the inner adjustments of the individual; that is, the degree to which the individual accepts and relates together his motivations, interests, attitudes, and all the other components making up the concept of personality. With this understanding of the term we would say that the typical paranoid patient has a good personality integration since his lack of adjustment is not within himself but between his well integrated self and other individuals. The schizophrenic, on the other hand, is poorly integrated since his conflict is not between himself and others but rather between the various components of his own personality. These explanations fit into the concept of schizophrenic behavior reaction as a regressive mechanism and the paranoid as a compensatory type of reaction.

---

* Wittman has referred to the Multiple Choice Test in her article as the "Harrower-Erickson Rorschach." To avoid confusion, however, we have substituted "Multiple Choice Test" in her quotations.

"We empirically interpret the Multiple Choice Test findings to indicate the degree of personality for the following reasons:

"1. Degree of personality integration is the most significant trait that differentiates those schizophrenic groups that do very poorly on the Multiple Choice Test from the other groups.

"2. Dissociation and lack of contact with reality are also factors affecting personality integration, and these factors also differentiate the groups at either extreme of test results.

"3. A negative argument to thinking of the Multiple Choice Test results as a measure of emotional adjustment or stability is obtained from the data for the cases diagnosed psychoneurotic or adult maladjustment. Certainly these are very poorly adjusted emotionally as a group, so poorly in fact, that they have become inmates of a state hospital. However, the scale findings do not classify the majority of cases as poor. Although emotional stability for psychoneurotic and maladjustment cases would be expected to be poor, their test results are variable.

"4. If we postulate differences in type as well as differences in degree of personality integration, this will explain the extreme differences in test results found among the psychoneurotic and the psychopathic groups.

"It is possible that certain psychoneurotic and psychopathic behavior reactions may be best understood as active compensatory reactions while others are of a passive, regressive nature. A preliminary study of the psychoneurotic and psychopathic cases at either extreme as far as their Multiple Choice Test results are concerned, appears to support this hypothesis. That is, those individuals with good scores present a type of behavior reaction that is compensatory, while those with poor scores show a regressive type of behavior. It would seem that the neurotic or psychopathic patient whose behavior reaction is mediated by a type of compensation is unable to adjust with his external environment; he projects conflicts out onto other people or onto the mores of the group, but he does not experience inner conflict. In other words, he does not lack personality integration although it is not a 'normal' type of integration but a compensating type. He has integrated his drives and their underlying motivations to his own satisfaction but not in a manner conducive to adjustment or conformity with the group.

"The psychoneurotics and psychopaths who have definitely poor Multiple Choice Test scores seem in general to lack personality integration. They are not able to coordinate their drives and methods of expressing these drives and the resultant conflict within themselves may produce a type of maladaptive behavior of either a neurotic or psychopathic type. Instead of rationalizing their own conflicts and projecting them outward upon others in a compensatory way, they develop a passive and regressive type of behavior reaction.

"Thus it may be possible to differentiate the psychoneurotic or psychotic individual whose difficulties in adjusting are due to inner conflicts and a lack of personality integration resulting in asocial, passive and avoiding reactions from those whose behavior reactions are associated with a compensatory, defensive mechanism that expresses itself outwardly in an active, anti-social way.

"5. If the Multiple Choice Rorschach can be considered a projective technique, then we might expect that the individual with a regressive type of behavior reaction, who is poorly integrated and out of touch with reality, would be unable to see the well-organized, good form responses to the Rorschach cards. On the other hand, the compensatingly well integrated person, both being in contact with reality and without dissociation, picks out a proportion of movement and good form responses and popular responses that yield a satisfactory score on the Multiple Choice Test."*

A second published study on the Multiple Choice Test done in conjunction with members of the Department of Student Health at a university clinic (10) is included because of the light which it throws on several factors. The 308 entering students at a university summer school were examined as part of the routine medical examination by the Multiple Choice Test. Five or more *poor answers*, when appearing as first choices, were considered the criterion for screening.

Using this cutting point, 79 students, or 26% of the total group, fell into this category. These 79 students were called in for a psychiatric interview and during this interview the Multiple Choice Test was repeated.

As a result of the repetition, a very clear distinction was found between persons who continued to give poor answers and those whose records improved on the second presentation. The duplication of a poor score was shown to correlate highly with a diagnosis based on the psychiatric interview. Of the 22 individuals who repeated a poor score, 21 (or 95%) were rated as having some significant psychopathology by a psychiatrist. These 21 were taken for treatment during the course of the semester. Psychiatric diagnoses are listed below:

Incipient schizophrenia	3
Anxiety tension state	5
Narcissistic regression pattern	1
Adolescent reaction	3
Psychopathic personality, schizoid	1
Psychopathic personality, paranoid	2
Menopausal syndrome	1
Compulsive obsessive neurosis	1
Diagnosis deferred	3

* Reprinted by permission from: The Use of the Multiple Choice Rorschach as a differential diagnostic tool. *J. Clin. Psychol., 1*:281-287, 1945.

Mentally dull 1

Total 21
Normal 1

Fifty-eight students improved on the repeat test. Of these, 39 (or 67%) were considered normal on psychiatric interview. Thirty-three per cent, however, were diagnosed as having some psycho-pathology.

The screening out of these individuals at the beginning of the semester was felt by the psychiatric staff to have been ample justifica-tion for the experimental study in that difficulties were caught early in the session and systematic therapy initiated.

In addition to this practical contribution, the program raised some questions of theoretical interest.

1. "False positives" were found to occur in individuals who had recently experienced serious physical illness or, let us say, a some-what legitimate preoccupation with the body, giving rise to frequent anatomical answers, was found to result from recent invalidism.

2. The menstrual period brought unsuspected and challenging findings. Taken at a different time of the month, many anatomical answers disappeared from these records.

3. What might be called "situational anxiety," that is, the fear that the medical examination per se might disqualify them for some reason, was found to be reflected in the initial records but was absent in the repeat performances.

The most important findings of this study are, clearly, that it is possible in situations where time and psychiatric help is limited to isolate persons with serious psychological disturbances in order that their problems may be handled as efficaciously as possible and with-out undue delay.

The need to repeat the Multiple Choice Test is not only of prac-tical importance but it raises the whole issue of whether or not the findings of any projective technique are significant if they occur at an isolated instance in time. It is highly significant that Szondi, whose test is one of rapid administration and scoring, has insisted that it is the pattern of ten-test-performances which can be considered diag-nostic whereas *a single presentation* may be highly misleading. Largely because of the cumbersomeness of the original Rorschach test, it has seemed to this writer, the assumption has grown up that the person-ality picture of an individual, John Doe, on January 1, 1949, is for better or for worse the picture of John Doe into eternity. Longitudinal studies rather than cross sectional studies are, however, possible with such an instrument as the Multiple Choice Test and may, in the last analysis, prove to be its particular contribution to the study of personality.

A discussion of the third group technique mentioned in this chapter may be pertinent at this point. The Stress Tolerance Test (2). which was conducted largely in hospitals, reflects an interesting tie-up with the foregoing discussion since this test is based on the assumption that an immediate dramatic and anxiety-producing situation, if it is sufficiently disturbing to the individual, will result in changed responses in the Rorschach record.

The following tables represent the extent to which the anxiety-producing war pictures evoked responses on the second presentation of the inkblots which reflected a personality disturbance.

TABLE V

SHOWING CHANGES IN RESPONSES TO INK-BLOTS AFTER EXPOSURE
TO TRAUMATIC WAR PICTURES

| | TOTAL NUMBER | SUBJECTS WHO SHOW AN INCREASE IN NUMBER OF FAILURES IN 2ND RECORD | |
		NUMBER	PER CENT
Controls	31	4	13
Patients	24	15	63
Chi Squared	14.72		

TABLE VI

SHOWING CHANGES IN RESPONSES TO INK-BLOTS AFTER EXPOSURE
TO NON-TRAUMATIC PICTURES

| | PATIENTS WHO SHOW AN INCREASE IN NUMBER OF FAILURES IN 2ND RECORD | |
TOTAL NUMBER	NUMBER	PER CENT
28	4	14

TABLE VII

SHOWING CHANGES IN RESPONSES TO INK-BLOTS AFTER EXPOSURE
TO WAR PICTURES—SEVERE VS. MILD

| | TOTAL NUMBER | PATIENTS WHO SHOW AN INCREASE IN NUMBER OF FAILURES IN 2ND RECORD | |
		NUMBER	PER CENT
Severe Cases	8	8	100
Mild Cases	9	2	21

TABLE VIII

EPITOMIZING DIFFERENT PERFORMANCE BETWEEN PATIENTS AND
CONTROLS ON ANSWERS TO WAR PICTURES

	TOTAL NUMBER	SUBJECTS WHO SHOW FAILURE AND/OR PERSONALIZATION IN ANSWERS	
		NUMBER	PER CENT
Controls	31	6	19
Patients	63	46	74
Chi Squared	24.22		

TABLE IX

COMPARISON OF PERFORMANCE OF CONTROL SUBJECTS AND PATIENTS
ON STRESS TOLERANCE TEST

CONTROL SUBJECTS		NUMBER	FIVE OR MORE FAILURES (PER CENT)	MORE THAN NINE FAILURES (PER CENT)
Applicants for service in Merchant Marine		106	3	0
Post-combat Aviators		35	9	0
Pre-combat Aviators		33	6	3
PATIENTS				
"Severe"	Officers	37	32	5
"Severe"	Enlisted men	46	43	20
"Severe and moderate improving"	Officers	17	6	0
"Severe and moderate improving"	Enlisted men	23	26	9
"Mild and mild improving"	Officers	22	5	0
"Mild and mild improving"	Enlisted men	20	30	5

TABLE X

COMPARISON OF PERFORMANCE OF CONTROL SUBJECTS AND PATIENTS:
TYPES OF ANSWERS GIVEN

	107 PATIENTS FROM REDISTRIBUTION CENTER		107 APPLICANTS FOR MERCHANT MARINE	
	NUMBER PERSONS	NUMBER INSTANCES	NUMBER PERSONS	NUMBER INSTANCES
Failures in first five ink-blots	43	84	16	23
Failures in second five ink-blots	55	123	16	27
Failures in War Pictures	40	85	13	14
Evasion	24	52	1	1
Details	5	12	0	0
Facetious Remarks	9	10	0	0
Universal Answers	41	223	26	54
Perseveration	9	29	0	0
Personalization	18	44	1	2
Feelings Expressed	27	51	1	1

A study by Chalke (11) shows a further use of the Stress Tolerance Test in hospital situations. The subjects used in this experiment were 23 officer candidates undergoing appraisal at an officers' selection camp, six soldiers hospitalized for psychosis, 18 soldiers under care in a neurosis treatment center.

"The psychoneurotic group was divided into two sub-groups on the basis of the history. The first group included men who had not been in action or whose neurotic breakdown did not appear from the history to be causally related to warfare. The second group were those who dated their symptoms from action or whose chief symptoms suggested an etiological relationship to battle."

The results in this study would indicate that the test was specifically oriented towards the detection of battle neurosis, nine of the ten "battle cases" showing a disturbance on this test. In contrast to this, only four per cent of the group of officer candidates and zero per cent of the psychotics showed a disturbance. The author suggests the following use of the test in other situations:

"In abnormal psychology the test has many possibilities. Patients suffering from similar psychiatric syndromes might be tested, by substituting various types of disturbing stimuli, to determine the presence of constant stressful situations characteristic of the syndrome. Moreover, with expert Rorschach interpretation the comparison of records would determine the pattern of the reaction to stress characteristic of the particular personality."

Chalke's conclusions state:

"Validation experiments have been carried out with the Harrower Stress Tolerance Test which indicate its value in screening persons susceptible to specific disturbing situations. Differentiation not only between 'normals' and 'neurotics' is noted, but also between cases presenting similar clinical pictures but of apparently different etiology."

Use of the Group Rorschach in medical research may be exemplified by the work of Brozek, Guetzkow, and Ancel Keys (12). In the *Study of Personality of Normal Young Men Maintained on Restricted Intakes of Vitamins of the B Complex,* the Group Rorschach Records along with the Minnesota Multiphasic Inventory, self ratings, man-to-man ratings, and the Cattell Miniature Situations Test were utilized. The procedure employed and the results obtained were as follows:

"The Rorschach test was given three times: at the beginning of the partial restriction, at its end, and at the termination of the acute deficiency. The procedure for group testing was employed; instead of using photographic reproductions, however, actual Rorschach cards were used. The responses were recorded by the subjects on the group Rorschach blanks which later were sent for analysis to M. R. Harrower. The records were scored according to the system utilized by Klopfer and the usual calculations were made in full for each record. Personality descriptions of the individuals based on the three successive records then were written. In the *Results,* passages taken from these original descriptions are presented. At no time did Dr. Harrower have personal contact with the subjects, nor was their nutritional status known to her when the original reports were made.

Results

"Work has been done on the effect of repeating the Rorschach which enables us to distinguish the effects due to repetition as contrasted with changes due to other causes. For example, repetition produces almost invariably an increase in the total number of responses. Therefore, it is not surprising to find that all eight subjects, regardless of their nutritional status, had a larger number of responses in their second record. Taking into account the uniform changes, we may ask whether successive records indicate alterations in personality. The records will be discussed in pairs with the men grouped according to their nutritional status.

"Jo and N (supplemented-supplemented): The subjects who were supplemented during both the partial restriction and the acute deficiency had different personality structures, as reflected in the initial Rorschach. Jo's record was relatively good; N's record, poor. The three tests of N showed no essential change. In this case the personality pattern did not improve during the six months period of relatively good nutrition. The second record of Jo, on the other hand, improved slightly, the original tenseness and lack of spontaneity being lessened. In the third record, a still more positive attitude towards the environment appeared.

"Ja and S (supplemented-deficient): In both Ja and S the second record showed an improvement, while the third record of subject S indicated that the 22 days of adverse nutritional conditions did not introduce any significant change in the Rorschach responses. The third record of subject Ja could not be obtained.

"Wa and T (restricted-supplemented): These men presented very different personality patterns at the start. Wa's first record was not a very satisfactory one; the record of T was better. In the case of Wa, a negative change occurred in the period of partial restriction; in the second record, *he was driving himself with a tight rein, being more punctilious, and paying greater attention to detail, showing more anxiety and less spontaneity.* The third record showed some relaxation of the tension. The same does not hold for subject T, whose three records were similar one to another.

"Wi and G (restricted-deficient): In the case of Wi, there was a change between the initial and final records. The third record indicated *considerably more constriction, as if the individual was having to watch his step more carefully or was combatting some difficult situation.* This tendency was already indicated in Wi's second record. The second and third records of G also reflected negative change, conscious control having been slightly increased. In G's records II and III there appeared an *increased preoccupation with bodily sensations.*

"The Rorschach test provided evidence of slight changes, paralleling the slight increases in the resting level of pyruvic acid which was taken as a specific indication of borderline dietary deficiency in the group on low vitamin intake. The fact that the Rorschach analyses were made 'blindly,' without knowledge of the subjects' nutritional status increases confidence in the results. It is methodologically important that these slight changes did not have a counterpart in the data obtained by the questionnaire-type procedures, i.e., the Multiphasic and the self-ratings which demand awareness of the changes."

Summary

"1. Various aspects of personality were studied in eight normal young men maintained 161 days on a partially restricted intake of B-complex vitamins, which was followed by 23 days of acute deficiency, and 10 days of thiamine supplementation.

"2. Self ratings and man-to-man ratings gave no evidence of change in the status of well being and adjustment during the partial restriction, but indicate consistent and striking deterioration during the acute deficiency. Supplementation of the diet by thiamine alone produced rapid recovery.

"3. The Minnesota Multiphasic Personality Inventory also gave no evidence of change in the partial restriction. During the acute deficiency significant changes were obtained in the scores on the three psychoneurotic scales—depression, hysteria, and hypochondriasis.

"4. In the Rorschach test records made at the end of the partial restriction, slight deteriorative changes were indicated in three out of the four experimental subjects. These changes increased in magnitude in the pair of subjects placed subsequently on the acutely deficient diet. The nature of this deterioration was loss of spontaneity, with an increase in tension. The Rorschach findings suggested that individuals with 'better' initial personality were better able to resist the dietary stress.

"5. Cattell's Cursive Miniature Situations Test during the partial restriction indicated a very slight and statistically *not* significant increase in the number of lines erroneously crossed ('emotionality' score). During the acute deficiency, there were evidences of further increased 'emotionality' and 'timidity.' On the other hand, those indices which have distinguished psychotics from normals showed no change in our deficient subjects.

"6. The personality changes were among the earliest symptoms of the experimentally produced borderline and acute deficiencies."

THE USE OF GROUP TECHNIQUES IN EDUCATION

Our original studies with the group test, although embarked on primarily with a view to establishing procedures and norms for a new method, netted us in addition some information in regard to the students who were our subjects when a comparison of their test records, academic performance, and general adjustment in college were obtainable. Utilizing general overall personality ratings of the type subsequently employed by Steiner and Abt and previously used for the individual method by Munroe, the 108 students whom we examined were estimated in terms of a scale including excellent, above-average, average, just below average, poor, and very poor personality resources. Findings have been discussed in Section I, Part I.

Munroe's initial findings at Sarah Lawrence (1, 13), also based on overall personality estimates, achieved approximately the same figures of correspondence between academic failure predicted by personality resources. Her contribution of the inspection technique whereby group Rorschach records can be scored rapidly allows for a much greater degree of uniformity between the findings of different investigators. Munroe's Check List is presented on page 255.

Although in our own large scale studies, we have never used the inspection technique, the writer feels that it is to be recommended in the majority of cases except where the examiner happens to have had an unusual amount of experience with any one type of subject or patient and where he is not intending to make direct comparisons between his own findings and those of others.

In an article entitled *The Application of the Group Rorschach Technique to the Problem of Achievement in College* (14) Montalto has made a very interesting study in relation to achievement in college. Her subjects were 90 women students in various colleges and universities in Cincinnati. These students were divided into achievers and non-achievers on the basis of their grade point average for two or three years of college residence. The achievers were those who had maintained an average of 1.5 or better; the non-achievers, those whose average fell below. Montalto studied the Group Rorschach records with a view to "signs of adjustment" which she describes as "a measure of quantitative features of the Rorschach protocol based on the interrelationship of certain factors." Her 14 signs of adjustment,

Number of R..	....
T/R > 60″ < 30″ (+, —) .... Refusal (√)	....
LOCATION	W (+, —, V, B) .... Dd (+) .... S (+) .... Suc (r, 1)	....
CONTENT	P, Com (—) .... O (+, B) .... At, Sex (+) .... Range (+, —)	....
FORM	F% (+, —) .... F (V, B, E)	....
SHADING	Shading Shock (±) (√) .... FK, Fc (+, —) .... c (+) .... C′ (+) .... K, k (+)	....
MOVEMENT	M (+, —, B, r, d) .... FM, FM:M (+, —) .... m (+) .... Total Movement (+, —)	....
COLOR	Color Shock (±) (√) .... FC (—, B) .... CF, CF:FC (+, —) .... C> 1, Cn (+) .... Total Color (+, —)	....
Color: Movement (+, —) .... Total Number of Checks	....

together with the frequency of their occurrence in achievers and non-achievers, is recorded in Table XI.

Two signs were outstanding in distinguishing the groups in that they occurred more frequently in the non-achieving group. The signs were the ratio of W:M, W to M being approximately two to one, and the percentages of responses on the last three color cards, these being between 40% and 60%.

Eliminating some of the signs and scoring the absence of two others as positive resulted in a "pattern of signs by which to make a quantitative attack on the problem of achievement in college through the

TABLE XI

FREQUENCY OF OCCURRENCE OF SIGNS OF ADJUSTMENT IN ACHIEVERS AND NON-ACHIEVERS

SIGNS	SIGN CATEGORY	ACHIEVERS	NON-ACHIEVERS	DIFFERENCE*
		%	%	%
1	M > FM or M = FM	83	80	3
2	M = 3 or more	85	82	3
3	W/M = 2/1 (approx.)	24	43	—19
4	F% = 50% or less	76	66	10
5	F + % = 75% or higher	59	55	4
6	FK + Fc = 2 or more	87	80	7
7	Dd + S = 10% or less	52	55	—3
8	Sum C > Fc + c + C'	35	30	5
9	FC > CF or FC = CF	91	86	5
10	FC = 2 or more	87	89	—2
11	No pure C	74	73	1
12	A% = 50% or less	91	82	9
13	P = 4 or more and 30%	65	68	—3
14	%R on VIII-X 40%-60%	24	41	—17

instrumentality of the Group Rorschach. These signs consist of: $F\% = 50\%$ or less, $FK + Fc = 2$ or more, $A\% = 50\%$ or less; in addition, these signs as 'negative ones,' namely: $W/M = 2/1$, and per cent of response to the last three cards 40% to 60%. These signs, then, would assign to the achiever (women) a personality which has good intellectual control without rigidity, posssesses a sense of tactfulness and social awareness, and is relatively free from stereotyped modes of thinking, but one which does not reveal the best balance between drive and creative capacity nor react in the optimal degree to environmental influences."

Montalto's findings are summarized as follows:

"The study is a purely quantitative one and the data were subjected to analysis using primarily the methods of correlation and partial correlation. On the basis of these results, the following conclusions were reached:

"1. Achievers possess more signs of adjustment than non-achievers.

---

* All differences are plus in favor of the Achievers except those with the minus sign which favor the Non-achievers.

"2. Achievers have a neurotic trend in their personality make-up which seems to be a pertinent factor contributing to their academic success.

"3. A pattern of signs of academic achievement was evolved which correlated highly with grade points when intelligence scores were held constant. This consisted of five signs, three of which are 'positive' and two of which are 'negative' with reference to norms of healthy adjustment.

"4. It is suggested that the method be subjected to further experiment in order to see if the 'pattern' would work with other groups."

The isolation of these two "neurotic" factors in achievement the present writer considers one of the most important contributions in this study.

The achievers "tend to overreach themselves in their intellectual pursuits or to have more nearly an unhealthy amount of drive. This would seem to be comparable with striving for college grades." The achievers show less response to environmental stimuli "which may mean less than average distractibility to external influence and hence more controlled concentration to self-imposed goals such as academic attainment." These might be seen as leading to emotional disturbances.

Thompson (15) administered the group Rorschach test to a beginning psychology class of 128 students, 63% male, 37% female, in an attempt to discover whether the test was a valid predictor of grades. Fifty-two Rorschach factors were considered of interpretative significance and used as a basis for summarizing protocols. Quantified scoring of the test yielded a correlation of .38 with the criterion of semester grades and a correlation of only .04 with a measure of verbal aptitude. She concludes:

". . . The group Rorschach may eventually prove useful as a large scale, practical and objective tool for the measurement of those factors influencing grades which are not purely intelligence factors in the sense that they are capable of measurement by our standard aptitude tests. It will remain to be seen, of course, whether the same items—and undoubtedly, not all of them—will remain valid under other conditions and in other college groups. Cross-validation of the Rorschach factors here isolated should be undertaken on further groups before conclusive diagnostic weighting can be assigned to any of them. . . .

"Several comments, however, appear justified: First, that the group Rorschach can be quantified and still retain diagnostic value—a finding which would corroborate that of Munroe and others. The advantages of quantification and the group method of administration would appear to be not only in the time of administration, one hour for a whole group, but also in the scoring, subjective elements being minimized by adherence to a predetermined set of categories which yielded an objective scoring that any experimenter could apply equally well. . . . In the event that objective scoring and interpretation could prove practical on a large scale, it would also seem probable that the present strict requirements for qualified Rorschach scorers would be lessened somewhat.

"Finally, then, it would appear that the group Rorschach could be used in the prediction of academic success above and beyond the prediction offered by a standard intelligence test, and it is hoped that further research will expand the practical use of the method."

Turning now to the use of the Multiple Choice Test as a means of screening in the educational set-up, mention may be made of two as yet unpublished studies. In collaboration with Walter Watson, Administration Officer, Carl Woodward, Psychiatrist, B. J. Fitch, Technical Assistant, the writer introduced a screening program on an experimental basis with the students at Cooper Union for the Advancement of Science and Art. This screening program included the Multiple Choice Test; drawing of the human figures, man and woman; a story or description of the figures drawn; and analysis of the graphological specimens obtained. The tests were administered by the present writer, scored by Miss Fitch, the work of correlating the findings between the tests and those students who had sought psychiatric aid being done entirely through the Department of Admissions. The following summary of the findings comes from the Admissions Office:

"The psychological tests located a group of 59 students with potential emotional or personality difficulties in a total of 632 students tested. Of this group of 59, *there were 54 who had been previously referred to the school psychiatrist.* The other five were then interviewed. Two of these were felt to need further help. On the other hand, only one student was referred to the psychiatrist, by the customary avenues, who had not been isolated by the psychological tests. Such agreement between test and counseling case finding procedures is definitely encouraging." (16)

There is a research problem involved in this particular project over and above the screening and the equation with the psychiatric findings. This project relates to an attempt to find "certain patterns of response typical of each group,* much as the interest inventories disclose such patterns. We also propose to study the response patterns

* The four groups of students referred to are art students who study by day; art students who study in the evening; engineering students who study by day; engineering students who study in the evening.

of selected deviates with each school, i.e., differences between very able artists as rated by instructors and unimaginative conformists or disorganized personalities. In the Engineering School, we hope to select, from instructor-rated students who have taken the tests, two groups differing in personality characteristics required of those in the engineering profession. We will also study the personality patterns of a group of engineers who equal or exceed their predicted grade averages, based on academic entrance tests compared with those of high predicted grades but who fall low on achievement, it having been felt at the impressionistic or hunch level by the instructors that there are very definitely different personality types involved in each of these groups.

In view of some of the disappointing findings in regard to the Multiple Choice Test when utilized as a screening method for acceptable recruits, the fact that 54 of the 59 students screened out by the tests had already sought psychiatric help or been referred to the psychiatrist is somewhat startling. The writer's suggestion is that this group approximates more closely those subjects who were utilized originally in the construction of the tests, since it would appear that more than we have realized the test must be altered in terms of the characteristics of the group to be screened.

Utilization of a battery of tests, amongst which the Multiple Choice is included, is also the procedure at Keuka College.* Amongst eight students screened out by the Multiple Choice for further consideration of the other test findings is the record of a student whom we shall designate as X. This student had an I. Q. of 119 on the Bellevue-Wechsler. Her performance on the Multiple Choice, however, indicated very obvious emotional difficulties. Quantitatively, 50% of her choices were poor answers, but a consideration of the actual choices is also of interest. On Card I, for instance, she sees twice "an x-ray of the chest" ignoring on all three groups of choices the popular bat. On Card II, there is overemphasis on the explosive type of emotional answer, "an erupting volcano," "an exploding firecracker," and "blood," being selected. On III, the human movement figures are seen, but on IV the choices of "a nasty, dirty mess," "a burnt mass," are highly significant. A very poor F— answer, "the lungs and the chest" is chosen for Card V; "gushing oil" on Card VI and VII

---

* The writer is greatly indebted to Dr. Donald R. Gorham for allowing the utilization of the following material.

reinforce the traumatic picture. "Fire and ice," "a medical picture," "the inside of the mouth," and "storm clouds at sunset" are amongst her choices on the last three cards.

If there is anything at all to the principle of projection, it must be clear that this individual is psychologically disturbed. Regardless of whether or not we speak of answers good or poor, it is clear that this girl finds an affinity with, chooses, endorses, considers acceptable answers those which reflect unstable, violent, and explosive inner emotional dynamics; that the whole area is fraught with guilt ("a nasty, dirty mess") and that she is insecure and anxious ("x-rays of the chest," "fog and mist.") A blind analysis of her TAT by Dr. Magda Arnold gives the additional corroborative evidence:

"This is the record of a seriously disturbed girl on the verge of psychotic incoherence. She has literally been 'shocked into incoherence' by life. Life has been too much for her for a long time; she still feels like a child, ill, lost in a strange land, has always felt 'different,' was able to find security only at home, protected by her mother. She suffers from her inability to cope with the world, and desperately hopes for a helper who will rescue her.

"She is quite sure that she will eventually find security in marriage if only a helper will come. In the meantime, she is afraid of life, for men to her are weak, degenerate, strangers who depend on women for their rescue. It is possible that there may have been a sexual trauma of some kind after adolescence, but that would seem to be the result rather than the cause of her attitude towards men and what they stand for. Her conviction that women have to help men by showing them the true vision might get her into all kinds of scrapes, for she has no feeling of relatedness either to men or to women, and would be quite incapable of judging what the effect of her actions would be on others, except that she recognizes that she is a source of worry, without, however, quite knowing why.

"Unless she can be helped, she might even decide to withdraw altogether, into detachment, so she can be amused at the antics of people instead of frightened, and into a haven of peace where wishes count instead of actions. In this record, religion is used as an escapist instead of a constructive solution, and, therefore, reinforces the danger of psychotic withdrawal.

"The only hopeful feature is the fact that she recognizes she needs help, and in fact is looking for it."

Turning now to the clinical data in regard to this particular girl, one finds the following comments: "She first came to the notice of the counselor as being completely irresponsible. Could not seem to realize college had rules, and could not seem to remember them overnight when told. Began excessive dating * * * changed major * * * confused about requirements in new course. Developed acute psychotic episode * * * paranoid ideas * * * actively hallucinated."

THE USE OF GROUP TECHNIQUES IN THE ARMED FORCES

With the noted exception of the study by Abt (17), to be reported in detail below, it must be stated that the findings by several investigators are frankly disappointing. Wittson, Hunt and Older (18), Jensen and Rotter (19), Winfield (20) and Springer (21) utilized the Multiple Choice Test with various groups. Wittson and Hunt, for example, contrasting "normal" Navy personnel with those who had been discharged for various neuropsychiatric reasons, found that whereas 59% of the dischargees gave more than four poor answers, as many as 44% of the "normal" group fell into this category also. Springer reports that "no reliable differentiation was found between those that were making a good adjustment in the service and those who were chronic offenders to Naval discipline." Winfield, using the test with women in the Marines, concludes that, "The Multiple Choice differentiates something other than it purports to do and that further research and standardization are necessary before the test can be used on a similarly selected sample for the screening of maladjusted individuals." Jensen and Rotter found that 45% of their officers and 36% of the officer candidates had four or more poor responses and naturally concludes the test was unsuitable for these groups.

It is quite clear, therefore, that the Multiple Choice Test in its original form with only ten choices for each card, administered once only under group conditions, could not in any sense be considered a sufficiently reliable diagnostic tool to be of value in military screening. As we shall discuss in a later section, however, these unsatisfactory findings have not led to the discarding of the whole idea but rather have stimulated modifications and refinements in the test itself and have forced certain investigators to think with great clarity of the whole question of underlying emotional disturbances in relation to the successful performance of a task.

Studies with the Rorschach administered under the usual individual conditions on the one hand and utilization of the group form with the results examined by experts on the other hand have both resulted in negative reports if one is to judge by findings of Guilford (22). Guilford states.

"The test was administered experimentally to several hundred students individually according to the prescribed procedure by members of the Rorschach Institute in one of the psychological units. Two methods of group administration were also tried, the Harrower, and our own version. The results were almost entirely negative. From the individual administration of the test, neither the 25 indicators, taken separately or collectively, nor the intuitive prediction of the examiner based upon the data he had from the administration of the tests gave significant indications of validity against the pass-fail criterion. There were two samples, one of nearly 300 and the other of nearly 200. The Harrower Group Administration Form also gave no evidence of being valid for pilot selection."

However, the actual reports (23, 24) from which Guilford takes his material are somewhat more cautious in their conclusions. Referring in particular to an experimental situation in which aviation students were contrasted with patients with diagnoses of severe anxiety, by means of the individual method, the authors state: "Generalizations based on these findings are not warranted since the samples are small and the statistical tests of significance were not applied."

An unpublished study by Glueck, Harrower, and Meta Steiner would support these negative findings, or perhaps one might say, throws light on the problem from a slightly different angle. In this study, no attempt was made to predict success, but the records of some 300 members of the Eighth Air Force which had been taken in England during the war were subsequently analyzed by the writer and Dr. Meta Steiner. The records of 30 aviators who had been decorated and had completed over 30 missions successfully were contrasted with those who had failed to complete more than five missions. No differences on any of the Rorschach findings or significant ratios were discovered. Moreover, amongst this group of highly decorated individuals were records which in the normal course of evaluation would have been termed frankly unstable or psychopathic personalities. Such records occurred with equal frequency in the two groups. Dr. Glueck's comment, made independently, was to the effect that in psychiatric examination of these men, there were amongst the highly successful and decorated group as many psychopathic personalities as there were in the unsuccessful-psychopathic personalities, that is, judged by our peacetime standards. Quite clearly, that which makes a successful pilot is not at present clearly envisaged in Rorschach terms. The too-naive assumption that the well balanced Rorschach personality in normal conditions must be the personality best adapted to an environment of severe strain may be an erroneous and dangerous one. Conversely, our concept that lack of balance within a stable, peacetime framework may again be misleading where environmental conditions are highly abnormal. We may well raise the question whether adjustment to one type of environment and condition of living, in and of itself, predicts adjustment under totally different conditions.

These negative findings have been emphasized for it has seemed to the writer that only by emphasizing what a test cannot do and where it is not relevant can one come to a realistic appraisal of its merits and assets.

That the Group Rorschach was an efficient instrument for one type of psychiatric screening, namely, for Marine Corps recruits can be seen by the excellent article of Abt (17) in which 1,000 subjects were investigated. In this instance, the Group Rorschach Test made up part of a battery which also included the Wilkins Miles Self-Description Inventory and the Kent Direction A Test, together with a personal information sheet. In this study Abt divided the records, after an inspection rating, into three groups classified as okay, suspicious, and bad. Abt checked his overall performance rating against a similar rating performed by another experienced Rorschach worker and obtained a mean square contingency coefficient of .80. He also checked his method against 141 records chosen at random which had been scored in detail and found here a mean square contingency coefficient of .91.

A breakdown of the 30 subjects who were discharged because of neuropsychiatric disabilities by a Recruit Aptitude Board showed that the test battery had already picked 26 or 86.6%. A combination of the Self-Description Inventory plus the Group Rorschach Test had detected 25, or 83.3%. Only four of the 30 subjects were not identified at all.

Abt found that "the most striking characteristic of the group records of the dischargees is the large amount of constriction or rigidity of personality." He feels that this suggests the dischargees have personalities which are too colorless, with mental lives too meagre and emotional responsiveness too poor to enable them to respond to the Rorschach slides in any other way, *i.e.,* than by form-dominated response. In short, there appeared a general impoverishment of personality among the dischargees.

Among the important features of this paper is the fact that the Group Rorschach Test was not expected to carry the full diagnostic load in and of itself. As the Group Test identified 56.6% of all dischargees, in combination with the Self-Descriptive Inventory the diagnostic strength of this combined instrument jumps to 83.3%. One of the fallacies too readily assumed by many enthusiasts is that any one testing technique is all-sufficient. It is the writer's belief that had more Rorschach programs been integrated properly with other types of tests, there would have been fewer negative findings in this field.

Abt's conclusion, therefore, "that the use of the Group Rorschach Test has been shown to identify neuropsychiatric misfits missed by a typical paper and pencil inventory" is justified. It is also his statement that the Group Rorschach Test is practical for use in the psychiatric screening of Marine Corps recruits and leads to the identification of over 86% of those neuropsychiatrically unfit when combined in a test battery with a psychometric test and a paper and pencil inventory.

SUGGESTED MODIFICATIONS IN TEST PROCEDURES

As pointed out previously, a number of investigators were challenged by the discrepancy which appeared in the findings of various authors in regard to the Multiple Choice Test. Different types of alterations of procedure and scoring methods have been suggested here.

The present writer made two major alterations as soon as the Multiple Choice in its original form appeared to be clearly inadequate; one was the introduction of additional responses for each of the ten cards; the other was an attempt to give weighted scores to certain responses (see Part 3, Section VIII). While these modifications are certainly no final solution, nor do they represent the highest degree of refinement of the test, they were unquestionably a step forward over the initial procedure and short list of choices.

A modification of the procedure which has been called "The Rorschach Ranking Test" was initiated by Eysenck (25) and may be described in his own words as follows:

"The Rorschach Ranking Test is a modification of the Harrower Multiple Choice Test. We found that the Multiple Choice Test had too low a reliability to be used as a screening test, and accordingly modified the procedure so as to increase its reliability. This was done by presenting the subjects with nine alternative responses to each inkblot, asking them to rank these in order of applicability, i.e., putting a 1 after the response most like the inkblot, a 2 after the second most likely response, etc., down through a number 9 after the response least like the inkblot. The actual responses used were taken from Harrower's list. Slight verbal modifications were introduced in some cases to suit the wording for English audiences. Four neurotic and five normal responses were offered for each blot, and the number of the position assigned the four neurotic responses by the subject constitute his score for that blot. The best score for each blot is therefore 30 (9 plus 8 plus 7 plus 6), and the worst score is 10 (1 plus 2 plus 3 plus 4). Scores for the ten blots are added, giving a range for the whole task of between 100 neurotic N and 300 normal N. The method of scoring increases the reliability to r = +0.84. This test does not correlate highly with intelligence, r = +0.08 but shows a slight correlation with vocabulary, r = +0.27. The critical level is at the score of 220; 74% of neurotics and 42% of normals score below this level."

In this study, Eysenck then utilized four tests: *Suggestibility, Dark Vision, Ranking Rorschach,* and a *Questionnaire.* He found that:

"While no one test by itself reaches a high level of prediction, a combination of the tests would considerably enhance their discriminative value. In clinical studies we have found that while the dark vision test is particularly discriminative with respect to anxiety states, the Ranking Rorschach test is particularly discriminative with regard to hysterics. Differences in selectivity of this kind may account for the fact that such correlations as we have found between the various tests have usually been rather small. They also argue in favor of the use of several tests in combination. We, therefore, put forward the whole battery as a useful measuring instrument for the general personality trait of neuroticism."

A study with constructive suggestions is that by Malamud and Malamud (26). These authors state that despite the lack of agreement on the findings in regard to the Multiple Choice Test it represents "an important methodological advance in projective testing." Their study "attempts to determine possible shortcomings of this test's scoring system in the light of an item analysis of its individual responses."

Utilizing the records of 488 normals as compared with 215 abnormal subjects, a breakdown of the scores in terms of the number of times any given response category was chosen was performed. The following significant findings were obtained:

"1. Using a critical ratio of 2.00 or over as the criterion, 21 good responses are found to be discriminative in the normal direction, 25 are neutral, and four discriminate in the abnormal direction. Good answers classified in the same category often vary in degree of direction of discrimination from card to card. For example, Response 4 discriminates in the normal direction on Card IV, is neutral on Card VII, and discriminates in the abnormal direction on Card VI."

This is a very interesting finding, and is closely allied to the recent work of Cox, reported above.

"2. Thirty-three poor responses are discriminative in the abnormal direction, 14 are neutral, and three discriminate in the normal direction. Poor answers classified in the same category vary in degree of direction of discrimination from card to card. For example, Response 8 discriminates in the abnormal direction on Card VII, is neutral on Card IV, and discriminates in a normal direction on Card VI.

"All in all, a total of 62 individual responses discriminate between normals and abnormals to the extent of a critical ratio of 2.00 or more. Of these responses 35 discriminate to the extent of a critical ratio of 3.00 or more."

In their discussion, the authors point out that the "appropriateness of assigning uniform weights to categories of responses is seriously questioned, since much depends on the type of response and the card on which it appears. Responses falling in the same category may deserve increased weights on some cards, decreased or even no weights on other cards. This would appear to be consistent with practice in the free Rorschach situation where the same response may vary in significance depending on the properties of the card to which it is given."

The authors feel further that "weighting in the normal as well as the abnormal direction seems desirable." They conclude that "the conditions affecting the choice of different responses vary significantly from one normal or abnormal group to another, a fact that may indicate that the test with a single scoring system cannot be applied universally with the expectation of getting consistently good results."

Challman (27) investigated three different scoring methods in a comparative study of the records of patients in a state hospital and student nurses. A considerable difference in the discriminative power of the same set of responses could be obtained by a change of method. Thus, according to Method I, 66% of the patients and 39% of the nurses were screened out; in Method II 61% of the patients and 31% of the nurses; in Method III, 57% of the patients and 19% of the nurses. Challman considered this last the more effective and makes as his conclusion the following statement: "With the methods of scoring recommended by Harrower for the amplified Multiple Choice Test (not for the present one), and with a critical score of 35, the test appears to have some usefulness as a screening device. The number of false positives would probably be reduced if the test were repeated, and only those scoring over the critical score both times screened out. Also, where it is feasible, using it with a personality inventory, such as Mittelmann* has done, appears to reduce the number of misclassifications."

Lawshe and Forster (7) utilized seven modifications of scoring in an endeavor "to raise the reliability of the test." "Those modifications were aimed at the scoring of only the most discriminative items and the development of separate scoring keys for males and females." The findings are as follows:

"1. The low reliability coefficients obtained from scores of college students on the Multiple Choice Test strongly indicate the unreliability of the standard scoring and reflect the weakness of the test as a screening instrument. However, in cases where a low selection ratio can be used, that is, when the object is to select few individuals from a large number of candidates, assuming validity to the obtained reliability, the test might be effectively used for selection.

"2. Significant sex differences in score distribution and items selection reveal the need for separate male and female scoring keys.

"3. For the restricted population studies, the intelligence factor does not seem to contribute significantly to the variability of the scores on the Multiple Choice test (compare Eysenck).

"4. The reversal of the intended discriminative power in some answers indicates a need for a review of the original classification of items (compare Malamud and Malamud).

"5. The insufficient number of strongly discriminative items in this test does not permit a significant raising of the reliability through the elimination of weak items. The suggestion is advanced that an increase in the number of ink-blots might render the test more useful in individual application."

A number of investigators (Watson, Gorham, and Zuckerman) have suggested the modification of scoring the Multiple Choice 300 items on an IBM scoring sheet. This type of study, however, has been most fully developed by Samuel Kellman† of the Detroit Civil Service Commission, who has combined this technical modification with several other important ones, including the development of what we originally termed the "expanded Multiple Choice Rorschach" (see Part 3, Section III).

---

* The reference to Mittelmann's work is found in: Proceedings of the Military Session, American Society for Research in Psychosomatic Problems. *Psychosomatic Medicine*, 5:4, 36-37, 1943.

† Adult Psychiatric Clinic, Harper Hospital, Detroit: a division of the Michigan Department of Mental Health.

Kellman (28) (29), beginning in 1945, concerned himself with the numerous practical, methodological, and philosophical questions raised by the amplified form of the test. His revisional work proceeded with three objectives in mind:

1. To determine the applicability to the test of the complex, multidimensional Rorschach "systems," such as those of Beck (30), Hertz (31), Klopfer-Kelley-Davidson (32).

2. To devise a method intermediate between such "full-range" treatment and the briefer "key number" system described in this volume.

3. To provide an objective, efficient scheme that would remove from the shoulders of the Rorschachist the great labor of scoring (whether "full-range," intermediate, or brief in nature; and particularly where the first of these is involved).

Historically the last objective was the first one to be tackled (29). An IBM (International Business Machines, Inc.) answer sheet was devised that reflected the multiple-choice answers selected by the subject, as to both *primary* and *secondary* reactivity. Machine scoring matrixes (scoring keys for intra-machine use) were constructed to cover location, determinant, and content scoring as well as "key number" categories.* Processing the Answer Sheets through the IBM Test Scoring Machine provides raw data in most of the usual scoring categories.†

Various correlational studies (28) were made between the "key number" results and the full-range scoring results, as well as between these two and Munroe's Inspection Technique (33), which was also applied. Validation studies are in progress at all levels.‡

A variety of clinical and other applications (mainly personnel selection and screening) were attempted. The multiple-judge method, generally as described for a clinical setting by Due, Wright, and Wright (Part 3, Section VI), was used to assess psychodiagnostic keenness of the procedure. Clinical and methodological studies are con-

---

* Originally Klopfer scoring was used (32). See Kellman's monograph (28) wherein charts are provided for matrix production according to scoring methods of Beck (30) and Hertz (31), as well as those of other investigators.

† The method described, particularly if used in clinical work, does not obviate the inspection of protocol for sequence analysis, perseveration of responses, nature of distribution of responses on a card-by-card basis, and qualitative factors and response dynamics.

‡ The first work, with emphasis on scoring techniques, was done under the auspices of the Detroit Civil Service Commission. Later work, on other levels of effort, was done (in part) under the terms of a special grant by William Scott Associates of Detroit to the Department of Clinical Psychology, Wayne University.

tinuing, with both the original amplified and later (revised) forms of the test.

As to the first objective: it became clear, during the early revisional work, that the 300 item form could not be subjected to objective scoring (as immediately above) unless certain aspects of it were altered. The changes involve administration, test booklet format, and response content. Kellman found the following to be the main areas of methodological difficulty:

1. Location scores could not be obtained for some of the responses because of vagueness of wording.

2. Determinant scoring, according to any of the current American "systems," was hindered for the same reason.

3. "Contamination" of reactivity by simultaneous exposure of all 300 responses.

4. Objections to the vagueness and/or all-inclusiveness of "Nothing at all" as a rejection choice.

5. Both overstress and understress on total scoring categories.

Considerable experimentation with these (and other factors) produced a revision of the 300 item form* in 1950. Its format, administration, and content now permit (among other things) more accurate location, determinant and content scoring; non-contaminated exposure of response choices; clear-cut rejection response choices; and show some correction of the over- and under-stress in certain of the scoring categories.

The revised instrument can be treated in a manner similar to that used with the individually administered, "classical" Rorschach. Many problems are left untouched, however, by this approach,† despite the hopefulness generated by preliminary studies. These have included full-range treatment, application of Munroe's technique, as well as the two "key number" approaches (the original 10 and Kellman's expanded proposal of 22). At this stage of the development, it can be reported that the most fruitful results have been obtained through the combination of results from full-range and briefer evaluations.

Despite the latter finding, work is in progress to sharpen the group application through more sensitive, albeit brief, evalutional methods.

---

* *Harrower Multiple-Choice Rorschach, as revised by S. Kellman.* Published by Wm. Scott Associates, Detroit, Michigan.

† For example: full proof of the assumption that the multiple-choice method can be a sensitive depth-sounding instrument; the rationale for interpreting primary-secondary response results, *etc.*

A new proposal is being tested, namely the expansion of the 10 key number system to 22 categories (28). Definition of each such category can now be clearer because of the revision of test content, as described above. In addition, the definitions themselves have been set up in the light of known clinical implications of the scoring factors, and are not based solely upon the dichotomy "good-bad" responses. Furthermore, the 22 *key* categories also reflect (a) scoring areas that lie in the no-man's-land between the "good-bad" sectors (their quantitative and qualitative characteristics determining in which of the two extremes they are to be interpreted); (b) three types of rejection response choices: rejection of the blot stimulus; implied refusal or inability to choose any of the offered answers; overt rejection of the printed choices as inadequate.

Throughout the history of the effort to provide a valid, quickly-scored instrument, the investigators have attempted to retain as much of the sensitivity, and to sacrifice as few of the nuances as possible, of the deeper Rorschach approaches to psychodiagnosis. Nevertheless, no such effort can adequately replace the simultaneity that is implied in a truly sensitive method between the collection of quantitative data and the working of insightful, clinical dynamics in the mind of the investigator.

Revised Harrower Multiple-Choice (Expanded) Rorschach*

Inkblot 1

A

1. *Whole Blot:* An army or navy emblem
2. *Whole Blot:* Crumbling cliffs
3. *Whole Blot:* A bat—just the shape of a bat
4. *The first three answers do not look like this inkblot*
5. *Right and Left Sides:* Two people
6. *Whole Blot:* A pelvis
7. *Whole Blot:* An x-ray picture
8. *Upper Center:* Pincers of a crab
9. *Whole Blot:* Messy, grimy stuff
10. *Lower Center:* Part of my body

---

* Prepared for purposes of review previous to copyrighting by M. R. Harrower and S. Kellman, June 15, 1948. A transitional revision. The final (1950) revision is in press: Wm. Scott Associates, 90 Edison Ave., Detroit 2, Mich.

B

11. *Middle, Plus Upper and Lower Centers:* Headless figure with arms up
12. *Whole Blot:* Vertebra
13. *Upper Center:* Tiny boxing gloves
14. *Whole Blot:* Spilt ink, dried up
15. *Whole Blot:* Someone's insides
16. *None of the 15 answers, above, look like any part of this inkblot*
17. *Whole Blot:* Butterfly flying
18. *Whole Blot:* Lava—hard, gray rocks
19. *Whole Blot:* Coat of arms
20. *Whole Blot:* An x-ray of the chest

C

21. *Whole Blot:* Hallowe'en mask
22. *Left and Right Sides:* Clouds
23. *Whole Blot:* A moth—shape of a moth
24. *Whole Blot:* Two people on a merry-go-round
25. *Lower Center:* A bell
26. *Whole Blot:* An x-ray picture of the spine
27. *Left and Right Sides:* Animal heads
28. *Lower Center:* The stomach
29. *No part of this inkblot looks like anything I've ever seen*
30. *Center:* Eyes glaring at me

Inkblot 2

A

1. *Whole Blot:* A bug somebody stepped on, bloody
2. *The first answer doesn't look like this inkblot*
3. *Whole Blot, Except for the Red Parts:* Two Scottie dogs standing with their noses up
4. *Right and Left Sides:* Little faces
5. *Whole Blot:* A bloody spinal column
6. *White, Center:* A white top
7. *Whole Blot:* A bursting bomb: smoke and fire
8. *Whole Blot, Except for Red Parts:* Two elephants, trunks lifted
9. *Whole Blot:* Two clowns with red hats
10. *Whole Blot:* Red and black ink, *still wet*

B

11. *Whole Blot, Except for Red Parts:* An animal skin
12. *Whole Blot, Except for Red Parts:* Two bears rubbing noses.
13. *Right and Left Sides:* Faces of Indians
14. *Upper or Lower Red Parts:* Blood
15. *None of the 14 answers, above, look like any part of this inkblot*
16. *Center White:* A white lamp
17. *Lower Center:* An exploding firecracker—lots of flame
18. *Lower Center:* A red butterfly
19. *Whole Blot, Except for Bottom Red Part:* Two people playing pat-a-cake
20. *Whole Blot:* Dried splotches of *red and black paint*

C

21. *Whole Blot, Except for Bottom Red Part:* Two witches
22. *Whole Blot:* Black and red paint, still wet
23. *Whole Blot, Except for Red Parts:* Bears' heads, black and furry
24. *Whole Blot, Except for Red Parts:* A deep empty hole
25. *Right and Left Sides:* Faces chiseled from stone
26. *Whole Blot:* Lungs and blood
27. *Center White:* A white sting-ray fish
28. *Above the White Center:* A little temple, high up
29. *No part of this inkblot looks like anything I've ever seen*
30. *Whole Blot:* A fiery erupting volcano

Inkblot 3

A

1. *Whole Blot, Minus Upper Center, Upper Corners:* Two birds fighting
2. *Upper Right and Left Corners:* Meat hanging in butcher shop
3. *Whole Blot, Minus Upper Center, Upper Corners:* Two men pulling something apart
4. *Whole Blot:* Part of my body
5. *Whole Blot:* Just colored blots
6. *Center:* A colored butterfly
7. *Upper Corners and Center:* Spots of blood and wet paint
8. *Upper Right and Left Corners:* Monkeys hanging by their tails
9. *Center:* A red bow tie
10. *The first nine answers don't look like any part of this inkblot*

B

11. *Center:* A red brooch
12. *Whole Blot:* A person's insides
13. *Whole Blot, Minus Upper Center and Upper Corners:* Two cannibals
14. *Whole Blot, Except for Center and Upper Corners:* Donald Ducks, playing together
15. *Whole Blot:* Fire, and smoke rising
16. *None of the 15 answers look like any part of this inkblot*
17. *Upper Corners and Center:* Spilt paint, all dried up
18. *Whole Blot, Minus Center and Upper Corners:* Two women quarreling
19. *Whole Blot:* Fresh blood and dirt.
20. *Whole Blot, Minus Center and Upper Corners:* Alphonse and Gaston—"after you"

C

21. *Center, Black Parts Only:* Two birds' heads
22. *Upper Right or Left Corners:* A bloody stomach
23. *Whole Blot, Minus Center and Upper Corners:* Two waiters bowing
24. *Lower Center:* An x-ray picture
25. *Whole Blot:* Dirty spots and bloody spots
26. *Center:* A colored hair ribbon
27. *Upper Corners and Center:* Lipstick splotches
28. *Upper Right and Left Corners:* Falling cats
29. *No part of this inkblot looks like anything I've ever seen*
30. *Lower Right and Left Sides:* Fish swimming

Inkblot 4

A

1. *Lower Center:* Head of an animal
2. *Whole Blot:* Lungs and chest
3. *Whole Blot:* Nasty, dirty slime
4. *Lower Right and Left Corners:* A pair of boots
5. *Whole Blot:* A burnt mass
6. *The first five answers don't look like any part of this inkblot*
7. *Whole Blot:* A giant in a fur coat
8. *Whole Blot:* An animal skin, fur side out

9. *Whole Blot:* A big gorilla
10. *Upper Center:* An x-ray picture

B

11. *Upper Center:* A little flower
12. *Entire Middle, From Top to Bottom:* The spine
13. *Whole Blot:* Dirty water after a rain
14. *Lower Right and Left Sides:* Charlie Chaplin's feet
15. *Whole Blot:* A person out of a nightmare
16. *Whole Blot:* A man sitting down
17. *Whole Blot:* A fur rug
18. *Lower Right and Left Corners:* Two Scottie dogs
19. *Whole Blot:* A black smudge
20. *None of the 19 answers look like any part of this inkblot*

C

21. *Lower Right and Left Sides:* Clouds
22. *Whole Blot:* A bat
23. *Whole Blot:* A man, seen from below
24. *No part of this inkblot looks like anything I've ever seen*
25. *Whole Blot:* Something squashed out of shape
26. *Whole Blot:* A frightening picture
27. *Upper Center:* A person's insides
28. *Upper Right and Left Corners:* Two little snakes
29. *Lower Right and Left Corners:* Big overshoes
30. *Lower Center:* A cow's head

Inkblot 5

A

1. *Lower Center:* A bird's beak
2. *Whole Blot:* Something squashed
3. *Whole Blot:* A ballet dancer
4. *The first three answers don't look like any part of this inkblot*
5. *Whole Blot:* A map
6. *Lower Center:* Sugar tongs
7. *Whole Blot:* A moth; the shape of a moth
8. *Entire Blot, Minus Upper and Lower Centers and Right and Left Corners:* The shape of shoulders
9. *Whole Blot:* A black smoke cloud
10. *Upper Center:* A rabbit's head

B

11. *Right or Left Side:* A man's face
12. *Whole Blot:* A black mess
13. *Entire Blot Except Entire Middle:* Two men with arms folded
14. *Whole Blot:* An island
15: *Center:* A policeman
16. *Whole Blot:* A bird flying
17. *Whole Blot:* A pelvis
18. *Whole Blot:* Tar or soot, smeared on something
19. *Lower Center:* Nutcrackers
20. *None of the 19 answers look like any part of this inkblot*

C

21. *Left or Right Corner:* An alligator's head
22. *No part of this inkblot looks like anything I've ever seen*
23. *Whole Blot:* A smashed body
24. *Whole Blot:* A fan dancer
25. *Entire Blot, Minus Right and Left Corners:* An x-ray picture
26. *Left and Right Corners:* Legs
27. *Whole Blot:* A bat or a butterfly at rest
28. *Whole Blot:* Lungs and chest
29. *Entire Blot, Minus Right and Left Corners:* Black clouds
30. *Lower Center:* A pair of pliers

Inkblot 6

A

1. *Right and Left Sides:* Two kings' heads with crowns
2. *Whole Blot:* An x-ray picture
3. *Upper Center, or Lower Two-thirds of the Blot:* Parts of the body
4. *Upper Center:* Totem pole
5. *Entire Blot, Except Upper Center:* A fur rug
6. *Whole Blot:* Mud and water
7. *Upper Center:* A polished post
8. *The first seven answers don't look like any part of this inkblot*
9. *Whole Blot:* A turtle
10. *Whole Blot, Except Upper Center:* A landslide

B

11. *Upper Center:* A dragon fly
12. *Upper Center and Down the Middle:* The spinal column

13. *Upper Center:* A cat's whiskers
14. *Upper Center and All of the Lower Part:* Male and female sex organs
15. *Whole Blot, Except Upper Center:* An animal skin
16. *Whole Blot:* Dirty water
17. *Upper Center:* A sceptre
18. *Upper Center, Very Top of:* A snake's head
19. *None of the 18 answers look like any part of this inkblot*
20. *Whole Blot:* Spattered, dried up mess

C

21. *Upper Center:* A butterfly
22. *Whole Blot:* An x-ray of the spine
23. *Upper Center:* Feathers
24. *Whole Blot, Except Upper Center:* A bear skin
25. *Whole Blot:* A leaf
26. *Upper Center:* A well-rounded table leg
27. *No part of this inkblot looks like anything I've ever seen*
28. *Upper Center:* Gushing oil
29. *Upper Center, Inside Portion:* A little man
30. *Whole Blot:* Part of the body.

Inkblot 7

A

1. *Whole Blot:* Smoke
2. *Whole Blot, Except Bottom Parts:* Two women
3. *Whole Blot:* Parts of the body
4. *Lower Two-thirds of Blot:* Animals
5. *The first four answers don't look like any part of this inkblot*
6. *Center, White:* A white chandelier
7. *Whole Blot:* Burning fragments
8. *Upper Left and Right Corners:* Woolly lambs' tails
9. *Whole Blot:* An x-ray picture
10. *Upper One-third of Blot:* Bookends

B

11. *Middle One-third of Blot:* Men's faces with big noses
12. *Lower One-third of Blot:* A butterfly flying
13. *Whole Blot:* Muck from the gutter
14. *Lower Center and Lower Sides:* Scottie dogs

15. *Whole Blot:* Pelvic bones
16. *Upper Two-thirds of Blot:* Indians with feathered caps
17. *None of the answers look like any part of this inkblot*
18. *Whole Blot:* Clouds
19. *Lower Center:* An x-ray of part of the body
20. *Whole Blot:* A necklace

C

21. *Whole Blot, Except Bottom Part:* Children playing
22. *Lower One-third of Blot:* The lower part of the torso
23. *Lower One-third of Blot:* Fog or mist
24. *No part of this inkblot looks like anything I've ever seen*
25. *Whole Blot:* A squashed frog
26. *Whole Blot, Except Bottom Part:* Statues
27. *Whole Blot:* Shapeless gray stuff
28. *Lower Center and Lower Sides:* Gray moth, at rest
29. *Upper Two-thirds of the Inkblot:* Dogs playing
30. *Center, White Part:* A white lamp

Inkblot 8

A

1. *Lower Center:* An orange or pink butterfly
2. *Whole Blot:* Shoulders, lungs, and stomach
3. *The first two answers don't look like any part of this inkblot*
4. *Whole Blot:* Just colors: can't find anything more
5. *Whole Blot:* A colorful emblem
6. *Lower Center:* A pretty flower, pink and orange petals
7. *Whole Blot:* Heaven and Hell: the colors suggest it
8. *Center:* Two blue cushions
9. *Right and Left Sides:* Two bears climbing
10. *Lower Center:* Colored clouds

B

11. *Whole Blot:* Flowers and leaves
12. *Center:* An x-ray picture
13. *Whole Blot:* Colored blobs of paint or ink
14. *Upper Center:* A horseshoe crab
15. *None of the 14 answers look like any part of this inkblot*
16. *Center:* Blue flags
17. *Right and Left Sides:* Animals climbing

18. *Whole Blot:* A colored coat of arms
19. *Whole Blot:* Fire and ice
20. *Whole Blot:* Parts of the body

C

21. *Whole Blot:* A Christmas tree with gay decorations
22. *Whole Blot:* This is similar to a medical picture in color and arrangement
23. *Lower Center:* Frogs' heads
24. *Whole Blot:* Life and Death because of the different colors
25. *Upper Center:* A mountain seen from the distance
26. *Whole Blot:* A nicely drawn, cheerful design for wallpaper
27. *Lower Center:* Inside the mouth—the pinkness of it
28. *Right and Left Sides and Lower Center:* Two beavers walking on colored rocks
29. *No part of this inkblot looks like anything I've ever seen*
30. *Whole Blot:* Colored ink splashed on paper, all dried up

Inkblot 9

A

1. *Upper Right and Left Sides:* Sea horses—the shape suggests it
2. *Whole Blot:* Just spilt paint, drying up
3. *Whole Blot:* Flowers of various kinds
4. *Whole Blot:* Parts of the body, on a doctor's chart
5. *Whole Blot:* Smoke and flames
6. *Upper Center:* Horns of a deer
7. *The first six answers don't look like any part of this inkblot*
8. *Upper Right and Left Corners:* Two witches
9. *Lower Center:* Bloody clouds
10. *Entire Middle:* An unlighted candle

B

11. *None of the 10 answers look like any part of this inkblot*
12. *Lower Center:* A pink jacket
13. *Whole Blot:* Meaningless colors: pink, orange, green, brown
14. *Whole Blot Minus Lower Center:* Bright tropical plant
15. *Whole Blot:* Stomach and intestines in a medical picture
16. *Whole Blot Minus Lower Center:* A forest fire, still burning
17. *Right and Left Sides:* Animal heads
18. *Upper Right and Left Sides:* Two gnomes

19. *Lower Right and Left Corners:* Bloody hands
20. *Upper Center:* A fountain, with the water flowing

C

21. *Whole Blot:* A beautiful orchid or other tropical flower
22. *Upper Right and Left Sides:* Boiled lobster, because of the color
23. *Whole Blot:* The insides of a person, when cut open
24. *Whole Blot:* An explosion in process
25. *Right and Left Sides:* Men's faces
26. *No part of this inkblot looks like anything I've ever seen*
27. *Upper Right and Left Sides:* Two Santa Clauses
28. *Whole Blot:* Storm clouds in a brilliant sunset
29. *Upper Center and Middle:* A violin
30. *Whole Blot:* Messy colors, all run together

Inkblot 10

A

1. *The Two Largest Areas in the Blot:* Two people
2. *Whole Blot:* Spilt paint, dried up
3. *Whole Blot:* A many-hued Chinese print
4. *Upper Center:* An x-ray picture
5. *Whole Blot:* All I can see are a bunch of colored ink spots
6. *Whole Blot:* Spiders, caterpillars, insects
7. *Whole Blot:* Parts from the inside of my body
8. *One of the Two Largest Areas in the Blot:* A colored map of California
9. *The first eight answers don't look like any part of this inkblot*
10. *Whole Blot:* A flower garden blooming in the spring

B

11. *Whole Blot:* Undersea pictures—coral, tropical fish, etc.
12. *Just Above Lower Center:* Two little dogs sitting up
13. *Upper Center, Middle, and Lower Center:* Stomach and intestines, as in medical text
14. *Whole Blot:* Just a lot of colors with no meaning at all
15. *Whole Blot:* A medical picture of the internal organs
16. *Whole Blot:* A bright design for wallpaper
17. *Whole Blot:* A child's painting, helter skelter
18. *The Two Largest Areas in the Blot:* Two ladies holding hands

19. *None of the 18 answers look like any part of this inkblot*
20. *Whole Blot:* Lots of animals running around

C

21. *Upper Right and Left Corners:* A blue flower
22. *Whole Blot:* Colored ink, still wet
23. *Whole Blot:* A picture of spring or fall: the colors suggest it
24. *Whole Blot:* Different parts of the insides of the human body
25. *Whole Blot:* Just colors, that's all I can see here
26. *Upper Center and Upper Right, Left Corners:* Octopus and crabs
27. *Upper Center:* Bones
28. *Whole Blot:* Pink coral and seaweed
29. *Whole Blot:* Flowers of many colors, all jumbled together
30. *No part of this inkblot looks like anything I've ever seen*

As illustration of Kellman's method, his full scoring chart for Card I on an IBM machine is given on next page.

CONCLUDING REMARKS

Let us sketch some developments which may be expected to take place. We may at the same time formulate some of the dangers which should be avoided and some of the prerequisites which may safeguard the most effective use of these group devices. Let us look into the future and make the assumption that there will be an ever-increasing rapprochement between the field of the physician and the field of the psychologist; where the physician, on the one hand, will become more aware of the kind of information that it would be helpful for him to have with patients, and where the psychologist, on the other hand, shall have cast off his academic seclusion, and sufficiently oriented himself in the field of medicine so that he can take the responsibility of bridging the gap and making his findings intelligible to the non-psychologically trained individual. Given this state of affairs, might it not be possible in large out-patient clinics, where persons may wait for several hours before being seen by the doctor, for certain types of group screening of the roughest kind to be conducted to highlight very obvious emotional disturbances?

It is certainly not beyond the realm of possibility that all colleges will require some kind of appraisal of the individual's emotional status at the time of entrance, over and above his academic achievement and acceptability on interview. As this is done with noteworthy success in several institutions once the student has entered, the possi-

CARD I

FULL SCORING OF HARROWER EXPANDED MULTIPLE-CHOICE RORSCHACH

Res. No.	Locations (WV W' D d Dd S)	Determinants (M FM m k FK F F– Fc c C' FC CF C)	Key No.	Content (H A Ad Hd SX / At Ob Cld Fre Drt Na Pt / Abs Ik Bld Art Other)	Dysp	P	O	Add Res.	Form LR*
1		F	3	Emb					
2	WV	m F	9	A Na		P			
3	WV	F	2						
4	Rejected		10						
5		M	1	H					
6		F	3	At					
7	WV	k F	7	Ad X-Ray					
8	d	F C'	4	Ad Mess					
9	WV	F–	9	At					
10		M	6	H					
11		F	1	At					
12		F	3	Obj Ink					
13	d	C'	4						
14	WV	F–	9	At					
15			6						
16	Rejected		10						
17		FM	11	A		P			
18	WV	C'	9	Na					
19		k F	3	Emb					
20		K F	7	X-Ray					
21		F	3	Obj					
22	WV	F	7	Cld					
23		M	2	A					
24		F	1	H Obj		P			
25		k F	3						
26		F–	7	X-Ray					
27	d	F	4	Ad At					
28		F–	6						
29	Rejected		10	Hd	Dy				
30	WV	M	9						
	7 3	4 1 1 3 1 11 3		3 3 2 1 5 1 3 5 3 1 1 2 1 5	1	3			

*Form Level Rating as per experimental proposal of B. Klopfer and H. H. Davidson.

bilities of utilizing rapid and accurate screening devices prior to entering may be envisaged.

Although still at the level of research, the emergence of vocational
characteristics, as seen in the work of Steiner, may be expected in
the future to play a greater and greater part in the actual placement
of the individual in industry.

Statistical norms for age levels, educational levels, and the like
should be compiled by some central research bureau.* While, ad-
mittedly, much remains to be done by the experimentalist in perfect-
ing his own tools, it is even more important that he take the time and
trouble to explain the relevance and significance of his tools in fields
outside his own.

References

1. Munroe, R. L.: The inspection technique: a method of rapid evaluation of
   the Rorschach protocol. *Rorschach Res. Exch., 8*:46-70, 1944.
2. Harrower, M. R., and Grinker, R. R.: The stress tolerance test: Preliminary
   experiments with a new projective technique utilizing both meaningful
   and meaningless stimuli. *Psychosom. Med., 8:1;*3-15, 1946.
3. Harrower, M. R., and Steiner, M. E.: *Manual for psychodiagnostic inkblots.*
   New York, Grune and Stratton, 1946, 112 pp.
4. Steiner, M. E.: The use of the Rorschach method in industry. *Rorschach Res.
   Exch. and J. Projective Techniques, 11:1;*46-52, 1947.
5. Steiner, M. E.: *The psychologist in industry.* American Lecture Series Monograph. Springfield, Thomas, 1949.
6. Cox, K.: The use of the Harrower multiple-choice Rorschach in a selection
   of sales personnel for a department store. (In publication.)
7. Lawshe, C. H., and Forster, M. H.: Studies in projective techniques: the
   reliability of a multiple-choice group Rorschach test. *J. Appl. Psychol.,
   31:2;*199-211, 1947.
8. Williams, G.: The possibilities of the Rorschach technique in industry.
   *Personnel, 24:*224-231, 1947.
9. Wittman, P.: The use of the multiple-choice Rorschach as a differential diagnostic tool. *J. Clin. Psychol., 1:4;*281-287, 1945.
10. Harrower, M. R., Washburne, A. C., and Jacobs, J. S. L.: A preliminary
    screening test for disturbance in personality. *Bull. Canad. Psychol., 44:*4-6,
    1944.
11. Chalke, F. R. C.: The Harrower Stress Tolerance Test. *Psychosom. Med.,
    8:3;*215-216, 1946.
12. Brozek, J., Guetzkow, H., and Keys, A.: A study of personality of normal
    young men maintained on restricted intakes of vitamins of the B complex.
    *Psychosom. Med., 8:2;*98-109, 1946.
13. Munroe, R. L.: Prediction of the adjustment and academic performance of
    college students by a modification of the Rorschach method. *Appl. Psychol.
    Monograph No. 7,* Stanford Univ. Press, 1945.

---

* See (34) for a proposal and method in implementing such a bureau or central file.

14. Montalto, F. D.: An application of the group Rorschach technique to the problem of achievement in college. *J. Clin. Psychol., 2:3;254-260,* 1946.
15. Thompson, G. M.: College grades and group Rorschach. *J. Appl. Psychol., 32:398-407,* 1948.
16. Cooper Union for the Advancement of Science and Art. Report from the Office of Admissions, New York, N. Y.
17. Abt, L. E.: The efficiency of the group Rorschach test in the psychiatric screening of Marine Corps recruits. *J. Psychol., 23:205-217,* 1947.
18. Wittson, C. L., Hunt, W. A., and Older, H. J.: The use of the multiple-choice group Rorschach test in military screening. *J. Psychol., 17:91-94,* 1944.
19. Jensen, M. B., and Rotter, J. B.: The validity of the multiple-choice Rorschach test in officer candidate selection. *Psychol. Bull., 42:3;182-185,* 1945.
20. Winfield, M. C.: The use of the Harrower multiple-choice Rorschach test with a selected group of women in military service. *J. Appl. Psychol., 30:481-487,* 1946.
21. Springer, N. N.: The validity of the multiple-choice group Rorschach test in the screening of naval personnel. *J. Gen. Psychol., 35:27-32,* 1946.
22. Guilford, J. P.: Some lessons from aviation psychology. *Am. Psychol., 3:1;3-11,* 1948.
23. Army Air Forces Aviation Psychology Program Research Reports. *Printed classification tests.* Washington, D. C., Government Printing Office, 1947, no. 5: 625-637.
24. Army Air Forces Aviation Psychology Program Research Reports. *The psychological program in the AAF convalescent hospitals.* Washington, D. C. Government Printing Office, 1947, no. 15: 145-149.
25. Eysenck, H. J.: A comparative study of four screening tests for neurotics. *Psychol. Bull., 42:9;659-662,* 1945.
26. Malamud, R. F., and Malamud, D. I.: The multiple-choice Rorschach: a critical explanation of its scoring system. *J. Psychol., 21:237-242,* 1946.
27. Challman, R. C.: Validity of Harrower multiple-choice test as a screening device. *J. Psychol., 20:41-48,* 1945.
28. Kellman, S.: *Modification of the Rorschach Method: Multiple-Choice Techniques.* American Lecture Series Monograph. Springfield, Thomas (In press).
29. Kellman, S.: *Scoring charts for the multiple-choice (amplified) Rorschach test.* Mimeographed. Detroit Civil Service Commission, 1946.
30. Beck, S.: *Rorschach's Test.* Two volumes. New York, Grune and Stratton, 1945.
31. Hertz, M.: The scoring of the Rorschach inkblot method as developed by the Brush Foundation. *Rorschach Res. Exch. 5:16-27,* 1942.
32. Klopfer, B., Kelley, D. M., and Davidson, H. H.: *The Rorschach Technique.* Second Edition. Yonkers, World Book Co., 1946.
33. Dryzer, E.: *Comparison of multiple-choice (amplified) and group Rorschach methods.* Unpublished M. A. thesis. Dept. Clin. Psychol., Wayne University, Detroit, 1949.
34. Kellman, S.: *The central Rorschach file.* Mimeographed. Dept. Clin. Psychol., Wayne University, Detroit, 1948.

Part V

AN ANALYSIS OF CONTENT

List of the Content of Responses, College Age Group

THE FIGURES which appear in the content list may be explained briefly. For example, Card I gave rise to 632 responses ($R = 632$). Of these, 284 were whole responses ($W = 284$) which constitutes 45% of the total number of responses to that card ($W = 45\%$). The first category, Anatomy (animal) constituted 2% of the 284W answers. Thus the relative frequency with which any specific content category occurred can be seen by a comparison of these percentages.*

Since this is apt to be confusing at first glance we may take another example, D2 on page 289. Here we find 40 such responses ($D2 = 40$). The D2 per cent, that is, the frequency with which D2, as a location, was selected, is 6% of the total number of answers given to Card I. ($D2\% = 6$). These 40 responses are distributed between six content categories. Anatomy (human), Animals, Human being, Human details, Natural objects and Objects.

We can, therefore, ask two questions about any given location. Is it utilized frequently or not? When utilized, are the responses apt to be drawn from a variety of content categories or from a few.

CARD I

COLLEGE AGE			
$R = 632$	backbone	skeleton	insect
	bone	spinal column	moth
W	bony structure	sternum	pelican
	costal cartilages	thorax	penguin
$W = 284$	hipbone	vertebra	phenix
$W\% = 45$	lungs	*Animals*	pigeon
Anatomy (animal)	nerve slice	46%	vampire
2%	pectoral girdle	*(Winged)*	*(Other than winged)*
anatomy of bird	pelvic bone	(40%)	(6%)
skeleton of bat	pelvic girdle	bat (22%)	animal
skull of dogfish	pelvis	beetle	cockroach
spine of animal	publis	bird	crab
	ribs	bug	crayfish
Anatomy (human)	sacral vertebra	butterfly (8%)	frog
30%	sacrum	dragon	mammal
axis vertebra	skeletal system	eagle (and N.R.A.)	reptile

---

* In certain cases additional percentages have been given. These have been added when any one item was given with unusual frequency in that particular location. For example, "bat" in this case constituted 22% of all the whole answers given to Card I.

CARD I—(Continued)

spider
turtle

Animal details
3%

antlers of moose
face of fox
head of dog
head of dragon
head of ox
head of wolf

Animal objects
.7%

shell
sponge

Fire, etc.
.3%

exploded object

Human beings
4%

angels
angels and devil
circus performer
dancer
diver hitting water
ghosts
goblins
god
King of the Mountain
masked men and
  prisoner
parachute troopist

Maps, etc.
1%

map
photograph of island

Natural objects
1%

iceberg
rock

Objects
10%

airplane
blouse
bomber
crest
⎰emblem
⎱insignia
kettle
mask (devil's)
paper doll
plane (shadow)
steel

Plants, etc.
1%

fungus growth
leaf
pansy

X-ray
.7%

x-ray
x-ray of bat

W'

W' = 38
W'% = 6

Anatomy (human)
50%

"anatomy" (part of)
bone
clavicle
pelvic girdle
pubis
ribs
sacrum
spinal column
sternum and vertebra
vertebra

Animals
26%

(Winged)
(16%)

bat
bird
eagle
insect
winged animal

(Other than winged)
(11%)

crab
pigs
ray fish

Human beings
11%

children in canoe
figures
ghosts
persons

Natural objects
3%

mountain crag

Objects
5%

emblem

Sex
3%

vagina

X-ray
3%

x-ray of body

W S

WS = 41
WS% = 6

Anatomy (human)
2%

part of the body

Animals
5%

(Winged)
(5%)

bat
phenix

Animal details
29%

face of cat
face of fox
face of green-eyed
  monster
head of cat

Human details
5%

face of heathen god
face of Satan

Maps, etc.
2%

Map

Natural objects
12%

avalanche
cave (entrance)
cave and high cliff
hills and lakes
hills and islands

Objects
44%

Hallowe'en cat
Hallowe'en lantern
Hallowe'en pumpkin
jack-o'-lantern
mask

W'S

W'S = 6
W'S% = .9

Animal details
33%

face of cat

Objects
66%

Hallowe'en cat
mask
Mask (Japanese)

D 1

D1 = 46
D1% = 7

Anatomy (human)
30%

bone
chest wall
costal cartilages
costal margin
nervous tract
skull
spinal cord
sternum
sternum and xiphoid
  process

Animals
20%

(Winged)
(11%)

bee
beetle
insect

(Other than winged)
(9%)

ant
frog
ogre (two headed)

Animal objects
2%

fossil

Human beings
39%

bat man
basketball player
comic-strip character
ghost
Ku-Klux Klan
lady
man
person
spirit
spooks
woman

CARD I—(Continued)

Objects
7%

dress pattern
idol
kettle

X-ray
2%

x-ray

D 2

D2 = 40
D2% = 6

Anatomy (human)
3%

sternum

Animals
50%

(Winged)
(28%)

bat
bird
vulture
winged horse

(Other than winged)
(23%)

animal
bear
frog
ground hog
rabbit
seahorses

Human beings
23%

figures
men
Santa Claus
witches

Human details
10%

face
face of Sherlock
Holmes

Natural objects
3%

clouds

Objects
13%

face of sphinx
gargoyle
keystone
totem pole
wings of airplane

D 3

D3 = 4
D3% = .6

Anatomy (human)
75%

body
pelvic bone
sternum

Human details
25%

torso of female

D 4

D4 = 7
D4% = 1

Anatomy (human)
14%

sternum and xiphoid
process

Objects
86%

bell

D 5

D5 = 28
D5% = 4

Anatomy (human)
4%

ribs

Animals
54%

(Winged)
(50%)

bat
bird
eagle
fowl
griffin

(Other than winged)
(4%)

fox

Animal details
21%

beak of bird
head of bird
head of dog
wings of bat

Maps, etc.
7%

map of England
map of South America

Natural objects
7%

rock

Objects
7%

hat
uniform

D 6

D6 = 16
D6% = 3

Anatomy (human)
13%

anus
vertebra

Animals
63%

(Winged)
(31%)

beetle
butterfly
insect

(Other than winged)
(31%)

crab
frog
lobster

Animal details
13%

head of beetle

Human beings
13%

figure
persons

D 7

D7 = 4
D7% = .6

Animals
25%

(Winged)
25%

bat

Objects
75%

airplane
emblem
totem pole

D 8

D8 = 8
D8% = 1

Anatomy (human)
25%

pelvic girdle
thoracic vertebra

Animals
38%

(Winged)
(38%)

bat
bird
eagle

Animal details
13%

antlers

Objects
25%

air force pin
flying wings

D 9

D9 = 4
D9% = .6

Anatomy (human)
100%

pelvis
sacrum
sacrum and coccyx
bone

D 10

D10 = 6
D10% = .9

Animals
67%

(Winged)
(67%

bat
bird
eagle

Objects
33%

airplane

D 11

D11 = 21
D11% = 3

Anatomy (human)
14%

attachment of ribs to
chest
ribs and intercostal
spaces

CARD I—(Continued)

throat (infected)
Animal details
5%
face of cat
Human details
19%
face
face of devil
Natural objects
10%
high cliff and cave
Objects
48%
Hallowe'en mask
jack-o'-lantern
mask of devil
X-ray
5%
x-ray

d 1

d1 = 11
d1% = 2
Animals
18%
(Winged)
(9%)
sea gull
(Other than winged)
(9%)
shark
Animal details
36%
beak of bird
claws
wings
Maps, etc.
9%
map of India
Natural objects
9%
rock of Gibraltar
Objects
27%
arrow
bayonet
weapon

d 2

d2 = 1
d2% = .1

Animal details
100%
head of animal

d 3

d3 = 10
d3% = 2
Animals
30%
snakes
turtles
worms
Animal details
40%
claws of crab
heads of eagles
heads of snakes
mouth of animal
Human beings
10%
monks
Human details
10%
thumbs
Natural objects
10%
waves

d 4

d4 = 4
d4% = .6
Animals
25%
(Winged)
(25%)
bird
Animal details
50%
head of dog
head of rat
Natural objects
25%
peak

d 5

d5 = 3
d5% = .4
Anatomy (human)
67%
jugular notch
tonsils

Animal details
33%
antennae

d 6

d6 = 4
d6% = .6
Anatomy (human)
50%
coccyx
xiphoid process
Maps, etc.
25%
geographical photo
Signs and symbols
25%
Fascist symbol

d 7

d7 = 1
d7% = .1
Objects
100%
breadmaker's mallet

d 3 + d 5

d3 + d5 = 9
d3 + d5% = 1
Animals
56%
(Winged)
(33%
birds
bugs
pigeons
(Other than winged)
(22%)
caterpillars
creatures from
"Frankenstein"
Animal details
22%
antlers
claws and mouth
Human beings
11%
people
Human details
11%
teeth

de

de = 3
de% = .4
Animal details
33%
face of monkey
Human details
33%
face of person
Natural objects
33%
coastline

di

di = 3
di% = .4
Human beings
67%
Old Man Winter
Minute Man
Maps, etc.
33%
geographical
photograph

dr

dr = 27
dr% = 4
Anatomy (human)
19%
scapula
sternum
vertebra
Animals
33%
(Winged)
(15%)
bat
(Other than winged)
(19%)
ant
cat
crab
ray
Animal objects
4%
sponge
Architecture
4%
church

CARD I—(Continued)

Maps, etc.
11%
aerial view of
  mountain
map of England
map of South America

Natural objects
7%
island masses

lava

Objects
22%
airplane
face of sphinx
jacket
remnant of jacket
shaving cream

S

$S = 3$
$S\% = .4$

Anatomy (human)
33%
scapula

Human details
33%
eyes

Objects
33%
gunshot hole

CARD II

COLLEGE AGE
$R = 540$

W

$W = 156$
$W\% = 29$

Anatomy (animal)
.6%
dissection of animal

Anatomy (human)
5%
cross section of spinal
  column
cross section of spinal
  cord
heart
pelvic bone
spinal column
transverse section of
  heart

Animals
28%

(Winged)
(15%)
bat
bird
butterfly
fly
insect
kite
moth
water bug

(Other than winged)
(13%)
animals
bears
cats
marine animals
ray fish
water flea

Art
.6%
water color painting

Color
1%
(color description)
(color naming)

Fire, etc.
2%
eruption
explosion
fire and coal

Human beings
55%
athletes
Buddha
children
Chinese
clowns
dancers
fencers
figures
ghosts
girls
Indians
men
monks
"Old Bill"
old maids
orientals
people
policemen
priests
rajahs
Russians
Santa Claus
tumblers
twins
witches
women

Human details
1%
face
painted face

Maps, etc.
.6%
anatomical slide

Natural objects
1%
clouds
lava

Objects
.6%
cauldron

Sex
2%
female sex organs
vagina and anus

Symbolism
.6%
murder in coal bin

X-ray
.6%
x-ray

W'

$W' = 127$
$W'\% = 24$

Anatomy (embryo)
.7%
foetal pigs

Anatomy (human)
3%
bones
lungs
pelvis

Animals
67%

(Winged)
(.7%)
birds

(Other than winged)
(66%)
animals
bears (23%)
beasts
bisons
buffalos
calves
cats
dogs (18%)
elephants
gorillas
rabbits

Animal details
5%
heads of bears
heads of bulls
heads of calves
heads of dogs

Animal objects
2%
bear rug
bear skin

Color
.7%
red spot and gray spot

Fire, etc.
2%
bomb exploding
explosion of rock

Human beings
10%
dancers
firemen
girls
men

CARD II—*(Continued)*

people

Maps, etc.
2%

map
map of Austria
map of Great Britain

Natural objects
2%

land
rock

Objects
4%

boots
fireplace
Japanese lantern
machinery
wig

Plants, etc.
.7%

plant

Sex
.7%

vagina

W S

WS = 7
WS% = 1

Animals
43%

(Winged)
(43%

butterfly
insect
winged animal

Architecture
29%

castle and impressive
walk
staircase

Objects
29%

breast plate
paper

W'S

W'S = 4
W'S% = .7

Architecture
50%

castle with surround-
ing territory

Natural objects
50%

smoke pattern
woods and lake

D 1

D1 = 36
D1% = 7

Anatomy
11%

blood

Animals
39%

(Winged)
(36%)

butterfly
insect
moth

(Other than winged)
(3%)

crab

Animal details
6%

tail of fish
tail of insect

Fire, etc.
31%

explosion
fire
flames
volcanic eruption
volcano

Human beings
3%

people

Natural objects
3%

comet (disintegrated)

Objects
8%

bullet
fan
ink

D 2

D2 = 71
D2% = 13

Anatomy (human)
6%

blood
blood vessels

---

chromosome spindle
sacrum

Animals
23%

(Winged)
(6%)

butterfly
cock
rooster

(Other than winged)
(17%)

animal
lion
rabbit
snake
worm

Animal details
1%

face of kitten

Animal objects
1%

shell

Architecture
1%

stairway

Color
3%

(color naming)

Fire, etc.
3%

fire

Human beings
13%

ghosts
girls
masqueraders
men
men (headless)
monks
Punch and Judy

Human details
28%

faces
hair
heads
noses
thumbs

Maps, etc.
6%

map of England
map of Ireland

Natural objects
1%

water

Objects
11%

balloon
lamp bulb
lipstick
mask
meat
shoes
silk fabric

Plants, etc.
1%

leaves

Symbolism
1%

a phenomenon

D 3 = 0

D 4

D4 = 1
D4% = .1

Animal details
100%

head of lamb

d 1

d1 = 23
d1% = 4

Anatomy (human)
9%

excretory organs
sternum

Animal details
4%

paws of animal

Architecture
22%

building
castle
church
staircase
stairway

Fire, etc.
4%

sky rocket (exploded)

Human beings
9%

children
Tibetans

CARD II—*(Continued)*

Human details
4%

head of Punch

Natural objects
4%

mountain

Objects
39%

altar
arrowhead
book end satyrs
bullet
fence
fire extinguisher
helmet

Sex
4%

sex organs

d 2

d2 = 3
d2% = .5

Animal details
67%

head of rooster
paw of cat

Human details
33%

head of man

d 3

d3 = 1
d3% = .1

Human details
100%

head of Old Man of
Mountain

d 4

d4 = 11
d4% = 2

Human details
100%

face of man
head of George
Washington
head of Indian
mouth (open) of
Father Time

d 2 + d 3

d2 + d3 = 1
d2 + d3% = .1

Animals
100%

monkey

d 1 + S

d1 + S = 7
d1 + S% = 1

Architecture
86%

chapel with walk
church with long walk
corridor leading to
stairway
palace and steps
shrine and steps
stairway and shrine

Objects
14%

bed with canopy

de

de = 3
de% = .5

Animal details
33%

bill of pelican

Human details
33%

head of woman

Natural objects
33%

mountain scene

di

di = 1
di% = .1

Miscellaneous
100%

rhythm

dr

dr = 13
dr% = 2

Anatomy (human)
8%

microscopic cell

Anatomy (embryo.)
8%

neural crest of embryo

Animals
15%

(Winged)
(8%)

butterfly

(Other than winged)
(8%)

worm

Animal details
8%

head of animal with
sharp beak

Fire, etc.
15%

fire and coal
furnace

Human details
15%

head of Indian

Maps, etc.
15%

map
slide

Objects
15%

nipple
nut-cracker

dr + S

dr + S = 8
dr + S% = 1

Fire, etc.
13%

explosion

Natural objects
63%

calcium structure and
water
cave
crater
passage
tunnel entrance

Objects
25%

flashlight
mask

S

S = 67
S% = 12

Anatomy (human)
6%

opening of thorax
spinal column
vertebral canal
vertebral foramen

Animals
15%

(Winged)
(4%)

bird
moth

(Other than winged)
(10%)

fish
ray-fish

Architecture
6%

castle and valley
church steeple with
slanting roof

Human beings
1%

ballet dancer

Natural objects
6%

lake
river

Objects
64%

ace of spades
bellows
birthday cake
bulb
bullet
bullet hole
centrifuge
drill
gear
head on metal lathe
incense burner
ink bottle
jar
lamp
light
parachute
ship
spade
spar in tent
spearhead
top

Plants, etc.
1%

beet

CARD III

COLLEGE AGE

R = 592

W

W = 49
W% = 8

Anatomy (animal)
2%
dissected frog

Anatomy (human)
8%
abdomen
kidneys
thoracic cavity
vertebra

Animals
14%
(Winged)
(6%)
bee (under
 microscope)
butterfly (under
 microscope)
fly (under
 microscope)
(Other than winged)
(8%)
crab
frog

Animal details
2%
mandible of
 grasshopper

Art
4%
design
painting

Human beings
59%
butlers
cannibals
cooks
diplomats
fellows
figures
Frenchmen
house boys
manikins
men
people
spiritualists
valets

waiters
women

Human details
2%
faces of women

Objects
6%
Hallowe'en mask
ornament
weapon made of rock

X-ray
2%
x-ray of cheekbone

W'

W' = 258
W'% = 44

Anatomy (animal)
.3%
ribs and head of
 animal

Anatomy (human)
2%
body
pelvic girdle
thorax

Animals
19%
(Winged)
(15%)
birds
chickens
cocks
ducks
hens
jays
penguins
roosters
wasps
(Other than winged)
(4%)
animals
crab
dogs
frog
mice
monkeys
spider

Animal details
.7%
face of animal
jaws of beetle

Human beings
75%
acrobats
Andy Gump
athletes
bojangles of Harlem
boxers
boys
bull fighters
butlers
cafe society
cannibals
characters
children
cooks
courtesans
dancers
dandies
darkies
devils
diplomats
doctors
Egyptians
English earls
figures
footmen
Fred Astaire
gentlemen
girls
horsemen
imps
Jiminy Cricket
lackeys
ladies
men
negroes
servants
skaters
South Sea Islanders
statesmen
waiters
women

Objects
2%
bowl
carvings of wood
mask
ornament
vase

Sex
.3%
vagina

Signs and Symbols
.3%
"M"

D 1

D1 = 101
D1% = 17

Anatomy (human)
13%
adrenals
blood
bone
kidneys
lobes of brain
pelvic girdle
scapula
vertebra

Animals
51%
(Winged)
(50%)
butterfly (48%)
moth
(Other than winged)
(2%)
lions
seahorses

Architecture
2%
bridge spanning
 chasm
corridor leading to
 door

Human beings
.9%
two buxom ladies

Objects
31%
bow }
bow tie }
(26%)
eye pad
pipes
sailboat
tongs
wallpaper

Plants, etc.
2%
tomatoes

D 2

D2 = 91
D2% = 15

CARD III—*(Continued)*

Anatomy (embryo.)
2%
embryo
Anatomy (human)
16%
blood
bone
kidney
oesophagus
skeleton of feet
stomach
stomach and
oesophagus
sweat glands
Animals
36%
(Winged)
(13%)
bat
bird
chicken
cock
parrot
(Other than winged)
(23%)
animal
cat
cobra
crab
dragon
fish
monkey
seahorses
snails
squirrels
Animal details
2%
head of animal
tail of fish
Fire, etc.
4%
fire
fiery atmosphere
Human beings
25%
athletes
clowns
devils
dwarfs
fairies
figures
girls
jitterbugs

men
skaters
spirits
swimmers
Human details
1%
legs of dancer
Natural objects
1%
sand bar
Objects
5%
ax covered with blood
gargoyle
saucepan
scarf
Plants, etc.
1%
watermelon
Signs and Symbols
1%
astrological signs
Symbolism
3%
conscience
nasty thoughts
suggestion that all is
not well

D 3
D3 = 30
D3% = 5
Anatomy (human)
37%
lungs
pelvic girdle
pelvis
pubic section
section of body
skull
sternum
thoracic region
Animals
30%
(Winged)
(7%)
chickens
roosters
(Other than winged)
(23%)
crab

crustacean
lobster
Animal details
7%
head of animal
jaws of animal
Objects
20%
basket
cauldron
hull of ship
mask
Plants, etc.
3%
plant growth
X-ray
3%
x-ray of kidneys

D 4
D4 = 5
D4% = .8
Anatomy (human)
40%
stomach
vertebra
Animals
20%
bears
Animal details
20%
eyes of fly
Objects
20%
boxing gloves

D 5
D5 = 12
D5% = 2
Anatomy (animal)
8%
bone of fish
Anatomy (human)
8%
clavicle
Animals
50%
(Winged)
(8%)
bird

(Other than winged)
(42%)
fish
seal
Human details
17%
legs
Maps, etc.
17%
map of Italy

D 6
D6 = 6
D6% = 1
Animals
67%
(Winged)
(67%)
bird
Human beings
17%
puppets
X-ray
17%
x-ray

D 7
D7 = 2
D7% = .3
Animals
50%
(Winged)
(50%)
bird
Animal details
50%
head of shark

D 8 = 0

D 9
D9 = 3
D9% = .5
Anatomy (human)
33%
dissected trachea
Animals
67%
crab
pediculus

CARD III—(Continued)

D 5 + D 7

$D5 + D7 = 2$
$D5 + D7\% = .3$

Animals
50%
(Winged)
(50%)

birds

Natural objects
50%

islands

D 1 + S

$D1 + S = 1$
$D1 + S\% = .1$

Objects
100%

bowl with red bow

D 1 + D 3 + S

$D1 + D3 + S = 1$
$D1 + D3 + S\% = .1$

Human details
100%

face of Chinese
emperor

d 1

$d1 = 4$
$d1\% = .6$

Animals
25%

fish

Human details
25%

feet

Objects
50%

shoes

d 2

$d2 = 5$
$d2\% = .8$

Animal details
60%

head of bird
head of chicken
head of rooster

Human details
40%

face of person

d 3

$d3 = 3$
$d3\% = .5$

Animal details
33%

head of mouse

Objects
33%

book on coat of arms

Plants, etc.
33%

pine tree

dd

$dd = 3$
$dd\% = .5$

Anatomy (animal)
33%

bone of fish

Objects
67%

collar
splinters

dr

$dr = 10$
$dr\% = 2$

Anatomy (human)
30%

artery and branch
commissure between
 brain lobes
sternum and ribs

Animals
20%
(Winged)
(10%)

blue jay

(Other than winged)
(10%)

worm

Animal details
20%

head of scottie
tail of fish

Human details
10%

elbow

Maps, etc.
10%

map of Italy

Sex
10%

vagina

S

$S = 6$
$S\% = 1$

Anatomy (human)
17%

sternum

Animals
17%
(Winged)
(17%)

insect

Natural objects
33%

cloud
land

Objects
33%

shirt

CARD IV

COLLEGE AGE
$R = 556$

W

$W = 241$
$W\% = 43$

Anatomy (animal)
.8%

skull of animal
skull of bat

Anatomy (human)
5%

bony structure
cell
dorsal aspect of body
manubrium

---

mouth (inside) of
 person
pectoral girdle
sacrum
scab from wound
sternum

Animals
31%
(Winged)
(12%)

bat
bug
butterfly
eagle
insect
mantis
moth

---

wasp

(Other than winged)
(19%)

animal
ant
ape
beaver
cat
crab
dog
dragon
fish
frog
gorilla
kangaroo
marine animal
monster

---

prehistoric animal
ray
skunk
squirrel

Animal details
5%

back of monkey
back of penguin
face of beetle
face of insect
head of bear
head of caterpillar
head of dog

Animal objects
25%

animal pelt

CARD IV—*(Continued)*

animal skin
fossil
fur
fur rug
shell of turtle
skin of bat
skin of bear
skin of buffalo
skin of deer
skin of muskrat

Architecture
.4%

station at night

Fire, etc.
.4%

shell exploding

Human beings
13%

Charlie Chaplin
clown
diver
football fan
Frankenstein
man
medicine man
person

Maps, etc.
.8%

photograph
slide

Natural objects
1%

smudge
soil
tunnel

Objects
8%

armor
book ends
carving of rock
coat
emblem
hat
metal (hammered)
object
paper
scarecrow
seaplane (smashed)
shrapnel
underwear
vase

Plants, etc.
3%

algae
morning glory
plant
sea anemone
seaweed

X-ray
5%

x-ray
x-ray of lung
x-ray of throat

W'

W' = 44
W'% = 8

Anatomy (animal)
2%

dissected rat

Anatomy (embryo.)
2%

embryo of chick

Anatomy (human)
2%

sphenoid of skull

Animals
27%
(Winged)
(9%)

bat
beetle
birds on post
bug
(Other than winged)
(18%)
animal
cow
dogs on post
Protozoa
rat
rodent

Animal details
7%

head of elephant
head of turtle
plastron of turtle

Animal objects
11%

skin of animal
skin of bear
skin of cat
rug of bear skin

Human beings
7%

comedian
person

Human details
2%

feet and trunk

Objects
32%

boots

Plants, etc.
5%

fungus plant
tree (Chinese)

X-ray
2%

x-ray

WS

WS = 1
WS% = .1

Plants, etc.
100%

tree cut to make
tunnel

D 1

D1 = 47
D1% = 8

Anatomy (animal)
2%

brain of frog

Animals
28%
(Winged)
(11%)

bat
bee
bug
insect
wasp
(Other than winged)
(17%)

animal
dragon
fish
Hydra
monster
sea monster

Animal details
64%

face of cat

head of bull
head of caterpillar
head of cow
head of dog
head of horse
head of insect
head of lobster
head of moose
head of serepent
head of snail
head of steer
tail of lobster

Plants, etc.
6%

orchid
plant growth
tiger lily

D 2

D2 = 59
D2% = 11

Anatomy (embryo.)
5%

embryo

Anatomy (human)
2%

skull

Animals
3%

calf
sea worm

Animal details
2%

head of dog

Human details
25%

feet
legs

Maps, etc.
8%

map
map of Italy

Objects
54%

boots (44%)
shoes

D 3

D3 = 3
D3% = .5

Objects
100%

hat (trampled)

CARD IV—*(Continued)*

shoes (wooden)
toy

D 4

D4 = 28
D4% = 5

Anatomy (animal)
7%

spinal cord of crayfish
spinal cord of fish

Anatomy (embryo.)
7%

embryonic chick
neural groove

Anatomy (human)
36%

backbone
body
spine
spinal cord
vertebral column

Animals
25%

caterpillar
fish
organism
prehistoric animal
rat and reflection

Architecture
4%

spire and clouds

Natural objects
7%

fountain

Objects
11%

bottle
lamp standard
torpedo

X-ray
4%

x-ray

D 5

D5 = 3
D5% = .5

Animals
67%

animal
fish

Objects
33%

armor

D 6

D6 = 10
D6% = 2

Anatomy (human)
30%

section of skull
sternum
thoracic wall

Animals
10%

fish

Animal details
10%

head of airedale

Maps, etc.
10%

map

Natural objects
30%

fountain
water and ornament

Plants, etc.
10%

plant

D 1 + S

D1 + S = 1
D1 + S% = .1

Natural objects
100%

den

d 1

d1 = 34
d1% = 6

Anatomy (animal)
3%

skull of bird

Anatomy (human)
15%

blood vessel (torn)
clavicle
scapula

Animals
26%

(Winged)
(12%)

bird
crane

duck
swan
(Other than winged)
(15%)
fish
serpent
snake
worm

Animal details
21%

head of bird
head of duck
head of horse
head of insect
tail
wing

Human details
6%

arm

Natural objects
3%

fountain

Objects
18%

handle
harp
sleeve
snap hook
trophy

Plants, etc.
3%

pistil of flower

Sex
3%

penis

Miscellaneous
3%

drooling

d 2

d2 = 27
d2% = 5

Anatomy (embryo.)
4%

embryo

Anatomy (human)
4%

chromosome spindle

Animal details
15%

head of animal

head of caterpillar
head of dragon
wings of eagle

Fire, etc.
4%

torch (flame)

Natural objects
33%

artesian well
fountain

Objects
7%

air corps wings
weather vane

Plants, etc.
30%

flower
fungus
lily
plant

Sex
4%

vagina

d 3

d3 = 4
d3% = .7

Animal objects
25%

pelt

Architecture
25%

castle on hillside

Human details
25%

head of man

Plants, etc.
25%

tree (snow-covered)

d 4

d4 = 2
d4% = .3

Animal details
100%

head of snail
head of wasp

dd

dd = 6
dd% = 1

CARD IV—(Continued)

Animal details
50%
eyes of cow
head of bat
horns

Architecture
17%
shrine in valley

Maps, etc.
17%
map of Mexico

Objects
17%
boot (furry)

de

de = 6
de% = 1

Human details
100%
face of person
profile

di

di = 7
di% = 1

Anatomy (embryo.)
14%
embryo

Anatomy (human)
29%
squamous cell
thorax (dissected)

Human details
29%
face

Natural objects
14%
clouds

X-ray
14%
x-ray

dr

dr = 27
dr% = 5

Anatomy (animal)
4%
skull of animal

Anatomy (embryo.)
11%
embryo
neural groove

Anatomy (human)
4%
part of vertebral
column

Animals
15%

(Winged)
(7%)
bat
eagle

(Other than winged)
(7%)
animal
skunk

Animal details
19%
back of cat
face of dog
head of dog

Animal objects
4%
shell

Architecture
4%
spire

Human beings
4%
person

Human details
7%
legs of woman
lips of woman

Maps, etc.
7%
map
map of South America

Objects
15%
head of arrow
object
shoes
vase

X-ray
7%
x-ray

S

S = 6
S% = 1

Anatomy (human)
17%
glenoid fossa of
scapula

Human beings
50%
king
man
person

Human details
17%
head of ghost

Maps, etc.
17%
map of Africa

CARD V

COLLEGE AGE
R = 489

W

W = 309
W% = 63

Anatomy (human)
1%
bones
muscles
pectoral region
vertebra

Animals
78%

(Winged)
(71%)
bat (30%)

bee
beetle
• bird
bug
butterfly (21%)
coleopter
crow
Donald Duck
grasshopper
insect
mosquito
moth (7%)
ostrich

(Other than winged)
(7%)
animal
antelope
bull

creature
deer
flying squirrel
hippopotamus
Minnie Mouse
mule
prehistoric animal
rabbit holding wings
slug
snail

Animal details
.3%
legs of mouse

Animal beings
.3%
skin of rabbit

Human beings
12%
angel
ballet dancer
bat man
clown
devil
ghost man
giant
girl
lady
man
man from Mars
Mr. Hyde
person
rabbit man
show girl
three thieves

CARD V—(Continued)

three people
Human details
.9%
face of god
head with bumps
knock-kneed legs
Maps, etc.
.3%
map of Denmark
Natural objects
1%
clouds
island
rock
shoreline
Objects
4%
airplane
arrowhead
balloon
brig with sails set
brooch
collar on coat
hat
jacket
shield
wreath
Plants, etc.
.9%
fungus
maple seed

W′

W′ = 29
W′% = 6
Anatomy (human)
3%
pelvic bones
Animals
41%
(Winged)
(34%)
bat
butterfly
insect
seahawk
(Other than winged)
(7%)
caterpillar
Architecture
7%
bridge

staircase
Human beings
3%
person
Human details
7%
heads of men
Natural objects
10%
clouds
dirt
smoke
Objects
21%
airplane
glider
gun
mask
pin
toupee
Signs and Symbols
3%
"V"
Miscellaneous
3%
Roman battle scene

D 1

D1 = 39
D1% = 8
Anatomy (human)
5%
rib
sternum
Animals
10%
(Winged)
(3%)
bird
(Other than winged)
(8%)
antelope
dog
mole
Animal details
8%
head of alligator
head of dragon
heads of bears in a
pile

Human beings
26%
dancer
girl
man
person
woman
Human details
38%
head of person
(and beard)
Natural objects
5%
shoreline
skyline
Objects
5%
high-heeled shoe
mask
Miscellaneous
3%
sulphite fibers

D 2

D2 = 28
D2% = 6
Anatomy (human)
4%
nerve cords
Animals
68%
(Winged)
(14%)
bug
grasshopper
insect
(Other than winged)
(54%)
antelope
deer
dog
donkey
fox terrier
rabbit
rat
snail
Human beings
29%
clown
dancer
devil
person

d 1

d1 = 22
d1% = 4
Anatomy (human)
9%
bones
part of brain
Animals
5%
fish
Animal details
27%
antennae
beak
feet of animal
legs of mouse
Animal objects
5%
wishbone
Objects
50%
forceps
handle of urn
hockey sticks
ice tongs
pliers
tweezers
Plants, etc.
5%
lily

d 2

d2 = 26
d2% = 5
Anatomy
12%
bone
fibia and tibia
Animal details
73%
claws of crab
head of alligator
head of crocodile
leg of cow
leg of ostrich
mouth of alligator
Animal objects
4%
drumstick
Human details
4%
leg of person

Card V—(Continued)

Objects 4%	Animal objects 5%	Human details 50%	Natural objects 17%
syringe	wishbone	face of god	skyline of hills
Plants, etc. 4%	Human details 5%	head of person Natural objects 25%	dr
twigs of tree	head of lady	cliff	dr = 3
d 3	Objects 5%	dd	dr% = .6
d3 = 20	statue	dd = 1	Anatomy 33%
d3% = 4	Plants, etc. 5%	dd% = .2	blood
Animals 10%	pollen grain	Anatomy (human) 100%	Human beings 33%
(Winged) (5%)	Signs and Symbols 20%	mammary glands	person
devil bird	"V"	de	Natural objects 33%
(Other than winged) (5%)	X-ray 5%	de = 6	mountain
worms	x-ray	de% = 1	S
Animal details 45%	d 4	Animal details 50%	S = 2
antennae	d4 = 4	face of ogre	S% = .4
beak	d4% = .8	head of dog	Human details 50%
head of caterpillar	Animal details 25%	hump of camel	face of woman
head of lion	head of bear	Human details 33%	Natural objects 50%
head of rabbit		face of John Bull	snow
head of snail		head of person	

Card VI

College Age R = 565	(Other than winged) (22%)	animal hide bear rug	Human beings .8%
W	animal beaver	bear skin beaver skin	ghost
W = 116	catfish	fox fur	Natural objects 10%
W% = 21	caterpillar (squashed)	fur rug	cross section of gusher
Anatomy (animal) 2%	crab fish	leopard skin	ditch
cross section of wasp	flying squirrel	skunk skin	fort
skeleton of chicken	hydra	tiger skin	fountain
Anatomy (human) 2%	jelly fish	Architecture 3%	Grand Canyon
cell	louse		oil well
part of the body	mammal	Aztec gate to village	river valley
Animals 28%	mouse	entrance to Egyptian	rock
	ray fish	mosque	section of land
(Winged) (5%)	squid	lighthouse	view of land
dragonfly	tortoise	Art .8%	Objects 16%
insect	turtle	Indian art	bomber
moth	worm	Color .8%	candle holder
	Animal objects 27%	black and gray splash	chandelier
	animal skin		crest
			crown with feathers

Card VI—(Continued)

decoration of copper
emblem
hinge
insignia
lamp
prow of ship
rack for magazines
relic
sceptre
tennis racquet
totem pole
warming pan

Plants, etc.
9%

flower with flower
  pot
leaf
maple leaf
plant in basket
seed pod
tree

X-ray
.8%

x-ray

Miscellaneous
.8%

something under dusty
  microscope

W′

W′ = 139
W′% = 25

Anatomy (animal)
.7%

dissection of pigeon

Anatomy (human)
4%

manubrium
sacrum and part of
  lumbar region
spinal cord
sternum

Animals
17%

animal
beaver
codfish
flying squirrel
frog
guinea pig
halibut
muskrat

primitive vertebrate
ray fish
tadpole
turtle
worm

Animal details
.7%

head of lizard

Animal objects
42%

animal skin
bear rug
bear skin
beaver skin
fox fur
hide
skin of mouse
skin of rabbit
skin of tiger
shell

Architecture
3%

church
house
lighthouse
tower

Fire, etc.
.7%

bomb exploding

Maps, etc.
2%

aerial map
map
relief map

Natural objects
10%

ditch
dust
geyser erupting
ground penetrated by
  drill
mine shaft
mountain and divide
rock
scaling from boiler
section of earth
smoke
substance

Objects
17%

beds
beef

bookends
bucket
cake
champagne bottle on
  ice
crown
decoration
drill
drinking trough
machinery
manuscript
pinafore
saddle and stirrups
shield
star
steamship
sweater

Plants, etc.
4%

flower
leaf

D 1

D1 = 18
D1% = 3

Animal details
11%

head of boar

Human details
56%

head of Barrymore
head of king
head of King Cole
head of Old Man of
  Mountain
head of Saint Nick

Maps, etc.
11%

map

Natural objects
6%

clouds

Objects
17%

chair
ship

D 2

D2 = 118
D2% = 21

Anatomy (human)
2%

nerve root
sternum

Animals
23%

(Winged)
(18%)

bird
bug
butterfly
dragon fly
duck
eagle
goose
insect
owl
penguin
prehistoric bird
"winged caterpillar"

(Other than winged)
(5%)

animal
fish
pneumococcus
prehistoric animal
tadpole
worm

Animal details
3%

face of animal
face of trout
head of owl
head of turkey

Architecture
8%

lighthouse
monument
steeple of church
tower

Fire, etc.
.8%

rocket

Human beings
.8%

pagan god

Human details
2%

clenched fist
head of man

Maps, etc.
2%

map

Natural objects
2%

fountain

CARD VI—*(Continued)*

Objects
57%

airplane
altar
ax
baton
bed post (decorated)
candle holder
cross
dart
drill
emblem
engine of airplane
handle of dagger
headdress (Indian)
idol
lamp
mace of pope
object with feathered
  appendages
pin
pole
post
sceptre
spearhead
sword
totem pole (25%)

X-ray
.8%

x-ray

D 3

D3 = 34
D3% = 6

Anatomy (animal)
3%

dorsal part of animal

Anatomy (embryo.)
9%

brain of embryo
primitive streak

Anatomy (human)
3%

vertebral column

Animals
9%

roach
seahorse
tadpole

Human beings
6%

man
soldier

Objects
71%

banister post
bed post
candlestick
club
drill
furniture leg
lamp stand
pan handle
rail spindle
stair rail
sword
table leg
thermometer
totem pole

D 4

D4 = 12
D4% = 2

Anatomy (embryo.)
17%

embryonic neural
  groove

Anatomy (human)
17%

spinal column
vertebral column

Objects
58%

bed post
drill
lamp post
pipe
statue
totem pole

Miscellaneous
8%

electrical impulses

D 5

D5 = 24
D5% = 4

Anatomy (human)
4%

macrophage

Animals
17%

(Winged)
(17%)

bird
insect

Animal details
17%

wings of bird
wings of hen
swimmerettes of crab

Animal objects
17%

ermine tails
feathers

Fire, etc.
4%

flame

Natural objects
13%

fountain
light
mud

Objects
4%

emblem

Plants, etc.
21%

leaves

Miscellaneous
4%

electricity waves

D 6

D6 = 29
D6% = 5

Anatomy (animal)
3%

neural system in
  worm

Anatomy (embryo.)
7%

embryo
embryo of chick

Animals
3%

(Winged)
(3%)

bug

Architecture
3%

monument

Human beings
3%

king with regalia

Natural objects
21%

canal and ship
fountain
oil well and pump
river

Objects
59%

brush
clothes tree
cross
drill
lamp
lamp post
lantern
sceptre
sword
torpedo
totem pole

D 7

D7 = 29
D7% = 5

Anatomy (animal)
3%

breastbone of turkey

Anatomy (embryo.)
3%

primitive streak

Anatomy (human)
14%

incision
slit throat
spinal cord with
  foramen

Architecture
10%

archway leading to
  corridor
gate

Natural objects
59%

canal and surrounding
  land
canyon
channel
creek
decay
mountains
pipe line and land
railroad and surround-
  ing territory
waterfall

Card VI—*(Continued)*

Objects 10%	*Natural objects* 33%	*Animal details* 100%	*Maps, etc.* 6%
hinge	agate	claws of animal	map

Objects 10%
hinge
steel
torpedo

d 1
d1 = 11
d1% = 2
Anatomy (human) 9%
sperm head
Animal details 91%
head of animal
head of cat
head of caterpillar
head of eagle
head of horsefly
head of lizard
head of owl
head of worm

d 2
d2 = 3
d2% = .5
Animal details 67%
paw of cat
tail of raccoon

Natural objects 33%
agate

d 3
d3 = 6
d3% = 1
Anatomy (human) 33%
ovaries
thyroid glands
Animals 17%
(Winged) (17%)
birds
Animal objects 17%
clamshell
Human beings 17%
persons
Human details 17%
hands

dd
dd = 5
dd% = .8

Animal details 100%
claws of animal
feelers
whiskers

di
di = 3
di% = .5
Anatomy (human) 33%
ducts
Human details 67%
face

dr
dr = 17
dr% = 3
Anatomy (embryo.) 6%
embryo of animal
Anatomy (human) 6%
vertebral notches
Architecture 12%
castle
doorway

Maps, etc. 6%
map
Natural objects 18%
beach
dust
ice
Objects 35%
bell
bomb
bullet head
chair
chess pawn
Sex 12%
sex organs
Miscellaneous 6%
industrial scene

dr + S
dr + S = 1
dr + S% = .1
Objects 100%
cotton

Card VII

COLLEGE AGE R = 482		*Animal details* 2%	Dopeys

COLLEGE AGE R = 482

W
W = 172
W% = 36
Anatomy (animal) .5%
dissected frog
Anatomy (embryo.) .5%
embryo
Anatomy (human) 8%
bony structure
cell
chest wall
pelvic bones
teeth and lower jaw
 of remains of man

thoracic region
vertebra
Animals 9%
(Winged) (1%)
geese
pelicans
(Other than winged) (8%)
animals
dogs
donkeys
elephants
frog
monkeys
rabbit
squirrels
starfish

Animal details 2%
head of bison with
 part missing
horns
Animal objects 2%
bear rug
rabbit skin
sea shell
Art 1%
design
Human beings 43%
acrobats
angels
babies
Cupids
dancers

Dopeys
dwarfs
figures
girls
gnomes
imps
Indians
jitterbugs
ladies
Little Lulu
nymphs
old ladies
old maids
people
Punch and Judy
Siamese twins
women
Maps, etc. 2%
map
relief map

CARD VII—*(Continued)*

Natural objects
10%
clouds
masses of land
rock
smoke
steam
tract of land
waterfall

Objects
20%
beard (false)
bomber
book-ends
bowl
bracelet
cast
cement wall hit by
  shell
chair
chicken (fried)
clams (fried)
clippers
collar
hanger for stockings
lamp
necklace
objects
paper (torn)
something broken
statue
velvet

Plants, etc.
2%
cactus
plant tissue
under sea growth

W′

W′ = 4
W′% = .8
Animals
25%
(*Winged*)
(25%)
bee in flight
Human beings
25%
women
Natural objects
25%
section of ground

X-ray
25%
x-ray of pelvis

WS

WS = 21
WS% = 4
Architecture
5%
church in a valley
Maps, etc.
5%
map of land and
  water
Natural objects
90%
bay and coastline
body of water and
  coast
canal and land
chasm and cliff
harbor
land and water
pass and cliff
reservoir and
  surrounding land
river and rock

D 1

D1 = 35
D1% = 7
Anatomy (human)
6%
brain stem
pelvic cavity
Animals
11%
(*Winged*)
(11%)
butterfly
moth
Animal details
9%
head of dog
head of scottie
Architecture
3%
street
Human details
6%
faces of women

heads
Maps, etc.
6%
map of Austria
map of Spain
Natural objects
26%
chasm and cliffs
clouds
gale
icebergs
mist
rock
sea coast with narrow
  lock
stone
valley
Objects
34%
balls
basketball trunks
collar
cradle
football pad
headdress (Russian)
hinge
steel
stools
sweater
swimming trunks

D 2

D2 = 23
D2% = 5
Anatomy (human)
9%
ribs
sternum
Animals
4%
(*Winged*)
4%
swanlike
Animal details
9%
face of monkey
head of bear
Human details
61%
face of puppet
head of Punch
heads

thumb
thumb and hand
thumbs up
Natural objects
9%
clouds
peninsula
Objects
9%
mask
watering can

D 3

D3 = 45
D3% = 9
Animals
7%
animals
cats
squirrels
Animal details
18%
feet of pig
heads of donkeys
heads of rabbits
horns
Human beings
2%
acrobats
Human details
56%
faces
faces, impudent
faces of children
faces of girls
faces of women
head of Indian
head of Victorian
  lady
thumb
thumbs up
Maps, etc.
7%
map
map of British Isles
map of Spain
Natural objects
2%
clouds
Objects
9%
pipe
rocking chair

CARD VII—(Continued)

seat
stamp

D 4

D4 = 95
D4% = 20

Animals
25%

(Winged)
(5%)

chicks
ducks
eagles
turkeys

(Other than winged)
(20%)

dogs
donkeys
elephants
ghosts with tails and
  horns
rabbits
satyrs
seals

Human beings
44%

cherubs
children
Chinese women
dancers
elves
girls
Indians
ladies
Mercury
old ladies
Venus
women

Human details
5%

hands
hands and shoulders
thumbs up

Maps, etc.
3%

map
map of France
relief map

Natural objects
7%

clouds
iceberg
island

rock
rocky promontory
smoke

Objects
15%

bust
gargoyle
radiator cap
statue
tin can
trousers, torn

D 5

D5 = 3
D5% = .6

Human beings
33%

jugglers' act

Maps, etc.
33%

map

Natural objects
33%

promontory

D 1 + D 2

D1 + D2 = 3
D1 + D2% = .6

Anatomy (human)
33%

skeleton of pelvic
  girdle

Human beings
33%

dancer

Natural objects
33%

rock

D 1 + D 2 + S

D1 + D2 + S = 1
D1 + D2 + S% = .2

Anatomy (human)
100%

mouth showing throat

D 4 + S

D4 + S = 1
D4 + S% = .2

Natural objects
100%

islands and water

d 1

d1 = 33
d1% = 7

Anatomy (human)
18%

blood vessel
capillary tube
cross-section of
  sternum
epiglottis
pectoral region and
  tissue
pubic symphysis

Architecture
3%

house

Human beings
9%

people
person
sentry

Natural objects
15%

canal and steamship
stream
Suez Canal

Objects
52%

airplane fuselage
bullet
candle
capsule
cigar
clamp
clasp
glue
hinge
lock
oil plates of fluid
  drive
pin
pot
zipper

Sex
3%

female genitalia

d 2

d2 = 8
d2% = 2

Animal details
38%

head of seal
horns
leg of cow

Human details
25%

finger
thumb

Maps, etc.
13%

map

Natural objects
13%

snow

Plants
13%

branch of tree

d 3

d3 = 3
d3% = .6

Animal details
67%

head of mouse
head of mule

Human details
33%

"V" hairdo

d 4

d4 = 6
d4% = 1

Anatomy (human)
17%

appendix

Animals
50%

snake
worm

Animal details
17%

tail of lamb

Objects
17%

handle of curling
  stone

dd

dd = 5
dd% = 1

CARD VII—*(Continued)*

Architecture
20%
house

Human beings
60%
figures
people

Natural objects
20%
tunnel

de

de = 2
de% = .4

Human details
100%
profile

profile from "funnies"

dr

dr = 5
dr% = 1

Anatomy (human)
20%
ligature

Animals
20%
dog

Human beings
20%
person

Human details
20%
face

Objects
20%
apparatus

dr + S

dr + S = 3
dr + S% = .6

Anatomy (human)
33%
portion leading into cervix

Natural objects
33%
bay with surrounding land

Sex
33%
vagina

S = 14
S% = 3

Human details
7%
head

Natural objects
7%
smoke

Objects
86%
arrowhead
image
sign on Heinz products

CARD VIII

COLLEGE AGE
R = 609

W

W = 127
W% = 21

Anatomy (animal)
7%
dissected animal
internal organs of animal
internal structure of chicken
section of sheep's maxillary region
skeleton of crab
skeleton of fish organs
transverse section through skull of insect

Anatomy (human)
10%
chest
dorsal section of body
organs
part of body
pectoral region
pelvis
plexus
skeleton of body
tissue

vertebra

Animals
9%
(Winged)
(.7%)
butterfly
(Other than winged)
(8%)
crab
flat fish
flounder
hermit crab
marine animal
sea fish
skate
spider

Animal details
.7%
face of horsefly

Animal objects
3%
fossil of shell
sea shell

Architecture
.7%
Chinese pagoda

Art
4%
design
painting
picture

Color
2%
(color naming)

Fire, etc.
2%
fire and smoke
skyrocket

Human beings
2%
madman
sorcerer from "Arabia Nights"

Human details
2%
face of oriental
face of person

Maps, etc.
14%
chart (anatomical)
map
slide

Natural objects
3%
aquatic scene
coral reef
fountain
pastoral scene

Objects
32%
bowl

bowl with ice cream
brooch
Chinese decoration
{coat of arms (23%)
{crest
crown
doodling
emblem
insignia
jewel
machine (Rube Goldberg)

Plants, etc.
7%
center portion of flower
flower
Japanese garden
orchid
sweet pea
tulip

Symbolism
2%
cool breeze blowing
represents Russian army driving out foe
something compelling

X-ray
.7%
x-ray

CARD VIII—(Continued)

W'

W' = 23
W'% = 4

Anatomy (animal)
22%
mouth of animal
skeleton of animal
spinal cavity of
  cricket
spinal cavity of fish

Animal objects
4%
coral

Anatomy (human)
4%
thoracic cavity

Animals
13%

(Winged)
(4%)
butterfly

(Other than winged)
(9%)
animals
seafish

Architecture
4%
castle on hill

Human beings
9%
children around a
  tree
women

Maps, etc.
9%
chart (anatomical)

Objects
22%
food
paint
sailing vessel
shield
ship

Plants, etc.
4%
flower

X-ray
9%
x-ray of throat
x-ray of upper part

D 1

D1 = 192
D1% = 32

Anatomy (animal)
.5%
skeleton of animal

Anatomy (embryo.)
2%
embryo

Anatomy (human)
1%
kidney
section through body

Animals
95%

(Winged)
(2%)
bats
birds
flies
insects

(Other than winged)
(93%)
animals (17%)
bears (17%)
beavers
boars
bulls
cats
chameleons
dogs
elephants (pink)
fishes
frogs
gophers
ground hogs
guinea pigs
lions
lizards
mice
prehistoric animals
rats (13%)
sloths
squirrels
tadpoles
toads
wolfs
woodchucks

Natural objects
.5%
stones

Objects
.5%
crest

Plants, etc.
.5%
parsnips

D 2

D2 = 64
D2% = 11

Anatomy (embryo.)
2%
embryo

Anatomy (human)
3%
kidneys
pelvic bones

Animals
52%

(Winged)
(44%)
butterfly (44%)

(Other than winged)
(8%)
frog

Animal details
3%
face of cat
face of donkey

Fire, etc.
3%
fire

Human beings
2%
tramp

Maps, etc.
2%
slide

Natural objects
11%
precious stone
rock
sea scene
stones

Objects
2%
beef steak

Plants, etc.
22%
flower
leaf

marine growth

D 3

D3 = 51
D3% = 8

Anatomy (human)
2%
cell

Animals
43%

(Winged)
(4%)
butterfly
dragonfly

(Other than winged)
(39%)
creature
devilfish
dragon
frog
lizard
louse
monster
octopus
scorpion
spider
unicorn

Animal details
2%
wings

Architecture
12%
castle
castle on hill
Chinese pagoda
hut
Japanese home
roof of house

Human beings
6%
devil
men
women

Maps, etc.
4%
map of England
map of Labrador

Natural objects
4%
froth
island

CARD VIII—(Continued)

Objects
10%

bird house
cap
crown
dunce cap
tent

Plants, etc.
18%

leaf
shrubbery
tree

D 4

D4 = 40
D4% = 7

Anatomy
3%

hemorrhage

Animals
13%

(Winged)
(3%)

butterfly

(Other than winged)
(10%)

animals
crab
jellyfish

Natural objects
3%

ice

Objects
80%

barrels
book
crown
cushions
dress (satin)
flags
football pad
heraldic sign
lingerie
material for dress
pillows
squares

Plants, etc.
3%

leaves

D 5

D5 = 22
D5% = 4

Anatomy (animal)
14%

skeleton of animal
skeleton of frog
skeleton of invertebrate

Anatomy (human)
36%

ribs
skeleton
vertebral column
vertebral column and nerves

Animals
5%

fish

Animal details
14%

face of dog
head of bison
head of cow

Animal objects
5%

sea-shell

Human details
14%

face
head of ghost
teeth

Objects
9%

arrow
roasted chicken

Plants, etc.
5%

flower

D 6

D6 = 14
D6% = 2

Anatomy (human)
14%

cytoplasm
pelvic girdle

Animal details
50%

head of frog

Natural objects
14%

boulder
stone

Objects
7%

flag

Plants, etc.
14%

flower
tulip

D 7

D7 = 5
D7% = .8

Animal details
20%

head of pig

Color
20%

(color naming)

Natural objects
60%

crystal
quartz
stone

D 3 + D 5

D3 + D5 = 4
D3 + D5% = .6

Anatomy (animal)
25%'

bone of chicken

Anatomy (human)
25%

vertebra

Objects
25%

umbrella

X-ray
25%

x-ray of breast

D 4 + D 5

D4 + D5 = 6
D4 + D5% = .9

Anatomy (human)
17%

skeleton

Animal
17%

crayfish

Human details
33%

head and shoulders of person

Objects
33%

corset

D 3 + D 4 + D 5

D3+D4+D5 = 18
D3+D4+D5% = 3

Anatomy (animal)
6%

dissected frog

Anatomy (human)
17%

backbone and ribs
pelvis and coccyx
skeleton

Animals
11%

bloodsucker
frog

Architecture
17%

building
castle
temple

Human beings
6%

ghostly figure

Human details
11%

head and shoulders of man
shoulders

Maps, etc.
6%

topographical map

Objects
22%

Chinese headdress
crown
sails of pirate ship

Plants, etc.
6%

tropical plant

D 4 + D 5 + D 6 + S

D4 + D5 + D6 + S = 1
D4 + D5 + D6 + S% = .1

CARD VIII—(Continued)

Anatomy (human)
100%
thoracic cavity

d 1

d1 = 3
d1% = .4

Animal details
100%
head of dog
head of fox terrier
head of pig

d 2

d2 = 4
d2% = .6

Anatomy (human)
50%
medulla oblongata
pubis

Maps, etc.
25%
chart (anatomical)

Objects
25%
vase

dd

dd = 8
dd% = 1

Anatomy
13%
bone

Animals
50%
(Winged)
(13%)
grasshopper
(Other than winged)
(38%)
animal
gopher
squirrel

Human beings
13%
people

Objects
25%
coat hook
forceps

di

di = 4
di% = .6

Human beings
25%
child

Human details
25%
eyes

Objects
50%
hieroglyphics
object (ghostly)

dr

dr = 21
dr% = 3

Anatomy (embryo.)
5%
embryo fold

Anatomy (human)
19%
ganglion
joints pulled apart
nerve root

Animals
29%
animal
bloodsucker
caterpillar
fish
frog

Animal details
5%
head of crayfish

Architecture
5%
dome

Art
5%
design

Human beings
5%
man diving

Human details
5%
head of Sherlock Holmes

Objects
19%
blowgun
propeller
shaft
thermometer

Plants, etc.
5%
tree

dr + S

dr + S = 1
dr + S% = .1

Anatomy (human)
100%
skeleton

S

S = 1
S% = .1

Human details
100%
head of Indian

CARD IX

COLLEGE AGE
R = 550

W

W = 99
W% = 18

Anatomy (animal)
2%
inside of animal
inside of cat

Anatomy (embryo.)
1%
embryo

Anatomy (human)
16%
abdomen
artery

---

chest cavity
hip bones
organs of person
scapula
vertebra

Animals
9%
(Winged)
(1%)
winged beasts
(Other than winged)
(8%)
animals
bulls
dragons
fish
jellyfish

---

reptile
sea horses

Animal details
2%
face of owl
wings of bird

Animal objects
1%
coral

Architecture
1%
entrance to tomb

Art
6%
cartoon
scene in technicolor
surrealist art

---

surrealist painting

Color
1%
(color naming)

Fire, etc.
15%
chemical experiment (explosion)
explosion
fire
flames
volcano

Human beings
7%
ballet scene
baseball catcher

CARD IX—*(Continued)*

characters on
horseback
farmers talking over
fence
men riding and
holding something
priests in flames
witches

Maps, etc.
7%

diagram of human
anatomy
map
maps of Norway
slide
topographical map

Natural objects
11%

deep sea formation
fountain
gases
geyser
incense
smoke

Objects
9%

candle in ornamental
globe
convertor
crest
emblem of K.K.K.
statue
tanks
vase

Plants, etc.
5%

flowers
plant
seaweed
tree

Signs and Symbols
1%

symbol

Symbolism
4%

elements—fire, water,
earth, air
nightmare
subjugation of a great
and glorious race
unseen powers
brewing

Miscellaneous
1%

symmetry

W'

$W' = 7$
$W'\% = 1$

Anatomy (animal)
14%

remains of animal

Anatomy (human)
29%

organs of person
skeleton of pelvis and
spine

Animal details
14%

head of pig

Fire, etc.
14%

fire

Maps, etc.
14%

map

Natural objects
14%

fountain

D 1

$D1 = 116$
$D1\% = 21$

Anatomy (human)
27%

bone
bladder
gall bladder
heart
heart and veins
kidney
liver
lungs
nerve
nerve fiber
nerve tissue
organs
pelvic bone
scapula
stomach
veins

Animals
30%
(Winged)
(3%)

bird
insect
rooster

(Other than winged)
(28%)

animal
bear
dogs
dragon
elephant
fish
horses
larva
lion
moose
oyster
parasite
pigs
rhinoceros
sea horses
undersea life
Winnie the Pooh

Animal details
3%

head of animal
head of boar

Animal objects
.8%

coral

Human beings
3%

girl
person
woman

Human details
10%

faces
heads

Maps, etc.
3%

map of Canada
map of Norway
map of Quebec

Natural objects
6%

clouds
islands
rock
smoke

Objects
10%

bag pipe
decoration
face of gargoyle
food
gas mask
pipes
pitchers
planes
shot
tank

Plants, etc.
8%

algae
cactus
flowers
fungus
leaves
plants
underwater plants

D 2

$D2 = 97$
$D2\% = 18$

Anatomy (human)
3%

artery
nerve tissue
tissue

Animals
32%
(Winged)
(1%)

birds

(Other than winged)
(31%)

crabs
crayfish
dragon
fish
gold fish
guinea pig
jungle cat
mice
moose
pig
scorpion
shrimp
squirrels
stags
unicorn

CARD IX—(Continued)

Animal details
10%

head of animal
head of donkey
head of moose
horns of reindeer
wings of bird
wings of eagle

Fire, etc.
10%

fire
flames

Human beings
33%

angels
characters
chiefs
clansmen
clowns
dancers
dwarfs
farmers
goblins
Jack Frost
jugglers
knights
men
people
Uriah Heep
witches

Maps, etc.
4%

map
map of Norway

Natural objects
2%

clouds
stellar body

Objects
1%

bomber

Plants, etc.
4%

flower

D 3

D3 = 1
D1% = .1

Animal details
100%

head of boar

D 4

D4 = 12
D4% = 2

Anatomy (embryo.)
8%

foetus

Anatomy (human)
8%

part of the anatomy

Human details
42%

face of man
head (bleeding)
head of man

Objects
17%

pillow
snowball

Plants, etc.
25%

apples
plant

D 5

D5 = 5
D5% = .9

Animals
20%

skate

Objects
60%

candle and stand
incense burner

Plants, etc.
20%

tree

D 6

D6 = 51
D6% = 9

Anatomy (embryo.)
4%

embryo
foetus

Anatomy (human)
14%

blood
blood cells
chromosomes
kidneys
ovaries
part of anatomy

section of brain

Animals
8%

(Winged)
(2%)

owl

(Other than winged)
(6%)

monster
sea fish

Animal objects
2%

coral

Fire, etc.
10%

fire
flames

Human beings
14%

babies
infants
men
people

Natural objects
16%

clouds
pebbles
smoke
vapor

Objects
14%

bricks
cotton (bloody)
pipes
pots
pottery
powder puff
weights

Plants, etc.
20%

apples
cherries
gourds
pears
potatoes

D 7

D7 = 27
D7% = 5

Anatomy (animal)
7%

backbone of animal

spinal cord of
caterpillar

Anatomy (embryo.)
4%

notochord

Anatomy (human)
19%

aesophagus
incision
nerve tissue
skeleton of cord
spinal column

Animals
4%

centipede

Fire, etc.
7%

rocket
shot (from gun)

Natural objects
26%

fountain
geyser
incense (smoke)
smoke

Objects
26%

arrow
candle
cannon
pole
rope

Plants, etc.
7%

plant
seaweed stalk

D 8

D8 = 2
D8% = .3

Anatomy (human)
50%

scapula

Animals
50%

crab

D 9

D9 = 22
D9% = 4

Anatomy (animal)
5%

skull of mouse

CARD IX—(Continued)

Anatomy (human)
18%

cell
skull of person

Animals
5%

fish

Animal details
45%

face of animal
face of cat
face of fish
face of monkey
face of rabbit

Human details
9%

head of man

Objects
18%

gas mask
lamp
mask
urn

D 10

D10 = 12
D10% = 2

Natural objects
8%

pool of water

Objects
92%

ball
glass
lantern
vase
world

D 1 + D 2

D1 + D2 = 12
D1 + D2% = 2

Animals
50%

bull
dog with bird in
  mouth
dragon

Animal details
8%

head of animal

Human beings
17%

beings from another
  world
girls

Maps, etc.
8%

medical chart

Natural objects
8%

sunset

Plants, etc.
8%

flower

D 7 + D 8

D7 + D8 = 1
D7 + D8% = .1

Anatomy (embryo.)
100%

embryo

D 5 + D 10

D5 + D10 = 1
D5 + D10% = .1

Natural objects
100%

fountain

D 7 + D 10

D7 + D10 = 1
D7 + D10% = .1

Objects
100%

oil lamp

D 2 + D 7 + D 10

D2 + D7 + D10 = 1
D2 + D7 + D10%
  = .1

Natural objects
100%

water and water jet

d 1

d1 = 8
d1% = 1

Animal details
38%

claws
horns of reindeer

Human beings
25%

figures

Human details
13%

Roosevelt's smile

Objects
25%

faucets
shoes

d 2

d2 = 6
d2% = 1

Anatomy (human)
17%

glands

Human details
83%

eyes

d 3

d3 = 6
d3% = 1

Animal details
17%

legs of grasshopper

Architecture
17%

bridge

Fire, etc.
17%

flame

Human details
17%

two hands folded

Objects
33%

rope
wands

d 1 + d 3

d1 + d3 = 1
d1 + d3% = .1

Human details
100%

thumb and forefinger

d 3 + S

d3 + S = 2
d3 + S% = .3

Anatomy (human)
50%

eye

Natural objects
50%

chasm and bridge

dd

dd = 9
dd% = 2

Anatomy (human)
22%

blood cells
ligament

Animal details
11%

feet of bird

Human beings
11%

person

Human details
55%

finger
hand

de

de = 2
de% = .3

Human details
100%

face
profile of Hitler

di

di = 8
di% = 1

Anatomy (animal)
13%

gill cleft

Anatomy
13%

blood stream

Human beings
25%

people

Human details
13%

eyes

Natural objects
25%

fountain

CARD IX—(Continued)

Sex
13%
genital organs

dr

dr = 41
dr% = 7

Anatomy (animal)
2%
bones of reptile

Anatomy (human)
12%
artery
bone

Animals
29%

(Winged)
(5%)
eagle
turkey

(Other than winged)
(24%)
dog
lion
monster
octopus
rabbit
sea-horse
squirrel

Animal details
7%
head of horse
head of rabbit

nose of pig

Human beings
7%
figure in uniform
person
man in "Buck
  Rogers" scene

Human details
12%
face of butler
face of W. C. Fields
hand
head of man
head and shoulders

Natural objects
2%
gases

Objects
17%
andirons
cannon
chemical apparatus
jacket
statues
wall

Signs and symbols
5%
"V" wings
wings of victory

X-ray
5%
x-ray of sternum
x-ray of vertebrate

CARD X

COLLEGE AGE
R = 791

W

W = 94
W% = 12

Anatomy (animal)
1%
dissection of animal

Anatomy (human)
2%
lungs and trachea
vertebra

Animals
26%

(Winged)
(14%)
bugs
cricket
insects

(Other than winged)
(12%)
animals
animal battle
animals in pool
dragon
lower forms of life
marine zoo
sea animals
water animals
worms

Animal objects
2%
coral
shells

Architecture
3%
bridges
castle in sky
World's Fair

Art
13%
Chinese painting
design
painting
painting by child

Color
2%
(color description)
(color naming)

Human beings
3%
dance of Bacchus
god
jousting match

Maps, etc.
10%
chart (anatomical)
slide
slide (histological)
slide in medical book
slide in zoology book

Natural objects
15%
ant hill
clouds
floor of sea
island formation
land
sea scene
underwater scene
waste land

Objects
9%
afghan
crest
idol
light bulb
object
wall paper

Plants, etc.
11%
ferns
Japanese garden
leaves
orchids
rock garden
seaweed
tree
tulip (cross section)

Symbolism
3%
bad dream
Gotterdammerung

Utopia

Miscellaneous
1%
pageant

W'

W' = 21
W'% = 3

Anatomy (animal)
5%
body of animal

Anatomy (human)
5%
lungs and trachea

Animals
19%

(Winged)
(5%)
butterfly

(Other than winged)
(14%)
animals
bacteria
creatures

Architecture
38%
estate
monument
Taj Maha!
temple

CARD X—*(Continued)*

Human beings
10%
figures (persons)
oriental deity

Natural objects
5%
bank of river

Objects
19%
Christmas decorations
wedding bells

D 1

D1 = 128
D1% = 16

Anatomy (animal)
.7%
skeleton of butterfly

Anatomy (human)
5%
alveoli
cells
nerve cells
neurons

Animals
81%

(Winged)
(7%)
bug
insect

(Other than winged)
(74%)
crab (32%)
crayfish
dragon
lobster
octopus
Portuguese man-of-
war
sea fish
shell fish
spider (23%)
starfish
tortoise

Animal objects
.7%
sponge

Human beings
5%
devils
figures
genie

witch doctor

Maps, etc.
.7%
slide

Objects
.7%
broom

Plants, etc.
5%
flowers
fungus
roots of plant
seaweed

D 2

D2 = 25
D2% = 3

Anatomy (human)
4%
vas diferens

Animals
84%

(Winged)
(4%)
insects

(Other than winged)
(80%)
caterpillars
eels
lizards
snails
snakes
worms

Human beings
8%
ladies
spooks

Objects
4%
curtains

D 3

D3 = 53
D3% = 7

Anatomy (animal)
6%
brain of frog
lungs of frog
skeleton of bears
with torpedo

Anatomy (human)
11%
bones
lungs and trachea
spinal cord
windpipe
vertebra

Animals
47%

(Winged)
(15%)
beetles
bugs
crickets
flies

(Other than winged)
(32%)
animals with pole
caterpillars
cockroaches
crabs
fishes
lobsters
monkeys
mouse-like animals

Architecture
13%
temple
tower

Human beings
6%
lady
man
people

Human details
2%
head of Hindenburg

Objects
4%
cannon
Christmas bells

Plants, etc.
6%
branch of tree with
acorns
sea anemones
tree

X-ray
6%
x-ray
x-ray of sternum

D 4

D4 = 52
D4% = 7

Anatomy (human)
4%
kidneys
stomach

Animals
79%

(Winged)
(48%)
beetles
birds
bugs
chickens
grasshoppers
insects
parrots
potato bug

(Other than winged)
(31%)
animals
caterpillars
crabs
crayfish
octopus
snails
squirrels

Animal objects
2%
coral

Art
2%
design

Human beings
4%
men
servants

Human details
4%
faces
heads of men

Plants, etc.
6%
flower
potatoes

D 5

D5 = 57
D5% = 7

CARD X—(Continued)

Animals
68%
(Winged)
(4%)
bug
insect
(Other than winged)
(65%)
alligators
caterpillars
dragons
eels
goat
jackal
larvae
lizards
mice
seahorses
sheep
slugs
snakes
worms

Animal details
5%
face of rabbit with antennae of insect
head of animal with whiskers
head of insect

Animal objects
2%
wishbone

Architecture
9%
archway
entrance
Gothic architecture
staircase
staircase with banisters

Human beings
2%
man

Objects
11%
harp
horseshoe
lyre
pincers
ship

Plants, etc.
4%
catkins

sea anemone

D 6

D6 = 62
D6% = 8

Anatomy (human)
5%
nerve ganglia
tissue cells

Animals
87%
(Winged)
(31%)
bat
beetle
birds
bugs
dragon fly
insects
(Other than winged)
(56%)
caterpillar
dragon
frog
moose
mouse
octopus
parasite
reindeer
seahorses

Animal objects
2%
cocoons

Human beings
2%
spies

Maps, etc.
2%
slide

Plants, etc.
3%
flowers

D 7

D7 = 9
D7% = 1

Animal details
89%
face of jackass
head of grasshopper
head of rabbit

Objects
11%
Indian feather

D 8

D8 = 18
D8% = 2

Anatomy (human)
61%
bone
cornea of eye
ganglia
pelvic bones
vertebra

Animals
28%
(Winged)
(17%)
birds
insects
swallows
(Other than winged)
(11%)
clam
oyster

Architecture
6%
dam

Plants, etc.
6%
sea anemone

D 9

D9 = 62
D9% = 8

Anatomy (embryo.)
5%
embryo

Anatomy (human)
8%
blood
blood smear
lungs
pelvic bone
wound

Animals
27%
(Winged)
(3%)
insects
(Other than winged)
(24%)
caterpillar

dragon
eels
fish
lobsters
seahorses
silkworms
snails

Animal objects
8%
coral

Fire, etc.
2%
fire

Human beings
24%
characters from "Alice in Wonderland"
children
Dopey
dwarfs
ghosts
goblins
mermaid
people
snake charmer
twins

Maps, etc.
3%
map
map of California

Natural objects
13%
cliff
clouds
coastline
land
rock

Objects
8%
brick
gargoyle
ink
molten metal
slip

Plants, etc.
2%
flower

D 10

D10 = 26
D10% = 3

Anatomy (human)
46%
cells

CARD X—(*Continued*)

cell tissue
cornea
lymphocytes
motor neurone
ovary

Animals
35%
(*Winged*)
(8%)

birds
insects

(*Other than winged*)
(27%)

amoeba
dogs
lions
poodles
seahorses

Human beings
4%

fairy

Maps, etc.
4%

slide

Objects
8%

fried eggs

Plants, etc.
4%

sea anemone

D 11

D11 = 12
D11% = 2

Anatomy
8%

blood smear

Animals
17%

amoeba
snail

Animal details
17%

head of dog

Human details
17%

head of Cupid
head of Indian

Maps, etc.
17%

map of Guam
map of New Jersey

Natural objects
17%

clouds
Isle of Man

Objects
8%

eggs (food)

D 12

D12 = 24
D12% = 3

Anatomy (human)
8%

glandular structure
vertebra

Animal details
4%

ears of Mickey
Mouse

Animal objects
21%

wishbone

Maps, etc.
4%

slide

Objects
42%

balls
governor
gyroscope
pawnshop symbol
pendulum
prize

Plants, etc.
17%

cherries
maple seed
oak seed
seed

Sex
4%

genitals

D 13

D13 = 8
D13% = 1

Animals
63%

(*Other than winged*)
(63%)

anthropoid
cow

crayfish

Animal details
25%

claws

Human beings
13%

figures

D 14

D14 = 12
D14% = 2

Anatomy (animal)
8%

brain of frog

Anatomy (human)
33%

blood vessel
spinal cord
trachea

Architecture
8%

tower

Objects
42%

chimney
smoke stack
Statue of Liberty
stove pipe
valve

X-ray
8%

x-ray of stalk of sea
plant

D 15

D15 = 17
D15% = 2

Anatomy (human)
24%

nerve cell
stomach

Animals
18%

(*Winged*)
(6%)

swan

(*Other than winged*)
(12%)

animal
fish

Animal objects
6%

coral

Natural objects
6%

island

Objects
6%

egg yolk

Plants, etc.
41%

cotton ball
flowers

D 16

D16 = 9
D16% = 1

Human beings
100%

bobby
divers
ghosts
glass blowers
ladies
men
people
person
policemen

D 17

D17 = 2
D17% = .2

Animal details
50%

horns of goat

Human beings
50%

fencers

D 18

D18 = 53
D18% = 7

Animals
96%

(*Winged*)
(4%)

birds
insects

(*Other than winged*)
(92%)

crabs (66%)
crayfish

CARD X—*(Continued)*

lobster
prehistoric animal
scorpion
spider

Human beings
4%

knights on dragon
wild person with tree
branch

D 3 + D 9

D3 + D9 = 2
D3 + D9% = .2

Animals
50%

octopus

Human beings
50%

Chinese god

D 5 + D 10

D5 + D10 = 1
D5 + D10% = .1

Plants, etc.
100%

cross-section of tulip

D 6 + D 15

D6 + D15 = 2
D6 + D15% = .2

Animals
50%
(Winged)
(50%)

birds

Plants, etc.
50%

flowers

D 8 + D 16

D8 + D16 = 2
D8 + D16% = .2

Human beings
100%

figures holding bottles
men

D 6 + D 11 + D 15

D6+D11+D15 = 3
D6+D11+D15%
= .3

Animals
33%
(Winged)
33%

birds

Human beings
33%

servants

Plants, etc.
33%

blooms

D 6 + D 11 + D 15 + D 18

D6+D11+D15
+D18 = 1
D6+D11+D15
+D18% = .1

Animals
100%

collection of
seahorses

D 8 + S

D8 + S = 1
D8 + S% = .1

Architecture
100%

bridge over chasm

D 3 + D 8 + S

D3+D8+S = 1
D3+D8+S% = .1

Architecture
100%

gates and road

dd

dd = 1
dd% = .1

Architecture
100%

factory with chimney

de

de = 1
de% = .1

Human details
100%

profile of boy

di

di = 1
di% = .1

Anatomy
100%

blood smear

dr = 14
dr% = 2

Anatomy (human)
21%

ligament
lungs and trachea

Animals
14%
(Winged)
(7%)

fly

(Other than winged)
(7%)

dog

Architecture
7%

Eiffel Tower

Human beings
7%

person

Human details
21%

face
face and hat

Maps, etc.
7%

map

Objects
14%

gauge
microscope

X-ray
7%

x-ray of spinal cord

dr + S

dr + S = 7
dr + S% = .8

Human details
43%

face
face with helmet

Natural objects
43%

canal and barges
ravine and bank

Objects
14%

moorhead and shaft

S

S = 10
S% = 2

Animals
20%

dog
teddy bear

Human beings
20%

man
oriental deity

Natural objects
20%

crevice
pit

Objects
40%

idol
pipe
wrench

A STATISTICAL STUDY OF "CARD-PULL"

A Statistical Study of "Card-Pull" for Comparison with Recently Produced Material for the Individual Method

IN 1943 WHEN WE first introduced the group Rorschach method there was little material available which might shed light on the potentialities of each card to draw out the various types of perceptual experiences or scoring variables. Thus, while we could present the "card-pull" material as derived from the group method, a card by card comparison of individual and group findings was not possible. It is quite clear that had such "individually" obtained material been available for comparison at the outset, we could have demonstrated the similarity between the two methods more easily. However, a study on adolescent groups with the individual method conducted at the Institute of Child Welfare, University of California, by Ranzoni, Grant and Ives (1) now makes comparison between the two methods possible.*

In the study of Ranzoni, Grant and Ives, the individual test was administered to groups of adolescents, male and female, the same subjects being examined at different age levels. Series A, with which the group test material is compared, constitutes two thirds of the total number of subjects to whom the individual Rorschach was administered at ages 11, 13 and 15 years. At age 18, all subjects were tested and the material is included with the Series A data.

The group test material which we use for comparative purposes was derived from 340 subjects discussed in Part II—224 College Age subjects, 34 Adults, 41 Prison Inmates and 41 Psychotics and Psychopathic Personalities.

In each of these investigations "card-pull" data is presented in terms of the per cent of each scoring variable based on total number of responses to each card. The per cents were compared *within each card* to obtain the variable rank by card and *among the cards* to obtain

---

* Quotations from this article are reprinted by permission of the editors of the *J. Projective Techniques*.

the card rank for each variable. The Edgerton and Paterson Table of Standard Errors and Probable Errors of Percentages for Varying Numbers of Cases was utilized in computing significant differences between ranks.*

Readers interested in a minute and detailed comparison of the material to follow with that derived from the individual method should compare each table with its counterpart in the investigation by Ranzoni, Grant and Ives (1). In order to make the present study uniform, the principal findings for the individual method are compared with those for the group method for each of the variables considered. Italic type in the tables indicates a significant difference at the 1% level of confidence between adjacent ranks tested, while an asterisk after the larger per cent denotes a non-significant difference. Per cents are based on the following number of responses to each card rather than on number of subjects tested.

NUMBER OF RESPONSES TO EACH CARD BY EACH GROUP
(Group Method)

CARD	COLLEGE AGE GROUP	ADULTS	PRISON INMATES	PSYCHOTICS AND PSYCHOPATHIC PERSONALITIES
	(N = 224)	(N = 34)	(N = 41)	(N = 41)
I	632	116	92	108
II	540	105	71	110
III	592	122	70	97
IV	556	110	66	81
V	489	96	70	76
VI	565	101	59	84
VII	482	96	58	69
VIII	609	90	68	106
IX	550	78	59	91
X	791	138	100	133
Total	5806	1052	713	955

Card I

In the group procedure W is the location category most frequently used. The difference between W and the next ranking location, D, is significant for all groups. Similarly, D, the second ranking location is significantly higher than d and Dd. F is the first ranking determinant while A is the highest ranking content category.

In the individual procedure, "W is by far the most frequently used location category. The difference between it and the second rank is

---

* The authors are grateful to Professor Harold A. Edgerton for making available a copy of the table appearing in *J. Appl. Psychol.,* 10:378-391, 1926.

significant at the 1% level for all ages and both sexes with the exception of the 18-year-old girls. D is next in rank. F is the outstanding determinant. A is the most frequently used content category." (1)

For both methods, then, the most usual responses given to this card appear to be of the W, F, A variety.

CARD I

TABLE I—PER CENT OF EACH VARIABLE BASED ON TOTAL RESPONSES TO CARD I
(Group Method)

LOCATION RANK	COLLEGE AGE GROUP		ADULTS		PRISON INMATES		PSYCHOTICS AND PSYCHOPATHIC PERSONALITIES	
		%		%		%		%
1	W	58	W	50	W	67	W	70
2	D	29	D	32	D	24	D	23
3	d	7	d	14	Dd	4	d	4
4	Dd	5	Dd	4	d	3	Dd	3
5	S	.4	S	0	S	1		
DETERMINANTS RANK		%		%		%		%
1	F	67	F	80	F	76	F	68
2	FM	15	k	4	FM	11	c*	12
3	M	7	FM	3	M	3	M	7
4	c*	5	m	3	c*	3	m	4
5	k	3	C'	3				
6			c*	3				
CONTENT RANK								
1	A	36	A	32	A	72	A	41
2	H	8	Ad	12	H	5	H	7
3	Ad	7	Hd	6	Hd	2	Ad	7
4	Hd	2	H	2	Ad	2	Hd	3

Italic type indicates significant difference between adjacent ranks.
*c = Fc + c

Card II

W is utilized significantly more often than any other location by all subjects participating in the group procedure. D is in second place in two groups but is only significantly higher than remaining locations in one instance. S, used more often in this card than in any other card, appears in third place in the College Age group and Psychotics, in fourth place in the Adult group and is tied for second place in the Prison Inmate group. F stands in first place in all groups while M and FM rank second in two groups each. A is the most frequently used content category with H standing in second place.

The individual method reveals the following location, determinant, and content choices: "W is used significantly more frequently in seven of eight groups reported. After age 11, D is significantly higher in rank than the remaining three location categories. S is either in third or fourth place in all but one group. The picture in regard to determinants is less clear in four of eight groups. After age 13, the ranks are consistent with F in first place, M in second place, and FM in third place. A is the most frequently used content category with H fairly consistently in second place." (1)

CARD II

TABLE II—PER CENT OF EACH VARIABLE BASED ON TOTAL RESPONSES TO CARD II
(Group Method)

LOCATION RANK	COLLEGE AGE GROUP		ADULTS		PRISON INMATES		PSYCHOTICS AND PSYCHOPATHIC PERSONALITIES	
		%		%		%		%
1	*W*	54	*W*	37	*W*	59	*W*	55
2	D	20	d	21	S	14	D	25*
3	S	12	D	20	Dd	14	S	13
4	d	9	S	14	D	11	d	6
5	Dd	5	Dd	8	d	1	Dd	1
DETERMI-NANTS RANK		%		%		%		%
1	F	29*	*F*	42	F	35*	*F*	39
2	FM	21	*M*	24	FM	28*	M	21*
3	*M*	20	CF	11	M	14	CF	15
4	CF	10	FM	9	CF	10	FK	4
5	c*	5	FC	4	m	6	m	3
6	FC	4	C'	4	C'	3	C'	3
7							FC	3
CONTENT RANK								
1	*A*	32	H	27*	*A*	38	A	27*
2	H	21	Hd	17	H	16*	*H*	21
3	Hd	7	A	10	Hd	6	Hd	5
4	Ad	3	Ad	5	Ad	6	Ad	5

Italic type indicates significant difference between adjacent ranks.
* Non-significant difference between adjacent ranks.
*c = Fc + c

Card III

When the group method is used, W stands in first place and D stands in second place in three of four groups. M holds first rank for determinants with F ranking second and FC third in three groups. For Psychotics, however, CF stands in third place. H is the content category most frequently given with A holding second place.

When the individual method is used, "W consistently occupies first rank at all ages and for both sexes except the 18-year-old girls. D ranks in second place. M is first in rank in the determinant category until the increasing trend toward F with age becomes apparent at age 18. FC and FM generally hold third or fourth ranks. H is the most frequently used content category and is significantly different from A, the second in rank." (1)

Both methods yield a standard response for this card which appears to be W, M, H.

CARD III

TABLE III—PER CENT OF EACH VARIABLE BASED ON TOTAL RESPONSES TO CARD III
(Group Method)

LOCATION RANK	COLLEGE AGE GROUP		ADULTS		PRISON INMATES		PSYCHOTICS AND PSYCHOPATHIC PERSONALITIES	
		%		%		%		%
1	*W*	*52*	D	55	*W*	63	W	52*
2	D	43	W	33	D	34	D	43
3	d	2	Dd	7	d	3	Dd	4
4	Dd	2	d	6	Dd	0	d	1
5	S	1	S	0	S	0	S	0
DETERMINANTS RANK		%		%		%		%
1	*M*	*41*	F	44	*M*	50	M	36
2	F	26	M	26	F	21*	F	35
3	FC	13	FC	17	FC	11	CF	11·
4	FM	11	CF	5	FM	11	FC	8
5	FC	4	m	4	CF	4	FM	4
6	C'	4					C'	3
CONTENT RANK								
1	*H*	*42*	H	28	H	50*	H	36*
2	*A*	*29*	A	27	A	31	A	28
3	Ad	3	Hd	6	Hd	3	Hd	5
4	Hd	2	Ad	4	Ad	1	Ad	5

Italic type indicates significant difference between adjacent ranks.
* Non-significant difference between adjacent ranks.

Card IV

W is significantly in first place in the group procedure with D in second place for all groups of subjects but one. Small d, Dd and S follow in order. For determinants, F ranks first with c following in second place. A is the content category most often used with Aobj standing in second or third place in three groups.

For the individual method, "W is first in rank consistently and significantly at all age levels. D is the next most frequently used category for the boys and, interestingly enough, d for the girls until age

18 when they use more D. F is consistently in first place in all groups. Texture responses are second in rank." (1)

CARD IV

TABLE IV—PER CENT OF EACH VARIABLE BASED ON TOTAL RESPONSES TO CARD IV
(Group Method)

LOCATION RANK	COLLEGE AGE GROUP		ADULTS		PRISON INMATES		PSYCHOTICS AND PSYCHOPATHIC PERSONALITIES	
		%		%		%		%
1	*W*	*51*	D	43*	*W*	*59*	*W*	*69*
2	*D*	*27*	W	31*	*D*	*26*	*D*	*22*
3	*d*	*12*	d	18	*d*	*6*	*d*	*5*
4	Dd	8	Dd	6	Dd	6	Dd	4
5	S	1	S	2	S	3	S	0
DETERMI-NANTS RANK		%		%		%		%
1	*F*	*41*	*F*	*63*	F	42*	*F*	*43**
2	*c**	*32*	*c**	*19**	*c**	*24**	*c**	*26*
3	FM	8	M	11	k	13	m	7
4	M	7	FM	3	M	8	k	7
5	k	5	m	2	FM	8	C'	7
6	K	3	FK	2				
CONTENT RANK								
1	*A*	*22*	Ad	19*	A	20*	*A*	*28*
2	Ad	12	Hd	14	Ad	15	Ad	10
3	H	7	H	11	H	8	H	2
4	Hd	7	A	9	Hd	3	Hd	2
	(Aobj. 12)		(Aobj. 8)		(Aobj. 14)		(Aobj. 22)	

Italic type indicates significant difference between adjacent ranks.
* Non-significant difference between adjacent ranks.
*c = Fc + c

Card V

Group test results show that W ranks first; d ranks second in three groups with D following in third place. F is significantly in first place for determinants with FM and M ranking second and third respectively. A is the most frequently used content.

The individual test reveals that "Card V even more than preceding cards, has a strong W pull. Small d is in second place consistently for all ages. F ranks highest in determinants. FM decreases in relation to F both in rank and in absolute per cent from age 11 on. The remaining two determinants (M and c) never contribute more than 8% of the total responses to this card. A is the most frequently used content category with no other category even approaching it in per cent.

The standard response for the groups is, therefore, not the popular W, FM, A but rather W, F, A." (1)

CARD V

TABLE V—PER CENT OF EACH VARIABLE BASED ON TOTAL RESPONSES TO CARD V
(Group Method)

LOCATION RANK	COLLEGE AGE GROUP		ADULTS		PRISON INMATES		PSYCHOTICS AND PSYCHOPATHIC PERSONALITIES	
		%		%		%		%
1	*W*	*69*	W	47*	*W*	88	*W*	72
2	d	15	*d*	36	D	9	d	13
3	D	14	D	11	d	3	D	12
4	Dd	2	Dd	4	Dd	0	Dd	3
5	S	.4	S	1	S	0	S	0
DETERMINANTS RANK		%		%		%		%
1	*F*	46	*F*	69	*F*	64	*F*	74
2	*FM*	27	FM	11	FM	19	FM	13
3	M	12	M	8	M	10	M	7
4	c*	10	C'	5	c*	6	c*	4
5	C'	2						
CONTENT RANK								
1	*A*	57	*A*	40	*A*	77	*A*	62
2	H	12	Ad	23	H	10	Ad	9
3	Ad	9	H	8	Hd	4	H	7
4	Hd	6	Hd	3	Ad	1	Hd	7

Italic type indicates significant difference between adjacent ranks.
* Non-significant difference between adjacent ranks.
*c = Fc + c

Card VI

Though D stands in first place in three of the groups, when the group method is used, it is not significantly higher than W which stands in second place. Percentage differences between D and W are slight except for Prison Inmates. Texture responses rank first for determinants with F following in second place. Amongst content categories, Aobj stands in first place in three groups with A in second place.

In the individual method, "W is emphatically the preferred location category. D is consistently in rank 2. The tendency for the use of F to increase with age is apparent. Ages 11 and 13 use texture significantly more often than F. There is a reversal of this pattern at age 15 which carries on through the 18 year records. In two groups (15-year-old boys and 18-year-old girls), F becomes significantly higher than the texture responses." (1)

The fact that W stands significantly in first place when the individual method is used while D stands in first place when the group method is used is of particular interest, since the group method has been considered to favor W's at the expense of D's.

CARD VI

TABLE VI—PER CENT OF EACH VARIABLE BASED ON TOTAL RESPONSES TO CARD VI
(Group Method)

LOCATION RANK	COLLEGE AGE GROUP		ADULTS		PRISON INMATES		PSYCHOTICS AND PSYCHOPATHIC PERSONALITIES	
		%		%		%		%
1	D	47	D	50*	*W*	*61*	D	47
2	*W*	*45*	*W*	*38*	D	36	*W*	*45*
3	Dd	5	d	8	d	3	Dd	5
4	d	4	Dd	4	Dd	0	d	4
5	S	0	S	0	S	0	S	0
DETERMI-NANTS RANK		%		%		%		%
1	c*	49	c*	43*	c*	63	c*	44*
2	*F*	*29*	F	35	C	18*	*F*	*31*
3	FK	6	FK	8	m	8	K	6
4	FM	6	C'	5	K	5	FM	6
5	C'	4	m	4	FK	3	FK	4
6							C'	4
CONTENT RANK								
1	*A*	*16*	A	13*	A	10	A	21
2	Ad	10	Ad	6	Ad	2	Ad	2
3	Hd	3	Hd	4	Hd	2	Hd	2
4	H	1	H	1	H	0	H	2
	(Aobj. 17)		(Aobj. 21)		(Aobj. 42)		(Aobj. 20)	

Italic type indicates significant difference between adjacent ranks.
* Non-significant difference between adjacent ranks.
*c = Fc + c

Card VII

Findings for the group procedure are as follows: D holds first place in three groups but is significantly greater than adjacent ranks in only two instances. W stands in second place in two groups and in first place in one group. F ranks first amongst determinants in all groups with M taking second place in three groups. The texture determinant stands in third place in two groups and in fourth place in two groups. H is the most frequently used content category with A ranking second.

For the individual method: "The tendency of the previous cards to pull a majority of W responses begins to break down in Card VII.

Although W still represents the largest percentage of responses, the differences between W and D are smaller. Pure form and human movement are the major determinants given at all ages. Animal movement holds third rank with texture responses occurring less frequently than any other determinant. While Card VII is considered a strongly shaded card, its surface texture pull for the group is negligible. After age 11, H is consistently in first rank for content." (1)

CARD VII

TABLE VII—PER CENT OF EACH VARIABLE BASED ON TOTAL RESPONSES TO CARD VII
(Group Method)

LOCATION RANK	COLLEGE AGE GROUP		ADULTS		PRISON INMATES		PSYCHOTICS AND PSYCHOPATHIC PERSONALITIES	
		%		%		%		%
1	D	68	D	49	D	57*	W	46
2	W	25	d	23	W	36	D	42
3	Dd	6	W	22	d	7	d	9
4	d	1	S	5	Dd	0	Dd	3
5	S	.1	Dd	1	S	0	S	0
DETERMI- NANTS RANK		%		%		%		%
1	F	39	F	50	F	41*	F	62
2	M	26	FK	12	M	26	M	7
3	c*	12	M	10	c*	10	FM	7
4	K	5	c*	9	FM	10	c*	7
5	FK	3	FM	8	m	5	FK	5
6	m	2	K	5	k	3	k	4
CONTENT RANK								
1	H	26	H	17*	H	28*	Hd	16
2	A	11	Hd	10	A	14	A	14
3	Hd	11	A	8	Hd	14	H	10
4	Ad	5	Ad	4	Ad	12	Ad	4

Italic type indicates significant difference between adjacent ranks.
* Non-significant difference between adjacent ranks.
*c = Fc + c

Card VIII

D is significantly in first place with W in second place for all subjects taking the test by the group method. F ranks first amongst determinants in two groups while FM ranks first in the two remaining groups. FC takes second place in the College Age group and Adults. For Psychotics, CF ranks second. Color pull (FC + CF) is significantly greater than F pull for the College Age group. A is the predominant content category.

For the individual procedure: "The per cent D is larger than the per cent W at all ages. W pull is still a second rank. FM and F are the determinants pulled most frequently. The comparisons of color pull to F pull show F to be significantly greater at ages 15 and 18. Only at age 11 is color pull greater than F. FC and CF rank above M and texture for this card. A is the predominant content." (1)

The "standard" response for both group and individual methods seems to be D, F or FM, A.

CARD VIII

TABLE VIII—PER CENT OF EACH VARIABLE BASED ON TOTAL RESPONSES TO CARD VIII
(Group Method)

LOCATION RANK	COLLEGE AGE GROUP		ADULTS		PRISON INMATES		PSYCHOTICS AND PSYCHOPATHIC PERSONALITIES	
		%		%		%		%
1	D	68	D	74	D	62	D	69
2	W	25	W	24	W	32	W	28
3	Dd	6	Dd	1	Dd	3	Dd	3
4	d	1	d	0	S	3	d	0
5	S	.1	S	0	d	0	S	0
DETERMINANTS RANK		%		%		%		%
1	FM	31	F	37	FM	38*	F	40
2	FC	23	FC	36	F	23	CF	23
3	F	23	CF	12	CF	20	FM	14
4	CF	16	FM	11	FC	13	FC	13
5	c*	3	c*	2	C'	3	c*	3
6	M	2	k	1	m	1	k	2
7					FK	1	C'	2
							C	2
	CΣ:F		CΣ*:F		CΣ*:F		CΣ*:F	
CONTENT RANK								
1	A	44	A	50	A	60	A	40
2	Ad	3	Hd	2	Ad	1	Ad	3
3	H	2	Ad	1	Hd	1	H	1
4	Hd	2	H	0	H	0	Hd	1

Italic type indicates significant difference between adjacent ranks.
* Non-significant difference between adjacent ranks.
*c = Fc + c

Card IX

The significant D pull of Card VIII continues in Card IX, for the group method, with W standing in second place. F ranks first for determinants with CF ranking second in three groups. *For Psychotics, however, the order is reversed.* When color pull (FC + CF) is compared with F pull, the latter is significantly greater in only one group. Color pull is greater than FM pull in all groups. Though

A content stands first in three groups, it is only significantly greater than its adjacent rank in the College Age group.

As in the group method, the individual method shows a significant Card IX D pull trend. "W is second in rank in all groups but one. F is the most frequently used determinant and has significantly more pull than even total color pull after age 11. There is no outstanding content category given." (1)

CARD IX

TABLE IX—PER CENT OF EACH VARIABLE BASED ON TOTAL RESPONSES TO CARD IX
(Group Method)

LOCATION RANK	COLLEGE AGE GROUP		ADULTS		PRISON INMATES		PSYCHOTICS AND PSYCHOPATHIC PERSONALITIES	
		%		%		%		%
1	D	66	D	58	D	56	D	57
2	W	19	W	24*	W	34	W	26*
3	Dd	11	Dd	12	Dd	10	Dd	15
4	d	4	d	6	d	0	d	1
5	S	0	S	0	S	0	S	0
DETERMINANTS RANK		%		%		%		%
1	F	32*	F	53	F	46*	CF	35*
2	CF	28	CF	22	CF	29	F	25*
3	M	10	FC	8	FM	10	M	12
4	FC	8	c*	5	M	5	FC	5
5	FM	8	FM	5	k	5	K	5
6	K	6	K	4	FC	3	FM	4
7							m	4
	F:CΣ		F:CΣ		F*:CΣ		CΣ*:F	
	CΣ:FM		CΣ:FM		CΣ:FM		CΣ:FM	
CONTENT RANK								
1	A	18	Ad	19*	A	19*	A	21*
2	H	11	A	15	Hd	12	H	11
3	Hd	7	Hd	5	Ad	8	Hd	5
4	Ad	7	H	3	H	7	Ad	4

Italic type indicates significant difference between adjacent ranks.
* Non-significant difference between adjacent ranks.
*c = Fc + c

Card X

D is by far the most preferred location category with W ranking second for all groups when the group method is used. F holds first place for determinants with FM and CF sharing second place. F has a stronger pull than color (FC + CF) in one group only but has a significantly stronger pull than FM in all groups. Color pull is greater than FM pull in three of the four groups. A content is used most frequently.

The individual method shows that "more than 82% of the responses fall into the D location category. W is second in rank. Even in this highly colored card, F ranks first in the determinants followed by FM. FC comes in a poor third in most of the groups with F or FM significantly higher than FC in all groups. A is by far the most popular content category." (1)

CARD X

TABLE X—PER CENT OF EACH VARIABLE BASED ON TOTAL RESPONSES TO CARD X
(Group Method)

LOCATION RANK	COLLEGE AGE GROUP		ADULTS		PRISON INMATES		PSYCHOTICS AND PSYCHOPATHIC PERSONALITIES	
		%		%		%		%
1	D	81	D	82	D	77	D	77
2	W	15	W	13	W	20	W	18
3	Dd	3	Dd	4	Dd	2	Dd	2
4	S	1	S	1	S	1	S	2
DETERMINANTS RANK		%		%		%		%
1	F	32	F	62	F	44	F	41
2	FM	25	CF	16*	FM	18	CF	24
3	FC	17	FC	7	CF	17	FM	12
4	CF	14	FM	4	FC	13	FC	9
5	M	6	M	3	M	6	M	6
6	FK	3	KF	3	FK	1	m	2
7							K	2
	F*:CΣ		F:CΣ		F*:CΣ		F*:CΣ	
	F:FM		F:FM		F:FM		F:FM	
	CΣ:FM		CΣ:FM		CΣ*:FM		CΣ:FM	
CONTENT RANK								
1	A	52	A	40	A	51	A	46
2	H	7	H	4	H	7	H	8
3	Hd	2	Ad	3	Ad	3	Ad	2
4	Ad	2	Hd	2	Hd	2	Hd	0

Italic type indicates significant difference between adjacent ranks.
* Non-significant difference between adjacent ranks.

Card Rank by Variable

The tables to follow present card rank for separate location, determinant and content variables. Critical ratios were computed between adjacent ranks and between ranks 3 and 8 of most variables in order to determine whether significant differences existed between the three top ranking and three bottom ranking cards.

Locations
W

Group test results show that W is highest for Card V in three groups, significantly so in two groups. Cards V and I hold first or second rank in all groups. Cards VII, VIII, IX and X have a lower W pull than do the remaining six cards. The difference between the top three and bottom three cards in rank is significant in three groups.

In the individual method, "Card V consistently pulls the highest number of W followed by Cards I and VI. Cards VIII, IX and X are significantly lower in W pull than the remaining seven cards. The difference between the top three and bottom three cards in rank is significant in every case." (1)

W

TABLE XI—PER CENT OF W TO EACH CARD BASED ON TOTAL RESPONSES PER CARD
(Group Method)

RANKS	COLLEGE AGE GROUP		ADULTS		PRISON INMATES		PSYCHOTICS AND PSYCHOPATHIC PERSONALITIES	
	CARD	%	CARD	%	CARD	%	CARD	%
1	V	69	I	50	V	88	V	72
2	I	58	V	47	I	67	I	70
3	II	54	VI	38	III	63	IV	69*
4	III	52	II	37	VI	61	II	55
5	IV	51	III	33	II	59	III	52
6	VI	45	IV	31	*IV*	59	VI	52
7	*VII*	*41*	VIII	24	VII	36	VII	46
8	*VIII*	25	IX	24	IX	34	VIII	28
9	IX	19	VII	22	VIII	32	IX	26
10	X	15	X	13	X	20	X	18
Ranks	3–8		3*–8		3–8		3–8	

Italic type indicates significant difference between adjacent ranks.
* Non-significant difference between adjacent ranks.

D

Card X ranks first for D pull with Card VIII ranking second in the group procedure. Card IX is in third place in three of the groups. Card V shows the least D pull with Card II ranking next lowest. The difference between rank 3 and 8 is significant in every case.

In the individual procedure, "Card X has the highest D pull. The three top-ranking cards (X, VIII, and IX) are consistent in all groups and are significantly different from the lowest three ranks which are generally Cards V, I and VI." (1)

D

TABLE XII—PER CENT OF D TO EACH CARD BASED ON TOTAL RESPONSES PER CARD
(Group Method)

RANKS	COLLEGE AGE GROUP		ADULTS		PRISON INMATES		PSYCHOTICS AND PSYCHOPATHIC PERSONALITIES	
	CARD	%	CARD	%	CARD	%	CARD	%
1	X	81	X	82*	X	77*	X	77
2	VIII	68	VIII	74	VIII	62	VIII	69
3	IX	66	IX	58	VII	57	IX	57
4	VI	47	III	55	IX	56	III	43
5	VII	43	VI	50	VI	36	VII	42
6	III	43	VII	49	III	34	VI	38
7	I	29	IV	43	IV	26	II	25
8	IV	27	I	32	I	24	I	23
9	II	20	II	20	II	11	IV	22
10	V	14	V	11	V	9	V	12
Ranks	3—8		3—8		3—8		3—8	

Italic type indicates significant difference between adjacent ranks.
* Non-significant difference between adjacent ranks.

d

Since few d were given to the test, the critical ratio was computed
between the top ranking card and lowest ranking card for which any
d was recorded. The differences between rank 1, which was Card V

d

TABLE XIII—PER CENT OF d TO EACH CARD BASED ON TOTAL RESPONSES PER CARD
(Group Method)

RANKS	COLLEGE AGE GROUP		ADULTS		PRISON INMATES		PSYCHOTICS AND PSYCHOPATHIC PERSONALITIES	
	CARD	%	CARD	%	CARD	%	CARD	%
1	V	15	V	36	VII	7	V	13
2	IV	12	VII	23	IV	6	VII	9
3	VII	10	II	21	III	3	II	6
4	II	9	IV	18	V	3	IV	5
5	I	7	I	14	VI	3	I	4
6	VI	4	VI	8	I	3	VI	2
7	IX	4	III	6	II	1	IX	1
8	III	2	IX	6	VIII	0	III	1
9	VIII	1	VIII	0	IX	0	VIII	0
10	X	0	X	0	X	0	X	0
	V:VIII		V:III, IX		VII:II*		V:III, IX	

Italic type indicates significant difference between adjacent ranks.
* Non-significant difference between adjacent ranks.

for three of the groups, and the lowest per cent were significant for all but one group when the group method was used.

Individual test findings show that "the differences between rank 1, consistently Card V for boys and Card IV for girls, and the lowest per cent were significant in every case. If Card X is eliminated from consideration, Card VIII ranks lowest in six of eight groups." (1)

Dd

Rare details, like d, were infrequently given, hence the critical ratio between highest and lowest ranking cards was computed. Card

Dd

TABLE XIV—PER CENT OF Dd TO EACH CARD BASED ON TOTAL RESPONSES PER CARD
(Group Method)

RANKS	COLLEGE AGE GROUP		ADULTS		PRISON INMATES		PSYCHOTICS AND PSYCHOPATHIC PERSONALITIES	
	CARD	%	CARD	%	CARD	%	CARD	%
1	IX	11	IX	12	II	14	IX	15
2	IV	8	II	8	IX	10	VI	7
3	VIII	6	III	7	IV	6	III	4
4	VI	5	IV	6	I	4	IV	4
5	I	5	I	4	VIII	3	I	3
6	II	5	V	4	X	2	V	3
7	VII	3	VI	4	III	0	VII	3
8	X	3	X	4	VI	0	VIII	3
9	III	2	VII	1	V	0	X	2
10	V	2	VIII	1	VII	0	II	1
	IX:III, V		*IX:VII, VIII**		*II:X*		*IX:II*	

Italic type indicates significant difference between adjacent ranks.
* Non-significant difference between adjacent ranks.

IX held first place in three groups. Differences between highest and lowest ranking cards were significant for three groups.

Rare details were infrequently given when the individual method was used. "Cards IX, I, and IV were usually the highest ranking cards and Card X and III most frequently among the bottom ranks. The differences between the cards in rank 1 and those in the lowest rank are significant for most age groups." (1)

S

In the group method, Card II ranks first in all groups for S pull with Card VII taking second place. The S pull of Cards II and VII

S

TABLE XV—PER CENT OF S TO EACH CARD BASED ON TOTAL RESPONSES PER CARD
(Group Method)

RANKS	COLLEGE AGE GROUP		ADULTS		PRISON INMATES		PSYCHOTICS AND PSYCHOPATHIC PERSONALITIES	
	CARD	%	CARD	%	CARD	%	CARD	%
1	*II*	*12*	II	14*	II	14*	*II*	*13*
2	VII	3	VII	5	IV	3	X	2
3	III	1	IV	2	VIII	3	I	0
4	IV	1	V	1	I	1	III	0
5	X	1	X	1	X	1	IV	0
6	I	.4	I	0	III	0	V	0
7	V	.4	III	0	V	0	VI	0
8	VIII	.1	VI	0	VI	0	VII	0
9	VI	0	VIII	0	VII	0	VIII	0
10	IX	0	IX	0	IX	0	IX	0
	II + VII: others		*II + VII: others*		II + VII*: others		*II + VII: others*	

Italic type indicates significant difference between adjacent ranks.
* Non-significant difference between adjacent ranks.

was combined and found to be significantly greater than that of all other cards in three of four groups.

Similarly, for the individual method, "Cards II and VII are the only cards of the series which have more than 4% white space responses. The S pull to Cards II and VII, combined, is significantly greater than that to other cards for most groups." (1)

M

TABLE XVI—PER CENT OF M TO EACH CARD BASED ON TOTAL RESPONSES PER CARD
(Group Method)

RANKS	COLLEGE AGE GROUP		ADULTS		PRISON INMATES		PSYCHOTICS AND PSYCHOPATHIC PERSONALITIES	
	CARD	%	CARD	%	CARD	%	CARD	%
1	*III*	*41*	III	26	*III*	*50*	III	36*
2	VII	26	*II*	*25*	VII	26*	II	21
3	II	20	IV	11	II	14	IX	12
4	V	12	VII	10	V	10	I	7
5	IX	10	V	8	IV	8	V	7
6	I	7	X	3	X	6	VII	7
7	IV	7	IX	3	IX	5	X	6
8	X	6	VI	1	I	3	IV	2
9	VIII	2	I	1	VI	0	VI	0
10	VI	1	VIII	0	VIII	0	VIII	0
Ranks	*3—8*		*3—8*		*3—8*		*3—8*	

Italic type indicates significant difference between adjacent ranks.
* Non-significant difference between adjacent ranks.

Determinants
M

Card III stands in first place for M pull in all groups with Cards VII and II following in second place. Cards VI and VIII are weakest in M production. The differences between ranks 3 and 8 are significant for all groups.

A similar trend for M production is seen when the individual method is used. "Card III holds first rank and Card VII, second rank. Cards III, VII and II are the strongest cards and Cards V, VIII, and VI the weakest in M with differences between third and eighth ranks significant in most groups." (1)

FM

Card VIII ranks first in FM production with Card V ranking second in three groups and Card X ranking third in two groups. Cards VI, IV and IX are most frequently amongst the lowest three ranks for all groups. The differences between the third and eighth ranks are significant for the College Age group only.

Cards VIII and V are the FM cards in the series when the individual method is used. "Card X ranks third. The per cent of FM to these three cards is always significantly greater than that to the last three. Cards IX and VI are consistently in the bottom ranks." (1)

FM

TABLE XVII—PER CENT OF FM TO EACH CARD BASED ON TOTAL RESPONSES PER CARD
(Group Method)

RANKS	COLLEGE AGE GROUP		ADULTS		PRISON INMATES		PSYCHOTICS AND PSYCHOPATHIC PERSONALITIES	
	CARD	%	CARD	%	CARD	%	CARD	%
1	VIII	31	VIII	11	VIII	38	VIII	14
2	V	27	V	11	II	28	V	13
3	X	25	II	9	V	19	X	12
4	II	21	VII	8	X	18	II	11
5	I	15	IX	5	III	11	VII	7
6	III	11	X	4	I	11	VI	6
7	VII	9	I	3	VII	10	IX	4
8	IV	8	VI	3	IX	10	III	4
9	IX	8	IV	3	IV	8	I	3
10	VI	5	III	.3	VI	2	IV	2
Ranks	3—8		3—8*		3—8*		3—8*	

Italic type indicates significant difference between adjacent ranks.
* Non-significant difference between adjacent ranks.

F

Card·I ranks first and Card V ranks second in F pull for three groups. In the fourth, Psychotics, the order is reversed. Cards II, III, VI and VIII rank lowest in F pull. There is a significant difference between ranks 3 and 8 in every group.

Individual test results show that "since all of the F% are high, it is not surprising to find that no one card pulls significantly more F than the next in rank. At 15 and 18 years, however, there is a significant difference between the top and bottom three ranks, with Cards I and V most frequently in top ranks and Cards VIII, III and II generally pulling the smallest percentage of F." (1)

F

TABLE XVIII—PER CENT OF F TO EACH CARD BASED ON TOTAL RESPONSES PER CARD
(Group Method)

RANKS	COLLEGE AGE GROUP		ADULTS		PRISON INMATES		PSYCHOTICS AND PSYCHOPATHIC PERSONALITIES	
	CARD	%	CARD	%	CARD	%	CARD	%
1	*I*	67	I	81*	I	76*	V	74*
2	V	46	V	69	V	64*	I	68
3	IV	41	IV	63	IX	46*	VII	62
4	VII	39	X	62	X	44	IV	43
5	X	32	IX	53	IV	42	X	41
6	IX	32	VII	50	VII	41	VIII	40
7	VI	29	III	44	II	35	II	39
8	II	29	II	43	VIII	23	III	35
9	III	26	VIII	37	III	21	VI	31
10	VIII	23	VI	35	VI	18	IX	25
Ranks	*3–8*		*3–8*		*3–8*		*3–8*	

Italic type indicates significant difference between adjacent ranks.
* Non-significant difference between adjacent ranks.

Fc + cF

Card VI ranks first with Card IV in second place for texture pull in all groups when the group method is used. In three of the groups significantly more texture responses are given to Card VI than to Card IV. Card VII stands in third place. Differences between ranks 3 and 8 are significant in all but one group.

For the individual method, "Cards VI and IV have the strongest texture-pull in the series. All of the groups except 15 and 18 year old boys give significantly more shading responses to VI than to IV.

The differences between the third and eighth ranks are significant
in only three groups although the differences between the second
rank and all other ranks are significant for most groups." (1)

Fc + cF

TABLE XIX—PER CENT OF Fc + cF TO EACH CARD BASED ON TOTAL RESPONSES PER CARD
(Group Method)

RANKS	COLLEGE AGE GROUP		ADULTS		PRISON INMATES		PSYCHOTICS AND PSYCHOPATHIC PERSONALITIES	
	CARD	%	CARD	%	CARD	%	CARD	%
1	VI	49	VI	43	VI	63	VI	44*
2	IV	32	IV	19*	IV	24	IV	26
3	VII	12	VII	9	VII	10	I	11
4	V	10	IX	5	V	6	VII	7
5	I	5	I	3	I	3	V	4
6	VIII	3	VIII	2	IX	2	IX	3
7	IX	3	II	2	II	1	VIII	3
8	II	3	V	2	III	0	II	2
9	X	1	III	1	VIII	0	X	1
10	III	1	X	0	X	0	VIII	0
Ranks	3–8		3–8*		3–8		3–8	

Italic type indicates significant difference between adjacent ranks.
* Non-significant difference between adjacent ranks.

Color

Card VIII stands in first place for FC pull in all groups, signifi-
cantly so in two groups with Card X in second place in three groups.
Card II is lowest in FC pull in all groups. Card IX ranks first for CF
pull with Cards VIII and X ranking second in two groups each. Card
VIII ranks first with Card IX ranking second in total color pull for
three groups. In the fourth group, Psychotics, the order is reversed.
Combined Cards VIII, IX and X pull more color responses than do
Cards II and III combined.

The individual method shows that "only one of the adjacent rank
differences for FC, CF or total color pull (FC + CF) is significant.
There is a general decrease in the amount of color used as age increases. Card III pulls consistently fewer color responses than any
other card. In regard to CF, while there are no significant differences
between the ranks, Card IX is always in first rank and Card III in the
last rank. Though no one card has outstanding color pull, Cards VIII,
IX and X combined do pull more color responses than Cards II
and III combined." (1)

Color

TABLE XX—PER CENT OF FC, CF, AND CΣ TO EACH CARD BASED ON TOTAL RESPONSES
PER CARD
(Group Method)

FC

RANKS	COLLEGE AGE GROUP		ADULTS		PRISON INMATES		PSYCHOTICS AND PSYCHOPATHIC PERSONALITIES	
	CARD	%	CARD	%	CARD	%	CARD	%
1	*VIII*	*23*	*VIII*	*36*	VIII	13	VIII	13
2	X	17	III	18*	X	13	X	9
3	III	13	IX	9	III	11	III	8
4	IX	8	X	7	IX	3	IX	5
5	II	4	II	4	II	0	II	3

CF

RANKS	CARD	%	CARD	%	CARD	%	CARD	%
1	*IX*	*28*	IX	22*	IX	29	IX	35*
2	VIII	16	X	16	VIII	20	X	24
3	X	14	VIII	12	X	17	VIII	23
4	II	10	II	11	II	10	II	15
5	III	3	III	5	III	4	III	11

CΣ

RANKS	CARD	%	CARD	%	CARD	%	CARD	%
1	VIII	39	VIII	38	VIII	33	IX	40
2	IX	36	IX	31	IX	32	VIII	36
3	X	31	X	23	X	30	X	33
4	III	16	III	23	III	15	III	19
5	II	14	II	15	II	10	II	18
Total	*VIII + IX + X:* II + III		*VIII + IX + X:* II + III		*VIII + IX + X:* II + III		*VIII + IX + X:* II + III	

Italic type indicates significant difference between adjacent ranks.
* Non-significant difference between adjacent ranks.

Content

H

Card III produces the greatest number of H responses with Cards II and VII standing in second place. Cards VI and VIII are lowest in H pull. Differences between ranks 3 and 8 are significant in three groups.

When the individual method is used "Cards III and VII show the highest proportion of H. The H pull of the first three ranks is significantly greater than that of the last three ranks." (1)

H

TABLE XXI—PER CENT OF H TO EACH CARD BASED ON TOTAL RESPONSES PER CARD
(Group Method)

RANKS	COLLEGE AGE GROUP		ADULTS		PRISON INMATES		PSYCHOTICS AND PSYCHOPATHIC PERSONALITIES	
	CARD	%	CARD	%	CARD	%	CARD	%
1	*III*	*42*	III	28	*III*	*50*	III	36*
2	VII	26	*II*	*27*	VII	28	II	21
3	*II*	*21*	IV	11	II	16	IX	11
4	V	12	V	8	V	10	VII	10
5	IX	11	VII	8	IV	8	X	8
6	I	8	X	4	IX	7	I	7
7	IV	7	IX	3	X	7	V	7
8	X	7	I	2	I	5	IV	2
9	VIII	2	VI	1	VIII	0	VI	2
10	VI	1	VIII	0	VI	0	VIII	1
Ranks	3−8		3−8		3−8		3−8	

Italic type indicates significant difference between adjacent ranks.
* Non-significant difference between adjacent ranks.

A

Cards V, VIII and X show the greatest A pull while Cards VI, VII and IX appear most frequently in the lowest ranks. Differences between ranks 3 and 8 are significant in two groups.

A

TABLE XXII—PER CENT OF A TO EACH CARD BASED ON TOTAL RESPONSES PER CARD
(Group Method)

RANKS	COLLEGE AGE GROUP		ADULTS		PRISON INMATES		PSYCHOTICS AND PSYCHOPATHIC PERSONALITIES	
	CARD	%	CARD	%	CARD	%	CARD	%
1	V	57	VIII	50	V	77	V	62*
2	X	52	V	40	I	72	X	46
3	VIII	44	X	40	VIII	60	I	41
4	I	36	I	32	X	51	VIII	40
5	II	32	III	27	II	38	III	28
6	III	29	IX	15	III	31	IV	28
7	IV	22	VI	13	IV	20	II	27
8	IX	18	II	10	IX	19	VI	21
9	VI	16	IV	9	VII	14	IX	21
10	VII	11	VII	8	VI	10	VII	14
Ranks	3−8		3−8		3−8		3−8	

Italic type indicates significant difference between adjacent ranks.
* Non-significant difference between adjacent ranks.

The individual method reveals an A pull trend similar to that for the group method. "Card V, VIII, and X pull the greatest number of A, while Cards VI and IX are most frequently in the bottom ranks. The A pull of the top three cards is significantly greater than that of the cards ranking eighth or below." (1)

Hd

Card VII stands first in three groups with Cards II and IX appearing more often in the first three ranks. Cards VIII and X are most frequently found in the bottom ranks. Differences between ranks 3 and 8 are significant in two groups.

The individual method presents "no significant differences among adjacent ranks and in only two of the groups are the differences between third and eighth ranks significant. Cards VII and IX are most frequently in the first two ranks." (1)

Hd

TABLE XXIII—Per Cent of Hd to Each Card Based on Total Responses per Card
(Group Method)

RANKS	COLLEGE AGE GROUP		ADULTS		PRISON INMATES		PSYCHOTICS AND PSYCHOPATHIC PERSONALITIES	
	CARD	%	CARD	%	CARD	%	CARD	%
1	VII	11	II	17	VII	14	VII	16
2	II	7	VII	17	IX	12	V	7
3	IX	7	IV	14	II	6	II	5
4	V	6	I	6	V	4	IX	5
5	IV	5	III	6	III	3	I	3
6	VI	3	IX	5	IV	3	III	3
7	I	2	VI	4	I	2	IV	2
8	III	2	V	3	VI	2	VI	2
9	VIII	2	VIII	2	X	2	VIII	1
10	X	2	X	2	VIII	1	X	0
Ranks	*3—8*		*3—8*		*3—8**		*3—8**	

Italic type indicates significant difference between adjacent ranks.
* Non-significant difference between adjacent ranks.

Ad

Cards I, IV, V, and IX appear most frequently in the upper ranks while Cards III, VIII and X are found most frequently in the bottom ranks. Differences between ranks 3 and 8 are significant in two groups.

No significant card-pull differences appear when the individual method is used. "Cards I, IX, and IV are most frequently in the first two ranks and Cards III and VIII in the last two." (1)

Ad

TABLE XXIV—PER CENT OF Ad TO EACH CARD BASED ON TOTAL RESPONSES PER CARD
(Group Method)

RANKS	COLLEGE AGE GROUP		ADULTS		PRISON INMATES		PSYCHOTICS AND PSYCHOPATHIC PERSONALITIES	
	CARD	%	CARD	%	CARD	%	CARD	%
1	IV	12	V	23	IV	15	IV	10
2	V	9	IV	19	VII	12	V	9
3	I	7	IX	19	IX	8	I	7
4	IX	7	I	12	II	6	II	5
5	VI	5	VI	6	X	3	VII	4
6	VII	5	II	5	I	2	IX	4
7	II	3	III	4	VI	2	III	3
8	III	3	VII	4	III	1	VIII	3
9	VIII	3	X	3	V	1	VI	2
10	X	2	VIII	1	VIII	1	X	2
Ranks	3−8		3−8		3−8*		3−8*	

Italic type indicates significant difference between adjacent ranks.
* Non-significant difference between adjacent ranks.

A survey of the preceding tables show us that except for very slight statistical differences between groups, strikingly similar "card-pull" patterns result for all variables when the group method is compared with the individual method. These similarities are even more striking in view of the heterogeneity of groups studied.

REFERENCE

1. Ranzoni, J. H., Grant, M. Q. and Ives, V.: Rorschach "card-pull" in a normal adolescent population. *J. Projective Techniques, 14*:107-133, 1950.

Index

This Book

LARGE SCALE
RORSCHACH TECHNIQUES
(Second Edition)

By

M. R. HARROWER, Ph.D.

AND

M. E. STEINER, M.A.

was set and printed by The Ovid Bell Press, Incorporated, of Fulton, Missouri. The binding was done by the Becktold Company of St. Louis, Missouri. The page size is 6 x 9 inches. The type page is 27 x 45 picas. The type face is Baskerville set 11 point on 13 point. The text paper is 70-pound Oxford Mainefold Enamel. The cover is Roxite L. S. Vellum—5175-11M, Two-tone Black.

With THOMAS BOOKS *careful attention is given to all details of manufacturing and design. It is the publisher's desire to present books that are satisfactory as to their physical qualities and artistic possibilities and appropriate for their particular use.* THOMAS BOOKS *will be true to those laws of quality that assure a good name and good will.*